Journey of Hope

The John Hope Franklin Series in African American History and Culture

Waldo E. Martin Jr. and Patricia Sullivan, editors

Journey of Hope

The Back-to-Africa Movement in
Arkansas in the Late 1800s

Kenneth C. Barnes

The University of North Carolina Press

Chapel Hill and London

Designed by April Leidig-Higgins
Set in Monotype Garamond by Copperline Book Services, Inc.

The paper in this book meets the guidelines for permanence and durability of the Committee on Production Guidelines for Book Longevity of the Council on Library Resources.

Library of Congress Cataloging-in-Publication Data
Barnes, Kenneth C., 1956–
Journey of hope: the Back to Africa movement in Arkansas in the late 1800s / Kenneth C. Barnes.
    p. cm.—(John Hope Franklin series in African American history and culture)
Includes bibliographical references and index.
ISBN 0-8078-2879-3 (cloth: alk. paper)
ISBN 0-8078-5550-2 (pbk.: alk. paper)
1. African Americans—Colonization—Liberia.   2. Liberia—History—1847–1944.   3. African Americans—Arkansas—History—19th century.   4. Sharecroppers—Arkansas—History—19th century.   5. Liberia—Emigration and immigration—History—19th century.   6. Arkansas—Emigration and immigration—History—19th century.   7. American Colonization Society—History.   8. Black nationalism—History—19th century.   I. Title.   II. Series.
DT634.B37 2004   966.62'004960730767—dc22   2003027748

cloth   08 07 06 05 04   5 4 3 2 1
paper   08 07 06 05 04   5 4 3 2 1

For Debbie

Contents

Illustrations, Maps, and Figures

Maps

Figures

Preface

As my plane touched down at Robertsfield outside Monrovia, Liberia, the passengers burst into applause. Some cheered, others cried. Most of the passengers were Liberian exiles who had fled their country during the brutal civil war of the 1990s, which displaced more than half of Liberia's people from their homes. Now it was the summer of 1998, about the first time since the war's end a year earlier that the country was considered safe enough for refugees to return or foreigners like myself to visit. For the exiles, who thought wrongly that the violence in Liberia had finally ended, it was a return to a homeland.

For me it was the culmination of a journey. I was studying the lives of approximately 600 people from my home state, Arkansas, who had emigrated to Liberia in the late 1800s. My main source of information was thousands of letters prospective emigrants wrote to the American Colonization Society, which arranged transportation and settlement in Liberia. When reading other people's mail over a period of years, one develops a relationship with the subjects of study. As I caught my first glimpse from the plane window of the lush green landscape of Liberia, my thoughts were of the emigrants and their first look at Africa from their steamboat railing, more than a hundred years ago. After twenty hours of travel, I was hot, tired, stubble-faced, and irritated that my luggage had not arrived and that I had to pay a bribe to get my carry-on bag past the customs desk. I felt it had been a long trip from Arkansas to Liberia, but then I imagined my subjects who made the same journey in a month instead of a day. And these people were coming for a lifetime. In my pocket I had a return ticket to fly back to the United States. After my first night in Liberia, as I counted the mosquito bites on my arms and legs (my net was in the luggage that had not arrived), I contemplated the mortality rates of the Arkansas emigrants. Perhaps a quarter died within the first year, most from malarial fevers. Again, my empathy was only partial, for I had chloroquinine and an arsenal of antibiotics in my bag of medications.

These privileges of modern life in a wealthy country form a gulf that separates me from my subjects of study, despite my excitement at seeing Liberia with my own two eyes. I remain aware that I am a voyeur, an outsider looking in. How can this white, middle-aged college professor really understand the life of black sharecropper families of a century before? Like my landing in West Africa, historians encounter the past as a foreign space where it is exceedingly difficult to understand the thinking of others. Was it courage or foolhardiness that brought these emigrants here? Was it the push of an increasingly hostile American South or the pull of an ancestral continent? Although answers are rarely certain, the message I heard in thousands of letters written by aspiring emigrants was of the power of hope, a power to inspire and delude. Emigrants were risk takers, optimists for whom despair over their difficult conditions in Arkansas was eclipsed by hope for a better life in Liberia. What follows is their story.

Acknowledgments

Generous institutional support enabled me to research and write this book. I thank the Historic Preservation Program, a division of the Department of Arkansas Heritage, and the University Research Council of the University of Central Arkansas for grants that financed my research in Liberia. I also thank the Arkansas Black History Advisory Committee for support of research travel for this project within the United States. The University of Central Arkansas also awarded me a summer stipend that enabled me to examine materials in the Library of Congress that were unavailable through interlibrary loan. And I especially thank my university for a sabbatical leave that allowed me to write the first draft of this book.

I am most grateful to Dr. Charles Wesley Ford Jr., a native Liberian who is a professor of computer science at the University of Arkansas, Little Rock. In addition to assisting with my research in Liberia, he became my friend and teacher about his homeland and its culture. I thank Charles's mother, the Reverend Mother Edna Mayson Ford, who opened her home to me in Monrovia, the many Ford relatives, especially Cecelia Ford, Lucy Appiah, and Byron Ross, who graciously welcomed me and took care of my needs in Liberia, and Jimmy Scotland Jr., who became my driver and guide.

I thank Dr. Evelyn S. Kandakai, Liberia's former minister of education, and administrators at the University of Liberia, particularly Dr. Frederick S. Gbegbe and Dr. Al-Hassan Conteh, for their welcome and support of my research.

Rich Corby, my friend and authority on Liberia and its history, assisted and encouraged me throughout the duration of this project and provided a critical reading of parts of the manuscript. I thank my colleague Lorien Foote, who read an earlier draft and discussed this project with me at various stages. I am indebted to Tom DeBlack and Sondra Gordy for sharing, on demand, their extensive knowledge about Arkansas history. I also thank the anonymous readers of the University of North Carolina Press for their insightful suggestions, and editors Chuck Grench, Amanda McMillan, and Mary Caviness for their help in many ways.

I am grateful for the assistance of staffs of libraries of the University of Arkansas, the Arkansas History Commission, and the University of Liberia and the staff at the Manuscripts Division of the Library of Congress. I especially thank Davie Bowie and Jimmy Bryant of the University of Central Arkansas Archives for their constant assistance in accessing Arkansas-related material, and Lisa Murphy, interlibrary loan librarian of the University of Central Arkansas, for her cheerful assistance in making the most obscure items miraculously appear. Graduate assistants Paul Anderson and Karen Lee assisted with several tasks. Without the help in so many ways from secretaries Donna Johnson and Judy Huff, I would never have had time to write a book.

I am especially grateful to my oral sources, named in the bibliography, who shared information about their families that could not be found in any written sources. In particular, I thank Alexander Smart of Cambria Heights, New York, who was the first descendant I located and who thereafter helped me in many ways. His nephew, Oscar Smart of Monrovia, Liberia, became my guide and research assistant in the township of Johnsonville and source of much information. Johnny Johnson kindly spent the day with me in Brewerville and introduced me to several other interviewees there. Henry Moore of Monrovia became my griot for the history of the Arkansas emigrants. I was constantly amazed at his knowledge of his family's history before emigration from Arkansas and after their arrival in Liberia, and I thank him for his kindness and hospitality.

Lastly, I thank my family for sharing me with this project. My children, Nick and Christina, for the first time, were old enough to take an interest in my work. My wife, Debbie, is always my sounding board, able reader, and faithful supporter, and to her I dedicate this book.

Conway, Arkansas
August 2003

Journey of Hope

Introduction

Give me your tired, your poor,
Your huddled masses yearning to be free,
The wretched refuse of your teeming shore.
Send these, the homeless, tempest-tost to me,
I lift my lamp beside the golden door!

Emma Lazarus, a Jewish immigrant from Russia, penned these famous lines in 1883 for the Statue of Liberty, then being constructed by the French Republic as a gift to the United States of America. Nearly a decade later, Lady Liberty would witness an ironic scene unfolding in New York Harbor. On the rainy afternoon of 10 March 1892, the Dutch steamer *Werkendam* arrived after a two-week voyage from Rotterdam on the North Sea. The 569 passengers speaking Dutch, German, Russian, Polish, Italian, and a host of other European languages must have chattered excitedly about their hope for a better life in America. One can imagine that many eyes became misty as they beheld Lady Liberty, torch held high, next to Ellis Island, which had opened just two months before. As the *Werkendam* made its way into the bay, it passed a much smaller, old-fashioned sailing ship, the *Liberia*, which had left Pier 6 on the East River earlier in the day. The *Liberia* was packed to the brim with black families from Morrilton, Arkansas, who were leaving the United States to return to their ancestral homeland of Africa.[1] Perhaps the passengers of the *Werkendam* and the *Liberia* waved to each other as they passed in the bay.

This image sums up the paradox of American society in the 1890s. While millions of Europeans were coming to the United States to follow their dream of political freedom and economic opportunity, thousands of black Americans, especially in Arkansas, were equally anxious to get *out* of this county. The hope for many African Americans centered on the Republic of Liberia in West Africa.

As Africa's only independent black republic, Liberia encouraged and symbolized race pride for African Americans in the late 1800s. With an elected black government that offered American settlers free land, Liberia represented a chance for a better life for the South's black farmers. Interest in African emigration peaked among black southerners in the 1890s, a time when cotton prices hit rock bottom and white racism reached its zenith. The 1890s saw the greatest number of lynchings in American history. As it became increasingly clear that black Americans would not get a seat at the table, Liberia posed an alternative to integration, an escape to an all-black world. One black man from central Arkansas asked in 1890: "Ar tha any White People over in liBery? if there is—none [of us] ar going there."[2]

Of all areas of the South, Liberia emigration fever was most intense during the late 1800s in Arkansas. More Liberia-bound emigrants left from Arkansas than from any other state—more than a third of all known black American emigrants to Africa in the years from 1879 to 1899—despite the fact that Arkansas's black population was smaller than that of any of its southern neighbors.[3] And for each one of the approximately 600 who left Arkansas for Africa, hundreds more applied unsuccessfully to go. To understand the back-to-Africa movement in the post-Reconstruction and Jim Crow years, one must examine Arkansas. Ironically, before the 1890s, Arkansas had served as a destination for black migrants leaving other southern states. A high percentage of African American men voted in Arkansas elections, and many held public offices on the county level. But Jim Crow measures, disfranchisement, and a wave of brutal racial violence dramatically changed the situation for black Arkansans. I will argue that the rapidity of this shift from relative well-being to subjugation, rather than the magnitude of the oppression, convinced many African Americans to leave not just Arkansas or the South but the entire United States. The Arkansas counties with the most competitive political environments, where white elites most targeted black voters, saw the most intense interest in African emigrations. Among sharecroppers and country preachers there swelled a remarkable wave of fascination with Africa—as a place of refuge from white oppression and as an ancestral land that helped define a black national identity. While middle-class blacks were more resolved to live as black Americans, many rural poor folk gave up on the United States and looked to Liberia to construct a better life. This study will compare the Liberian dreams to the reality Arkansas emigrants found in their African fatherland. For those who left, and for those who stayed behind, the meaning of Liberian emigration was simple: it was a journey of hope.

EARLIER IN THE nineteenth century, Liberia evoked mixed images in the minds of black Americans. People of color must have pondered a return to Africa as soon as they arrived in the New World, but an organized back-to-Africa movement began in the late 1700s. British abolitionists worked together with free black immigrants to found Sierra Leone on the continent's west coast as a place for the return of black people from British territory. The first black settlers arrived from England in 1787, and others came afterward from Nova Scotia and Jamaica. Sierra Leone became a British crown colony in 1808.[4] In the United States, black Americans' discussion of African colonization originated among New England religious circles that opposed slavery and the slave trade. Paul Cuffe, a prosperous half-black, half-Indian Quaker of Massachusetts who owned a small fleet of whaling ships, transported thirty-eight free blacks to Sierra Leone, largely at his own expense, late in 1815. Cuffe died two years later, but he had inspired a movement.[5]

Humanitarian concerns, like those of Cuffe, joined with very different motives to found the American Colonization Society, just before Cuffe's death. Slave owners in the South had become increasingly worried about the presence of a free black population clustering in southern towns. Some whites thought the very existence of a free black community undermined the slavery system and inspired slaves to revolt. In 1816, the Virginia legislature, dominated by slave owners, asked the U.S. Congress to find a territory on the African coast to become a place of asylum for free blacks and emancipated American slaves. Slave owners and antislavery forces gathered at the Davis Hotel in December 1816 in Washington, D.C., and founded the American Society for Colonizing Free People of Color in the United States, a name later shortened to the American Colonization Society (ACS). At this first meeting, antislavery leaders, such as Daniel Webster, promoted the idea of an African colony as a place of protection for a persecuted people while slave owners, such as Henry Clay, who chaired the first assembly, saw an African colony as a dumping ground for free blacks who had no place in America. Through its early years, the ACS struggled with this tension between humanitarian and racist motivations. Black

Americans stood divided on the issue of emigration. A few black church leaders gave signals of support for the ACS, and free blacks in Richmond, Virginia, made the first public pronouncement in January 1817 favoring emigration. But most free blacks in northern communities such as Philadelphia, New York, and Boston united against emigration, seeing it as a ploy to expel free blacks from the United States.[6]

On 21 January 1820, the ship *Elizabeth* sailed from New York carrying a party of eighty-six free blacks from the Illinois Territory who had volunteered to resettle in Africa. The ACS had received financial and moral support for this expedition from President James Monroe. Nearly a decade after Congress had outlawed the slave trade, American ships were still capturing and confiscating cargoes of illegal slaves bound for the New World, and by 1819 a new slave trade act had authorized the president to establish a place in coastal West Africa where recaptured slaves could be returned. Thus, the ACS began its resettlement work as a private agency carrying out a public policy. The *Elizabeth* arrived in Sierra Leone, where the settlers waited for more than a year while white agents acting on behalf of the U.S. government and the ACS located a site for a colony. They found one at Cape Mesurrado, more than 200 miles south of Freetown, Sierra Leone, where a rocky promontory juts out into the sea near the mouth of the mighty St. Paul River. After much discussion with the local African ruler—the agents ultimately put a gun to his head to encourage cooperation—the ACS received the cape in exchange for an assorted package of rum, muskets, beads, tobacco, and other items worth in total less than $300. The settlers in Sierra Leone, augmented by another group recently arrived from the United States, first set foot in the colony on 25 April 1822. The ACS named the colony Liberia, after the Latin *liber*, meaning free man. The colonists choose the name Monrovia for their first permanent settlement, in honor of the president's support for the colonization effort.[7]

The first settlers, and virtually all the emigrants from America, struggled to survive in their new environment. The ACS agents had chosen one of the most inhospitable locations in West Africa for their colony. Beyond the rocky hill overlooking the coast, mosquito-infested swamps surrounded the new town of Monrovia. Settlers invariably came down with malaria in the first months after arrival. Nearly a quarter of the early settlers to Liberia died within the first year of settlement. Those who survived the "seasoning" found it difficult to make a living. The thin, leached soil did not easily yield American food crops, and settlers found local foods unpalatable. The early settlers eschewed agriculture and largely subsisted on imported foods. They searched in vain for some commodity in demand on the world market, first looking for gold or ivory, then finding camwood, used in the dye industry. But the venture never became economically profitable.[8] Nevertheless, yearly reinforcements brought settlers to Liberia, which remained a colony of the ACS for the next twenty-five years. The society's resident agent in Monrovia presided over the colony, assisted by an elected council of settlers.

The emigration of free blacks to Liberia particularly increased after the Nat Turner rebellion in 1831. During the next year in Maryland, for example, the state legislature passed laws restricting the liberties of free people of color and even appropriated money to pay for their resettlement outside the state's boundaries. In 1832, the American Colonization Society resettled 796 emigrants to Liberia, more than in any year of its history, and the Maryland auxiliary of the ACS itself sent another 146. As the movement became increasingly dominated in the 1830s by slave owners who wanted Liberia to absorb the free blacks of the South, antislavery forces largely turned against the society. William Lloyd Garrison led the charge, decrying African colonization as a plot to continue the slave system in America. Prominent free black leaders, such as David Walker, loudly and consistently denounced the colonization enterprise through the emerging black press, from pulpits, and at every national Negro convention of the 1830s. In a time of conflict within the ACS, state auxiliaries, such as the one in Maryland, began to go their own ways and even establish their own resettlement colonies along the coast southeast of Monrovia. Despite this internal dissension in the society, some free blacks, mostly from slaveholding states, continued to apply for emigration. A few slave owners emancipated slaves with the expressed goal of sending them to Liberia. In addition, more than 5,000 African slaves, confiscated by the U.S. Navy on the high seas, were returned to Africa and left in the colony of Liberia.[9]

Liberia's status changed when the colony gave way to an independent republic on 26 July 1847, a day still celebrated as Liberia's national holiday. It had become evident that a colony owned by a private philanthropic society had little legal and diplomatic standing. Under ACS direction, the settlers drew up a constitution based on that of the United States and designed a flag, again emulating the American model. Thus, beginning in 1847, an elected president and congress of black American settlers governed Liberia, and the ACS's role became virtually that of an emigration agency, transporting settlers and assisting them once they arrived in country.

Emigration picked up in the 1850s when the new Fugitive Slave Act encouraged runaway slaves to seek a destination outside the United States. And then

The Liberian coast. Painting by Robert K. Griffin, ca. 1856. Courtesy Library of Congress.

the Supreme Court's *Dred Scott* decision in 1857 demonstrated that people of color possessed no rights that white people of America were obligated to respect. Many free blacks became even more pessimistic about any future in the United States. Free black leaders, still viewing the ACS as a racist organization in league with white slave owners, sought other locations for black emigration. Martin R. Delany, a prominent black physician, tried to establish a colony in the Yoruba region of today's Nigeria as an area for American settlement. Others looked to Haiti or Central America as destinations. But these movements had leaders but few followers. No settlers actually emigrated to Delany's Nigeria colony, and only a few North Americans moved to Haiti.[10] However, by the beginning of the Civil War, nearly 13,000 black American settlers had come to Liberia, and the black republic controlled a strip of English-speaking settlements scattered along 250 miles of coastline, a few miles deep. Indigenous Africans, who always formed the majority of Liberia's residents, were considered neither "Liberians" nor citizens, and they had no voice in the republic's affairs.

By 1861, the Republic of Liberia had emerged as a symbol that could unite or divide black public opinion. Some black Americans, as well as white abolitionists, believed Liberia's very existence suggested that persons of African descent had no place in America outside of slavery. Prominent black leaders saw the American Colonization Society as a white man's movement that was part of America's racial problem, not its solution. Others saw in the Liberian Republic a symbol of black nationalism, a place where "civilized" black people ruled themselves. At the end of her famous novel, *Uncle Tom's Cabin*, Harriet Beecher Stowe sent George and Eliza off to Liberia with their family but kept some of her black characters home in the United States. George, the strong and angry black man, cannot live in America but expresses his black nationalist feelings by building up the black Republic of Liberia. Likewise, in real life, some emigrants applied to the ACS every year willing to trade in their residence in the United States to follow their African dreams.

Black interest in Liberia emigration plummeted when the Civil War promised the end of slavery and meaningful change to the status of black Americans. Ironically, President Abraham Lincoln's administration suddenly became interested in colonizing freed slaves, especially those who trailed behind occupying Union armies throughout the South. Looking past Liberia, Lincoln's officials searched for locations closer at hand, in the Caribbean or Central America, for the resettlement of freed persons. Despite a congressional appropriation for colonization, the Lincoln administration mustered only one small unsuccessful colonization expedition to Haiti. Likewise, the ACS during the war had difficulty finding emigrants for Liberia and ultimately had to recruit settlers from Barbados instead of the United States.[11]

The end of the Civil War saw significant change in the fortunes of the American Colonization Society and the idea of African colonization. By the time the society celebrated its fiftieth birthday in 1867, its revenues had sharply declined, its loyal following of wealthy white men had largely grown old and died, and the state auxiliaries for the most part had ceased their operations. The ACS had really become the work of one man, William Coppinger, the society's corresponding secretary, who after 1872 worked out of an office on Pennsylvania Avenue in Washington, D.C. Coppinger, a white Quaker, had begun work with the colonization movement in 1838 as a ten-year-old office boy in the Pennsylvania auxiliary. By 1864, he became corresponding secretary of the ACS and devoted the rest of his life, until his death in 1892, to the work of Liberia emigration. He single-handedly administered the ACS's dwindling resources, edited the society's quarterly journal, the *African Repository*, corresponded with the people who desired to resettle in Liberia, and made the arrangements for those accepted for emigration. A dedicated, humble, self-effacing man, Coppinger appeared to believe sincerely that freed people of the American South could better their lives through emigration to Liberia, and he worked tirelessly to that end. No longer a big-budget institution, the American Colonization Society had become virtually a one-man show.[12]

William Coppinger. From *Li-beria Bulletin*, November 1892.

But at the same time, the momentum in the back-to-Africa movement was shifting from white northerners to poor black farmers in the South. Freedom's rewards were slow in coming and fewer than expected. The Liberian govern-ment promised twenty-five acres of free land for each emigrant family, ten acres for a single adult, who came to the black republic. After the war's end, Sec-retary Coppinger made yearly trips to Georgia and the Carolinas recruiting em-igrants. Between 1865 and 1869, the ACS expended much of its remaining funds and transported a record number of 2,394 emigrants to Liberia, more than the society would send over the next thirty years. Through the 1870s, with even less money in its treasury, the ACS sent a yearly average of only ninety-eight emigrants, and that average dropped to seventy-four in the 1880s. Finally, in 1892, the society decided to stop sending groups of emigrants entirely.[13] How-ever, the decline in the number of emigrants in the post-Reconstruction years reflects the dwindling financial resources of the society, not motivation among African Americans. In fact, the most intense black interest in emigration, as measured by the volume of the ACS's incoming correspondence, came in the late 1870s and early 1890s. Both of these periods were moments of sharp racial conflict, and nowhere was the desire for African emigration greater than Arkansas.

African Americans' desire to move out of the South swelled as Reconstruction came to a halt in 1877. Reconstruction had been winding down gradually before its final closure. White Democrats had reclaimed state governments in Tennessee by 1869; in North Carolina, Georgia, and Virginia by 1870; in Arkansas, Alabama, and Texas by 1874; and in Mississippi by 1875. By 1877, the party of Lincoln controlled only the statehouses of Florida, South Carolina, and Louisiana. Public opinion in the North had begun to sour on military occupation of the South, and business interests in the Republican Party pushed for the reintegration of southern states into the national economy. The election of Rutherford B. Hayes as president in 1876 signaled the end of federal oversight of local affairs in the South. Ironically, Hayes's campaign platform called for strong protection of black citizens in the South. But when the election mired down in controversy because of disputed returns in Florida, South Carolina, and Louisiana, Republicans worked out a compromise that gave them the presidency in exchange for measures formally ending Reconstruction. In an extremely complex turn of events, the necessary electoral votes went to Hayes while the statehouses in the disputed states went to the Democrats. Hayes withdrew the federal troops from South Carolina and Louisiana and included some southern Democrats, even ex-Confederates, in his federal patronage and cabinet appointments. Historians have debated whether Hayes's policy reflected a genuine attempt to heal sectional strife or a mere ploy to win a disputed election and consolidate power. In any case, Reconstruction, with its use of force to protect the rights of black citizens, had come to an end.[14]

The symbolic meaning of Hayes's policy seemed clear to white southern Democrats. The federal government, while it would use troops to fight Indians in the West and to break a railroad strike in northern cities in the summer of 1877, would not intervene in southern affairs. In black-majority areas, white Democrats had already begun using terror tactics against black Republican voters in the elections of 1875 and 1876. Before the state elections in Mississippi in 1875, white military companies in Yazoo and Coahoma Counties, deep in the delta, attacked black Republican meetings and murdered several black leaders.[15] In South Carolina's piedmont area, gangs of white men rode through the countryside before the 1876 election terrorizing black neighborhoods and keeping Republican voters home on election day. Obviously, Hayes's actions of 1877 further emboldened white Democrats. The violence and fraud in the next election, the state and congressional races of 1878, shocked many northern Republicans into admitting the failure of the president's southern policy. Again the atrocities were greatest in black-majority states where white Democrats needed to suppress black Republican votes to get or maintain power. Reports from Louisiana suggested that animals preyed upon the unburied bodies of African Americans slain on election day. The number of Republican ballots cast in South Carolina dropped from 90,000 in the fraudulent 1876 election to a mere 4,000 in 1878. The Republican Party thus crumbled in the Black Belt southern states that had the largest number of potential Republican voters.[16]

The pattern would continue in the 1880 elections. Only two Republican votes were recorded in Yazoo County, Mississippi, a county that was 75 percent black. The Republican presidential candidate of 1880, James A. Garfield, received his lowest percentage of votes in states that had the highest proportion of black residents, while he polled the greatest percentage of southern votes in border states with the lowest black populations.[17] Thus, African Americans virtually lost voting rights in the areas where their numbers threatened white control.

African Americans understood the meaning of the president's retreat from Reconstruction. In the same areas where Reconstruction's end brought sudden change to their political status, a black migration movement took root quickly and sprouted in the last three years of the 1870s. The day after President Hayes withdrew federal troops from South Carolina, John Mardenborough, a black lawyer in Edgefield County, wrote to the American Colonization Society's office in Washington begging the society to send a group of seventy-five local black residents to Liberia. Edgefield County, in fact, was known throughout South Carolina for the most extreme political violence against black citizens. Mardenborough explained why his group wished to leave Edgefield County: "While I write a colored woman comes and tells me her husband was killed last night in her presence by white men and her children burned to death in the house; she says her person was outraged by these men and then she was whipped —such things as these are common occurrences. In the name of God can not the Society send us to Africa or some where else where we can live without ill treatment?"[18]

By the summer of 1877, interest in Liberia emigration had spread throughout South Carolina. One of the black leaders from Edgefield County, Harrison N. Bouey, traveled to Charleston to serve on a federal jury, and there he linked up with others interested in emigration. When Bouey arrived in Charleston, "Professor" J. C. Hazeley, a native African, was in town to deliver lectures promoting African emigration at the Morris Brown African Methodist Episcopal

(AME) Church. Apparently displeased with the ACS's response to prospective emigrants, leaders at these meetings proposed the formation of a joint stock company to purchase their own ship and to transport emigrants to Africa. Thus was born the Liberian Exodus Joint Stock Steamship Company, which sold stock at ten dollars a share. By early 1878, the company had raised $6,000 and purchased a ship in Boston, the *Azor*, which arrived in the port of Charleston in March. Five thousand people turned out for the worship service that consecrated the vessel into service. The elderly Martin R. Delany, eminent Charlestonian and longtime promoter of African emigration, spoke, as did the Reverend Henry McNeal Turner, future bishop of the AME Church and the coming generation's spokesman for the emigration cause. A month later, the *Azor* finally set sail with 206 passengers, and 175 more remained behind awaiting a second voyage. But the *Azor* would never sail again. Upon its return, bills from the first voyage came due, and the ship was sold at auction the next year to pay the company's debts.[19]

At the same time that black South Carolinians were organizing for African emigration, a similar movement broke out in Louisiana. As early as December 1875, a group of black clergymen from Louisiana, Texas, Arkansas, Mississippi, Alabama, and Georgia had held a conference in New Orleans to assess the situation for southern blacks. The group discussed migration to the western territories or to Liberia. One of the delegates to the meeting, Henry Adams, a tireless political organizer from Caddo Parish, in northwest Louisiana, returned home and founded the Colonization Council to plan a way to go somewhere, anywhere, outside of the South. In July 1877, Adams's council drew up a petition to President Hayes asking for the government either to protect rights of black citizens or to give them a territory of their own. If Hayes could do neither, the petition asked for a federal appropriation of funds to send them back to their own land, Africa. The next month, Adams wrote to the American Colonization Society claiming to speak for 69,000 African Americans in Louisiana, southern Arkansas, and eastern Texas who wished to move to Liberia. The aspiring emigrants even proposed to send a delegation to Liberia to investigate the conditions there and report back to the group. Coppinger made it clear that the ACS could not fund a mass migration to Liberia and that any investigative delegation must travel at its own expense. He encouraged the group to keep organized, collect dues, and send a few settlers each year. Given the impoverished conditions under which they lived, this advice could hardly satisfy. Only seven known emigrants left Louisiana for Liberia, a group from New Orleans settled by the ACS in 1876.[20]

As possibilities for emigration to Liberia were waning, interest shifted to a destination closer at hand: Kansas. Benjamin "Pap" Singleton, a former slave from Tennessee, had arrived in Kansas in the mid-1870s and immediately begun work to promote the state as a haven for black settlers. Singleton and other land developers circulated handbills throughout the South encouraging black people to consider Kansas. Political actions further inspired black southerners to move west. In January of 1879, Senator William Windom of Minnesota introduced a resolution calling for a U.S. Senate committee to study the feasibility of federal aid for migration of black citizens from areas where their rights were denied to western territories where they would be respected. After much debate in the Senate, the Windom resolution eventually died from inaction, but rumors about the resolution swept through the South and further inspired black interest in migration and the possibility of governmental assistance. By spring 1879, Liberia fever in the lower South had become Kansas fever, and hundreds of migrants camped along the Mississippi River waiting for steamboats to take them north. Reports of a mass migration from Louisiana, Mississippi, and Texas in particular aroused much interest among politicians and newspaper editors. The U.S. Senate even established a select committee to investigate the situation. However, informed estimates suggest that only around 8,000 black migrants actually moved to Kansas in 1879 and 1880. Poverty rather than lack of interest probably best explains the modest numbers, for few rural blacks could afford the steamboat and railroad passage needed to get to Kansas.[21]

The Kansas exodus of 1879, like the Liberia emigration movement, illustrates the keen interest among African Americans in escaping political oppression in the South. While in antebellum years, free black Americans had criticized the American Colonization Society as a racist organization hell-bent on removing the country's free black population, one can only wonder what slaves may have thought or said about Liberia in the years before freedom. After Reconstruction's end in 1877, most prominent black leaders continued to oppose African migration, but for ordinary black Americans, many whose lives had begun as slaves, Liberia became a symbol of a new life, free from white oppression. These men and women were more than willing to work with the ACS to get to Africa. During the late 1800s, as the back-to-Africa movement shifted from being a white man's institution to a black grassroots movement, interest would be no greater anywhere than in Arkansas. The story of Arkansas's African emigration movement will illustrate not just the severe realities for black southerners in the late 1800s but also their hopes and dreams for a better life.

The Liberia Exodus Arkansas Colony, 1877–1880

On 23 November 1877, a convention of nearly one hundred black delegates and observers assembled at the Third Baptist Church of Helena, Arkansas, to make plans for a mass migration to Liberia. Calling themselves the Liberia Exodus Arkansas Colony, the delegates resolved:

> That we hold these truths to be self-evident, that all men are created equal; that they are endowed by their creator with certain inalienable rights, that among these are life, liberty, and the pursuit of happiness. And WHEREAS, In the United States of North America many of our people have been debarred by law from the rights and privileges of freemen, and even now public sentiment—more powerful than law—frowns us down. We are made a separate and distinct class, and against us many avenues to improvement and eminence are effectually closed. Strangers from all lands, of a color different from ours, are preferred before us. Therefore, Resolved, That we continue to seek an asylum from this deep degradation by going to Liberia, on the western coast of Africa, where we will be permitted to more fully exercise and improve those faculties which impart to man his dignity, and to evince to all who despise, ridicule and oppress our race, that we possess with them a common nature, and are susceptible of equal refinement and equal advancement in all that dignifies man, and that we are capable of self-government.[1]

This eloquent statement reveals both the push and the pull motivations for emigration: the deteriorating racial climate of the American South combined with the magnetic attraction of Liberia, a stirring symbol for black hopes. Conditions in Arkansas's delta region, near the Mississippi River, provided the motivations for the state's first back-to-Africa movement, although it would prove to be short-lived.

In some ways, Arkansas would seem a less probable location for an African emigration movement than other southern states. Under the firm hand of so-called carpetbagger Republican governor Powell Clayton, Reconstruction policies had achieved more success in Arkansas than elsewhere in the South. Clayton's first months as governor in the fall of 1868 saw an intense confrontation with conservative Democratic forces organized as the Ku Klux Klan. But Clayton met the challenge decisively by declaring martial law and organizing militia companies of local black and white Republicans to police a large part of the state. Clayton's willingness to use force distinguished him from most other Republican governors in the South. The heavy-handed tactics made him a hated figure to white Democrats for several generations, but Reconstruction in Arkansas after 1868 was relatively peaceful.[2] With more than 8,000 white men serving in Union blue during the Civil War, more than any other Confederate state except Tennessee, Arkansas had many white Unionists joining with freedmen to form a sizable block of Republican voters. Arkansas's Reconstruction struggles of the 1870s resulted more from factions within the Republican Party than from an overpowering Democratic opposition. Reconstruction ended in Arkansas in 1874 with one last blowout, the Brooks-Baxter War, fought by two rival groups who supported two Republican politicians, each claiming to be the lawful governor.[3]

Elections that followed in 1874 brought Democrats into control of both the statehouse and legislature. But the Democratic takeover did not mean the end of black political power, as in some other southern states. No evidence suggests a decline in black voting or political officeholding, or a violent backlash against people of color immediately following Reconstruction's end. The new Democratic governor, Augustus H. Garland, campaigned on promises to protect black voting rights and provide access to free public schools. As governor, he opened the Branch Normal College in Pine Bluff to train black teachers and named an African American, Joseph C. Corbin, as its first principal. After Democrats had firmly reestablished control of state government, some whites in black-majority Lee County tried to oust the black elected sheriff, W. H. Furbush. However, Governor Garland refused to allow it, saying they had no legal grounds on which to remove him. Black Republicans so highly regarded the Democratic gover-

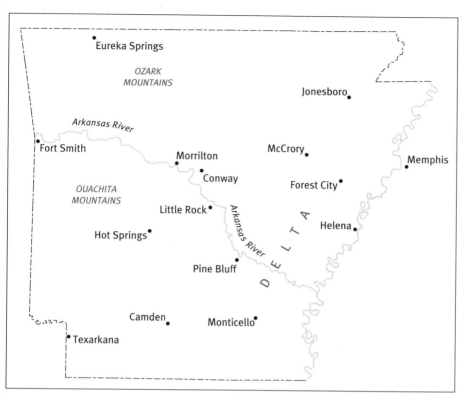

Arkansas

nor that five black representatives in the Arkansas legislature broke ranks with their party in 1877 to vote for Garland in his bid to become a U.S. senator. Some northerners held up the Redeemer government of Arkansas as a model for other southern states, and even Arkansas Republican leaders admitted that Democratic rule had been peaceful and fair after the end of Reconstruction.

African Americans made up just over a quarter of Arkansas's population in the 1870s, so Democrats did not need to worry, as they did in South Carolina and Louisiana, about black votes controlling state politics. In the 1876 presidential election, the Republican candidate polled about 40 percent of the state's popular vote, which suggests that blacks voted freely and in large numbers. African Americans formed a majority of the population in about a dozen counties in the delta area of eastern Arkansas. There the democratic process enabled black politicians to occupy many county offices and take seats in the state legislature. Ned Hill, for example, headed the Republican legislative ticket in black-majority Jefferson County for the first post-Reconstruction General Assembly in 1875. A man who knew him said Hill was a black man "who could neither read nor write, but whose fighting weight was two hundred pounds, drunk or sober. His ticket was overwhelmingly elected."[4]

Rather than restricting black political rights, the new Democratic state government took more subtle but damaging economic measures. In 1875, lawmakers passed two new acts that gave planters and persons with wealth more control over the rural poor, black or white, who worked the land. One law approved a system of mortgages granted on future crops whereby small farmers could borrow in the spring from a landlord or merchant using the expected fall harvest, preferably cotton, as collateral. Farmers dubbed these mortgages "anaconda" mortgages after the snake that squeezes its victim to death. The second law gave landlords a lien on the crops of an indebted tenant and forbade the worker to leave until the agreed-upon terms of service had expired. Taken together, the laws encouraged landless farmers into debt and then gave more control to the planters and merchants to whom they were indebted. In the same legislative session in 1875, the assembly passed another draconian measure aimed specifically at the poor, a larceny law that made the theft of any goods worth more than two dollars punishable by up to a five-year prison term. The state prison population jumped dramatically in the late 1870s, with black prisoners outnumbering white. Without space to house all the inmates, state officials increasingly leased out convicts as virtual slave labor under deplorable conditions.[5]

Thus, even though black Arkansans retained political rights after Reconstruction's end, their economic position and freedom of movement sustained losses. But with the federal retreat in 1877 indicated by President Hayes's southern policy, African Americans immediately perceived a significant change in their status and well-being. In the black-majority Arkansas delta, some people responded with efforts to escape to Africa.

On 15 August 1877, just shortly after the clamor for African migration had begun in South Carolina and Louisiana, the Reverend Anthony L. Stanford, a Methodist preacher and physician, inquired about the terms to resettle about 5,000 black Arkansans in Liberia. He addressed his questions to AME Church leader Henry M. Turner, who held the honorary position of vice president of the American Colonization Society (ACS). Turner passed on the letter to ACS secretary William Coppinger, who asked Stanford how many of his 5,000 emigrants could pay the one hundred dollars it cost the ACS to transport and provision each settler. Not put off by this response, Stanford busily prepared for a convention in November to discuss a mass migration to Liberia.[6]

A flamboyant man of questionable character, Stanford proved to be an able leader of the emigration movement. Born free in Greenwich, New Jersey, in 1830, by the close of the Civil War he served as pastor of Savannah's St. Phillip Church, the first African Methodist Episcopal congregation in Georgia. There he met Henry Turner, who arrived in 1865 to organize AME churches elsewhere in the state. By the later 1860s, Stanford had moved to Philadelphia, where he claimed to have graduated from the Eclectic Medical College, a school closed down in 1880 for selling and giving away diplomas.[7] In the early 1870s, Stanford worked at the AME Church headquarters in Philadelphia, managing the publications department. However, in early 1872, allegations surfaced that he had embezzled money, left his wife, and disappeared in the company of a young woman who clerked in his office.[8] Evidently, Stanford made his way to Jackson, Mississippi, where he practiced medicine. After serving a jail sentence in Canton, Mississippi, he had by the fall of 1872 moved west to Helena, Arkansas, an old port town on the Mississippi River. There he entered politics and was elected in 1876 to a four-year term as state senator, representing the black-majority counties of Lee and Phillips.[9] Scott Bond, a prosperous black farmer in eastern Arkansas, later remembered that Stanford came through his neighborhood recruiting emigrants for Liberia. Stanford was such an effective salesman for his cause, Bond said, he could "almost talk the horns off a frozen cow."[10]

By the time of the emigration convention in November, Stanford had disseminated the information about Liberia he received from the ACS and had apparently organized at least twenty-eight emigration clubs in eastern Arkansas.[11] The clubs, under Stanford's leadership, had drafted a constitution for the movement, which called itself the Liberia Exodus Arkansas Colony, obviously following the lead of the South Carolina group of a few months earlier. According to the constitution, the colony would be divided into companies of no more than one hundred; each would be represented at the convention, with one delegate per fifty members. As in a secret society, one could not join the club without the sponsorship of an existing member and acceptance by the group. Five black balls in the vote would be sufficient to exclude someone. Members would pay an initiation fee of $1.25 and then monthly dues of a quarter. Upon membership, one kissed the Bible and took a loyalty oath that included a clause requiring secrecy about the business of the organization. Members could be expelled for immoral, drunken, or felonious behavior. Once organized, clubs would hold monthly meetings, each following an established order of business beginning with the singing of the missionary hymn "From Greenland's Icy Mountains."

Anthony L. Stanford. Courtesy
Arkansas History Commission.

While Stanford's letters to the ACS had made allusions to poverty and political oppression as motives for emigration, the constitution of the Liberia Exodus Colony spoke less of black desire to leave the United States than about a
responsibility to redeem and elevate Africa. The colony pledged to take to Liberia "the implements of husbandry, mechanics, artizens, school-teachers,
preachers, doctors and lawyers, wealth and refinement, a higher and nobler christian manhood to develop the resources of that country . . . and to redeem its
tens of millions to Christ." As if to help elevate the material standards of Liberia, the constitution directed emigrants to take with them "stoves, pans, ket-
tles, bedsteads, bedding, chairs, sofas, lounges, pianos and organs, carpets, pictures, and everything that conduces to refinement and education, with books
in vast number and variety." These words clearly reflected Dr. Stanford's middle-
class vision. While the poor farmers who formed the bulk of the colony's membership may have lacked the pianos, carpets, and instruments of refinement,
apparently they, too, believed they could do much, as Christian Americans, to
bring civilization to a dark continent.[12]

At the two-day convention that convened in Helena in November, delegates representing clubs in Phillips, Lee, Cross, and St. Francis Counties quickly elected Stanford as chairman of the Liberia Exodus Arkansas Colony. After considerable speechmaking—each speaker limited to five minutes—the delegates spent most of their time deliberating about the choice of two of their number to travel to Liberia as "commissioners" to scout out the land, choose a suitable location for settlement, and then return to Arkansas and report to the group. Delegates resolved to pay the commissioners a salary of $1,000 if married men, or $700 if single, and up to one $100 each for transportation. Dr. Stanford was unanimously elected as one commissioner. Brother A. Dennis was proposed as the second, but after much discussion, he was deemed too old to stand up to the rigors of such travel and replaced by a younger man, Charles F. Hicks. As a last act before adjourning, the all-male convention resolved that women could join the colony and were asked to pay reduced dues of fifty cents.[13]

After the meeting, Stanford sent the ACS $175 to book cabin passage for himself and Hicks aboard the bark *Liberia*, chartered by the ACS to transport fifty-three settlers in less commodious steerage accommodations. The *Liberia* sailed from New York on the morning of 9 January 1878 and arrived in Monrovia in early February. Stanford and Hicks spent two months in Liberia, traveling throughout the settlements near Monrovia and along the coast as far south as Cape Palmas. Just before the *Azor* arrived from South Carolina, Stanford and Hicks returned to the United States, enthusiastic about Africa and emigration. Hicks said: "Africa is the home for the freeman, and his able sons and daughters where-ever they may be found in the United States." Stanford was somewhat more chastened in his views. While he still viewed Africa as the black man's home, he concluded that emigrants required means of support in their new land or they easily became a burden on the ACS and the country itself. Stanford recommended that emigrants come from the "more enterprising, hardworking, moral and intelligent class," not the "indolent, ignorant, and immoral class of American Negroes." Upon his return voyage to New York, Stanford worked his way back to Arkansas by lecturing about Africa in cities such as Philadelphia, Wilmington, Baltimore, and Washington. Stanford declared that he planned to gather his family and prepare for permanent emigration to Liberia.[14]

By the time the commissioners returned home in May with their favorable report, Liberia fever had broken out in eastern Arkansas. Interest had spread west into the central part of the state. One applicant for emigration from Pulaski County, near Little Rock, claimed that a hundred people were ready to go immediately, and 5,000 more would emigrate if the ACS would provide some assistance. The state's leading newspaper, the *Arkansas Gazette*, reported that 1,600 black residents in Phillips and adjoining counties were organizing to go to Liberia. In August, Berry Colman, a black farmer and Baptist preacher who had served as Phillips County's elected representative to the state legislature, wrote the ACS asking for passage to Liberia. Colman recognized that hopes had outpaced realities, explaining that "Dr. Stanford and Hicks is laboren away. . . . They have enBold about 10,000 of whom will never see Liberia."[15]

Interest in emigration reached panic proportions in Phillips County with the state and local elections of September 1878. In the weeks before the election, white Democrats decided the time had come to reclaim their county from the black Republicans, like Anthony Stanford and Berry Colman, who held all local offices. Using tactics found successful in Mississippi, Louisiana, and South Carolina, white Democrats early in August organized military companies, complete with cavalry, infantry, and breach-loading rifles. Democrats called their company, which reportedly enlisted a thousand men wearing red shirts, the Phillips County Legion. When black citizens tried to hold a mass meeting in Poplar Grove, the white company arrived on horseback and broke up the assembly.[16] Just before the election, the group's leader, W. R. Burke, editor of the *Helena World* and the Democratic candidate for the legislature, traveled to Memphis, where he secured two artillery pieces owned by the state of Tennessee, leaving a bond and pledge to return them in thirty days, after the election. Democrats apparently positioned one cannon in an open square in Helena and pulled the other one around through black settlements in rural areas of the county. One planter noted that the streets of Helena were filled with armed men in the days before the election, reminding him of war days of the previous decade.[17]

According to Republican reports, Democrats had announced they would win the upcoming elections no matter how much bloodshed would be required and that "no colored man will be permitted to go near the polls on election day, unless he intends to vote the Democratic ticket." If Republicans refused to abstain from voting, they were threatened with death. The leaders of the military clubs reportedly banned any Republican meetings and by one account threatened to kill the Republican county judge, Samuel Clark, if he appointed anyone but Democratic men as election judges throughout the county. As if these measures were not enough, Democrats expected assistance on election day from rifle clubs and extra voters coming from across the river in Mississippi.[18] Democrats claimed they had organized their military companies to protect against threats "made boldly by negroes against the whites" who live "in daily peril of their lives." In an even less believable claim, Democrats said that their rifle clubs aimed to protect from retaliation any black citizens who wanted to break ranks with Republican leaders and vote Democratic.[19] Under such pressure, the county's Republican organization, led by black county sheriff H. B. Robinson, offered to divide local offices in a fusion arrangement, with the Democrats getting the offices of judge, treasurer, and assessor and part of the representation in the state legislature. Republicans even offered to vote the Democratic judicial and state tickets. Feeling confident that they could have it all, Democrats refused the fusion offer.[20]

Given the southern policy of President Hayes's administration, the disheartened Republicans of Phillips County expected no help from the national government. A local correspondent lamented: "In the eyes of a Northern Republican, a Southern Republican is fit for only one thing, i.e., to be a martyr for the party."[21] Ironically, their only support came from the Democratic governor of Arkansas, William Miller. Sheriff Robinson and black Republican county clerk D. W. Ellison traveled to Little Rock to complain personally to the governor about the intimidation and threat of violence by the rifle clubs. Democratic leaders from the county also met with Governor Miller to respond to the Republican complaints. On 19 August, the governor telegraphed orders to Phillips County that the Democratic military clubs must disband. While his orders denied that the clubs were armed or were anything more than political organizations, he forbade them on the grounds that they invited "misrepresentation" and set a precedent for future abuses.[22]

The intimidation by Democrats apparently worked nonetheless, for the election on 2 September brought a resounding defeat for Republicans in Phillips County. The election day coincided with an outbreak of yellow fever, and Democrats reportedly corralled potential black voters under the pretext of quarantine. Some white Republicans claimed later that they, too, were turned away at the point of a musket when they tried to vote that day. James Hanks, a Democratic planter of Helena, recorded in his diary on election day: "We have had an election so-called. Any was permitted to vote the Democratic ticket—no one was permitted to vote any other. . . . It is the first time in a long while that we have had the presence of the military overawing the civil authorities." Democrats claimed two-thirds of the votes of a county that had gone Republican by a majority of 1,800 in the presidential election two years before.[23] Although the Phillips County election was the most spectacular case of fraud and violence, Democrats in neighboring east Arkansas counties successfully suppressed the black vote as well. No Republican candidates won seats to the state legislature in the September 1878 election from any black-majority county except Jefferson, where Democrats and Republicans had entered on a fusion agreement to split the representation between them.[24]

Thus for African Americans in the black-majority counties of Arkansas, the promises of Reconstruction quickly faded in 1878 as they did in Mississippi, Louisiana, and South Carolina. Escape to Liberia only seemed the more attractive. Letters to the ACS office in Washington poured in from the delta region of Arkansas, especially from Phillips County. Some applicants wrote just for their own families; others applied on behalf of a whole club. George Hayden wrote for seventy-eight others in Poplar Grove who, he said, could pay fifteen dollars each toward their passage. H. H. Robinson, a teacher and former state representative for Monroe County, sent an application for eighty-one residents in the rural hamlet of Duncan Station. Schoolteacher Ben McKeever, from North Creek in rural Phillips County, asked if pregnant women could travel to Liberia, for his wife Mary was expecting a child.[25] Leaders of the Liberia Exodus Arkansas Colony inquired about possibilities of chartering their own ship and traveling down the Mississippi River and onward to Africa via New Orleans. Obviously aware of the voyage of the *Azor* from Charleston earlier in 1878, some black Arkansans asked the ACS for news about the passengers after the ship's arrival in Liberia. Coppinger assured correspondents that the ACS's chartered vessels provided the cheapest manner to get to Liberia. Most applicants hoped the ACS would provide some subsidy toward the cost of their passage.[26]

The ship passage from New York to Liberia, along with provisions to last the first six months, cost the ACS approximately one hundred dollars per adult passenger. Emigrants were expected to pay their own way to the port of New York. Thus, secretary Coppinger encouraged applicants who said they could pay at least a portion of the cost of the transatlantic passage. He told Shadrach Jenkins of Poplar Grove that the society would give preference to those who could contribute at least twenty-five dollars a head. When Coppinger promised passage to George Hayden and his wife for seventy-five dollars, he angered other applicants who had been told they must pay fifty dollars per person.[27]

Throughout 1878 and 1879, the would-be emigrants were thus preoccupied with raising enough money to get accepted by the ACS. Shadrach Jenkins wanted to know if emigrants could pay off their passage to the ACS over ten years after emigration or if the ACS would take their personal property in exchange.[28] With the need for hard cash, those wanting to emigrate competed with each other to sell their land and/or possessions. George Hayden complained that he could not sell his land for its true value and that he would take a financial sacrifice to go to Liberia. Berry Colman explained that he failed to collect the $500 he needed for his homestead but that he would try again next fall: "Nothen will stop me but Death." Despite his resolve, Colman never made it to Liberia.[29] Others hoped to sell enough of their crops to raise the necessary cash. But the sinking prices for cotton, corn, and stock meant few could get the money they needed. As one Arkansas applicant informed Coppinger, "a large number of people would leave now if they had money."[30]

Another difficulty for the prospective settlers concerned the timing of the voyage. Coppinger could not promise a departure before June 1879. That response created a problem, for most of those interested in emigrating were renters or sharecroppers who, around the first of January, had to make contracts for a year's labor or leave their farms. If they could not depart until June they would lose a half year's labor. The land and labor system, buttressed by the new laws in Arkansas, worked to keep rural black laborers tied to the land. One farmer who was most enthusiastic about emigration said that when he went to his landlord to close his contract, he "was defeated and failed to raise the money needed to emigrate." Apparently his landlord promised him that if he would stay and raise one more crop, then he would have enough to go to Liberia.[31]

By spring 1789, McKeever and the Lucas, Johnson, and Yancey families of Poplar Grove were finalizing their plans to emigrate. William Lucas sent the ACS a post office order for $125 toward the passage of his family of six.[32] Dr. Stanford intended to depart for New York immediately after the spring session of the Arkansas General Assembly. As Stanford served out the last leg of his four-year term, he was the only Republican and the only black man left in the Arkansas Senate.[33] By 1879, he seemed to have stopped recruiting large numbers of emigrants for Liberia, having decided that only the better class of citizens, like himself, should go there. However, this educated professional man had to beg the ACS for aid to emigrate. Unable to pay his way, Stanford asked for employment as an attending physician aboard the chartered ship in exchange for cabin passage for himself, his wife, and son. Coppinger agreed to the terms, and Stanford's family left for New York in April.[34] Ben McKeever, who had seemed the most anxious of all to emigrate to Liberia, wrote Coppinger in May despairing that even though he had sold all that he owned, he had only forty dollars, just enough to get to New York. None of his friends could help him, he said, because they all had their own mortgages. Begging the ACS for help, McKeever said, "I believe I had almost as soon die as stay here amid such showers of censure contempt and vexation." Coppinger took pity on McKeever and told him to come anyway, even though he had no money to contribute toward his African passage.[35]

By the end of May, all five Arkansas families were on their way to New York, an ordeal certainly for Mrs. McKeever and Mrs. Lucas, who were both seven months pregnant, and Mrs. Johnson, who was due to give birth any day. The McKeever, Johnson, and Lucas families traveled by steamship from Helena to Cincinnati, where they met Parker and Jane Yancey and their three children, who had left earlier by train. From Cincinnati the whole group traveled by rail to New York, arriving on 9 June. They went directly aboard the bark *Monrovia* to their steerage accommodations, as they had no other place to stay. The Stanfords arrived on 13 June, and the ship set sail the next day with forty-six passengers, half of them from Arkansas. Sarah Johnson gave birth to her baby, a boy named Aberdeen, aboard the ship. The passengers sailed into port in Monrovia, exactly a month later, on 14 July. The Johnsons, McKeevers, Lucases, and Yanceys all eventually settled in Brewerville, a farm community on the St. Paul River, about ten miles from Monrovia, while the Stanfords stayed in the capital. Within a month after their arrival Mary McKeever and Susan Lucas had each given birth to a baby boy, who became automatically citizens of the Republic of Liberia.[36]

The departure of the first Arkansas emigrants to Liberia took place just as the Kansas exodus was at its height elsewhere in the South. H. H. Robinson, the black politician whom the ACS turned down for African emigration, asked Secretary Coppinger, "If not Liberia, how about Kansas?"[37] Some Arkansans anxious to get out of the South looked north and west instead of across the Atlantic. A black state convention met in April in Little Rock to discuss the Windom resolution, at that time stalled in Congress. The meeting adopted statements declaring that, as black citizens do not enjoy their constitutional rights in many parts of Arkansas, they wished to move to another state or territory "where the elective franchise can be enjoyed unmolested." Delegates endorsed the Windom resolution, specifically calling for federal aid for black migrants leaving the South. Before adjourning, they formed an auxiliary State Emigration Aid Society with the goal of sending commissioners to find a suitable place for relocation. An Arkansas delegate at a national black meeting in Nashville, Tennessee, a few weeks later, called for emigration from the South to a place "where they could enjoy the fruits of their labor and social and political equality." The delegate also shared the proposal calling for state commissioners to scout locations for migration.[38] Despite this interest in domestic migration, few from Arkansas apparently left their homes. The number of black residents of Kansas born in Arkansas was less in 1880 than at the census ten years before.[39] While many wanted to leave, Africa, not Kansas, seems to have captured the dreams of African Americans in eastern Arkansas. G. A. Walker, the pastor of Mt. Zion Church in Poplar Grove, spoke for many when he said: "I think that it would be a good thing for the corler race all to com out of the south, but myself I want to go ther to my father land."[40]

Local interest in emigration to Liberia only increased after the departure of the first emigrants. By the following September, letters from William Lucas and Ben McKeever had arrived back in Phillips County indicating satisfaction with their new surroundings. Correspondents representing dozens of other families in Phillips, Lee, Woodruff, and Monroe Counties wrote to the ACS applying to go.[41] W. H. Green wrote pleadingly to the ACS, asking to be accepted as an emigrant for Africa, saying, "In this part of the Countery we is not Living here we ar jest Being and do be leve there is a beter Cuntery for us and from all accounts Liberia is the plase for us cullard pepels." Green, who, despite his poor spelling, claimed to be a schoolteacher in North Creek, Phillips County, indicated that he was one of nearly sixty people in his community ready to emigrate to Liberia.[42]

After the fall harvests were in, some families in teacher Green's neighborhood began to sell out their possessions to get ready to go. When other farmers gave their landlords notice of their intention later in the year to leave for Liberia, they said they were turned out of their houses and off the plantations.[43] With no place else to go, some set out for the North. By the middle of February, Austin Barrow and his family of seven from Helena arrived at the New York office of Yates and Porterfield, the shipping company the ACS used for its Liberia voyages. Told that the next chartered vessel would not leave for some time, Barrow and his family rented rooms in the city and began to look for temporary work.[44] Around the same time, a group of twenty led by Elijah and Caroline Parker, who had sold their 125-acre farm the previous December, showed up in Philadelphia, spending all their money just to get that far north. Coppinger said they were swayed solely by letters from their relatives and friends in Liberia. By the end of the month, another family from the Helena area, Isaac Dickson, his wife, Martha, and their two grown sons, one of whom had his own wife and four children, had arrived in New York, like the others, neither invited nor expected by the ACS. They, too, had spent most of their money to get to New York and hoped to find some work to tide them over until they could take their ship to Liberia.[45] Another group of eleven, the McCarty and Lee families, arrived unannounced in New York a few weeks later. More alarmingly for the ACS, rumors circulated that a large party in excess of a hundred emigrants was on its way north from Arkansas.[46]

The rumors proved correct, for on 17 March 1880, a group of farmers in Phillips County gathered in Helena to catch a steamer up the Mississippi River. The group's leader, Richard Newton, claimed that when white authorities learned of the planned departure, county sheriff Bart Turner, in an effort to keep them from leaving, confiscated some of their luggage and demanded payment of a tax ranging from $2.50 to $8 per person. The departing emigrants protested that they had paid all their property taxes; some even had receipts to prove it. The leaders consulted lawyers, who advised them to pay the taxes even though they might be illegal ones. The group clubbed together, those who could pay sharing money with those who had none. After satisfying the sheriff's demand, the emigrants boarded their steamer and departed the next day, 18 March. On Friday morning, eight days later, the party arrived at Pennsylvania Depot in Jersey City and made their way into New York. A reporter for the *New York Times* described them as "dusty, travel-worn, and scantily-clad. . . . There were old black men with snowy wool, roughened cheeks, and hard, cracked hands, little molasses-colored pickaninnies with frightened faces, clutching hold of the mothers' skirts, good-looking young mulatto and quadroon girls, old women with sunken cheeks and bowed heads, anxious fathers toil-worn and husky-voiced, clad in rough homespun and keeping an anxious look-out for their charges." Numbering 100 exactly, 24 men, 33 women, and the rest children, they came with assorted boxes and bags containing everything from furniture to bedding, clothing to food.[47]

With no one from the ACS expecting them and in New York to greet them, the tired travelers marched north up Sixth Avenue looking for lodging until they secured a room in the Young Men's Colored Christian Association at 124 West Twenty-Sixth Street. There, all 100 of them crowded into a room some thirty feet long and only thirteen feet wide, packed almost to the point of suffocation and made more chaotic by the ceaseless crying of a half dozen babies. Some of the neighboring businessmen took pity on the group and brought food; a baker donated two barrels of bread. The travelers set up a table of boards in the middle of the room to eat and then lay down on the floor to sleep. Within a few days, the "Arkansas refugees," as the New York newspapers called them, had moved down the street to the basement of the Shiloh Colored Presbyterian Church, before finding more spacious rented quarters at 118 West Thirty-Seventh Street. Here in a squalid precinct of the city the emigrants had four

Arkansas emigrants in New York City awaiting transportation to Liberia. From *Frank Leslie's Illustrated Newspaper*, 24 April 1880.

sleeping rooms with some beds and a large public room for cooking and eating and for the overflow to sleep. Within a week, more families had arrived from Woodruff County, Arkansas. The number of black Arkansans stranded in New York had grown to 136 with 20 more in Philadelphia.[48]

With New York newspapers, such as the *Times*, the *Herald*, and the *Evening Telegram*, describing the plight of the refugees in poignant detail, the emigrants quickly captured the sympathy of the city. Black churches in the city, led by Reverend Henry Highland Garnet, pastor of Shiloh Presbyterian and a black leader of national renown, joined together with the relief committee of the colored YMCA to attend to the physical needs of the refugees. Ministers collected money and organized a relief committee composed of one woman from each congregation to distribute food and necessities. One member of the committee spent an average of fourteen dollars each day purchasing food for the group, while another directed the women in cooking their meals. Other women of the committee set up sewing machines on the premises to make bedclothes for those who lacked these basic items. Businessmen of Wall Street planned a meeting to raise money for the refugees. Garnet said assistance came in from all directions: "White people, black people, Americans, English, Irish—all classes and nationalities brought clothing, baskets of provisions." Nonetheless, after the long trip from Arkansas and several days living in wretched conditions in the city, several members of the party became sick. Adults and children lay ill with measles in a makeshift sick ward in the rented lodgings, and two others were hospitalized with pneumonia. Within two weeks of their arrival, four people, including two elderly men, Benjamin Jordan and Jason Clobton, had died. The church relief committee paid twenty-five dollars for each to be buried side by side in New York's Evergreen cemetery.[49]

Similarly, in Philadelphia, the group of twenty who had arrived there in February were cared for by compassionate citizens of the city of brotherly love. Supporters of the ACS in Pennsylvania, led by the Reverend Henry L. Phillips and Edward Morris, who ran an import business of Liberian products, took responsibility for caring for the refugees in Philadelphia. One devout Christian man, Thomas Malcolm, visited the Arkansas refugees more than thirty times in the three months they stayed in the city.[50]

Besides their difficult conditions, the refugees garnered sympathy by their grim accounts of the life they had fled back home. The leader of the New York group of refugees, Richard Newton, described as an "intelligent, hardworking black man," told reporters about the violence and bulldozing of the 1878 election when black voters were terrorized into staying home on election day. One old woman, he said, had her hayrick and house burned to the ground because she sheltered some "radical niggers" at election time. The Reverend Simon Davis, one of two ministers of the gospel among the Arkansas refugees, took the Reverend Garnet's pulpit at Shiloh Presbyterian on the evening of Sunday, 4 April, and described floggings and murders that took place during the election time. Davis said whites had exclaimed: "Your Northern friends have gone and left you in our hands, and we are going to do just what suits us, and stuff ballot-boxes as we please." Economic tyranny, the refugees explained, had become as bad as the political oppression. Ephraim Holmes, second in command to Newton, said he had seen a black man knocked down and beaten in Dr. Jack's store in Helena when he refused to take $2 worth of goods and $1.50 in change for a $10 bill. All commented that people of color could never get out of debt because their crops were always mortgaged beforehand and landlords claimed up to half of the cotton they produced as rent. From the remainder they had to pay their expenses and their bill at the local store. "Hundreds were thus brought to the verge of starvation," Davis explained with a reference to Arkansas's new larceny law, "and if to preserve life they confiscated food they were sent to the Penitentiary." Newton summed up their condition: "I would not treat a dog as colored men are treated in Arkansas. We humbly beg the people at large to help us out of the South." The Reverend Davis declared that people of color "were so oppressed in the South that sometimes they almost doubted whether they were human beings."[51]

By the middle of April, reports had come back to Arkansas concerning the refugees in Philadelphia and New York and the extensive coverage northern newspapers had given to their plight. The *Arkansas Gazette*, as the mouthpiece for the white Democratic establishment, denied that the impoverished black travelers living off of charity in New York had come from Arkansas: "We can assure the people of the North that there are no negroes leaving Arkansas for Liberia or anywhere else. They are all satisfied with their condition here, and know that they cannot better it anywhere else, and least of all in Liberia. Those claiming to be Arkansas refugees are swindlers and impostors, and should be accordingly treated."[52] White Arkansans evidently wanted to discourage a black migration movement that would exacerbate an existing shortage of agricultural labor.

As the refugees' stay dragged on, however, some New Yorkers began to raise similar questions. Many of the Arkansas refugees were obviously penniless, having expended all their resources in getting to New York. But others had some money and numerous possessions with them. Austin Barrow, the first to arrive in February, had brought $400 and 1,000 pounds of salted meat with him from Arkansas.[53] Rumors also circulated that the refugees had turned over $478 of their own money to the ACS toward their Liberian passage. Some New Yorkers charged that the refugees were stubborn and independent and that several had turned down job offers after arriving in New York. With such grumbling, a recommendation came to the relief committee that the aid cease to those who had money and that these refugees be asked to give back food and supplies. After a lengthy debate, the committee decided to continue the assistance. Henry Garnet defended the refugees, suggesting that any stubbornness on their part simply reflected their single-minded resolve to get to Africa. Although some New Yorkers had tried to dissuade them, even intimidate them to do otherwise, they would not budge on their dream, Garnet said.[54]

While compassionate citizens in New York and Philadelphia cared for the physical needs of the Arkansas refugees, a resolution to the crisis fell to the American Colonization Society. Secretary Coppinger left the charity to others and concentrated on raising the necessary funds to transport the refugees to Liberia. He began a letter-writing campaign begging for money, an effort that culminated in a special appeal mailed out to prospective donors by the executive committee of the ACS. The leaflet included a letter signed by the leaders of the

Arkansas refugees in New York—Simon Davis, Richard Newton, Ephraim Holmes, and Benjamin Manual—in which they implored Christians and philanthropists to help them reach Africa, as "experience has taught us that it is impossible to make homes of our own in Arkansas." Donations for the Arkansas refugees could be sent to the president of the Mechanics Bank on Wall Street.[55] And the money poured in. Checks of one, five, twenty, and one hundred dollars arrived in the mail from towns large and small in the mid-Atlantic and northeastern states. One anonymous note enclosed twenty dollars, signed "Friend of the Oppressed." A donor from Harrisburg, Pennsylvania, gave $500 specifically to transport and settle the McDuffy family, one of the largest Arkansas families stranded in Philadelphia.[56] Although the Pennsylvania auxiliary of the ACS alone donated several thousand dollars, the executive committee eventually had to sell half of the society's stock in the Chesapeake and Ohio Canal Company to pay for the remaining transportation of the Arkansas refugees.[57]

Coppinger had already promised some places on the next regular voyage, scheduled for May, to emigrant groups from North Carolina and Texas. With the extra money, he chartered an additional ship to handle the overflow from Arkansas. But Coppinger and others in the ACS feared that their success in raising money to aid and transport the refugees would only inspire others to leave their homes in the South and descend uninvited on northern ports. During the thick of their efforts in April, Berry Colman wrote ominously from Phillips County that from 5,000 to 10,000 people in the area were preparing to leave for Africa. ACS leaders in Philadelphia composed a statement, which they tried to publish throughout the South, warning people against leaving their homes uninvited for the North in hopes of Liberian passage. The ACS could give no guarantee of support, they said.[58]

Meanwhile, as the ACS raised money and tried to contain any imminent new migration, the Arkansas refugees prepared for their departure for Liberia. Shortly before the first ship sailed, Edward W. Blyden, the famous Liberian patriot and educator, passed through New York on a speaking tour of America. In an address at Dr. Garnet's church on 16 May, he directed his closing remarks to the Arkansas refugees. He assured them that Liberia would warmly welcome them in many ways: "the beaming rays of the sun; the whispers of the gentle breezes; the murmur of the rippling brooks; the melodious songs of the birds; the voice that comes from the recesses of the woods and from the shadowy hills; the soft light of the stars and the silver glory of the moon; flowers and fruits; the waving sugar-cane and the fragrant coffee trees; and, above all, the untarnished man of the forest, your brother." Blyden directed the emigrants to teach the native Africans "the elements of the civilization and religion you have learned here, and they can teach you the manhood you have lost." Blyden's rhetoric made Liberia sound like a veritable paradise. "The air which brings disease and death to the white man," Blyden said, "will bring health and strength to you." The emigrants would soon find that Blyden's promises did not entirely ring true. But there in Shiloh Presbyterian Church in New York, their hopes soared.[59]

The Philadelphia group could hardly contain their enthusiasm as they headed for New York accompanied by their "shepherd," the Reverend Henry L. Phillips, on Friday, 21 May. The refugees had been in Philadelphia long enough to establish friendships with those who assisted them, and tears were shed at the time of departure. One woman, Mrs. Melvina Crosston, almost missed the train when she went to say goodbye to a friend and lost track of time. When the emigrants arrived in New York, they went directly aboard the old-fashioned sailing ship *Liberia* at Pier 27, and the ship sailed the next day.[60] The bark *Monrovia*, a slightly larger sailing ship than the *Liberia*, left a week later, on Saturday morning, 29 May, with seventy-six emigrants. The two ships left thirty-one of the Arkansas refugees behind in New York. Four families decided to wait for more friends and relatives from Arkansas, while a few others had changed their mind and decided to stay permanently in the North. One family of eleven was simply too large for the ACS to accommodate; the society had run out of money and refused to go into debt to send them.[61] The 118 Arkansas refugees who left aboard the *Liberia* and *Monrovia* arrived in Africa slightly more than a month later, and they joined the others who had come from Arkansas the year before in Brewerville.[62] The first wave of Arkansas's emigration to Liberia had ended.

The experience of these families and their efforts to emigrate to Africa demonstrated several themes. The beginnings of the back-to-Africa movement in 1877 suggest just how meaningful was the end of Reconstruction that year. While Reconstruction ended locally in Arkansas in 1874, it was the final federal retreat with President Hayes's southern policy in 1877 that signaled real change. Black citizens understood that their status and rights had been redefined in Arkansas, just as in South Carolina, Louisiana, and elsewhere. The founding of the Liberia Exodus Arkansas Colony, obviously modeled after the Liberia Exodus Association of South Carolina, shows how the national politics of 1877 resonated throughout the South. But the retreat from Reconstruction was more than just black perception. White Democrats in Arkansas counties with large black populations, such as Phillips County, took their cues as well. In the next election, they boldly used force and fraud to take back control of local government. In the 1880 gubernatorial election, just two months after the Arkansas refugees had arrived in Liberia, the black vote in the delta counties of Arkansas was nearly gone. Returns showed only ten Republican votes of the 1,654 votes cast in Phillips County, a county with more than 15,000 black residents in 1880. Neighboring Lee County recorded only one Republican vote, and Crittenden County, none, even though both counties had large black majorities.[63] Political oppression had combined with economic measures that gave advantages to creditors and landlords. A black man or woman could well ask whether slavery had returned to the black-majority areas of the South by the late 1870s. And in this difficult environment, some black Arkansans took the huge gamble that life could be better if they could just get to the African Republic of Liberia.

2

A Movement Ebbs and Flows
The 1880s

The year of the attempted mass migration to Liberia, 1880, formed a peak in Arkansas's back-to-Africa movement. However, as letters from Liberia arrived back in Arkansas in the early 1880s, the report was apparently mixed; two of the emigrant families of 1880, in fact, returned to the United States dissatisfied with Liberia. Meanwhile, conditions began to improve in Phillips County and neighboring areas of the delta. The franchise appears to have returned to African Americans in the 1882 elections throughout most of the delta and, by 1884, even in stubborn Phillips County. A large black migration from southeastern states swelled into Arkansas in the 1880s, and a biracial agrarian populist movement brought hope for meaningful political and economic reform. The 1880s in many ways seemed a decade of promise for both poor black and poor white farmers in Arkansas. In this more hopeful environment, interest in a Liberia exodus waxed and waned according to local conditions and motivations. By the end of the decade, however, stiff repression returned to motivate a new back-to-Africa movement throughout Arkansas.

After the fiasco of the 1880 elections in the delta counties, black Republicans took deliberate action to improve their situation. In early January of 1882, black leaders convened a statewide meeting to organize themselves as a distinct faction within the party. They drafted a circular letter to black voters, who, the conference claimed, made up 80 percent of the state's Republican ranks, calling for immediate action to shape politics for the good of all citizens. The delegates also called for cooperation with white Republicans.[1] The actual impact of this organization remains uncertain.

Another factor that worked to improve political conditions on the local level was pressure from the governor's office in Little Rock. Although Democratic governor Thomas J. Churchill's administration had been plagued with accounting scandals, Churchill showed his willingness to use force to curb attacks by conservative Democrats. In the summer of 1881, he sent the Quapaw Guards, a unit of state militia, to Perry County when local whites identifying themselves as the Ku Klux burned down the newspaper office of John Matthews, a former Union officer and local Republican leader from Reconstruction days, and then brutally murdered him. When the militia restored order three weeks later, Churchill recalled them to Little Rock.[2] In black-majority Jefferson County that same summer, Churchill ordered militia captain Sam Hilzheim to muster into service a group of black soldiers who called themselves the Neel Guards. When Hilzheim refused to accept the black troops, Churchill had the captain court-martialed on the charges of disobedience, disrespect to the commanding officer, and conduct unbecoming an officer. Hilzheim was found guilty and suspended from office for six months.[3]

When the 1882 campaign rolled around, Churchill, James Berry, the Democratic nominee for governor, and the state's leading Democratic newspaper, the *Arkansas Gazette*, all loudly called for "a free ballot and a fair count." Admitting that their party in post-Reconstruction elections had fought fire with fire, Democratic leaders now said the time had come for the rule of law and the right of each citizen to cast an "untrammeled ballot." Governor Churchill even met with a delegation of Republican leaders from Phillips County who expressed concerns that Democrats there would prevent black citizens from nominating or voting for a Republican ticket in the coming election. Churchill promised them he would use all powers at his disposal to achieve a fair election in Phillips County. If any military companies undertook to intimidate or interfere with the vote, he promised to muster them out of service at once. To make his position eminently clear to Democrats in Phillips County, Churchill even sent his private secretary, R. H. Johnson, and General R. L. Newton, the commander of the Quapaw Guards, to Helena two weeks before the election.[4]

The governor's rhetoric and show of force may have worked. In the 4 September state election, Republicans carried the black-majority counties of Crittenden, Lee, Desha, and Lincoln, where the black vote had been suppressed two years before. Jefferson County, which polled 7 Republican votes in the 1880 governor's race, returned a Republican majority of nearly 3,000 votes in 1882. Democrats still won in Phillips County, the area most notorious for bulldozing, but the county recorded more than 1,000 Republican (presumably black) votes, as compared to 10 Republican votes two years before.[5] Charges of fraud and intimidation surfaced again in 1882, especially in Phillips County, but clearly the situation had improved for black voters in 1882.[6] In the state elections that followed in the 1880s, African Americans in black-majority counties appear to have received back the voting rights they had lost in 1878 and 1880. Republicans carried almost all the black-majority counties in the 1884, 1886, and 1888 gubernatorial elections. Even in Phillips County, the *Arkansas Gazette* almost sighed in 1884 that the election there had "passed off very quietly."[7]

To elect local officials, Republican and Democratic leaders in black-majority counties during the 1880s often struck compromise agreements by which the two parties divided up offices between them through a joint "fusion" ticket. In Jefferson County, for example, Democrats usually chose the county judge, the county clerk, the assessor, and the state senator while Republicans picked the sheriff, the circuit clerk, and the three state representatives. The Republican officials were usually a combination of white and black leaders. By 1882, fusion tickets succeeded in Hempstead, Jefferson, Little River, Mississippi, Monroe, Miller, Lafayette, Crittenden, and Lincoln Counties.[8] Even Phillips County moved to a fusion system by 1886, with a black Republican, J. N. Donohoo, elected as representative. In a few counties with the largest black majorities, the Republican Party won all the local offices. For example, Republicans swept everything during the 1884 and 1886 elections in Chicot County (85 percent black) and in 1886 in Crittenden County (80 percent black). In these areas, black men governed.[9] While the political situation for black citizens varied from county to county and from election to election, clearly the black disfranchisement experienced in the delta counties in 1878 and 1880 generally reversed in the 1880s. Black families thus had less political motivations to leave Arkansas for destinations such as Liberia.

The improving conditions for African Americans in Arkansas also led to a large black inmigration in the 1880s. Arkansas had already become a destination for black migrants in the late 1870s, but the arrivals mushroomed in the 1880s. The black population of the state in the 1880s increased by 98,451, an aggregate growth second only to that of Georgia among the forty-nine American states and territories. The rate of increase of the black population in Arkansas (46.7 percent) exceeded that of all other southern states. While Arkansas's white population also grew rapidly, the state's percentage of blacks grew from 26.3 to 27.4 during the decade.[10] The increased black population was dispersed throughout the state. Nearly all of Arkansas's seventy-five counties gained black residents in the 1880s, with decline only in seven counties, mostly located

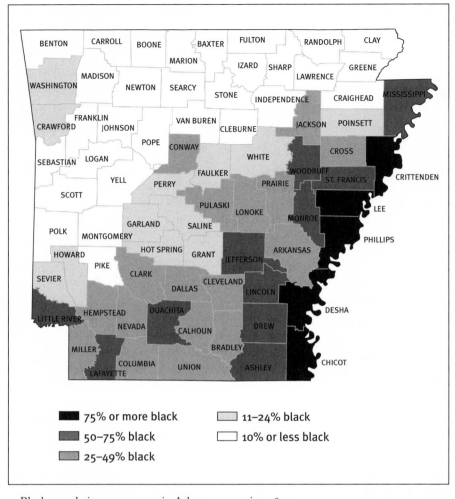

Black population percentage in Arkansas counties, 1890

in the Ozark and Ouachita Mountain regions, which earlier had minuscule black populations. The greatest growth took place in the cotton-growing regions of eastern Arkansas and the Arkansas River valley in the central part of the state. By 1890, the number of black-majority counties had grown to fifteen, with Mississippi, St. Francis, and Drew Counties in eastern Arkansas passing that threshold for the first time.[11]

In the late 1870s and the 1880s, land and labor agents traveled the southeastern states, encouraging people to move to Arkansas. Federal land grants to railroad companies before the Civil War had tied up thousands of acres of land that came onto the market after the construction of railroad lines through the state in the 1870s. Other land became available for settlement via the Home-stead Act. As new land went under the plow, the amount of improved farm acreage in Arkansas shot up by nearly two-thirds in the 1880s. A labor shortage in plantation districts motivated planters to hire labor agents to recruit workers and tenants who lacked the ability to purchase land. One of the most flamboyant agents, Robert A. "Peg Leg" Williams, claimed to have relocated some 80,000 black workers from the south Atlantic states to the Mississippi Valley area and Texas between 1883 and 1890.[12] Williams and another labor agent, C. A. Rideout, were so successful in recruiting migrants that white residents of Newberry, South Carolina, hustled the two men out of town. Williams left on the next train, while Rideout, a black lawyer from Morrilton, Arkansas, took to the woods.[13] Newspapers reported that roads and train stations, especially in the Carolinas, were jammed with black settlers on the move to Arkansas. One correspondent from Little Rock wrote to a black Methodist newspaper in June 1885 that the trains arriving in Little Rock from points east were "loaded to their utmost ca-pacity with men, women, and children seeking homes in Arkansas." The 11:40 A.M. train from Memphis, he said, brought black settlers from Georgia, South Carolina, North Carolina, Tennessee, and Alabama.[14]

The story of William Pickens, who was later a field secretary for the NAACP, serves as a vivid example of the experiences of thousands of black migrants to Arkansas in the 1880s. Pickens was born in 1881 near Pendleton, South Car-olina, in an area of worn-out red soil. His family heard stories from western immigration agents of the fertile land and high wages on the other side of the Mississippi River. In 1887, an agent representing a planter in eastern Arkansas induced Pickens's father to sign a contract putting him into debt to the planter in exchange for the family's railroad fares west. According to Pickens, the agent was quite persuasive, describing Arkansas as "a tropical country of soft and balmy air, where cocoanuts, oranges, lemons, and bananas grew" and "ordinary things like corn and cotton, with little cultivation, grew an enormous yield." On 15 January 1888, the agent saw the family off at the train station in South Car-olina for their trip to Arkansas, via Atlanta, Birmingham, and Memphis, with agents at each stop to help them make their connections. The family had no suitcases but carried all their worldly possessions in sacks, bundled quilts, and baskets.

The closer they came to Arkansas, Pickens said, the colder the weather be-came. "In Memphis snow was deep and the wind biting." By the time the fam-ily arrived at small station in eastern Arkansas, they had seen no orange blos-soms or coconuts. Instead, their hiring planter's double-team wagon hauled them through snow and ice in the canebrakes of Woodruff County to their new home. There they received a one-room hut and sufficient provisions while they waited for spring to begin cultivating their fields. That fall, after the family's first crop of fifty bales of cotton had been sold by the planter, Pickens said, "Father came home with sad, faraway eyes, having been told that we were deeper in debt than on the day of our arrival."[15]

The experience of William Pickens's family was doubtless like that of many black migrants enticed by labor agents into Arkansas under the yoke of peonage debt. Others came to Arkansas in the 1880s fleeing worsening political conditions in the Deep South. Edgefield County, South Carolina, had experienced some of the worst political violence following the end of Reconstruction in 1877, and black residents there organized a Liberia emigration movement that led to the *Azor* expedition in 1878. But after the *Azor* was sold in November 1879 and South Carolina's Liberia Exodus Joint Steamship Company folded, unhappy black families of Edgefield County began to place their hopes on Arkansas instead of Liberia.[16] In 1881, John Hammond, a black preacher, and William Lawson, a black schoolteacher, organized a club with twice-weekly meetings to plan a mass migration to Arkansas. The club sent Hammond and two other men to Arkansas that fall to scout the area and report back. By December, the party had returned, reporting a great demand for labor, good wages, and cheap available land. The club took a vote and resolved to go. During the week of Christmas 1881, the roads between Edgefield County and Augusta, Georgia, the nearest railway point, were packed with people bound for "Rockansas." One observer said of the mass exodus, "There has been nothing like it since the days of Pharaoh." By early January, whole townships in the county stood practically vacant. Several planters reported that not a Negro was left on their plantations. One newspaper estimated that some 20,000 acres in the county would go uncultivated in the next year for want of laborers. Estimates of the size of this mass migration ranged from 2,000 to 10,000. After this initial migration, "Arkansas fever" remained high for the next few years in neighboring counties, such as Lauren, Newberry, and Barnwell.[17]

The largest number of Edgefield migrants settled along the Arkansas River valley in Faulkner and Conway Counties, where they worked on plantations or, if they had some cash money, found cheap railroad land in good supply. One settler, N. D. Bryan, reported that agents met the new arrivals at the Morrilton depot and transported them to large buildings erected specifically to accommodate the settlers until they could buy land or find work. Bryan said work was plentiful, with wages for farmhands ranging between twelve and twenty dollars a month, and that Arkansas soil gave higher yields than that of South Carolina, even without fertilizer. Another newcomer, Sam Raiford, wrote back to a friend in Edgefield County, urging him and others to make the move, saying, "Arkansas is the best place for negroes this side of heaven." With this sudden inmigration and more South Carolinians following later, Conway County's black population more than doubled between 1880 and 1890, with the black proportion growing from a quarter to nearly 40 percent of the county.[18] In fact, this greater number of black Republican voters in elections later in the 1880s would spell a formidable challenge to the white Democratic control over county offices. The arrivals from Edgefield may have brought with them their African dreams, for Conway County would become the center of the next Liberia exodus movement a decade later.

The black migration to Arkansas continued through the 1880s. A black Methodist newspaper in Tennessee, the *Christian Index*, instructed its readers that "the State of Arkansas seems to us to be the future great state for the negroes," citing the good farm land, timber, water, and mineral resources of the state. As late as 1888, Bishop Henry McNeal Turner of Atlanta, who supervised the Eighth District of the AME Church, which included Arkansas, told his large reading audience: "Arkansas is destined to be the great Negro state of the country. . . . The meagre prejudice compared to some states, and opportunity to acquire wealth, all conspire to make it inviting to the colored man. The colored people now have a better start than in any other state in the Union."[19] By the time Turner said this in 1888, the political and racial climate in Arkansas was becoming much more conflicted, but his statement held some truth for most of the 1880s. The improved political conditions for black Arkansans and the dreams for a better life in "Rockansas" imparted by newly arrived African Americans from other southern states may have temporarily muted interest in a return to an African homeland.

Despite the optimism of such advocates and new arrivals, life was hard for black farmers in Arkansas. A conspiracy of factors worked together to challenge rural folk. While the 1870s had been known for favorable weather, the 1880s brought various problems. Most parts of the state experienced drought during the summer and fall of 1881, followed by heavy rains in the winter and spring of 1882. Flooding occurred throughout the eastern lowlands and delayed farmers at planting time. This pattern unfortunately prevailed through much of the decade—too much rain in the spring followed by insufficient moisture in late summer and fall.[20]

As the population increased in the 1880s and more land went under the plow, farmers also became further dependent on cotton rather than food crops. Railroad lines opened up rural Arkansas to national markets, further encouraging farmers to grow fiber to sell rather than food to eat. But while the number of acres devoted to cotton increased, production moved into more marginal landscapes, and average yield per acre actually declined. In Phillips County, the productivity declined from .68 bales per acre cultivated in 1879 to .47 bales per acre a decade later.[21] Other counties experienced similar declines. Moreover, the Arkansas farmers turned to cotton production just when expanded production in the South combined with output in India and Egypt collectively to erode the world price of the fiber. Wholesale cotton prices declined throughout the 1880s before bottoming out in the 1890s.[22]

The influx of settlers and economic pressures caused the size of the average Arkansas farm to shrink and the rate of tenancy, rather than farm ownership, to rise. At the census of 1880, 30.9 percent of Arkansas farms were hired rather than owned, but by 1890 the percentage of families who rented had risen to 46.1.[23] Black farm families were even more likely to rent than own, with 76.1 percent of black farm homes rented in Arkansas in 1890.[24] In the eastern Arkansas counties most devoted to cotton agriculture, black farms were small, and the overwhelming majority of farm families rented their land either for a fixed cash sum or for a share of produce. Sharecroppers had to give up to half of the cotton and a third of the corn produced to the landlord. Tenants might incur further debt in the neighboring store, probably also owned by the local planter.[25] So it was that Arkansas, a place of such promise to new settlers, became so sparing in her rewards. The improved political conditions in the 1880s would certainly mean less when one had to struggle so hard merely to survive.

Many families doubtless experienced the disappointment of the Pickens family when they found life in Arkansas as difficult as the one they had left elsewhere in the South. While generalization invites exceptions, the experiences of William Pickens's family probably epitomized that of most poor black farmers in the 1880s. Living in a one-room house on hired land, they tried desperately to get out of debt. The Pickens children worked alongside their parents in the fields with William's elder sister even guiding a plow. Large families were the rule for black farm families as the children provided valuable labor. In slow seasons, William's father cut trees in the canebrakes to make rails and boards, and his mother cooked and washed for white families to bring extra income to the family. Despite their hard work, they fell further behind. When they supplemented their monotonous diet of salt pork, cornbread, and molasses with occasional store-bought commodities like sugar, coffee, and flour, it only added to their growing debt. Similarly, the swampy landscape of eastern Arkansas brought chills and fevers. When William's father had to pay for medicine and doctors' bills, the indebtedness further increased. Finally, after two years, he slipped off to scout for a better situation. He found a landowner near Little Rock who would advance fares for the family to sneak away from their debt. The entire family left Woodruff County, an area that would be enthusiastic for African emigration just a few years later, and traveled by train to their new rented farm in rural Pulaski County.[26]

The kind of rural difficulties the Pickenses faced gave rise to an agrarian populist movement that began in 1882 and swept through the state in the rest of the decade. The movement rested upon a foundation of farmer unrest in the 1870s, organized as the Grange movement. Angry that banks, town merchants, and railroads held the balance of the farm economy, farmers had organized to protest, educate, and mobilize farm families into a united front. The group even ran candidates under the Greenback Party for local and state offices in the late 1870s and early 1880s. This movement gave way to more radical homegrown groups of white farmers. In February 1882, nine farmers gathered in east central Arkansas and founded the Agricultural Wheel. In western Arkansas a few months later, white farmers organized as the Brothers of Freedom. These two new groups absorbed the older Grange agenda but took a more class-conscious and politically activist approach. The Brothers of Freedom formally excluded merchants, bankers, and lawyers from membership; both organizations encouraged members to establish cooperative stores, cotton gins, and mills to remove the capitalist middleman from the agricultural economy.[27]

As white farmers founded the Agricultural Wheel in Prairie County in 1882, a group of black farmers there organized the first lodge of black farmers. By 1885, several black lodges had organized in the delta region of Arkansas, calling themselves collectively the Sons of the Agricultural Star. Later that year, the two white farmers' organizations formally merged, keeping the name Agricultural Wheel, and the next year the Wheel revised its bylaws to absorb the black Sons of the Agricultural Star into separate local chapters. At the 1887 state Wheel meeting, white farmers voted to seat the organization's first black delegation. Arkansas's Agricultural Wheel had become a biracial organization of the rural poor, and the organization grew rapidly in the state. By 1888, the Wheel claimed more than 75,000 members in Arkansas and had spread to neighboring states, swelling to a total membership of half a million. Two hundred of the nearly two thousand local Wheels in Arkansas were black.[28]

Arkansas's agrarian populist movement was much more than a grassroots economic organization; it quickly became a political movement. As early as 1884, the Brothers of Freedom in several northern and western counties ran candidates for local offices and won positions in county government. By 1886, the united Wheel prepared tickets for local and state offices, placing Charles E. Cunningham, a former Greenbacker, as candidate for governor. Cunningham lost to the Democratic incumbent, Simon P. Hughes, but the Wheel won several seats in the state legislature and an even larger number of county offices. In some counties, Wheel candidates pulled away sufficient white votes from the Democratic ticket to allow Republicans to win local elections. In Conway County, for example, Democrats had reigned supreme since Reconstruction, but the fractured white vote of 1886 allowed mostly black voters to achieve a clean Republican sweep, and even to send a black Methodist preacher, the Reverend G. E. Trower, to represent the county in the General Assembly.[29] With a biracial agrarian populist movement working for economic and political reform, and widespread officeholding in Black Belt counties in eastern Arkansas, people of color had less reason to think about African emigration.

Although interest in Liberian emigration declined after the mass expedition from East Arkansas in 1880, it had never disappeared. One factor that kept the movement alive was the regular appearance in the state of Bishop Henry McNeal Turner, the leading black propagandist of his generation for African emigration. Born free in South Carolina in 1834, Turner had served as a chaplain for a regiment of United States Colored Troops and after the war worked for the Freedmen's Bureau. A turning point in his life came when he was expelled from the Georgia House of Representatives in 1868 when white legislators refused to allow black delegates to take their seats. Even though he reclaimed his seat the next year, this experience and the end of Reconstruction convinced him that blacks could not have full citizenship in the United States. Thereafter, he chose confrontation and strong language over polite accommodation as his strategy. By the 1870s, through his position as a leader in the AME Church, he preached race pride and a manifest destiny for black Americans that pointed to the African continent. In 1876, he received the appointment as honorary vice president of the American Colonization Society in recognition of his work for African emigration. Through his blunt language in countless sermons throughout the South and his frequent contributions to black newspapers and the AME Church periodical, the *Christian Recorder*, Turner had an enormous audience, especially among lower-class blacks. In 1883, Turner announced that the U.S. government owed, by his calculation, some forty billion dollars to black people as a compensation for services rendered under slavery and that Congress should appropriate this money to assist blacks in emigrating to Africa. Clearly, by the 1880s, he had emerged as the Moses of the African exodus movement, calling for his people to leave their land of bondage for their ancestral homeland.[30]

Although some of the older AME Church leaders opposed Turner's fiery nationalism, in 1880 he was elected as one of the twelve bishops of the church, governing the Eighth District, composed of Arkansas, Mississippi, and the Indian Territory. While Turner kept his home in Atlanta—like most of the AME bishops, Turner did not reside in the district he served—he came to his district often for the annual conferences, staying in the homes of local church leaders.[31] The Arkansas Methodists warmly received Turner at his first episcopal visit to the state at the annual conference in 1881, welcoming him "as a brother beloved, an ardent lover of his church and his race." When he returned the next year, the annual meeting was in Morrilton in Conway County, where the Liberia Exodus Association was already working to send club members to Africa. In his opening sermon on 15 November 1882 at Morrilton's AME church, Turner "spoke earnestly on the African mission field and the Dark Continent in general."[32]

On Turner's next visit to Arkansas, he used his pulpit to address a nation. In November 1883, Turner arrived in Arkansas for the annual church conference just after an important U.S. Supreme Court decision regarding civil rights. The Court had declared unconstitutional the Civil Rights Act of 1875, which had prohibited discrimination by race in public facilities such as restaurants and hotels, arguing that the law restricted the rights of private individuals. Turner was fuming about the recent decision at the time he arrived in Arkansas. He said the decision absolved people of color from any allegiance to the United States and that the Constitution had become nothing more than "a dirty rag, a cheat, a libel and ought to be spit upon by every Negro in the land." Under Turner's direction, the conference devoted one of its sessions, a full evening at the AME Zion Church in Little Rock, to a discussion of the civil rights law and the court decision. Turner's strong words burned bridges between himself and the established black leadership, but it apparently brought him a much greater following among the poor.[33]

While Turner's annual visits kept Africa in the minds of black Arkansans, clearly an emigration movement survived in the 1880s in areas of localized racial conflict. Letters had continued to pour into the ACS office from Phillips County, where racial tensions remained high. Berry Coleman, the former state representative who failed to emigrate in 1880, kept trying to raise enough money to send his family to Liberia, always hoping that the next harvest would bring

Bishop Henry McNeal
Turner. From Bowen,
ed., *Africa and the American Negro*, 1896.

sufficient cash to allow him to go. In April 1881, he wrote that about a thousand good, respectable families in his area were thinking of going to Liberia.[34] Letters and applications also came in from various areas in eastern Arkansas. A schoolteacher named E. S. Hughes wanted to emigrate and teach school in the "dark continent," and he even asked if he could complete a college degree at Monrovia College.[35] Another black teacher, after reading copies of the *African Repository* lent to him by the local AME pastor, wrote to the ACS asking to emigrate to Liberia as a teacher and missionary.[36] Two more groups of black eastern Arkansans actually made it to Liberia: a family from Union in Lee County, Stewart and Mary Ann Dorsey and son, Robert, along with a Henry Jones, a schoolteacher from Fort Smith, left for Liberia in 1882. Four years later, Richard and Lucinda Bankhead of Helena paid the American Colonization Society a hundred dollars to get themselves and their six children to Liberia.[37]

But as political affairs settled down in the Arkansas delta by the middle part of the decade, the focus of the Liberia emigration movement shifted from eastern to north central Arkansas. Conway and Faulkner Counties, in the Arkansas River valley northwest of Little Rock, had received most of the new settlers from the South Carolina mass migration of 1881. The sudden increase in black population brought intense political competition and a rise in racial tensions in the area. Street fights between gangs of white and black men broke out in Morrilton in August 1881, and Democratic officials swore in extra policemen to protect against reported black threats to burn down the town. With the large black vote and a third-party ticket, Republicans managed to win the Conway County elections in 1884. Soon afterward, Democrats formed a military company. Some whites apparently went a step further and began night riding through black districts as the Ku Klux Klan. Black citizens formed their own military company to defend themselves, and Republican officials built a barbed-wire fence around the courthouse in Morrilton, the white Democratic stronghold.[38]

Perhaps new arrivals brought Liberia fever with them from South Carolina, or possibly people had just heard of the expedition from eastern Arkansas, but in this environment of conflict, local black residents in Conway County began to organize a Liberia emigration movement. By July 1881, Andrew Flowers had formed the Liberia Exodus Association in Plumerville, a railroad town in the southern part of the county, and asked the ACS for circulars and information to distribute in the area. "We can't do any good in this country is our final conclusion," Flowers said, "and we believe that Africa is our intended home as it is our father and mother home."[39] Within a year, the club had enrolled about twenty families who were planning to depart after the next harvest.[40] By the beginning of 1883, Flowers had raised $170 in cash, surrendered his land, and moved to Little Rock to await the journey to Liberia. Coppinger agreed to take Flowers's family of three for $100. Flowers bargained him down to $75 and sent the money by postal order to Washington. Second-class train fare from Little Rock to New York cost another $33.60. Flowers, his wife, Maria, and nineteen-year-old Alice Johnson, Maria's sister, sailed on 1 December 1883 aboard the *Monrovia* with thirty-five other passengers bound for Liberia.[41]

Interest in Liberia spread from Plumerville to neighboring communities in Conway County. M. E. Childress organized a club in Springfield, a few miles to the north, and reported that he "had got the people here in a stir for Liberia. . . . For we are bound to leave this country soon or later." Childress had organized a mass meeting in 1881 of black citizens of Conway, Faulkner, and Van Buren Counties and sent the proceedings to the U.S. attorney general, telling him that anything he could do "to better our conditions will be highly appreciated by the colored element in the south."[42] In Morrilton, the county seat, M. H. Keen organized an exodus club early in 1884 and wrote to Coppinger:

Dear Sir: I take much pleasure in writing you a letter in regards to colonizing from the United States to the Republic of Liberia. The time has become so inbearant in the Western portion of Arkansas that colored men can not get any protection before the Law, and our Sons and Daughters are not hardly recognized as human, and it seams as the Earth has refused to yeal us substance to sustain the body, and we the freemen of Conway County Arkansas has almost become demorilized over our condition and it seams from the very nature of things in the United States our way looks dark and gloomey. So we have come to conclusion to colonize to Liberia as soon as we can get ready to go.

In July, Keen insisted that 500 would be ready to leave Morrilton at once, if people were only able.[43]

Back in Plumerville, the Liberia Exodus Association kept going without Andrew Flowers's leadership. The new corresponding secretary, R. R. Walting, assured the ACS that the club still held regular monthly meetings and continued to receive more applications: "The African fever is burning her Very High and . . . there Will not be less then 150 or 200 People sending to go to Africa from the County of Conway." By early 1884, Walting had sent $237 to the ACS for his passage and that of other members of the club.[44] The ACS approved Walting and fourteen others for the April 1884 voyage to Liberia, so they sold their possessions, gave up their land, and moved to Little Rock to await departure. Three members of the club, J. A. and Luvenia Allington and Allin Green, traveled on ahead to wait in New York.[45] Walting failed to leave in April when several members of his family fell sick, and the other members of the party would not go without him. By the time the next voyage came around in September, Andrew and Maria Flowers and Alice Johnson had come back to the United States, dissatisfied with life in Liberia. The return of the Flowers family apparently caused the rest of the Plumerville party to change their mind, and they refused to depart.[46] The Flowers family came back to Little Rock, and the Allingtons and Allin Green returned from New York and resumed farming in Conway County. People from Plumerville asked Coppinger to send back their money back, and correspondence with the ACS from the area virtually ceased.[47]

Some interest in Africa revived late in 1886 when a traveling promoter, self-proclaimed professor Jacob C. Hazeley, came to Arkansas to recruit emigrants and educate residents about the "dark continent." A native of Sierra Leone who had also lived in Liberia, Hazeley made his living by traveling throughout the country giving public lectures and shows about Africa. Hazeley had stirred up black South Carolinians for African emigration in 1877, which led to the *Azor* expedition to Liberia the next year. Although he had no formal connection to the ACS, he worked with the organization to distribute its information and materials. After touring Texas, Hazeley arrived in Arkansas in November and wrote the ACS office, requesting Coppinger to send copies of the *African Repository* and other information about Liberian emigration to interested parties in rural hamlets throughout southwestern Arkansas.[48] By December, Professor Hazeley had arrived in Little Rock, which he made his base for trips throughout central Arkansas in the next five months.[49] Apparently, Hazeley's standard show was a lecture and panorama, which, according to one handbill, displayed more than a hundred pictures of palm and coffee trees, "the Heathen African Woman" and her various hairstyles, a Zulu king, sympathetic heathens carrying missionaries on their backs across a river, and more. Hazeley held his programs in black churches and charged admission of fifteen cents for adults and a dime for children under twelve.[50]

In the weeks after Hazeley had passed through any Arkansas town, letters would arrive in the ACS office from citizens there, usually asking for information about emigration to Liberia. In some cases, Hazeley himself wrote the ACS asking Coppinger to send circulars and copies of the *African Repository* directly to interested parties he had met.[51] For example, a group of twenty-four people from Conway, the county seat of Faulkner County, formally applied for emigration in February, shortly after several of them had attended Hazeley's show, and another forty applied in August 1887.[52] Faulkner County, which was next door to troubled Conway County and whose black population had more than doubled after the mass inmigration of black South Carolinians in the early 1880s, experienced periodic racial conflict throughout the decade.[53] John Johnson, one of the Conway men who had listened to Professor Hazeley, became so enthused about Liberia that he named his baby daughter Monrovia. Johnson, a poor farmer, was persistent about leaving Faulkner County. He sent $70 of his hard-earned cash to the ACS office over the next two years. On 6 April 1889, he, his wife, Malissa, and the couple's six children, including baby Monrovia, sailed for Liberia.[54]

By the time the Johnson family departed for Liberia, the back-to-Africa movement had revived among a mass audience in Arkansas. While generally improved political conditions and a massive black migration to Arkansas in the 1880s had eroded the motivations for African emigration, the idea had never really died. The high expectations black migrants brought with them to Arkansas may have, in fact, contributed to a back-to-Africa movement when the reality west of the Mississippi River did not match up to people's dreams. Localized flare-ups of racial violence, the yearly visits of Bishop Henry Turner, and the publicity work of Professor Hazeley kept the idea of Liberia emigration alive in Arkansas through the decade. However, it was the failure of biracial agrarian populism beginning with the elections of 1888 that re-ignited the African emigration movement in a general way throughout the state.

3

Hope Ignites
Liberia Fever, 1888–1891

The back-to-Africa movement, which had ebbed and flowed during the 1880s, came roaring back at the end of the decade. With heightened political and racial tension after 1888, thousands of black Arkansans aimed to leave the state and the country, and they placed their hopes on a vaguely perceived ancestral home-land, Africa. A black farmer in Conway County, W. D. Leslie, voiced the concerns of many in August of 1890: "We do here By disire to know if you can let us know if you will make some arrangements for a bought a hundred familys to embark the ship next May, making a bought one thousand people. We want to leave here as soon as we can for the times gets no better Here for the negro race and we want to get out from . . . the land of Slavery and how happy we will Be when we get on that old Ship and our Song will Be I am going home to die no more . . . we see that we can not prosper here in the U.S."[1] When the Arkansas General Assembly authored disfranchisement and Jim Crow segregation laws in early 1891, this interest in emigration became, in the words of black Arkansans, "Liberia fever."

Mr. Leslie's despair concerning conditions of his life resulted from some specific turn of events in Arkansas, and especially in his particular region. By the late 1880s, the real potential of the biracial farmers movement had become clear. It threatened to unseat the Democratic officeholders on the state and local levels. If the mobilization of small farmers into the Agricultural Wheel was not threatening enough, Democratic leaders faced an even greater threat in the election of 1888. Rural Wheelers negotiated with members of the Knights of Labor in the state's few cities to organize under the mantle of the Union Labor Party. The party chose a one-legged Confederate veteran, C. M. Norwood, as its candidate for governor. Republican leaders shocked Democrats when they declined to run a candidate and instead supported Norwood against the Democrat James P. Eagle, a planter who, with his plantation store, anaconda mortgages, and tenant farmers, represented everything the Wheel opposed. In several counties, Republicans and Wheelers followed suit and entered fusion agreements to unseat Democrats. In Faulkner County, for example, Republicans demanded three places on the fusion ticket as the price for their alliance with the Wheel. While such an alliance of the parties of business and labor might seem incongruous in northern states, it made perfect sense in Arkansas in 1888.[2]

The state and federal elections that followed in September and November 1888 were perhaps the most fraudulent in Arkansas history. Some Democrats apparently became convinced they could never defeat the Wheel/Republican alliance fairly through the casting of ballots. In many areas of the state, they resorted instead to fraud and violence to achieve victory. Democratic leaders apparently viewed black Republican voters as the weakest link in the coalition of the rural poor, and they decided to bring back the tactics that had worked in the delta counties in 1878 and 1880. In Crittenden County, which was more than four-fifths black, fusion agreements had brought Republicans, including several black men, into local offices. However, in July, a group of about a hundred white men armed with Winchester rifles assembled in the county seat Marion. Led by W. F. Werner, the white Democratic sheriff, they rounded up all the black officeholders and some other prominent black citizens, including a minister, a newspaper editor, and a teacher, and escorted the group of about twenty to the railway station, placed them on a train to Memphis, and ordered them never to return. The son of Daniel Lewis, the black county judge forcibly removed from office, remembered that his father never again slept in a darkened room after his experience with white terror in 1888.[3] Two weeks before the September election, Democratic governor Simon P. Hughes sent two boxes of guns and two thousand rounds of ammunition to Conway County to arm a seventy-five-man Democratic club so the men could drill and parade through the streets. Similar shipments of arms reportedly went to Woodruff and St. Francis Counties.[4]

After this sort of buildup, election day on 3 September erupted in violence. A fight between blacks and whites at the polls in Monroe County left one black man dead, another wounded. In a rural black precinct in St. Francis County, a row occurred while the votes were counted, leaving seven men shot, one dead. In Conway County, the scene of some of the most flagrant abuses, Democrats arrested a white Republican election judge on his way to the polls in Morrilton and roughed up a Republican party worker when he tried to distribute ballots outside the polls. At Plumerville, where most of the county's black residents voted, white Democrats arrived early at the polls, and by a voice vote, unseated and replaced the two black Republican judges with two white Democrats. With only Democrats running the election, Democrats won back all the county offices that had been held by Republicans for the past four years. Some of the worst fraud occurred right under the noses of state officials in Little Rock. When it appeared that Republicans would win in Pulaski County, the state's most populous county, someone broke into the county clerk's office and took the poll books of nine heavily Republican townships. Not surprisingly, Republicans claimed fraud before, during, and after the election. Besides their local tickets being counted out in many counties, the Republican/Wheel candidate for governor, Norwood, lost the race by just 13,000 votes. When the state legislature met the following January, Norwood filed a contest, claiming he had been counted out of votes in a number of counties. When the Democratic-controlled legislature required Norwood to post a $40,000 bond to cover the costs of the investigation, he reluctantly withdrew his case.[5]

Democrats in some counties became overconfident with their success and tried to use such strategies again in the November federal election. In Conway County, when officials had just begun to count the votes in Plumerville, the county's main black precinct, a party of five masked men burst in and stole the ballot box at gunpoint. The Republican/Wheel candidate for Arkansas's Second Congressional District, John M. Clayton, brother of Reconstruction governor and Republican Party boss Powell Clayton, lost the race by the slimmest of margins, a mere 846 votes, to Democratic incumbent Clifton Breckinridge. Similarly, Louis Featherston, the Republican/Wheel candidate for Congress in eastern Arkansas's First Congressional District and president of the state Wheel, lost to the Democratic candidate W. H. Cate after several flagrant cases of ballot-box stuffing. Both candidates announced they would contest the election because of such irregularities. Clayton's contest, however, would bring about his death. When he came to the Conway County in January to take depositions reconstructing the stolen ballots, two assassins blasted him with a load of buckshot through his hotel window in Plumerville.[6]

The outrageous political violence and fraud in the 1888 elections did not take place in all parts of Arkansas. Democratic state leaders may have targeted just enough counties to bring in necessary majorities for their candidates to win. Or possibly the election fraud was planned and executed entirely on a local level. The worst problems were in counties where the black share of population ranged from 40 to 55 percent, such as Conway, Woodruff, St. Francis, and Pulaski, and thus black voters held a balance of power. African Americans in these politically competitive counties would show the most intense interest in Liberia emigration in the late 1880s and early 1890s. However, in several black-majority counties in eastern Arkansas, Republican or the traditional Democratic/Republican compromise tickets still carried majorities, and in other counties, the Republican/Wheel alliance prevailed. The state legislature elected in 1888 included at least nine Republican and six Union-Labor representatives, some of them black men from the delta area. The irregularities were selective but sufficient to insure a Democratic victory on the state level; they did not entirely eliminate black officeholding in county governments.[7] Nonetheless, the 1888 elections turned a page in race relations in Arkansas from an atmosphere of relative tranquility to one of conflict in which white Democrats again used tactics of terror and fraud, as in the late 1870s, to keep power.

Black residents in the counties that experienced the worst election violence almost immediately began to inquire to the ACS about emigration to Liberia. Just two weeks after the election fiasco in Conway County, where Democrats took back all county offices, William H. King of Morrilton, the county seat, wrote for information about African emigration, explaining that "almost the entire county of colored people is enraged on the subject." And from Crittenden County, also where some of the worst abuses took place, a correspondent explained in early October that he wrote for a group of 200 black families who wanted to leave the United States for Africa. A group of twenty-three people from neighboring Lee County later that month formally applied to emigrated to Liberia.[8]

Interest in emigration had diffused to other parts of the state by 1889. From locations throughout Arkansas, correspondents wrote for information about emigration, often claiming to speak for large groups of people who wished to go. Even in Eureka Springs, a new resort town in the Ozark Mountains where few blacks lived (only eighty-three blacks lived in the whole county in 1890), a man wrote for information to circulate about Liberian emigration. Farther east, in the black-majority delta, Pink Blair claimed he had fifty families organized for emigration in Osceola (Mississippi County) late in 1889—before angry whites chased him out of the county. Blair fled to Memphis, where he wrote the ACS begging Coppinger to pay his and his wife's way to New York and give them passage onward to Liberia. Claiming he was destitute, pushed to the point of begging money from churches to survive, Blair insisted he would repay the society afterward if it would only send him to Liberia.[9] Coppinger did not advance Mr. and Mrs. Blair any money.

While interest in African emigration had spread throughout Arkansas, it was clearly most keen during 1889 and 1890 in Conway County, perhaps the toughest political environment in the state. In April 1889, soon after the assassination of Republican congressional candidate Clayton, Abner Downs, a black schoolteacher in Morrilton, explained: "We are having a great deal of trouble in our Town and Community three colored men have been killed with in the last four months. So I am going to try by God's help to go home." Another Morrilton man, Anthony Lipscomb, applied to emigrate and, after harvesting and settling his crops at the end of the year, moved his family to Little Rock to await their departure for Liberia. He said he went to the post office every day just waiting for his order of passage to come through. Finally, Lipscomb, his wife, and his five children left for New York and sailed for Liberia on 14 June 1890.[10] By the time the Lipscomb family emigrated to Liberia, back home in Conway County black residents had formed exodus clubs in Morrilton, Plumerville, and Menifee.[11] An emigration society had also been organized in the neighboring town of Conway (Faulkner County), which claimed fifty families as members. One member there, J. P. Douglas, exclaimed, "Sir there is a great many of us who would start at once . . . for we have a great deal of strife between the white and colored race and grows more every year."[12]

Also, by the spring of 1890, the ACS approved for emigration a group from Jefferson County, the home county of slain Republican candidate Clayton. Several families in Humphrey had formed an association of about forty-five people led by a Baptist minister, William Moss, and they voted to embark for Liberia. Coppinger promised passage to twenty of the Humphrey group for the fall voyage, leaving 1 November. At the last minute before catching their train for New York, however, some of the party fell ill, and the whole group decided to stay home. The Humphrey folks did not telegraph the ACS that they were not coming, and Coppinger had no time to replace them with other passengers. The ship sailed to Liberia half empty.[13]

African migration was much on the minds of blacks in the First and Second Congressional Districts, for the hubbub following the stolen election of 1888 and Clayton's assassination kept tensions high. Despite their misfortunes in Arkansas in November 1888, Republicans had won the presidency and both houses of Congress in that election. The House of Representatives sent a com-

mittee of congressmen to Arkansas to gather evidence about the two con-
tested elections. After lengthy investigations in Arkansas and partisan debate in
Washington, the House voted to take away the seat from Democratic congressman Cate and give it to Featherston, and similarly to remove Congressman
Breckinridge, leaving the seat vacant on account of Clayton's murder.[14]

To prevent such election fraud in the future, Representative Henry Cabot
Lodge of Massachusetts introduced a bill in June 1890 that demanded federal
control over elections. Called the "Force bill" by southerners, the bill aimed to
stop the rampant fraud that had taken place in Arkansas and other states and
to re-enfranchise many black citizens who had ceased to vote in the Deep South.
The Lodge bill would have allowed for one hundred voters in a congressional
district who believed fraud had taken place in an election to petition the federal
courts to investigate. The bill brought more discussion and excitement in the
South than any federal measure since the end of Reconstruction. Throughout
the South, newspaper editors and Democratic politicians discussed the Lodge
bill, raising the specter of Negro domination.[15]

The debate about the bill was raging during the September 1890 state elections and the congressional vote two months later. Again Democrats faced a
formidable challenge from a populist/Republican alliance. By 1890, the Agricultural Wheel had merged with the national Farmers Alliance but in the process lost its black lodges, for the Alliance segregated blacks into the separate
Colored Farmers Alliance. Again the farmers supported the Union Labor Party
in a fusion ticket with the Republicans. And once more Democrats resorted to
fraud and intimidation to win elections in many counties in Arkansas. Conway
County led the way, as it had in 1888. In the week before the September 1890
election, a Democratic gang burst onto the train arriving at the depot in Morrilton and wrested from the hands of a Republican leader the valise that contained the printed Republican/Union Labor ballots. This time they tried to
steal the ballots *before* rather than *after* the election as in 1888. Congressman
John F. Lacey of Ohio, who chaired the committee that had investigated Clayton's murder, read a *New York Tribune* account of the affair on the floor of the
House of Representatives. Other northern newspapers reported that the 1890
election in Arkansas saw more violent and illegal crimes than the election of
1888.[16] While the Democratic incumbent, James P. Eagle, defeated his Repub-
lican/Union Labor challenger, Napoleon B. Fizer, by more than 20,000 votes,
Fizer managed still to carry most of the black-majority counties of the delta
region.[17]

When the Arkansas General Assembly convened in January of 1891, Democratic lawmakers were resolved to action. Setting the tone for this legislative session, one of the first acts of the new House was to remove the portrait of George Washington from behind the speaker's rostrum and replace it with one of Jefferson Davis. As one of its first legislative moves, the Assembly proposed a Jim Crow segregation law. Modeled after a Mississippi statute of a few years earlier, the law ordered railroad companies in Arkansas to provide separate coaches and waiting rooms for black and white patrons. Railroad officers who chose not to enforce the law, or passengers who refused to obey it, would be assessed a fine. Supporters argued that the measure was needed to protect white travelers from drunken, rowdy, and unwashed black passengers. In Arkansas, as throughout the South, blacks and whites had close physical associations in fields, nurseries, kitchens, and other spaces of everyday life. Clearly the legislature, which included black men, crafted the separate coach law for its symbolic value.

Black citizens held two mass meetings in Little Rock in January to denounce the separate coach bill. The African American members of the legislature, eleven in the House and one in the Senate, led the gatherings and spoke eloquently against the proposed law in the Assembly chambers. The lone black senator, George W. Bell of Desha County, argued that blacks and whites had ridden the same trains without incident since the time railroads came to Arkansas. In the House, John Gray Lucas, a twenty-six-year-old representative from Jefferson County, led the rhetorical assault. Lucas had grown up in Pine Bluff but had attended law school at Boston University, where he was the only black graduate of his class. Lucas pointed out that while some Democrats accused the black race of using insufficient amounts of "soap and God's pure water," thus necessitating separate coaches, other Democrats also have said "that the more money, intelligence, and gentility, the more objectionable the negro." Lucas asked, "Which is the truth?" When the matter finally came to a vote, only the black legislators and a few white Republican and Union-Labor legislators voted against the bill. The one black Democratic representative, P. F. Adair of Pulaski County, actually voted with his fellow Democrats for the segregation measure. By 1891, Jim Crow had arrived in Arkansas.[18]

After passing the separate coach act, the General Assembly went on to rewrite the election laws to put an end at last to the fusion alliance of poor farmers and Republicans. Two years before, the Arkansas Senate had passed secret-ballot and poll-tax bills, designed to remove votes of poor and illiterate citizens. But the bills never came to a vote in the House, where Republicans and Union-Labor representatives held a third of the seats. In 1891, however, Democrats had success. The new law, this time passed by both houses, proposed a secret, or "Australian," ballot system, which Democrats were pushing throughout the South in the early 1890s. Before 1891, men voted by receiving a preprinted ballot from a party worker outside the polling place, and the voter simply had to sign or make a mark in the poll book and drop the party ballot into the ballot box. Republican and Democratic ballots would be of different colors; thus one did not need to be able to read to vote. Under the new law, ballots would be printed by the state and would list the names of all candidates, providing no symbols to identify party affiliation for illiterate voters. The bill even forbade the use of a party label, as illiterates could easily learn to recognize the words "Republican" or "Union Labor." The law also kept party workers from assisting voters in marking their ballots, mandating that only election judges could render this assistance. This provision would not help illiterate white populist or black Republican voters, however. The new election law made sure Democratic officials kept control over the choice of election judges. The law directed the governor, the auditor, and the secretary of state to name election commissioners for each county, and these commissioners would then choose the election judges. With the Democrats always winning these state offices, the party could now control appointment of election officials even in the black counties of the delta that had Republican majorities. The Assembly voted down an amendment from a Union Labor legislator from Faulkner County that proposed a $100 fine for county commissioners if they failed to name persons of different parties as election judges and clerks. Thus the secret ballot, usually considered a safeguard of the democratic process, aimed to thwart real democracy in Arkansas, as in other southern states. The legislature also passed a poll tax bill obviously aimed to reduce further the black and poor white farmer vote. This measure, however, required a constitutional amendment and did not become law until it was passed by a voter referendum in 1892.[19]

Arkansas's segregation and disfranchisement laws were enacted in 1891 just weeks after Congress voted down the Lodge election bill. Black citizens truly had reasons to be anxious from these cues on the state and federal levels.[20] The early 1890s saw not just a change of law but a change in the culture of racism, in Arkansas and throughout the South. While the white Arkansas press had previously referred to African Americans as Negroes, darkies, or coloreds, public language increasingly turned to more derisive terms such as coon or nigger. Racial segregation moved beyond railway coaches to other arenas. Around the time the separate coach bill took effect, the city council of Searcy passed an ordinance prohibiting black citizens from drinking from the city's sulfur spring.

If blacks wanted the water, they had to carry a bucket to dip from the ditch down the way. Similarly, the Texarkana City Council prohibited black people from using the city's only public park.[21]

The new laws and the more stridently racist atmosphere convinced many black citizens in Arkansas that their future lay in emigration. One speaker at the black rally in Little Rock held to oppose the separate coach bill in 1891 argued that the new legislation "would drive his race in Arkansas to Oklahoma or Africa, where they are being invited."[22] Indeed, the social and political changes fueled the already widespread interest in Liberian emigration.

After the fall 1890 elections, letters and applications from Arkansas poured into the ACS office in Washington, and in early 1891, as the General Assembly wrote and debated racist legislation, the correspondence became a flood. The great majority of the letters the ACS received in the early part of 1891, in fact, came from black Arkansans seeking to emigrate.[23] Secretary Coppinger finally prepared a standardized form letter to send to the Arkansas applicants. And the letters and applications came from all parts of the state, from Miller County in the southwest to Mississippi County in the state's northeastern corner, from Washington County in the northwest to Chicot County in extreme southeast Arkansas. From the September 1890 elections through the end of 1891, the would-be emigrants corresponded to the ACS from ninety-nine different post offices representing thirty-seven of the state's seventy-five counties. The most intense interest came from the Arkansas River valley region and a corridor of cotton lands in eastern Arkansas stretching from Jefferson County northward to Jackson County, regions that experienced a high degree of political competition and violence in the 1888 and 1890 elections. Of all these areas, the one still on fire for emigration was Conway County in west central Arkansas.[24]

The voluminous correspondence shows how political developments motivated people to take drastic action. After the September 1890 election, H. C. Cade wrote to the ACS begging for emigration. He told Coppinger that a band of about fifty white Democrats had ridden through his township near Camden on the day before the election, threatening to kill blacks if they went out to vote. They did shoot one man and blasted his house in twenty places. When some black men persisted in trying to vote, they were told at the point of a gun that they could not cast a ballot unless they voted as the Democrats directed. Whites drove about 200 black citizens away from the polls that day, and Cade said, the "courts fails to take any notice of it." His group wanted to leave for Africa from New Orleans in the next year: "We will have to go somewhere as

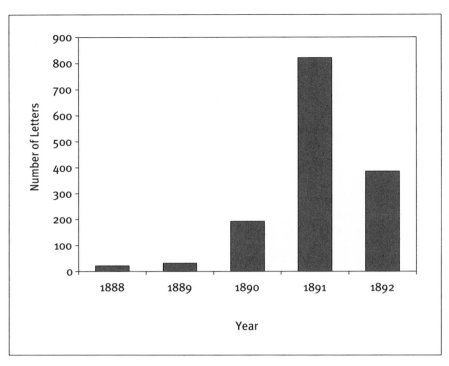

Number of letters from Arkansas to the ACS, 1888–1892. *Source:* ACS Records, Library of Congress, Washington, D.C.

we do not feel safe to stay here." Soon after the fraudulent election in September, B. H. Miller wrote from Morrilton requesting emigration, saying, "I can't feel like this Country is my home." Also from Morrilton, William Jones agreed: "We are in the South appress [oppressed] on every hand and we found out that this is a white man's country, and we can't do any good among them. Mr Coppinger . . . we wants to goe to our ancestry land Africa . . . we means business." From eastern Arkansas another man wrote: "We can see clearly that we can not stay here. They tell us this is the white man's country and that he is going to rule it."[25]

Just a few weeks after Arkansas's General Assembly passed the separate coach bill, the Reverend G. W. Waters, a preacher who also practiced medicine, wrote Bishop Henry McNeal Turner, asking for his aid to go to Liberia. Waters explained that although he was "doing well as a Negro can in Ark.," after the segregation law he was convinced "there is but little left for Negroes here. So I am going and all the Negroes in Johnson [County] will go with me." G. W. Lowe, a Baptist preacher and state representative for Monroe County, 1888–

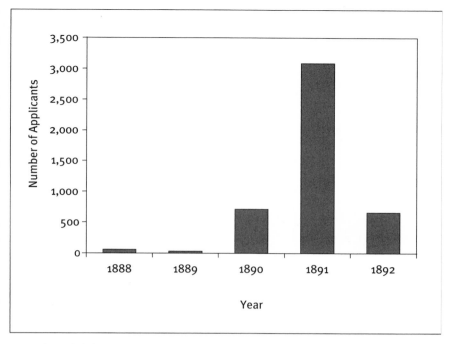

Number of Arkansas applicants for emigration to Liberia, 1888–1892.
Source: ACS Records, Library of Congress, Washington, D.C.

92, wrote for 500 people who wished to emigrate, saying, "There is a great rest-lessness among them on accoun of discriminating laws that are being made."[26]

Racial oppression was clearly the most significant factor motivating this emigration movement. Applicants to the ACS continually spoke of white prejudice as the reason they wished to leave not just Arkansas but the entire United States. The Reverend J. S. Smith, a black preacher in Conway, wrote, "Your all Dont know how we air treated this is the reasing we all want to git a way." From Augusta (Woodruff County), I. W. Penn wrote that he was using all his energies to "deliverate" his people from the pressure they lived under in Arkansas: "We are tyerd of Race Problem and Mob Rules and we believe that there are peace and happiness and prosterity in a nother section of the world." From neighboring McCrory, another man explained that he could be no more despised by other races than where he was and that he just wanted "to be recognized as human." About the time that the separate coach law took effect, John Jimison said, "We do not want to spend twenty-four months longer in America, we have long thought it was not our home and now it is proven to us more and

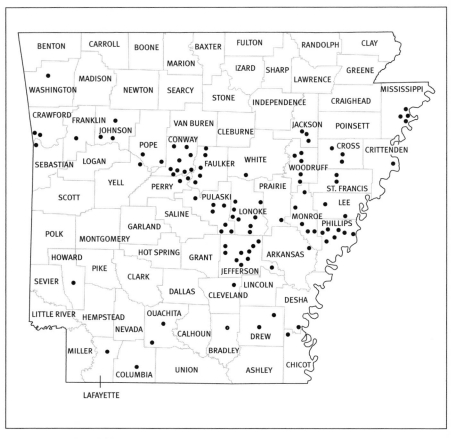

Arkansas post offices from which letters were sent to the ACS, 1891

more every day of our lives here around Plumersville, Ark."[27] F. M. Gilmore complained that in his neighborhood in Jefferson County, whites killed black men and then molested their wives at gunpoint, while they would not even permit blacks to own a firearm. The greatest frustration for Gilmore clearly was that "we have no pertexsion in Law."[28]

Would-be emigrants were motivated by economic problems as well as the deteriorating political situation. But they clearly saw the relationship between economic and political oppression. Applicants bemoaned the springtime floods and droughts in late summer that diminished their crop.[29] But black farmers saw man-made impediments, rather than acts of nature, as their worst problems. Farmers complained about the low prices of cotton and low wages for cotton picking on the one hand and steep rents and the exorbitant prices of goods they had to buy, such as flour and meat, on the other.[30] Many applicants desperately wanted to emigrate but admitted they could not scrape together the cash for their train fare to New York. One Morrilton man suggested this was because they were cheated at settlement time: "If they had their Rights they would be able to pay all their fare." In late 1890, a group of thirteen men from Pine Bluff wrote the ACS for assistance, saying, "We are in a suffering condishion and likely For Werst. The merchans says thay are gonter take our Stock away from us in the Spring we don't see how we are to live without help." F. M. Gilmore lamented that in his neighborhood landlords had black renters "bound to do just as they say or git off of his land." Whites believed the only land intended for a black man to own in the South, Gilmore concluded, was six feet long, four feet wide, and four feet deep.[31]

Besides the low wages and cotton prices, the high rates in stores, and the land lien system, other farmers complained of excessive taxation. One farmer from a hamlet on the Mississippi River ironically named Sans Souci, the French phrase meaning "carefree," complained of financial oppression, saying his people's conditions could not improve until they were freed from "the enormous taxation." Another farmer lamented that while his people had no rights, they were still taxed "on every thing from a wash Board up."[32] With state laws regulating labor and debt, with enforcement in the hands of county officials who received their offices through fraudulent elections, and with any legal redress subject to local courts, black farmers could clearly see that white power led to their economic oppression. As one black preacher despaired to the ACS, "We are greatly imposed on in America by our white Brethrens. We work hard and gets nothing from them but poverty sorrow and death from one year on to another and we are a crying now for aid to get back home and to our fathers happy land."[33]

The economic stranglehold made it extremely difficult for people who wanted to emigrate to get away. Sharecroppers and renters had to wait until the fall cotton harvest to get cash money. Settlement time for sharecroppers usually came in December. Many applicants wrote that after their crop was sold, they still were in debt and thus planned to stay another year, grow one more crop, and emigrate the following year. In January, those who had some cash after settlement were required either to sign new leases for the next year or to give up their homes. Unless applicants had a commitment for passage from the ACS, they were reluctant to give up possession of their farms to be left homeless while they waited, hoping for acceptance on the next voyage.

By late 1890, several black families nonetheless were willing to take the risk. One leader in Conway reported that his people had sold out their possessions and were prepared to leave. Near Camden, families had given up their farms and in early January 1891 were "camping out" waiting to hear from the ACS. If they could not go to Liberia, these people still had to go somewhere. They either made leases with other farmers or left for towns. One black man in Conway, J. M. Suggs, wrote the ACS that all he owned was packed in trunks ready to go, for he had "sold out everything I possessed . . . all my dishes too." By February, Suggs had drifted off to Forrest City, where he found a new house and work.[34] Several applicants from rural areas moved to Little Rock, where they sought wage labor and from where they could leave for Liberia at quick notice.

Although it is difficult to estimate how many black men and women dreamed of African emigration, available information suggests that interest was wide and deep in Arkansas. The correspondents who wrote to the ACS often claimed to speak for large numbers of people. In Arkansas, most African Americans could neither read nor write (55.2 percent of black adult males were illiterate at the 1890 census).[35] Thus, schoolteachers or preachers often corresponded for whole groups of people. In late September 1890, for example, E. H. Tate of Jefferson County wrote on behalf of twenty-five to thirty others in rural Noble Lake who wanted to emigrate. In neighboring Nubia, the Reverend W. P. Pennington claimed to speak for nearly a hundred men, each with families ranging in size between two and thirteen, who wanted to go. From McCrory in Woodruff County, a physician, Dr. Eph. Jones, wrote in early 1891 that from 1,500 to 2,000 there wanted to leave. Anderson Barnes, claiming to write for hundreds in Crittenden County, asked Coppinger how much it cost to charter a train for 500 people.[36] One correspondent from Fort Smith declared that black men intended to organize in every county of the state for emigration to Liberia and that "we have men that wants every colard man woman and children to go." From Phillips County, another declared, "Nearly every intelligent negro wants to go."[37]

Black people throughout Arkansas held meetings to discuss communal migration to Liberia in 1890 and 1891 and in many areas organized back-to-Africa clubs. Leaders called the organizations lodges, companies, associations, or clubs and gave them several names, such as the Communal Exodus Association or Colonization Association. At Menifee, in Conway County, members decided to call their club the Young Men's Association to disguise the true purpose of the society from any hostile neighbors. This name spread to several other clubs in the county and the Arkansas River valley.[38] Clubs usually had from twenty to a hundred members. When membership swelled, new clubs were formed in the same communities. In Conway County, at least two clubs existed in each of the rural communities of Menifee, Plumerville, and Germantown, as well as Morrilton. Members of a church sometimes formed their own association. Formal clubs were organized in the early 1890s in at least thirty-five communities in sixteen counties of Arkansas. The clubs elected officers, usually president, vice president, recording secretary, corresponding secretary, and treasurer. Leaders collected money from members who were serious about emigration and sent it via postal money order to the ACS office for safekeeping as a contribution toward the applicant's passage to Africa. Usually monthly, clubs held regular meetings. The Young Men's Association of Menifee, for example, met on the "Saturday night before the second Lord's day of each month." The assemblies consisted of rousing oration, singing of songs, the dissemination of information, and open discussion sessions. Following meetings, correspondence often flowed to the ACS office asking questions that members raised, along with requests for circulars, copies of the *African Repository* and other information, and application blanks. The president or corresponding secretary passed information back to the club, distributed the circulars, and read aloud the written material to the club at the next meeting. The club in McCrory pooled their money to buy a copy of Henry Morton Stanley's best seller, *In Darkest Africa*. Some clubs even had designated speakers whose job was to recruit new members and organize other lodges.[39]

Word about possibilities of African emigration spread in a variety of ways. Some enthusiastic individuals traveled the countryside preaching emigration. The Reverend Joseph Harris wrote Coppinger that besides working to organize people in his home area of Conway, he had traveled to Holly Springs, Mississippi, and aroused people there. A black schoolteacher in southern Arkansas, E. W. Wofford of Camden, claimed to have influenced seven counties for the movement. Several men asked Secretary Coppinger to hire them or authorize them to act as agents of the ACS to recruit emigrants and organize clubs in Arkansas. Coppinger consistently responded that the ACS did not hire local agents.[40] Informal and social contacts surely spread the word about African emigration. One poor speller in Lonoke County said he had heard "a good deal about Library by the word of moth." In northwest Arkansas, a black man wrote that he had learned about the company in Morrilton and wanted to start a similar club in his hometown of Fayetteville. And in Fort Smith, the Reverend Daniel Simpson wrote to the ACS that he had friends in Conway County who were going to Liberia and he wished to go with them.[41] Some black Arkansans had received letters from acquaintances who had already emigrated to Liberia and were satisfied with the country. Such letters only inspired more interest in the back-to-Africa movement.[42] In addition, Bishop Henry Turner had visited Arkansas at the annual AME Church conference in Forrest City in November 1889, and a year later in Fort Smith, where he preached to large congregations about African missions.[43]

In the fall of 1890, around the same time Turner came to Arkansas, black people held conventions in southwest and northeast Arkansas to discuss mass migration to Africa. On 2 October, a group of fifty-four delegates in southwest Arkansas assembled to devise "some plan by which we can get up a concerted action in regard to our imigrating to some country where our race can receive some protection, and where the laws are enforced equally against all its violators." Organizers planned a second meeting for 6 November at Mt. Olivet Baptist Church, five miles southwest of Camden, and printed handbills to publicize the meeting. The day after this meeting, H. C. Cade wrote the ACS from Camden that eighty-two families wanted to go to Liberia.[44] Another gathering was held somewhere in eastern Arkansas, and one delegate, L. W. Wyatt of Cross County, said this meeting represented 1,000 people in Arkansas, Mississippi, and Tennessee. The convention was apparently organized by J. W. Wells, a man who claimed to be the Arkansas agent of the U.S. and Congo National Emigration Steamship Company, a private corporation that purported to arrange emigration to Africa on chartered vessels. Although the U.S. and Congo Company never transported one person to Africa, its publicity work only fueled the feverish interest of black Arkansans in 1891 about an exodus to Africa. Wyatt said he was the only man of the 1,000 represented at the meeting who had corresponded with the ACS. Thus, the back-to-Africa movement may have been more widespread and deep than the records of the ACS indicate, for no records of this rival emigration organization have survived.[45]

This shady company had been founded by three white businessmen in 1886 who sought to capitalize on the keen interest in the Congo region following the Berlin Congress of 1884–85. This international meeting, attended by a representative of the United States, decided the terms under which Africa would be colonized by western powers, and it specifically called for free access to the Congo River, which ran into the resource-laden tropical interior of the continent. The U.S. and Congo Company proposed to transport emigrants on the eastbound voyage and bring back African products for trade on the return trip. By 1889, the white owners of the company had tired of the venture and turned over the business to some black men in Washington, D.C., who had purchased most of the stock. They hired as their chief agent a Georgia-born missionary

Notice! - Notice!

THE COLORED CITIZENS
Of Ouachita and Adjoining Counties

Are hereby invited to send Delegates to a Convention to be held at the Mt. Olivet Baptist Church, five miles Southwest of Camden, NOVEMBER 6, 1890, for the purpose of devising some plan by which we can get up a concerted action in regard to our imigrating to some country where our race can receive some protection, and where the laws are enforced equally against all its violators. We deny, and uttterly scout the idea, that there is now, properly speaking, any such thing as a NEGRO PROBLEM before the American people. It is not the Negro, educated, or illiterate, intelligent or ignorant who is on trial, or whose qualities are giving trouble to the Nation. The real problem lies in the other direciton. It is not so much what the Negro is, what he has been, or what he might be that constitutes the problem here, as elsewhere; the lesser is included in the greater. The real question, the all-absorbing question is whether American civilization, American law and American christianity can be made to include and protect alike. The Bible tells us that God has made of one blood all Nations of men to dwell on all the face of the Earth. This comprehends the Fatherhood of God and Brotherhood of Man.

Fifty-four Delegates were in the first Convention October 2d, 1890, and it is hoped there will be one hundred and fifty at the November Meeting.

THE COMMITTEE.

Handbill notice of black emigration meeting in Ouachita County, Arkansas, 1890. Courtesy Library of Congress.

who had returned from twenty years in Liberia, and he began to publicize Liberia as the destination, instead of the Congo, although the company kept the same name. By the time agents of the company had made it to Arkansas in 1890, the company had devised a plan whereby blacks could buy a membership for one dollar, plus two cents for return postage, so that the member could be informed when the chartered vessel was ready for its Atlantic voyage. After the November convention, letters poured into Coppinger from eastern Arkansas, inquiring about the legitimacy of the U.S. and Congo Company. The company's handbills, and apparently agent Wells, claimed that for the price of $1.02 a person could get passage from the United States to Liberia. Buried in the text at the bottom of the circular, was the statement: "Unless a subsidy shall be appropriated by Congress to aid the exodus, we reserve to ourselves the right, as to other applicants, to raise the price of passage."[46]

The company's plan was based on the possibility of a congressional appropriation to fund black emigration from the United States. This idea had been around for years. Whenever it came back into public discussion, it only inspired a new round of hopes for impoverished blacks who could never pay their own way to leave the United States. The U.S. and Congo Company believed it might get such funds based on a neglected federal law enacted during the Civil War calling for a quarter of the funds raised from the sale of abandoned lands in Confederate states to be used to fund black emigration from the United States. By 1890, the company had succeeded in getting a bill introduced in the House of Representatives that would provide $100 to each black adult who wished to leave the country. The company's offer to send an emigrant for $1.02 was predicated on the passage of this bill, which was referred to the House Judiciary Committee and never seen again.

The House bill appeared at the same time that Senator Matthew Butler of South Carolina introduced a bill to appropriate five million dollars of federal money to fund black emigration from the United States. The bill gained the support of some conservative southern Democrats, who wished to reduce the black population, and the number of black voters, in the South. Strangely, Butler found himself on the same side of an issue with Bishop Henry Turner, who, having already called for federal reparations to compensate for slavery, now loudly supported the bill. The Senate extensively debated the Butler bill, and it received a great deal of coverage in black and white newspapers as well. The black press, reflecting the views of educated, middle-class black Americans, uniformly opposed the bill, for it implied that black people had no future or claim to life in the United States.[47] Although the bill never came to a vote, the public discussion diffused to the local landscape in Arkansas and elsewhere in the South.

The possibility of federal aid for black emigration ignited the hopes of black Arkansas farmers who knew they could contribute little or nothing toward their passage to Africa. One farmer wrote the ACS in January 1891 explaining that rumors were passing through the country that Congress had appropriated money for Negro emigration. He wanted to know if it was true. From rural

Faulkner County, J. L. Woodard asked Coppinger for information about a law that "Congress shall aid to insist the collard population" in emigration. Coppinger wrote Woodard and others explaining that Congress had not appropriated any money for emigration and that he did not expect that it would do so. Apparently dissatisfied with this answer, Woodard wrote again asking if the government of England offered any assistance.[48]

As interest in African emigration swelled in Arkansas in the early 1890s, black people inundated the ACS with all kinds of questions and requests on issues besides federal aid. Many asked practical questions about the particulars of emigration. Some correspondents, apparently afraid of inquiring directly at their local train depot about fares and arrangements, asked Coppinger how much it would cost to get to New York, or if they could get a reduced group rate for rail travel. Because emigrants had to pay their own way to the port of embarkation, many wanted the ACS to take them from a southern port like New Orleans instead of New York.[49] Others wished to know what they could take with them on their journey. One man wanted to take his team of fine horses to Liberia, while another fretted about whether he could take a seven-foot-long wooden box containing his carpentry tools.[50] Several applicants who had trouble selling land or personal possessions for what they were worth asked if the federal government or the ACS would buy their property at fair market prices.[51]

Many people asked detailed questions about Liberia. Applicants wanted to know about the soil, timber, water, climate, and crops. Would corn, wheat, rice, barley, and rye grow in Liberia, one applicant asked, and could emigrants take seed for these products to raise there? "Is there any Horses An murels [mules] in Africa we has not seen any account off them over there?" asked George Moore, president of the Menifee Young Men's Association. A Pine Bluff man had a long list of questions: Does a big river like the Congo run through Liberia? Are there good plains for grazing stock? Any fruit farms? How much does an acre of soil produce? How much does coffee, the main cash crop of Liberia, sell for per pound in Africa? He asked Coppinger to answer as nearly as he could, for he was "answering questions for a thousand people or more." Several people asked if Liberia had any railroads, a measuring stick of modern development in late-nineteenth-century America.[52] Others asked questions about the government and laws of Liberia. People requested maps of the country, books about Liberian history, and photographs of presidents, ministers, and prominent Liberian places. Several correspondents requested copies of the constitution and laws of Liberia and asked about the particulars of citizenship and landownership.[53] Because Liberian law forbade non-Negro ownership of land, M. J. Miller was concerned about the rights of white spouses in mixed-race marriages. He wanted to know before going if the white spouse could co-own land, and if the white person would be left with no means of support or legal rights if the black spouse died first. Speaking for his club in Argenta, Miller said, "We are so badly mixed up by marriage and other ways that this question is of importance."[54] A few men asked about Liberian currency, with one reflecting America's political preoccupation of the time, inquiring: "Is it silverised?" A Brinkley man asked about educational opportunities in Liberia and how much schoolteachers were paid there.[55] Several correspondents wanted to subscribe to a Liberian newspaper and were disappointed to learn that Liberia had none in the early 1890s. One well-read black man wrote Coppinger asking about the future of Africa in regard to territorial wars between European states in the area.[56]

Not everyone was so well informed, however. One black farmer asked if Liberia was connected to Africa. Wild rumors circulated, and people often requested that the ACS confirm or deny them. "When the ship lands in Liberia," Miles West asked, "will they make slaves of us?" One man reported that black folks in Conway feared they would starve to death in Liberia. A black preacher said his people in Mississippi County were worried about newspaper reports of cannibalism in Africa. Another correspondent apparently most feared the sea journey across the Atlantic. He asked detailed questions about the length of the ocean voyage, dangers of storms or getting lost at sea, and seasickness.[57]

The people who wanted to emigrate to Africa were ordinary working folk. Almost all of those who inquired or applied to emigrate earned their living as farmers. While many had postal addresses in towns, their letters indicate that the great majority lived in the surrounding countryside and worked on the land. A few actually lived in town, like the members of the club in Argenta, today's North Little Rock. But a good number of these town dwellers had recently arrived from the countryside, many from Conway County, and appeared to have given up their leases and moved to town to take up wage labor in order to leave more easily at short notice. While most applicants clearly were tenants or sharecroppers, a few owned small farms. But the property owners also complained of their difficult economic situation. R. W. Haffold, for example, said that even though he owned sixty acres of ridge land in Johnson County, as well as four horses, seven cattle, and fourteen hogs, poverty still stared him in the face every day, and he did not see a way to turn his property into cash money. Harvey Hopson said that although he owned 120 acres of land in Faulkner County worth about $600, he could not sell it "now for no money." Another black landowner, J. W. Waters of Jefferson County, reported that he owned his house and 160 acres of land but he would give it all up to go to Liberia.[58] The letters to the ACS from potential emigrants may exaggerate the role of more prosperous and literate black farmers who could afford pen, ink, and postage, for these men often wrote on behalf of clubs or groups of people who could not write for themselves.

Most of those who applied and nearly all who were accepted for emigration were families containing a father, a mother, and several children. The applicants mirrored the average black American family, which in 1880 contained two parents and 2.7 children.[59] But the application lists also contained names of elderly men and women, orphaned children, widows, single men, and female heads of households. Coppinger clearly discouraged the applications of people who would not be able to support themselves in Liberia, such as the elderly. This stance reflected not just the middle-class bias of the ACS but also the historical reality that families with children meant extra laborers for the farm economy emigrants would face in Liberia. He told one man that the ACS would not send people over seventy to Liberia. In 1891, Juda Parker, who described herself as a "poor wider woman," wrote to the ACS wanting to emigrate to Liberia. Coppinger responded that the ACS did not aid widows in settling in Liberia. But some single mothers persisted and managed to get their families to Liberia. Narcissie Moore, a thirty-two-year-old widow in Argenta, was accepted with her four children, and they emigrated on 31 October 1891.[60] Coppinger's outgoing letters and the ACS's promotional material made it clear that those who could contribute toward their Atlantic passage would receive priority in the selection process. This policy favored smaller families, people with some means, and those who were willing to gamble by turning their livestock and meager possessions into cash to send on to Washington. From the voluminous correspondence and the thousands of applications returned, the composite portrait of a would-be Arkansas emigrant to Liberia would look much like the typical African American family in the state: two parents with several children, living on the land, unable to make ends meet through cotton farming. Those chosen by the ACS were most often in a group led by risk takers who converted some possessions into cash, which they sent on to the ACS as a contribution toward the African voyage.

By late 1890, a large group of people in Conway and Faulkner Counties were doing just that: selling out and sending money to the ACS, expecting to emigrate. One applicant from the western edge of Conway County wrote that "the

Liberia questions has got the people of my cuntry aroused they think that they will bea out from under the yoke of Bondage." From Morrilton, James Dargan exclaimed, "We live in a most horrible place it vexes the soul of a richous man." In August 1890, W. D. Leslie of Menifee said his group wanted to leave "the land of slavery and how happy we will be when we get to that old ship and our song will be I am going home to die no more . . . there can be no worse a plase in the world than this place."[61] By the fall of 1890, W. K. Fortson guaranteed that 1,500 black people from the Menifee area would be ready to emigrate. From Germantown, on the other side of the county, W. H. King assured the ACS of another one hundred families. The Morrilton club promised from 500 to 600 more settlers.[62] Eventually, more than 1,500 black residents of Conway County formally applied to emigrate to Liberia, about 20 percent of the county's entire black population. The exodus movement was well organized in the county, with at least eight clubs in five communities in the southern part of the county, where most of the black population resided.

By the end of 1890, black people in Conway County were sending the ACS money toward their African passage by postal order in small amounts and large —$.50, $1, $5, $27, $29.10, $48.[63] While Coppinger indicated he would accept the application of the company of James Dargan, a schoolteacher in Morrilton, for the spring voyage, he told other people they could not be accommodated.[64] People kept sending in their money orders anyway. The exodus club in the town of Conway sent $189 and applications for fifty-nine people. When Coppinger explained to members of the Conway emigration club that the ACS could not take them in the spring, the group fell into "considerable panic," for most of the applicants had "disposed of nearly all they had at a very great sacrifice."[65] Even Dargan's party had its problems. Coppinger first said that only sixty could be accommodated, which would have left a portion of the company behind, some who had already sold their possessions. Then he further reduced the number accepted to forty and gave Dargan the onerous job of choosing who would go from his party. Dargan's group finally sailed from New York aboard the bark *Liberia* on 14 February.[66]

Coppinger promised he would do what he could to take others in the Morrilton party in the fall. But he was telling the same to other applicants in Plumerville, Menifee, Germantown, and Conway. W. D. Leslie, a frequent correspondent, responded: "I hope to the time come when you will give us vorges a nuff so as we can get on and leave the U.S.A." John L. Rilhard wrote that he was sorry they could not go to Liberia in the spring, but "we still stand organized as a club in Conway, Ark."[67] Some, however, could not be patient and wait.

Daniel and Lucy Brown of Plumerville and another couple, John Sandling and wife, sold their things and had no place to go. They left in late March heading north. A few weeks later, they arrived at the ACS office in Washington to beg Coppinger personally for passage. The Browns, who had previously sent $50 to the ACS, were taken on the next voyage in May. The Sandlings, deemed by Coppinger as too old, were refused passage.[68]

The back-to-Africa movement in Conway County faced a challenge when James Dargan returned to the area from Liberia. Apparently, he had begun to get cold feet before going, for he gave up his own family's space on the ship to others he said were in "worse shape." He explained to Coppinger that he planned to lead his party on the African voyage and then return to get his family after preparing a place for them in Liberia.[69] When he came back in early May 1891, he told people that the ACS's circulars had lied to them and that settlers were forcibly and inhumanely treated once in Liberia. Dargan said the country was no place for an American person; in fact, it was "not fiting for a horse to live much less of a person." Settlers were not allowed, Dargan said, to write back the truth about the country. He insisted he had left the other Morrilton colonists "holering and cring wanting to come back, but they wouden let them." Immediately the prospective emigrants of Conway County besieged the ACS with letters asking Coppinger if Dargan's account was really true.[70] Coppinger assured the anxious applicants that Dargan had been in Liberia for only three days before he took the same vessel directly back to the United States. Dargan had stayed in Monrovia the entire time and was drunk most of that time, Coppinger said, and he deserted his party without even seeing where they settled some ten miles into the interior. Dargan's account was simply untrue, Coppinger said, and Dargan knew it was untrue.[71] By June, when letters from Morrilton settlers began to arrive back in Conway County denouncing Dargan and indicating their satisfaction with Liberia and its prospects, people seem convinced that Dargan indeed had been lying. One black man even decided that Dargan had conspired with white people on a mission to discredit the emigration movement.[72] While the return of Andrew Flowers from Liberia in 1884 had brought the emigration movement in Conway County to a virtual halt, Dargan's return proved merely a temporary setback. Either Dargan's credibility was low or the desire to emigrate was overwhelming, for black people in the Conway County area resumed sending their applications and money to the ACS office in Washington.

By late 1891, some of the black families from Conway County, including the Moore, Rogers, and Ficklin families, had moved to Little Rock and its sister city, Argenta, just across the Arkansas River. They and others in Pulaski County began to organize a ninety-member emigration club. By July, Coppinger was promising passage on the fall voyage to several members of the club, such as Andrew Ficklin, whose brother Stephen had gone with the Morrilton party in February.[73] By early October, Ficklin and several of the families from Pulaski County and two families from Morrilton took off for New York without waiting to receive their order of passage for the fall voyage.

Several of the party lived close to each other in Argenta. Narcissie Moore lived on Hazel Street, between Green and Astra streets, just a stone's throw from the Davids and Streets, who also left for New York. Moore, a dark-skinned woman of mixed Creek Indian and African descent, was the single mother of four children, her husband having died the year before. She apparently kept secret her plans to leave for Liberia until the day before departure. When Willie Shaw, a young neighbor desperately in love with Narcissie's teenaged daughter, Dora, learned of the family's plans, he decided to leave with them. (Willie and Dora were married in Liberia and lived there together as husband and wife for sixty years.) After a Sunday morning Baptist service, the party left for New York. Upon arrival in the city, several of these families found lodgings on West 30th Street to wait out their departure for Liberia. Three weeks later, the group of at least twenty people were begging Coppinger for support, for rent was high in New York and they had spent all the money they had.[74]

Just before the 31 October departure, another unauthorized group from Arkansas arrived in New York, a family of six from Little Rock and a married couple with the wife's elderly mother from Keo in Lonoke County. But the ship could not accommodate the whole group; the new arrivals and two families that had come earlier were left behind. The ship sailed on the morning of the 31st with the emigrants reported as "perfectly contented." The twenty-one Arkansans left standing at the port must have felt quite differently. Some of this party stayed for a while in New York at 13 Cornelia Street, but their ultimate fate is unknown. The ACS never transported them to Liberia.[75]

As the Jim Crow laws began to take effect in the fall of 1891, interest in African emigration, already at fever pitch, only intensified. In various parts of the state, applicants were selling their possessions, preparing to emigrate to Liberia. Liberia hysteria remained at the highest level in Conway County. Wertevious Mack Wilson printed a handbill announcing the public sale on 25 November 1891 of his seventy-nine acres near Menifee, two mules, one Mitchell wagon, one cow, twenty hogs, farming tools, and several hundred bushels of corn. All was to go for cash to the highest bidder. Others were selling out and sending in their money to the ACS. Emigration clubs in Morrilton, Plumerville, and Menifee sent more than a thousand dollars to Coppinger in the fall of 1891 toward the passage of hundreds of applicants for emigration. From Atkins, just across the county line in Pope County, came another $190. The ACS had not seen more than a thousand dollars contributed by emigrants toward passage since 1880, the last year African migration had swelled into a mass movement in Arkansas.[76]

Abner Downs of Morrilton, who had been corresponding with the ACS for two years, finally received notice that Coppinger had approved his group for the spring voyage. Although Coppinger seemed to procrastinate in sending firm rejections, eventually he informed other club leaders that the ACS could not accommodate any more applicants. W. A. Diggs became distraught upon hearing the news, for his group in Plumerville had sold out everything and had even made travel arrangements with the railroad. From Lonoke County, F. J. Jones would not take no for an answer. Jones scolded Coppinger: "You ant talking to sute me . . . and you will hafter talk to me better then that because we all here have don got ride of all our things and sould out all we have here we just hafter come for we can not stay here."[77] W. H. Holloway explained to the William Coppinger that it had "struck my people like a thunderbolt" when his emigration club in Cleveland County learned the ACS would not be able to send them to Liberia. A great many of his people, he said, had "sold their farms and homes and disarranged all their Business in this country preparing for Liberia." Holloway concluded, "Brother Coppinger, we are in dead ernest and mean what we say and do."[78]

Feelings of hope, fear, and desperation resonate through Holloway's letter and make up a complex set of emotions that must have been shared by many of the black men and women in Arkansas who wanted to emigrate to Africa. In 1891, the year of Arkansas's segregation and disfranchisement laws, 86 of the 154 black men, women, and children that the ACS settled in Liberia had come from Arkansas. The keenest interest in African emigration had begun in the counties, such as Conway and Woodruff, where black voters had been most defrauded by white Democrats. But with the racist legislation of 1891, the back-to-Africa movement had spread statewide. By the end of that year, thousands were waiting for the word to go. A large number of black Arkansans, despairing of a good life in the United States, had placed their hopes for a better one on the Republic of Liberia. One wonders just how many would have emigrated to Liberia if the ACS had sufficient ships and resources to take them.

4

Gaw'n t' 'Beria
The Crisis of 1892

When 1892 arrived, black neighborhoods throughout Arkansas were enthused about emigration to Africa. While the party of approved emigrants from Morrilton prepared for their departure, elsewhere in the state people sought every measure to get the ACS's favor. However, the death of the ACS leader William Coppinger in February 1892 and the arrival in New York of a large group of desperate would-be emigrants brought a turning point in the ACS's long history of promoting African emigration. The ACS stepped out of the emigration enterprise just as interest in Arkansas approached hysteria. As a spate of lynchings swept through Arkansas in 1892 combined with the first election under the new disfranchisement law, people of color had more reasons than ever to leave the state. With the door to Liberia closing on them, the problem became one of where else to go.

Many aspiring emigrants sold homes, stock, and/or possessions in late 1891 and early 1892 and had to go somewhere. As these refugees drifted from Arkansas to New York City, hoping for transportation to Liberia, they became a financial and public relations problem for the ACS. In early November, George Angram left Little Rock to join the party of stranded aspiring emigrants whom the October voyage had left behind. Angram wrote Coppinger from New York explaining that he had to take his family out of Arkansas because they feared for their lives: "White people wanted to harm me for leaving the country." Others in Little Rock told Coppinger they planned to leave for the North and would just settle in New York if the ship could not take them to Africa. Coppinger repeatedly warned applicants of the high cost of living in the city and instructed them to wait for the ACS's order of passage directing them to leave for New York. But the desperate applicants complained that after selling off their possessions, they were just spending their money by staying in Little Rock. If they waited any longer, they feared they would lack the money to travel to New York. One correspondent exclaimed, "I love to obey orders, but we are compel to lieve here."[1]

The story of stranded emigrants and Coppinger's stern warnings fueled rumors in various parts of Arkansas. Samuel Graham of Woodruff County wrote Coppinger in January asking if it was true that 10,000 or more homeless emigrants were at port waiting to go to Liberia. Another correspondent reported that stories were circulating in Conway County of thousands of people starving in New York as they waited for their ships. Adding to the confusion, Coppinger fell seriously ill with pneumonia in the middle of January and was unable to answer his voluminous mail from Arkansas.[2]

Bishop Henry Turner added fuel to the emigration fires by traveling to West Africa at the end of 1891, a trip widely publicized in the black press. For Turner, visiting Sierra Leone and Liberia was a religious experience, and he wrote back a series of fourteen letters describing Africa in the most glowing of terms. In his seventh letter, published in the *Christian Recorder*, Turner declared that Sierra Leone was far healthier than Memphis, Tennessee, or Pine Bluff or Helena, Arkansas. And Liberia, Turner said, was "one of the most paradisical portions of earth my eyes have ever beheld." Meeting Turner at the docks upon his arrival in Monrovia were William Patterson, James Slocum, and Stephen Ficklin, who had arrived earlier in the year from Morrilton, Arkansas. One black man in Conway wrote in March 1892 after reading of Turner's trip, "He makes me each [ache] all over with gladness to heare of him."[3]

At the height of this interest in Liberian emigration in Arkansas, William Coppinger died on 9 February. One of the members of the executive committee of the ACS, a Washington lawyer named Reginald Fendall, stepped in to manage ACS affairs. Fendall knew little about the day-to-day work of the ACS, for his committee met infrequently. Coppinger had handled the actual business of the society from its office in Washington. In Coppinger's last days he was so sick that he could not even discuss ACS business with Fendall or show him any records. With the *Liberia* then coming in to port, Fendall contemplated canceling the next expedition. But shortly after Coppinger's death, Fendall decided instead to delay the sailing until 10 March, and he telegraphed the order of passage to the Morrilton emigrants. By the 24th of February the settlers from Conway County had arrived in the city.[4]

By that time, a full-scale crisis had broken out for the ACS. Besides the party of authorized emigrants from Morrilton, two groups of black families from Indian Territory and Woodruff County, Arkansas, had descended on New York. Nearly 200 impoverished folk from Muldrow and Redland, Indian Territory, communities just west of the Arkansas line near Fort Smith, had come without warning the ACS office. Newspaper reports suggested that the party had been duped by a black preacher from Arkansas, the Reverend Frank Priestly, who had organized and led the party but feigned illness at the last minute and stayed behind in Fort Smith. The group stepped off their train in New York with no one there to meet them, and they wandered around lower Manhattan, half frozen, wet, hungry, and bewildered. They found accommodations in a cheap hotel, where they paid from $.50 to $1.50 for the privilege of sleeping on the floor. The next day a policeman directed them to shelter in Merritt's Mission for Homeless Men on 8th Avenue. They announced to quizzical New Yorkers that they were "gaw'n t' 'Beria'."[5]

On the following day, 22 February, another group of thirty-four unauthorized emigrants arrived from McCrory in Woodruff County, Arkansas. Hundreds of black families from the McCrory area had applied to emigrate in late 1891, but Coppinger had written back that the ACS could not take them in 1892. By February, the members of the Liberia exodus club of McCrory, mostly tenant farmers, had sold out their stock and possessions and purchased tickets to New York, at $19.35 per adult and half that for a child. They traveled by train to Savannah, Georgia, where they caught a steamer that took them to New York. Seasick from a rough ocean voyage, they arrived at the port of New York five days after they left home. They had subsisted on bananas, bread, and molasses from the time of their arrival in Savannah. One leader of the group, a bowlegged, wizened Baptist preacher named Judge Thornton, stepped off the gangplank of the steamer carrying a lantern. The McCrory club had pooled their money to buy a copy of Henry Morton Stanley's book, *In Darkest Africa*, and with his lantern Thornton aimed to be prepared for the "dark continent." The other leader, George Washington, carried all his earthly possessions in a ragged yellow valise and a bed quilt full of old clothes. The *New York Herald* quipped that Washington was delighted at being told that the flags and bunting he saw displayed on that 22nd day of February were in his honor of his birthday. Behind them filed a procession of black men, barefoot children, and women in gingham dresses and poke bonnets. With no one there to meet them, the new arrivals spent their first night in New York on their steamer and then found lodgings at a boardinghouse at 27 Sullivan Street.[6]

Reporters for the New York daily papers swarmed the wharf to cover this refugee crisis that was reminiscent of the arrival of the Arkansas refugees in 1880. Headlines blamed the ACS and Bishop Turner's "glowing pictures of the promised land" for luring the emigrants north. In fact, Judge Thornton explained that "every one down in our country's talking of going to Africa. The only ones who don't come haven't got the money. Bishop Turner wrote right smart about Liberia, and we all thought that was the place for us to go." Another McCrory man, Coleman Williams, who arrived with his wife and ten children, noted the low price of cotton as a motivation for departure. "When the year comes around we's mostly in debt," Williams said. "We's alway in debt down there. We just makes enough to keep in debt." The emigrants created quite an alarm when they explained to reporters that "thousands and thousands were always talking of going and ready to sell out what property they had at any time, and start for New York." The whole event quickly became a fiasco of bad publicity for the ACS and the back-to-Africa movement.[7]

Upon reading about the refugee crisis in the newspaper, members of the ACS executive committee held an emergency meeting in Washington. The committee named Reginald Fendall as acting secretary and directed him to go to New York to manage the situation. Fendall feared that the more than 200 emigrants in New York had been authorized by Coppinger to depart. After he returned to New York, he ascertained that they had not been promised passage by the ACS. At first Fendall planned to conduct a fund-raising campaign, as the ACS had done in 1880, to collect the necessary money to charter additional ships to send the refugees to Liberia. The executive committee of the ACS had appropriated $2,000 toward that end but estimated it would require $18,000 more to send the entire group to Africa. Fendall met with the refugees from McCrory and decided that they were just the sort to make fine emigrants to Liberia. He also talked with reporters, trying hard to convince the press that the ACS had not been at fault. Thinking matters were under control, Fendall returned to Washington.[8]

In the meantime, black church and community leaders in New York discussed the situation at two meetings held on 28 February and 3 March at the Bethel AME Church, just down the street from where the McCrory refugees were staying. Leading the meetings were influential black men such as W. B. Derrick, the secretary of the AME Church's Foreign Mission Society who came from Philadelphia; the Reverend Theodore Gould, pastor of Bethel Church; and T. Thomas Fortune, the editor of the black newspaper the *New York Age*. The second meeting resolved that the refugees should not be sent onward to Liberia but back to the South. Black community leaders of New York clearly feared that thousands of impoverished southern blacks might descend on their city and become burdens to the city's charitable organizations. But the meeting went further, denouncing the entire African colonization movement as a fraud and those connected to it as "ignorant or malicious disturbers of the public peace and understanding." Turner responded by castigating the comfortable northern black leaders who would send the stranded refugees in New York "back to the devil-ridden region of the country from whence they came—trying to escape from the jaws of slaughter and death." Turner concluded, "May God hurl thunderbolts at the head of every Negro who would advise those people to return, is my prayer."[9]

Given the negative publicity and high cost of resettling the stranded refugees from Arkansas and Indian Territory in Africa, Reginald Fendall and the executive committee of the ACS decided to ignore their plight. The *Liberia* sailed at 7:30 on Thursday morning, the 10th of March, packed to the rafters with the fifty authorized emigrants from Morrilton. The refugees from McCrory and Indian Territory apparently melted into the population of New York. Two years later, T. Thomas Fortune said the refugees had found work in New York and Brooklyn, determined to raise money to go on to Africa, but then had become contented where they were. At least one family, that of George Washington, one of the McCrory leaders, traveled on to Liberia from New York in 1896. The fate of the rest of the party is unknown.[10]

The 10 March 1892 expedition of emigrants from Arkansas was the last group settlement in the long history of the American Colonization Society. At a meeting later in the month, the executive committee voted to reorganize the society and its policies. The ACS suspended publication of the *African Repository*, replacing it with a scaled-down biyearly publication, the *Liberia Bulletin*, which had its first issue in November. The committee fired the ACS's agent in Monrovia, C. T. O. King, deeming him derelict in his duties, and replaced him with Ezekial E. Smith, a black man from Goldsboro, North Carolina, who had been a former U.S. minister to Liberia. But most important, the committee decided to abandon the society's seven-decades-long program of group migration to Africa. Instead of sending large numbers of permanent settlers, the ACS decided to thereafter send only a few select emigrants with particular skills needed in the Republic of Liberia. Through the remaining eight years of the century, the ACS would send only twenty people to Liberia, most of them teachers and missionaries. The society hired Coppinger's daughter, Miss Ida Coppinger, to work for a month to catch up on the voluminous correspondence. She diligently wrote hundreds of formulaic letters to applicants, most of them in Arkansas, giving them the news of her father's death and communicating no hope for any passage to Liberia in 1892 or 1893. By April, the executive committee had chosen James Ormond Wilson, a Washington educator, as the acting secretary of the society and named Fendall as treasurer. Wilson and Fendall began returning the money applicants had sent toward their passage and instructed people to send no more funds to Washington. Nonetheless, the letters and applications for emigration continued to flow in from Arkansas and elsewhere in the South.[11]

William Coppinger had so personified the ACS that it virtually ceased to exist after his death. The ACS withdrew from the emigration business just when interest in a back-to-Africa movement was at its peak in Arkansas. Conditions for black people only worsened in 1892, and blacks had even more reason to leave the state. While the previous year had seen new levels of legal and political discrimination against black people in Arkansas, 1892 became known for its violent physical attacks against people of color.

While the number of known lynchings had increased dramatically in the late 1880s and early 1890s, 1892 had the dubious distinction as the peak year for lynchings in American history. Those who counted lynchings, such as Ida B. Wells, the black woman from Memphis who led the antilynching campaign in the 1890s, and later the NAACP, relied mainly on newspaper accounts to prepare their lists. Doubtless many lynchings went unreported. The counts of lynching victims varied considerably from one list to another, for the very term "lynching" defied precise definition. What one might count as a lynching, another might disregard. Although the lists do not provide conclusive evidence, they suggest patterns. Wells counted 241 lynchings in the United States in 1892, and she said 25 of these took place in Arkansas. According to the NAACP's list, prepared about thirty years later, 155 black lynchings occurred in 1892, 19 of them in Arkansas. Only Louisiana, whose black population was almost double that of Arkansas, saw more black victims in this year, with 22 lynchings.[12] From all the available records, the pattern appears clear: a black person in 1892 stood a greater risk of falling victim to lynching in Arkansas than anywhere else in the United States.

Some of the most dramatic and grotesque lynchings in Arkansas occurred in February while the Liberia emigration crisis was unfolding in New York, and collectively they represented the state of race relations in Arkansas. On 14 February, five days after William Coppinger died, a white mob in downtown Pine Bluff lynched John Kelly, a black man accused of murder, and his alleged accomplice. The mob strung up the two victims forty feet in the air from the cross arm of a telegraph pole immediately in front of the Jefferson County courthouse. As the second largest town in the state, in a county that was three-quarters black, Pine Bluff could perhaps make the claim to be capital of black Arkansas. The city hosted an annual black state fair, was home to the state's only public black institution of higher education, the Branch Normal School, and contained a thriving black business district. A black newspaper, the *Echo*, was published there. Many middle-class blacks and several wealthy black citizens called Pine Bluff home. John Gray Lucas, the Boston-educated legislator who so eloquently opposed the separate coach bill the year before, lived there. So did Wiley Jones, a rich black man who had been born a slave. Jones owned Pine Bluff's only streetcar line, as well as a racetrack with a stable of trotting horses worth $50,000. Another black man, Ferd Havis, owned tenements, businesses, and warehouses in town and 2,000 acres of farmland in the county. The public lynching of two black men at the seat of government in mostly black Pine Bluff resonated with symbolic power.[13]

On 20 February, just a week after the Pine Bluff lynchings, a black man named Edward Coy was arrested for sexual assault of a white woman, Mrs. Henry Jewel, in Texarkana, a town straddling the Arkansas-Texas border. He proclaimed his innocence, suggesting that the two had been involved in a consensual affair for the previous year. Nonetheless, a crowd estimated variously between 1,000 and 15,000 people (in a town that claimed only 3,528 citizens in 1890) turned out to witness Coy's death. A white mob carried him out of jail in the middle of the afternoon, tied him to a ten-foot-high cedar stump, doused him with coal oil, and burned him alive. Mrs. Jewel, his accuser, lit the first flame. It took Coy seven minutes to die. Afterward, souvenir hunters carved buttons and a policeman's club from the charred tree stump that remained.[14]

In Little Rock, the state capital, three months later, a similar spectacle unfolded. Henry James, a black handyman, was accused of raping a five-year-old white girl in the house where he worked. James was arrested and transferred to the state penitentiary for safekeeping. On the evening of 13 May, a white mob broke down the gates of the prison with sledgehammers, forcibly took James from his cell, marched him to downtown Little Rock and hanged him from a telegraph pole at Fifth and Main streets, just a few blocks from the state capital building. Newspaper reports suggested the mob exceeded 500 people. Gov-

A lynching in Arkansas, ca. 1890. Courtesy Allen-Littlefield Collection.

ernor James Eagle had been passing nearby on a street car and heard the commotion. When he tried to stop the mob and arrest one of the leaders, the crowd knocked him off his feet and rescued the white man from his grip. The governor later explained that he sprained his hand in the fistfighting that followed. While some in the mob desisted when they saw Eagle, others said they "didn't care a d— if it was the Governor." Henry James's body remained hanging in downtown Little Rock until the next morning. Thousands of spectators reportedly filed by for the lurid view and even braved a thunderstorm that tossed the dead body about at the end of the rope. A photographer took pictures. When the coroner took down the corpse of Henry James, the 125-foot-long rope used to lynch him was cut in pieces as souvenirs. All the pieces disappeared within twenty minutes.[15]

These communal murders in Arkansas show classic ritual patterns of spectacle lynchings. Complex phenomena, lynchings defy easy explanation. Social scientists have offered theories explaining such outbursts of collective violence, ranging from the collapse of cotton prices, to psychosexual frustration, to class conflict. Edward Ayers, in his book *Promise of the New South*, notes that the greatest number of late-nineteenth-century lynchings generally occurred not in the blackest areas of the deep delta and plantation South but in the areas of rapid black population growth, specifically the Gulf Plain, which stretches from Florida to Texas and the cotton uplands of Mississippi, Louisiana, Arkansas, and Texas. He theorizes that in these areas, newly arrived blacks had fewer social connections with local whites and blacks and fewer people to vouch for them and thus they became more vulnerable in rough times. This argument may well fit the Arkansas lynchings of 1892, most of which occurred in counties where blacks formed a sizable but not a dominant portion of the population.[16]

However, the timing of this dramatic rise in lynchings in Arkansas in 1892, following shortly after the application of disfranchisement and segregation laws, underscores the political situation for black Arkansans. It was almost as if the lynchings took place to confirm for whites that taking away black votes and rights had been the right thing to do. After declaring blacks unwashed and unfit through segregation and disfranchisement laws, the public seizure of accused black criminals, especially in the wake of crimes considered dirty like rape and murder, and then lynching them as an act of public justice, simply reaffirmed what laws had just done the year before. After the new laws, in effect, made blacks noncitizens, whites could mistreat people of color with impunity. The mobs that killed John Kelly, Edward Coy, and Henry James had not even bothered to wear masks or hoods to conceal their identities. Yet in all cases, coroners' verdicts concluded that the deaths were at the hands of unknown parties. Ida B. Wells saw clearly the relationship between discriminatory laws and lynchings, writing in 1898: "With no sacredness of the ballot there can be no sacredness of human life itself. For if the strong can take the weak man's ballot, when it suits his purposes to do so, he will take his life also. . . . Therefore, the more complete the disfranchisement, the more frequent and horrible has been the hangings, shootings, and burnings."[17]

The first application of Arkansas's disfranchisement law came soon after this rampage of lynchings. Following years of heated competition, the biyearly stealing or stuffing of ballot boxes, and physical intimidation of black voters, the September 1892 state and local elections took place calmly. The *Arkansas Gazette* observed that "a more quiet election was never before held." With deputy sheriffs stationed at polling places, some black men were apparently not willing to test the new election law. A few black voters in Jefferson County refused to allow Democratic judges to make out their ballots for them. Others who permitted white judges to mark their ballots apparently ended up voting inadvertently for the opposition. Reports from Conway County said many black men voted Democratic who were not accustomed to doing so; Democrats there said that "the new law works like a charm." Not only black voters were affected in Conway County; the new law also kept from voting a number of immigrants who could not read or write English. Leaders of the People's Party, which had replaced the Union Labor Party by 1892 as the party of the farmers, charged that the Democratic monopoly over positions of election judge and clerk made manipulation of votes easy even in black-majority areas. One populist leader complained that judges routinely marked ballots for the Democratic candidates with no regard to the expressed wish of illiterate voters. Democrats denied these charges, but the results of the election speak for themselves.[18]

The number of votes cast in the gubernatorial race dropped by 17 percent from the previous election. This decline in voter turnout cut across both races. But it disproportionately hurt the black Republican vote, for the majority of black Arkansans were illiterate at the 1890 census, a rate five times higher than for whites. Several delta counties, which had for decades elected Republican or compromise tickets in county elections, went Democratic in 1892. Democrats took all the county offices in black-majority Desha, Lafayette, Phillips, Monroe, and St. Francis Counties. Even in Chicot County, which was 88 percent black in 1890, the local white newspaper's headline read: "After Negro Rule for Twenty-Eight Years—Democracy on Top." Moreover, the September election saw the passage by voters of a constitutional amendment allowing a poll tax, which would further diminish the votes of poor, and especially black, Arkansans. When the poll tax law came into effect in the 1894 election, the number of voters declined by almost a third from the number that had turned out in 1890, a fraction just slightly higher than the black proportion of Arkansas's population in the early 1890s. After the 1894 election, Democrats ruled in the remaining black-majority counties, such as Jefferson and Phillips. For the first time in twenty-five years, no black man would serve in Arkansas's General Assembly. Not until 1973 would a black person again occupy a seat in the state legislature.[19] Disfranchisement in Arkansas had become thorough and near complete.

With the heightened racial violence and the application of the disfranchisement laws, 1892 brought a new level of desperation to the back-to-Africa movement in Arkansas.[20] Two black men of Plumerville wrote to the ACS in May that "the present condition of the country is torn up so bad here and all around. . . . We must soon get some where for voyage for ar linching and threating al the time." A few weeks after the Kelly lynching in Pine Bluff, a correspondent there begged the ACS for passage, explaining that "the time has come that the colored people will have to go somewhere." The *Indianapolis Freeman* reported that black families around Gurdon, in southwestern Arkansas, were disposing of their property and clandestinely planning a mass exodus to Africa because of the Coy lynching in Texarkana. From Lonoke County, the site of a brutal lynching of a black family in February, a correspondent wrote the ACS that a thousand families would leave Arkansas in the winter and spring. Another Lonoke County man, Robert Davis, explained that "we are anxsious to leave this state now and go in libeare time are getten hard with us now the white people are shouting us down ever day and the ante nothen siad about it. We are going Bake in slavery ever day."[21]

Thus black Arkansans had the greatest motivation to leave just as the ACS slammed shut the door to African migration. Desperate for somewhere to go, many turned their sights on the Oklahoma Territory. Congress had authorized the opening of western and largely unoccupied portions of Indian Territory to settlement, commencing with the famous land run of 22 April 1889. In the next year, these lands were organized as the Oklahoma Territory, with the remaining Indian Territory to the east occupied by the Five Civilized Nations. In the early 1890s, Oklahoma fever struck both blacks and whites who thirsted for the vast tracts of land becoming available. Two prominent black Kansans, Edward P. McCabe and William L. Eagleson, began promoting black migration from the South into the new Oklahoma Territory. McCabe had moved to Oklahoma and, by 1890, had taken over the town of Langston, which he billed as an all-black town. McCabe also had political ambitions. Early in 1890, he campaigned for the appointment as territorial governor and met with President Benjamin Harrison to discuss his plans for black migration to Oklahoma. McCabe promoted a plan for black settlement in such concentrations that black voters would be able to control each representative and senate district in the new territorial legislature. Although he failed to get the appointment as governor, McCabe, as editor of the *Langston Herald* and chief promoter of black migration, inspired blacks with his talk of Oklahoma becoming the first black state. Eventually, several dozen all-black communities were established in Oklahoma. McCabe boasted that these all-black towns, like his Langston, offered safety and society for black people, but most important, they offered "absolute political liberty and the enjoyment of every right and privilege every other man enjoys under the constitution of the country." In retrospect, black settlers were naive to believe that they would come in sufficient numbers to control the government of Oklahoma. But in 1892, such talk of freedom and rights, combined with the possibility of free land, became the stuff of dreams for poor blacks throughout the South.[22]

As many black people made efforts to leave Arkansas after the Jim Crow and disfranchisement laws, Oklahoma became the alternate destination to Liberia. Some black Arkansans had participated in the run for land of April 1889. While Arkansas's General Assembly debated the disfranchisement and segregation laws in February 1891, agents promoting migration to Oklahoma were traveling throughout Arkansas, reportedly telling black people that they would receive free land, mules, and transportation there. A black preacher in Little Rock traveled to Jefferson, Desha, Chicot, and other counties of southeast Arkansas to speak against the movement. At a public meeting in early March, black citizens debated the merits of Oklahoma migration, with Dr. J. H. Smith, a black dentist, speaking for Oklahoma, and George W. Bell of Desha County, the only black state senator, telling black people to stay home.[23]

As possibilities of emigration to Liberia lessened and the pressures intensified in 1892, many black Arkansans made the move to Oklahoma. Several hundred destitute black farmers, mostly from Jefferson County, passed through Little Rock and Fort Smith on their way to Oklahoma in March 1892. By the end of the month, a party of more than 100 penniless blacks from eastern Arkansas were traveling on foot, with two wagons, to get to Oklahoma, and more were said to be following. When they met the White River at Newport, they had no money to pay for a ferry crossing. Some charitable citizens in Newport chipped in to pay for their passage across the river, and the travelers went on their way rejoicing. One Arkansas correspondent wrote to the *Indianapolis Freeman* in April that "every train for Oklahoma is loaded down, and wagon trains can be seen a mile in length going in that direction. It is nothing strange for the inhabitants to wake and find his back yard full of emigrants cooking breakfast and having a lively chat."[24] By the end of April, 500 Oklahoma-bound settlers left Argenta. Forty-five families were reported leaving Phillips County on their way to Oklahoma, and another thirty families followed later in May. In January 1893, a wagon train of black families from Cleveland County passed through Little Rock on its way to Oklahoma, the second such train to pass in a few days. The party of young and old black women and men traveled with all their worldly possessions piled high on their covered wagons. When asked why they were leaving Arkansas, they answered: "We is tired of having the white folks rule us and we are gwine where the nigger has some say."[25]

In Conway County, where people had sold out their possessions in late 1891 and early 1892 expecting passage to Liberia, many now set their sights on Oklahoma. Two men wrote the ACS from Plumerville, saying black people there started out for Oklahoma in droves of fifty and sixty, knowing they could not go to Liberia. Applicants who had sent money to the ACS toward their Liberian passage were asking for it back so they could use it for domestic migration. In 1892, W. D. Leslie, a frequent correspondent from Menifee, wrote the ACS: "We are trying to get away from here as soon as we can . . . we had jest well have our money back and go some wheres else for it a show thing we are not living here." Some of the people who moved west continued their correspondence with the ACS. W. H. King, the leader of a club in Conway County, had moved to McAlister, in Indian Territory, by early 1892, but he insisted that he would do all he could "to encourage the movement of emigration to Liberia" just as he had before.[26]

Some of the frustrated applicants for Liberian emigration did not find Oklahoma an inviting destination, for they were determined to leave the United States entirely. Would-be emigrants in Alma, Crawford County, late in 1892, talked of traveling to New York, like the McCrory group had done, and waiting there for assistance onward to Liberia. Several applicants explored the possibility of purchasing their own passage through commercial steamship lines. Yates and Porterfield, the New York company that owned the *Monrovia* and *Liberia* ships chartered by the ACS for its expeditions, operated the only vessels that connected directly the United States and Liberia. For years the company had been content with its arrangement with the ACS, carrying an expedition of settlers to Liberia and on the return voyage bringing a cargo primarily composed of coffee, with smaller amounts of ginger and animal hides, for trade. When the ACS stopped planning further expeditions, the acting secretary referred many Arkansas applicants to Yates and Porterfield to book and pay for their own transportation. But the company did not wish to make engagements with individuals. Yates and Porterfield eventually complained to the ACS that they were receiving numerous letters from would-be emigrants but that they had no plans to engage in passenger service.[27] Some Arkansas applicants asked the ACS for advice on other ways to get to Liberia. What would it cost to charter or buy a boat, one man asked from Monticello, "for we must get a way from the south." C. E. Dixon of Carlisle, who had been refunded the hundred dollars he had sent the ACS toward his Liberian passage, by the fall was asking for the name and address of an independent shipping company in New York. By early 1893, the ACS was referring applicants to private companies that transported travelers to Liberia via Liverpool, England, for seventy-five dollars per person.[28]

With Yates and Porterfield's ships no longer carrying passengers, the only way to travel to Liberia was through a steamer to Europe and there making a connection to a ship bound for West Africa. Although this was an expensive and time-consuming option, some people were willing to try. A Little Rock man named Daniel Walker claimed he had left home on 29 December 1891 with sixty-five cents in his pocket and the clear understanding that he was going to Africa. The following July, he wrote to his brother that he had arrived in Liberia, having worked his way to New York, from there to Liverpool, and then to Africa, stopping in Spain and the Canary Islands along the way. Early the next year, C. E. Dixon, along with several family members and friends, left Lonoke County for New York, hoping to make their own arrangements to Liberia. Half of the group found passage on a steamer to Hamburg, Germany, and arrived in Liberia in April, while the others traveled through Liverpool and arrived in May. Each paid seventy-five dollars for the passage from New York to Liberia. The Dixons then wrote the ACS begging for assistance in sending the rest of their family to join them in Liberia. It is impossible to know how many people traveled on their own to Liberia. However, the ACS estimated in its annual report for 1893 that more than fifty emigrants had gone at their own expense to Liberia that year.[29]

While Arkansas had served for two decades as a destination for black migration, by the early 1890s race relations in the state had come to mirror the notorious oppression of Mississippi, Louisiana, and South Carolina. In March 1892, John Mitchell, editor of the black newspaper the *Richmond Planet* and an antilynching crusader, prepared a cartoon reflecting on the lynchings in Arkansas in early 1892. His crude drawing depicted the Gates of Hell and was accompanied by the caption: "Mississippi, Louisiana and Texas have been considered as the main entrance to Hell's Gate, but a Sinner from that region is told to enter by way of Arkansas."[30] Joseph Harris, a black preacher in Conway, wrote the ACS in June 1892: "I don't believe there would be any exaggeration at all, were I to say, that there are no less than two million negroes in the South who would leave America for Africa this fall were they able."[31] But just when black Arkansans had the most powerful motivations to leave the United States, they lost the opportunity as the ACS shut down its emigration enterprise. However, black dreams of a better life in Liberia refused to die. Determined individuals, such as the Dixons and Dan Walker, would look for other ways to get to Africa, the land of their dreams.

5

Troublemakers

Although thousands of black Arkansans had become anxious to leave for Africa, not everyone supported the idea of a black mass migration outside the United States. Many white people recognized the need for labor that a black exodus would take away. Some people of color, particularly middle-class and educated black leaders, opposed the movement, claiming that African Americans should build a future on American soil. A small number of both races actively worked to thwart black migration. A few charlatans even took advantage of people's desperation to leave and executed scams to steal poor people's money. These various groups spelled trouble for the back-to-Africa movement.

White Arkansans expressed ambivalent feelings about a back-to-Africa movement from its beginnings. A few whites had assisted black neighbors in emigration in one way or another. During the Phillips County exodus in 1879, a white man wrote letters to the ACS on behalf of black neighbors who presumably could not write for themselves. Some white neighbors, landlords, and merchants occasionally wrote testimonials of good character for applicants to help them get serious consideration by the ACS.[1] In 1892, J. L. Cloninger, a white man in Atkins, wrote to Albion Tourgée of New York, the well-known white lawyer and activist for black civil rights, asking him about the Liberia emigration movement. Cloninger's letter suggested a concern that somebody was swindling uneducated black people in his area. Thousands have gone, Cloninger said, and they were never heard from ever again.[2]

Another group of white Arkansans supported the back-to-Africa movement with more self-serving motives, especially in the 1880s. If blacks departed in sufficient numbers, some argued, then the political balance in many eastern Arkansas counties could dramatically change. Whites who advocated a black exodus naively believed that black labor could be replaced by white immigration, especially of foreign workers. As black people in Phillips County were preparing for their departure in March 1880, the *Arkansas Gazette* editorialized, "we are glad to note that the exodus is booming," for large numbers of European immigrants would not move to Arkansas if the black population was so high. White citizens of Helena, in fact, held a public meeting on 26 March 1880 to establish an immigration bureau to encourage foreigners to come to that county. Counties even competed with each other to attract white laborers in the 1880s. In 1888, at least twenty Arkansas counties established immigration societies or held conventions to discuss ways to attract new residents.[3]

Woodruff County, in east central Arkansas, illustrates how white immigration efforts stemmed from a deep-seated hostility toward the local black population. In May 1889, some 200 white farmers and planters gathered at Riverside to form an immigration society to recruit white laborers to the area. The assembly even passed a resolution to boycott people who worked against the interests of the white race. By August, the society had sent two of the county's leading men to the Carolinas and Georgia, where they secured 400 white workers, and they expected an additional 400 families to come to the county in time for the fall cotton picking. From the perspective of the immigration society, "the day of the sleepy, lazy, indolent Negro is numbered in Woodruff. No more midnight, bloody-shirt, nihilistic speeches during political years, so say the good citizens of Woodruff." At another meeting of the society in September, one white speaker explained to a number of black people in attendance that the society wished to bring laborers to the county because black men had made themselves obnoxious by voting with a "scalawag" faction and attempting to control the county government. The promotion of white immigration in Woodruff County achieved some success. As white laborers moved in, some landowners refused to renew their leases with black tenants, asserting that "the majority of our cotton land will be cultivated by white, in stead of negro labor in the future." By January 1890, a hundred black families were reported to have left Woodruff County, with more expected to follow in the near future. It is no wonder, then, that Woodruff County, like Conway County in west central Arkansas, became so intensely interested in Liberian emigration in the next few years.[4]

Although the idea of replacing black laborers with white workers had tremendous appeal to some whites, it proved unrealistic at a time when labor generally was in short supply. In fact, a planter from Lee County and the manager of Richardson plantation in Mississippi, claimed to be the world's largest cotton plantation, came to Woodruff County to recruit the same black farmers local whites were encouraging to leave. In January 1890, reports appeared that 5,000 blacks were leaving the southeastern United States for Arkansas to farm as sharecroppers on plantations in the eastern and southern parts of the state. While some Arkansans denounced the movement, saying that only white immigrants should be encouraged, planters who hired blacks countered that whites alone could not provide the necessary labor.[5]

While some whites encouraged local blacks to leave, white planters more commonly wanted African Americans to stay on the land and work. One way whites opposed the back-to-Africa movement was through selective reporting in newspapers. White papers usually simply ignored black migration or concentrated on the bad news associated with the movement: stories of frauds and swindles or accounts of hapless refugees starving in crowded conditions in New York.[6] The papers carried reports of emigrants who did not like Liberia and returned to criticize the country and the ACS. One black man in Lonoke County wrote to the ACS asking the organization to confirm the truth of a Democratic paper's report that a ship carrying 5,000 emigrants for Africa had sunk in the Atlantic.[7] In general, white newspapers tried to discredit the whole back-to-Africa enterprise.

In areas needing black labor, whites more actively tried to thwart a Liberian emigration. During the first exodus of black Arkansas in 1879 from Phillips County, white neighbors wanted to keep black workers on the plantations. Ben McKeever, for example, complained that when "our southern (white) brethren learned of the Exodus" they "rendered everything so gloomy that none can go." By February 1879, McKeever indicated to the ACS, he was trying to find temporary farm work in Pennsylvania for his family and the others who planned to leave for Liberia in the summer, fearing it was no longer safe to remain in Phillips County: "The Ku Klux are so numberous in this portion until our lives are in jeapardy every hour. hence we want to go somewhere norh of the mason and Dicy [Dixon] line." A few days later, he reported to Coppinger that the Ku Klux had taken out and whipped E. T. Rone, the clerk of the Liberia Exodus Club, number sixteen. After enduring two heavy blows on the head from a pistol, Rone fortunately got away.[8]

Applicants for emigration frequently complained to the ACS that local postmasters tampered with mail when they suspected it related to Liberia or emigration. In 1890, Joseph Harris complained that in Conway "whites are doing

On a trade card of the late 1800s, a racist caricature of a black husband and wife on their way to Liberia. Courtesy John Kemler.

all they can to prevent the movement. . . . Our mail is being intercepted, and opened, just how and by whom we can not tell." Correspondents from several parts of the state asked the ACS to send its mail and circulars to them in unmarked envelopes or wrapped in plain paper "so no one will notice it." Correspondents in Plumerville believed their local postmaster was intercepting their mail and asked the ACS office to send it to the post office in neighboring all-black Menifee. The Reverend James Miller said his postmaster in Osceola opened his mail, read it, and passed it on, writing his name and "Liberia" on the contents. Frank Little wished to correspond directly with Liberia, but he sent his letter and stamps to the ACS office in Washington, asking the secretary to mail it on to Liberia. In his hometown, Crawfordsville (Crittenden County), Little said an outgoing letter addressed to Liberia gets no further than the post office.[9]

Black people generally tried to keep the Liberia exodus movement a secret from white neighbors. Disguised names for their clubs, such as the Young Men's Association, became one way to do this. In Monroe County, one man explained that he wished to go but did not want to create a sensation and arouse the curiosities of white neighbors. Andrew Thompson of Lee County wanted the ACS to purchase the property of his group of emigrants because they did not want to announce locally their intentions of leaving by putting their property up for sale. They wished to keep their Liberia business "concealed till we get away from here," Thompson said.[10] Debt probably trapped most potential migrants, and they faced prosecution if they tried to skip town for Liberia. Others clearly feared that if their plans to emigrate became known, their personal safety would be at risk. P. S. Buckingham of Forrest City corresponded with the ACS through a friend in Caldwell, a neighboring community, and even then insisted that the ACS mail come in plain wrappers and envelopes. "If this is found out," he wrote, "some of us will be killed." One man in Little Rock begged Coppinger not to say anything about him in public until he was gone. Similarly, a Morrilton man, Shelton Leaphart, instructed Coppinger: "Dont publish my name or I may be hung for Example to other poor black men." In Auvergne in Jackson County, Marion Babb explained that "the landholders are very hard on the Negro for working to go [to] Liberia it will bring bote death if a man do not hold a watchful eye." A leader of the club in Atkins complained to the ACS that several of his people had decided against emigration "out of fear of getting killed." By 1892, even in Woodruff County, where whites had earlier tried to recruit immigrants to replace black labor, George Johnson of Riverside lamented, "We are in deplorable condition our lives are parshally threaten for wanting to go to Africa."[11]

Some of the local emigration leaders were forced to flee from their homes when whites learned of their business. William King, who led a club in Germantown in Conway County, explained that he had to leave Arkansas for Indian Territory because whites threatened him with death for his emigration work. Whites ran Pink Blair out of Mississippi County for promoting Liberia emigration. When he later tried to organize people to move to Oklahoma, he was arrested and sent to the Phillips County penal farm. At least some members of the emigration club in Little Rock/Argenta who left for New York in the fall of 1891 did so because they feared for their lives if they stayed any longer in Pulaski County. George Angram said whites had tried to break into his home and kill him because he was known to be a member of the club.[12]

Besides threats of physical force, whites also used economic measures to dissuade black people from emigrating. Knowing that emigrants were desperate to sell livestock, possessions, or land, whites refused to buy them unless they were at rock-bottom prices. W. M. Wilson of Menifee estimated his farm was worth $1,000, but he was only offered $200 for it. Adaline Bailey of neighboring Solgohatchia said that "the whites will not give us anything for our land and stock." From Lee County, Andrew Thompson, another black landowner, also complained that "the white people of this cuntry will not by any thing we have to sell and pay us what it is worth . . . these people are afraid we are going away from this cuntry." Thompson, who claimed to own land worth $1,200 and whose brother, William, owned eighty acres of prime delta farmland worth $3,000, said they would come to Liberia at their own expense if they could just sell their property for its worth.[13] From Lonoke County, R. T. Winters said that rumors circulated that the county's entire black population planned to leave for Liberia. Landholders organized to thwart the movement, Winters said, and were "working to keep us half slave and ant letting us having Any monies to do any thing at all." If black people stayed there, he lamented, they would most certainly starve. One African American from Sans Souci in the Mississippi delta region charged that white planters conspired to keep their poorest black laborers from being able to leave. The correspondent said planters there had clubbed together and determined to pay cotton pickers no more than fifty cents for a hundred pounds of cotton picked, instead of the customary rates, which ranged between seventy-five cents and a dollar. While they kept wages low, the planters kept prices for cornmeal and flour high, all with the intent of keeping black laborers from earning enough cash to travel from Arkansas to the shipping port for Liberia.[14]

In the late 1800s, the conspiracy among white planters to keep wages for cotton picking low prompted one of the most dramatic and deadly events in eastern Arkansas's history. The Colored Farmers Alliance had been working with little success in late summer 1891 to organize cotton pickers to strike throughout the South. In Lee County, Arkansas, on 20 September, pickers working on the Rodgers plantation demanded seventy-five instead of fifty cents per hundred pounds for their labor. After they were ordered off the premises, they went to neighboring plantations talking strike. The strikers even threatened pickers who refused to strike. The group became a mob, killing two black pickers and a white plantation manager, and they burned another planter's cotton gin to the ground. A posse of white men from several eastern Arkansas counties organized to put down the revolt. By the time the white mob had found all the strikers hiding out in the swamps and canebrakes alongside the Mississippi River, fifteen black men had been killed, most of them hanged by the mob, and another six men were in jail. A St. Louis newspaper said that after the incident, a Liberia craze broke out among cotton pickers in Arkansas. The correspondent to the ACS from Sans Souci, however, suggested that Liberia fever had been a cause, rather than effect, of the cotton pickers' revolt.[15]

Not just white people opposed the back-to-Africa movement. About a week after the dust settled from the cotton pickers' strike and massacre, a group of black Pine Bluff businessmen filed the articles of incorporation for the Colored Farmers' and Laborers' Joint Stock Association. The new corporation reportedly expected to establish branches throughout the state and began with working capital of $50,000. The stated purpose of the association was to assist members in buying homes and obtaining employment, to discourage strikes and emigration to foreign countries, to furnish laborers and supplies by contract, and to create a fund for distressed black farmers and laborers.[16] These black businessmen obviously were taking proactive steps to keep black workers from striking again or leaving for Liberia. Educated and middle-class black people had greater stakes in the United States and, in general, felt that black Americans should stay right where they were.

In his vocal call for people of color to return to their ancestral homeland, Bishop Henry McNeal Turner was a lone voice among prominent black leaders in the United States. The black nationalist leaders of an earlier generation who had supported the idea of an African repatriation were gone by the 1890s. Martin R. Delany had died in 1885. Henry H. Garnet, after assisting the Arkansas refugees when they were stranded in New York in 1880, took the appointment as U.S. minister to Liberia the next year, and within a month of his arrival in Liberia came down with fever and died. The other aging black leaders, such as Frederick Douglass and Alexander Crummell, consistently opposed African emigration. Crummell, even though he had lived in Liberia from 1853 to 1872, lobbied for missionary work in Africa, not an exodus to the continent. Until his death in 1895, Douglass would bicker with Turner over African emigration. Douglass had attacked Turner for his emigration stance as early as 1873, when he accused Turner of supporting the ACS, which Douglass believed to be a racist organization. Douglass believed the future for blacks lay in America, not in an African exile. Turner countered that the ACS had done much good.[17]

Most African American leaders sincerely believed that the back-to-Africa movement undermined black claims for full citizenship in the United States. The debate about emigration became particularly spirited on three occasions. In the first half of 1883, the AME Church's weekly *Christian Recorder*, probably the most widely distributed black newspaper in the country, published a lengthy exchange between Turner and his opponents. Frederick Douglass restated his view that blacks owed no allegiance to Africa whatsoever. The paper's editor, Benjamin Tanner, suggested that emigration expressed cowardice at a time when African Americans should take their stand in America. Other educated black citizens chimed in to oppose Turner's emigration schemes.[18]

The public debate was renewed in spring 1892 when hundreds of would-be emigrants from Arkansas and Indian Territory became stranded in New York. Bishop Turner had never been popular among the AME leadership, and he received much of the blame for inspiring large numbers of poor blacks of the South to emigrate. The public meetings held in New York to discuss the refugee problem elicited a firestorm of criticism of Bishop Turner and the ACS. After T. Thomas Fortune's *New York Age* published the resolutions of the meeting, other black newspapers reprinted them, and the discussion continued nationwide. Fortune's comments were especially brutal. He called Turner the agent, the "hired man," of a white man's corporation, the ACS, and said, "I wish I could take a bludgeon and smash the head of that American Colonization Society flat, oh so flat." Turner, never one to take criticism lying down, responded with both barrels. In a letter to the *Indianapolis Freeman*, he vigorously denied that he had been a paid agent of the ASC and explained that, even though he was an honorary vice president since 1876, he had never actually attended a meeting of the society. Nonetheless, he strongly defended the Liberia emigration movement as the only hope for black people in the United States and said, "Thank God for the Colonization Society," for it had founded the only nation for black Americans on the continent of Africa.[19]

In the following year, Turner and his detractors had two opportunities to debate African emigration at large meetings held in Chicago and Cincinnati. In August 1893, the American Missionary Association sponsored the World's Congress on Africa in conjunction with the World's Columbian Exposition in Chicago. Attended by missionaries, scholars, anthropologists, and politicians from America and Europe, and even a few Africans, the week-long congress may have been the first scholarly conference ever held about Africa. Turner spoke several times at the meeting, first shocking delegates by announcing that Adam in the biblical Garden of Eden had been a black man, then moving on to his usual condemnation of mob rule in the South, which justified a mass migration to Liberia. Other speakers disagreed with Turner, especially Fortune, who argued that the African Americans should no more return to Africa than German Americans to Germany. Black people in the audience, mostly middle-class northerners, clearly agreed with Fortune.[20]

While in Chicago, Bishop Turner and other delegates visited the courts of the Columbian Exposition, where the Republic of Liberia hosted an exhibit in a prime location sandwiched between the displays from Mexico and Curaçao. Liberian officials had collected thirty tons of materials, which they boxed and shipped to the United States to construct the exhibit. With backdrop walls decorated with African woods, woven fabrics, ropes, and elephant tusks, the exhibits showcased Liberian products and native cultures, as well as development by American settlers. Glass jars contained coffee beans, ginger, various peppers, cocoa, and other products, while showboards displayed maps and photographs of the country. Liberian officials claimed that as many as 12,000 people visited their exhibit daily. More popular and exotic than the Liberian court, however, was the Dahomey exhibit, which included an entire village of thatched huts constructed on the exposition's grand midway. Some eighty-five Africans in traditional dress manned the exhibit and raced their canoes on the lagoon. After viewing the exhibit, Frederick Douglass expressed a middle-class disdain for Africa, complaining that the black race was represented at the exposition by "African savages brought in to act the monkey." Bishop Turner, on the other hand, reminded his audience that those Africans "are my folks, we all came from the same stock."[21]

After returning to Atlanta from the Chicago Congress, Bishop Turner decided to call his own national conference to discuss the issue of African emigration. The Turner Conference, as it was called, convened in Cincinnati on 28 November 1893 with nearly 800 delegates present. Turner spoke in his usual bombastic style at the beginning and end of the meeting. He reiterated his call that the U.S. government owed its black citizens $40 billion for unpaid labor

The Liberian exhibit at the Columbian Exposition in Chicago, 1893. Courtesy Library of Congress.

performed under slavery and suggested that a down payment of $500 million of that sum would enable his longed-for African exodus to begin. But the tenor of the meeting went against Turner and emigration. Only a few delegates came to Cincinnati from the rural South; elected delegates from Crittenden and Woodruff Counties in Arkansas were among them.[22] Most of the attendees at the conference, as at the Chicago Congress, were urban middle-class African Americans from the North and Midwest who had greater stakes in staying in the United States. Had Turner held the meeting elsewhere—Jackson, Birmingham, or Little Rock, perhaps—the outcome may have been different. However, even the southern black leader Booker T. Washington, who had yet to appear on the national stage, wrote from Tuskegee that "this talk of any appreciable number of our people going to Africa is the merest nonsense."[23]

Some of the strongest opposition to Bishop Turner's emigration plans came from black newspaper editors throughout the country. They typically described Liberia in the most derogatory fashion—as a land of sultry weather and deadly fevers, a place lacking in civilization and opportunities but abounding in insects and snakes.[24] Like their white counterparts, black newspapers gave extensive coverage to the disgruntled settlers who returned to the United States telling of economic misery, slavery, ill health, and other problems on the "dark continent." In fact, at a meeting in 1891 of the Colored Press Association, black editors took a formal stand against any expatriation of black Americans.[25]

In addition to T. Thomas Fortune, other editors were downright hostile to Bishop Turner for his work as a Moses for the exodus movement. During Turner's Cincinnati convention in 1893, the nationally distributed *Indianapolis Freeman* railed against Turner and his emigration scheme with the headline: "Better Struggle in Civilized America than Die in Jungles of Africa."[26] Charles Henry James Taylor, the editor of *American Citizen*, a black newspaper in Kansas City, said if Turner was such an advocate of emigration, he should move to Liberia himself. Then the bishop could say "come, rather than go." Taylor, a rare black Democrat who had been appointed by President Grover Cleveland as U.S. minister to Liberia, called Liberia a "Death Hole to be Shunned" and denounced Turner's talk of Liberia as simply crazy. Taylor had stayed in Liberia only four months in 1887 as U.S. minister and, as he admitted himself, never left the city of Monrovia.[27] Nonetheless, his negative portrait of Liberia appeared in black and white newspapers throughout the United States.

Besides this black opposition to emigration on the national level, some local black leaders worked against the movement in Arkansas. Black newspapers in the state have not survived in sufficient numbers to allow one to generalize about the local black press. But clearly some individuals worked to thwart Liberian emigration. When Dr. Anthony Stanford organized the first group of Arkansas emigrants in 1877, the Reverend J. T. Jennifer, a prominent Methodist preacher in Helena, spoke against emigration and its leaders. In his Sunday evening sermon just before the emigration convention convened in November, Jennifer said that certain leaders of the emigration movement, including Henry McNeal Turner and Stanford, "should have a rope put on their necks, led to the woods and made promise to leave the country, or the rope tightened until they did." The convention passed a resolution condemning Jennifer for "soiling his clerical garments" with such malicious words.[28] In Conway in 1891, the Reverend Joseph Harris complained that some blacks there were conspiring with whites to oppose the movement and Harris's leadership. Similarly, in neighboring Menifee, W. A. Diggs said whites had paid several men in the area to make public speeches against Liberia and the ACS. What disturbed him most, Diggs said, was "they are my color."[29]

The most serious trouble posed by African Americans to the emigration movement did not come through editorializing, speechmaking, or debates. More damaging was a series of frauds by which some black people tried to make money off people's desperation to leave the United States. When emigration clubs collected what would have been large sums of cash to rural farmers, even otherwise honest individuals could easily yield to temptation. For example, the Reverend W. A. Diggs led one of the Young Men's Associations in Plumerville in collecting the sum of $255.25, which he forwarded in fall 1891 to the ACS toward Liberian passage. But when it became clear that the ACS could not take the Plumerville party to Liberia, Diggs left Arkansas for Graham, South Carolina. From there, in January 1892, he wrote the ACS asking for the group's money back. He implied that the entire group had moved there and that he would distribute the money to those who contributed it. In the meantime, however, members of Diggs's club back in Plumerville had written Coppinger explaining that Diggs had gone and that they wanted the ACS to send back their money to Arkansas. Consequently, Coppinger refused to send Diggs the money. After Coppinger's death in February 1892, however, the new acting secretary of the ACS sent Diggs the $255.25. Diggs apparently never dispersed the funds, for members of Diggs's club continued to write the ACS asking for their money.[30]

Preacher Diggs appears to have been a dedicated emigrationist who simply yielded to temptation. This type of dishonesty from within the ranks of would-be emigrants seems to have been rare. More common were deliberate schemes to take advantage of people's keen desire to leave Arkansas. As the interest in Liberia intensified, charlatans found bold ways to take people's money. On several occasions in different areas of Arkansas, some individuals claimed to be agents of the ACS, organized people for emigration, and collected their money. For example, a man named McHaney in Pine Bluff went about organizing "lodges" and told people they had to pay him one dollar to be a member. In northeastern Arkansas in 1892, an elderly black man calling himself the Reverend William Thomas claimed to be a representative of the "Africa Commission of Emigration of the Colored People," as if the nations of Africa had banded together to invite black Americans to come over. Skeptical black Arkansans frequently wrote the ACS asking if such self-proclaimed agents were authentic. The ACS consistently responded that it hired or appointed no agents and that anyone purporting to be an agent was an impostor.[31]

One of the most blatant fraud attempts came in the late summer of 1891 when a black man, claiming to be Edward Blyden, traveled throughout central and eastern Arkansas organizing emigration clubs and collecting money. The real Edward W. Blyden, an educator and fiery nationalist, was probably the most famous Liberian of his day. Born free on the island of St. Thomas, which was then part of the Danish West Indies, he had come to the United States for a brief period in the 1850s before emigrating to Liberia. He became a teacher, college president, Presbyterian pastor, and sometime politician. But, most of all, he was a scholar and propagandist for Africa. He traveled to the United States several times in the 1880s and 1890s, giving speeches and encouraging blacks to come to Liberia.[32] In July 1891, the Blyden impostor was in Little Rock claiming that the ACS had sent him to Arkansas to make speeches and organize people for Liberia. Some would-be emigrants in Little Rock and Argenta had already formed an exodus club and had raised money for their departure in the fall. The impostor suggested that they give him the money to deposit in a bank rather than send it on to the ACS. He also collected $1.50 from each member for society membership and explained that for $57 one could get to Africa. He told people that upon arrival in Liberia, emigrants would receive 150 acres of land and a team of horses. His tales and confidence expanded as time passed. To get to Liberia, he explained, emigrants had to cross three oceans, one around Europe, another around Asia, and a third around "Austrailer." By September, the fake Blyden claimed he had been commissioned by President Benjamin Harrison and that Congress had appropriated $200,000 to send black people to Africa.[33]

In July and August, the impostor traveled through rural areas of Pulaski and Lonoke Counties organizing lodges and collecting money. He then moved on to work the black communities of Prairie, Monroe, and Phillips Counties in eastern Arkansas. Although the faux Blyden fooled many people, some skeptical souls noticed the discrepancy between the information they already had received about Liberia and the man's grand tales, and they wrote the ACS inquiring about him. No one, however, seemed to wonder why "Professor Blyden" spoke with a southern plantation accent rather than Caribbean- and African-inflected English. "Blyden" was bold and naive enough to write the ACS himself, bragging about how many lodges he had organized and the large number of emigrants he had inspired for Liberia. Coppinger quickly wrote letters and sent telegrams informing people in Arkansas that this Blyden was a fraud. By the end of August, one correspondent from Monroe County told the ACS that the "creature calling himself Blyden is named Meingault" and another reported that he was arrested but had escaped and disappeared.[34]

The Blyden incident provides remarkable evidence of the knowledge rural black Arkansans possessed about the Republic of Liberia. The real Edward Blyden clearly had a reputation and following among poor Arkansas farmers. The impostor obviously knew about this spokesman for black nationalism and assumed his identity with the expectation that others in Arkansas were familiar with Blyden. While elite, educated black Americans had shown the greatest interest in Africa earlier in the century, by 1891 this knowledge about, and interest in, Africa was shifting to poor, working-class folk.

In the following year, another scam artist tried to capitalize on this grassroots fascination with Africa, this time with more deadly results. Around September 1892, a black Baptist preacher who called himself Brother G. P. F. Lightfoot appeared in northeastern Arkansas. He told some people he had come from Africa, while he claimed to others that he had received a special commission from Queen Victoria. Her Majesty's government, Lightfoot explained, echoing Martin Delany's plan of a generation earlier, wished to enter the cotton business and wanted their labor. He claimed he had made arrangements with railroads and steamships to take blacks to New York and then Liberia for the rate of three dollars per person. A family of five could go for five dollars, he maintained, while a whole club of ten people could travel for just eight dollars. Lightfoot organized clubs he called Home Circles, sold memberships, and encouraged people to sell out their possessions and prepare to go. By early December of 1892, Lightfoot had worked people into a frenzy in Woodruff, Jackson, and Cross Counties. Some had sold their livestock and land for "little of nothing" to be ready to go, even though the ACS had told them earlier they could not be accommodated. One report suggested that as many as ninety-two families in Jackson County and half that many in Woodruff had sold out and given their money over to Lightfoot. Some were sleeping on floors waiting for his summons to go to Liberia.[35]

When Lightfoot failed to meet some of his scheduled appointments, his followers grew suspicious. On Friday, 9 December, Lightfoot met some of the would-be emigrants at the Mt. Zion Church, in the southern part of Jackson County. When he received less than a hospitable welcome, he pulled out a revolver. Shooting began, and after the smoke had cleared, Lightfoot was dead, his body riddled with bullets, and his face, throat, and hands hacked with knives and razors. Blacks in Jackson County were so disgusted by Lightfoot's fraud that none could be induced to give his body a proper burial after the official inquest, and white men reportedly had to perform the service. Blacks in neighboring Woodruff County, on the other hand, refused to believe Lightfoot was a fraud, and they began to organize to avenge his death. The white sheriff of Woodruff County had to pacify an armed crowd that had assembled near the county line. A few weeks later, two black men from Woodruff County accused twelve black men of Jackson County of murdering Lightfoot. However, the grand jury dismissed the charges against them and instead indicted one of the accusers for perjury. He was later sentenced to three years in the state penitentiary. The case was promptly forgotten by the courts, but the threat of fraud, or, as one black Arkansan put it, "humbuging" poor folks out of their money, lingered in people's memory.[36]

The black crowd in Woodruff County, however, had become either so gullible or so desperate to leave that they quickly fell victim to another scam. In late January 1893, a month after Lightfoot's murder, some swindlers were making arrangements to send a group of Woodruff County blacks to Brunswick, Georgia, to meet a nonexistent ship that was to take them to Liberia. Newspaper accounts differed as to who was responsible. The local newspaper said a passenger agent for the East Tennessee and West Virginia Railroad was in the county making arrangements for the group to leave, while another account put the blame on a pair of unnamed black preachers.[37] Local whites in Woodruff County, who had tried to recruit foreigners to replace black labor a few years before, now evidently wanted their black population to stay home. The local newspaper threatened that "Arkansas is not a safe place for men to interfere with hands who have contracted," and the white sheriff tried to disband a group of black emigrants who camped at the depot in Augusta waiting for their train to arrive. By one account, as many as 400 emigrants boarded seven chartered coaches around 11 February, paying an estimated total of $3,000 for their tickets to Brunswick. As the party passed through Atlanta, newspaper reports suggested they were in a state of religious ecstasy, praying and singing, "carried away with the idea that they were going back to the promised land." Presumably their enthusiasm dampened when they arrived in Brunswick to find no ship and no agents to meet them. Unlike Lightfoot, the swindlers this time physically removed their victims from the area so they could not exact retribution. What ultimately happened to the group is unknown.[38]

Black people of Arkansas who wished to emigrate to Africa thus had many obstacles to overcome. Of the large number who wanted to go, only a few were chosen to be among the 100–150 people transported by the ACS each year, and only a few also possessed the money to travel to the port of embarkation. And after March 1892, the ACS stopped sending parties of emigrant settlers entirely. Besides these challenges of opportunity, would-be emigrants faced the opposition of whites who needed their labor and worked to thwart any emigration movement. They also had to deal with division within their own community and the opposing views of prosperous and prominent black leaders. Perhaps most crushing were the scams perpetrated by swindlers trying to profit on others' misery. In late 1893 in Monroe County, yet another charlatan, reported to be a white man, promised people passage to Liberia for $300 a person, and he convinced some 300 to 400 people to hand over their money. By January of the next year, a train-car load of emigrants left Brinkley, the main depot in Monroe County, for New York City. Theodore Steele, a wise and sad black man who watched the emigrants go, wrote to the ACS describing this event as just another of the "many frauds that are intended to deceive and rob the poor ignorant colored people." He wished "such men could be exposed as frauds and their names published in every news paper in the U.S." Steele concluded: "This is why so many become victims of Injustice we are ready to grasp at the least shadow of hope."[39] As Steele and the scam artists well understood, the magnetic power of Liberia rested in the black republic's ability to inspire dreams of a better life.

Missions

By the early 1890s, the Liberia emigration movement had stirred tremendous interest in Africa in the black settlements of Arkansas. But after the ACS shut down its emigration program in March 1892, African Americans had little opportunity to pursue an actual relocation to Liberia. Not until three years later, in March 1895, would it become again possible for a large group of emigrants to depart for Africa. In the meantime, people channeled their fascination with Africa into missionary endeavors. Many black Christians who could not, or did not wish to, emigrate instead organized missionary societies and raised money for African missions. Several clergy and lay folk offered themselves as missionary workers, and about a dozen black Arkansans and their families actually crossed the Atlantic to win Africans for Jesus Christ. African missionary work swelled in black churches throughout the South in the 1890s, but nowhere more so than in Arkansas. While the state claimed slightly more than 4 percent of the black population of the United States in 1890, nearly a quarter of all known black American missionaries to Africa in the 1890s came from Arkansas.[1]

The late nineteenth century had seen an explosion of Christian missionary work around the world. As Europeans staked out empires in Africa and Asia, and as the United States collected territories in the Pacific region, missionaries followed, and sometimes led, colonial administrators and traders to the far corners of the planet. The number of Christian missionaries in foreign lands increased from around 2,000 in 1876 to more than 15,000 by the end of the century.[2] After the Berlin Congress of 1884–85 established the ground rules for the claiming and development of colonies there, Africa especially emerged as a ripe field for the Christian harvest. Several white-majority denominations in the late nineteenth century had tried to recruit black missionaries for Africa, working under the delusion that black Americans were better suited than whites for the tropical climate and disease environment of Africa and could more easily evangelize people of their own color. By the 1870s, several black missionaries had served in Africa on behalf of mostly white denominations, most famously Alexander Crummell, who worked for twenty years as an Episcopal missionary in Liberia. Even more African Americans had served with various mission societies, some as far afield as Angola, Rhodesia, and the Congo region.[3]

By the 1880s, black churches also became interested in African missions, although they lacked the financial resources of white denominations. A pastor of the AME Zion Church, a black Methodist body, emigrated to Liberia via the ACS in 1876 and established several congregations among American settlers. Two black clergymen, one a Baptist preacher and the other an AME pastor, had emigrated to Liberia in 1878 on the *Azor*, and they organized black churches of their denominations among the American settlers. They made few overtures toward indigenous African populations.

While most black Christians in the United States worshiped as Baptists, the black Baptist churches were so badly disorganized that they could hardly muster any missionary endeavors. Black Baptist leaders from several states, including three delegates from Arkansas, met together in Montgomery, Alabama, in 1880 to found the Baptist Foreign Mission Convention. The Reverend Elias C. Morris of Helena, the president of the Arkansas Baptist Association, regularly attended the annual mission meetings and hosted the 1887 convocation, which met at Little Rock's First Baptist Church. Morris went on to become the president of the Baptist Foreign Mission Convention in 1894. Although the organization managed to send a few missionaries to Liberia in the 1880s, regional competition and a lack of financial support hampered Baptist efforts for African missions.[4]

The AME Church had sent two missionaries to Sierra Leone to work with indigenous Africans in the late 1880s, but the real beginning of the AME Church's African missions work came with Bishop Henry McNeal Turner's trip to West Africa in 1891. In addition to his touring and bombastic preaching, Turner organized followers in Sierra Leone and Liberia into two annual conferences of the AME Church. He brought with him the Reverend T. R. Geda, whom he left behind in Liberia as a missionary to look after the new AME organization in that country. In 1893, Turner received the formal appointment as AME bishop of Africa, a development that would serve as a pretext for his return to West

Africa in 1893 and 1895 and a trip to South Africa in 1898, where he ordained clergy and organized AME congregations in the Cape Colony, the Transvaal, and the Orange Free State. Back in Atlanta in 1893, Turner established an AME monthly newspaper, the *Voice of Missions*, which served as his own pulpit to promote Africa as a mission field and destination for emigration. Largely as a result of Turner's tireless work and magnetic personality, the AME Church made more of a commitment to African missionary work than any other black church in America.[5]

In Arkansas, both black Methodists and black Baptists began to organize formally and raise money for African missions in 1892.[6] The Baptist State Sunday School Convention, which met in Texarkana in June, recommended that each Sunday school raise money for African missions, and the meeting itself collected $1,500 for Africa. The Arkansas Conference of the AME Church held its annual meeting in 1892 in Newport at the same time that Reverend Lightfoot passed through the rural areas nearby, preaching African emigration and fraudulently taking people's money. The AME assembly overflowed with enthusiasm for African missions. A committee on foreign missions submitted a report declaring the goal to "send the gospel to the heathen land; yes to darkest Africa," recommending that each congregation give ten dollars for that specific purpose. The convention also passed a resolution encouraging Dr. Charles Spencer Smith, the AME Sunday School superintendent who was in attendance, to visit the African continent. Smith made his well-publicized trip two years later, which resulted in a book, *Glimpses of Africa*. As a climax to the meeting, the presiding bishop, B. W. Arnett, read a letter from Turner, who, in his role as bishop of Africa, announced the appointment of one of the Arkansas pastors, the Reverend Alfred Lee Ridgel of Brinkley, as a new missionary to Africa and the presiding elder of the Liberian Conference of the AME Church. Ridgel was called forward amid cheers to speak about why he wished to go to Africa. The assembly gave that night's offering of thirty dollars to assist Ridgel in getting to Africa and then adjourned after singing the mission hymn, "On the Shore Beyond the Sea," and "Praise God From Whom All Blessings Flow."[7]

The black Baptists and the AME Church continued to discuss Africa and raise mission funds at their annual conferences through the rest of the decade. At the Baptist State Sunday School Convention in 1893 in Newport, the corresponding secretary read a letter from Lewis R. Johnson, who described in detail the Baptist congregations and associations in Liberia and the church's educational mission outside Monrovia, a boarding school called Rick's Institute, which had three grades of study and its own coffee farm for students to work.

At the 1895 meeting, G. W. D. Gaines, the president of the state association, reported on a foreign missions convention in Montgomery, Alabama, he had attended as the Arkansas delegate. Although he spoke against Bishop Turner and mass emigration to Africa, he preached that black Americans possessed a special God-given role to civilize and Christianize the "dark continent."[8] Bishop Turner attended AME annual meetings in Arkansas in 1894, 1895, and 1896 and always worked Africa into his sermons before packed crowds. The meeting in Little Rock in 1895 passed a resolution declaring that Turner had endeared himself to members of the conference and asking that he be reassigned to Arkansas for another four years. One AME pastor from Augusta, the Reverend S. T. Brown, said that Turner had so inspired him at the Little Rock meeting that he returned home to organize "missionary sociables" in private homes and thus raised forty dollars for the African work.[9]

Although male bishops, presiding elders, and clergymen conducted the annual meetings of black church bodies, much of the interest generated and money raised for African missions in the 1890s came through the endeavors of women. Most white Protestant denominations in the United States had women's missionary societies. Black Baptist women in Arkansas also were organizing societies by the end of the 1880s, even though they encountered some resistance from male church leaders who believed men should exercise leadership in the clubs and control over finances.[10] The AME Church had organized the Widow's Mite Missionary Society in 1874, mostly in northern states, to raise money for missionary work, particularly in Haiti and Sierra Leone. But, around 1892 or 1893, Bishop Turner began another organization that spread quickly throughout the South, the Women's Home and Foreign Missionary Society (WMFMS). His second wife, Martha (Turner married four times), became very active in the society, and local chapters were often led by pastors' wives.[11] In the 1890s, these societies turned their support primarily to the Liberian missions. With Arkansas missionary Alfred Ridgel presiding over the Liberian Conference of the AME Church and the emigration of hundreds of black Arkansans to Liberia in the 1890s, this effort in particular resonated among black women in the state.

Chapters of both the Widow's Mite Missionary Society and the Women's Home and Foreign Missionary Society were organized in Arkansas. In their meetings, the women held devotions, read essays, raised money, and discussed African missions and women's roles. Mrs. Callie Swan, the Helena pastor's wife, organized two children's mission societies in 1894, one with fourteen boys and the other with nineteen girls under the leadership of three women. The children saved their nickels and dimes, eventually raising twenty-five dollars for African missions, and Mrs. Swan added another eighteen dollars specifically earmarked for the Reverend Ridgel's work. A convention of Widow's Mite societies in northeastern Arkansas convened in August 1895 at St. Mark's AME Church in Osceola. With some male clergy present to lead prayers, women conducted business of the convention and gave speeches on such topics as "Women as Missionaries," "Shall Africa Be Redeemed? If So by Whom?" "Women's Place in the Church," and "Liberian Mission and Its Needs." In April 1896, the first statewide convention of the WHFMS was held in Little Rock, with delegates attending from all parts of Arkansas. Although clergymen were present to provide pastoral guidance, the main sermon was presented by the Reverend Mrs. G. T. Thurman of Jackson, Michigan, a missions superintendent for the AME Church. Mrs. Thurman was apparently a powerful speaker, for one delegate described her sermon as "full, rich and sweet as it rolled in unchecked streams from the lips of the speaker, bringing down the pentacostal showers of blessings."[12]

Even the male-dominated annual conferences of the AME Church in Arkansas recognized foreign missions as a special domain for women's work. In 1895, Mrs. Thurman preached about African missions to packed crowds at all three annual AME Church conferences in Arkansas and was reported to have "displayed an oratory in her lectures and sermons that thrilled the ministers and people." The women's missionary societies presented their funds raised for Africa, donations that ranged from a dollar to $127.25, the sum raised by the women of the Jonesboro AME congregation. The money represented the work of women and children including Mrs. Swan's children's clubs in Helena, which gave thirty dollars, and ninety-year-old Sister Cicely Hill, who donated ten dollars to Reverend Ridgel in Liberia. The women's societies in the three Arkansas conferences raised a total of $473.70 for African missions in 1895.[13] At a district meeting of AME congregations in northeastern Arkansas, three women spoke on the topic "The Redemption of Africa," as the male clergy sat and listened.[14]

While women had not taken a leadership role in the Liberia emigration movement—men wrote almost all the letters to the ACS and, in all known cases, held the offices in exodus clubs—they dominated the work on behalf of African missions. The missionary societies were arenas in which black women could exercise leadership, where they could speak, preach, pray, and manage money. Clearly the women's missionary movement fits into the club women context of the late nineteenth century, a time when black and white women organized to improve the health and morality of their communities in a variety of ways.[15]

While Jim Crow laws and white oppression were crushing rights and opportunities, black women in missionary societies were able to work for racial uplift, albeit outside the United States. While African emigration work required a shroud of secrecy because of white opposition to the movement, missionary work gave women a safe way to take action and express their race pride.

The women, pastors, and missionaries from the Arkansas conferences of the AME Church had done so much for African missions that the missions department of the denomination dedicated its new "African Mission Song," penned by Bishop Turner and published in 1895, to the ministers and missionaries of Arkansas. Appropriately, the hymn touched all the requisite themes of this missionary movement, including God's call for black Americans to return to a native land, the "wilds" of Africa.[16]

This hymn very well reflected the thinking of Reverend Ridgel, the most prominent missionary to Liberia of that day. In 1884, as a young man of twenty-three, he was accepted into the ministry by the annual AME conference in Helena, presided over by Bishop Henry Turner. Turner gave Ridgel his first preaching appointment at Walnut Lake Mission, and Ridgel thereafter moved on to several congregations in eastern and southern Arkansas. Early in his career, he preached at four stations, traveling on horseback from place to place, carrying two suits of clothes, a Methodist hymnal, and a Bible.[17] Ridgel clearly was inspired for missionary work by his mentor, Bishop Turner, whom he heard speak at the annual AME conferences in Arkansas. In the summer of 1892, when Ridgel served a parish at Brinkley, Monroe County, he participated in a public debate of clergymen on the question of African emigration. Ridgel's side won the debate: the assembly resolved that the Negro should emigrate to Africa. Ridgel made good on his rhetoric, for he began a correspondence with Turner about a missionary appointment. A few weeks before he formally received his orders from Turner at the annual conference in Newport in November, Ridgel had already asked the ACS for transportation to Liberia.[18]

By the beginning of 1893, Ridgel had left his wife and two daughters behind in Arkansas and commenced an ambitious speaking tour through the southern states on his way to New York to take ship for Africa. Starting out to tearful goodbyes in his home conference of South Arkansas, Ridgel traveled through Mississippi and Alabama on his way to Atlanta, where he visited Bishop Turner before traveling up the east coast to Philadelphia, speaking in churches and collecting money along the way. Passing out his flyers with the heading "Off to Africa," Ridgel eventually raised more than $500 to support his African work. He spent a month in Philadelphia, the headquarters of the AME Church, where he met with church officials, including Dr. W. B. Derrick, the general secretary for missions of the denomination. Ridgel, with a combative personality like his mentor Bishop Turner's, immediately fell into conflict with Derrick over his missionary appointment. Derrick felt that all appointments should come from him. To some extent, Ridgel fell victim to a power struggle over who would control AME Church missions, but his choleric temperament intensified the struggle. He battled against Derrick during the whole time of his service in Africa.[19]

While Ridgel waited to sail for Africa, he met a young woman, Fannie Worthington, a schoolteacher in Camden, New Jersey, who also hailed from Arkansas. Fannie's father was the mulatto son of a slave and her master, Elisha Worthington, antebellum Arkansas's most wealthy plantation owner. Apparently Fannie did not know that Ridgel had left a wife behind in Arkansas, nor apparently did the officials of the AME Church, for the two were married on 7 February 1893 by the Reverend H. T. Johnson, the editor of church's leading journal, the *Christian Recorder*.[20]

Two weeks after their marriage, the couple met Bishop Turner in New York, and they sailed on the *Majestic*. Turner was making his second African voyage and, in addition to Mr. and Mrs. Ridgel, took along another missionary, the Reverend L. L. Vreeland, for the African mission fields. Possibly yielding to pressure from AME officials, Turner posted the Ridgels to Sierra Leone and gave Ridgel's original appointment as presiding elder of the Liberian conference to Vreeland.

For Alfred Ridgel, the preacher from small-town Arkansas, the trip was filled with wonders. The *Majestic* docked in Liverpool, and Ridgel reported his amazement that he could walk the streets and eat in restaurants without any sign of race prejudice. The ship then stopped in the Canary Islands and then at Gorée, off the port of Dakar, where Ridgel caught his first glimpse of native Africans: Muslims, wearing flowing loose gowns, boarding the ship to sail farther south. On 4 April 1893, just a few days after Easter, the ship landed in Freetown, Sierra Leone.[21]

Within a few weeks, Fannie and Alfred Ridgel settled into their new roles. Alfred reported that Freetown reminded him very much of Helena, Arkansas, and three hundred worshipers attended his first church service. Before long, he was preaching to Africans through an interpreter speaking the Temne dialect. Fannie headed a school for local children. Both were laid low with malaria within their first month in Africa.[22]

Ridgel's work had hardly begun when he became embroiled in controversy with the church body back home. He complained of poverty almost as soon as he arrived in Africa, and he blamed Dr. Derrick for failing to pay a salary to the missionary family. Even some Methodists of Sierra Leone wrote to American newspapers on Ridgel's behalf, arguing that he was mistreated by the AME Missions Board.[23] In his battle with the church missions department, which he waged primarily through letters home to black newspapers, Ridgel suggested that his lack of financial support stemmed from the rivalry between Derrick and Turner over control of African missions. Actually, Derrick had more serious concerns. By the fall of 1893, charges surfaced that Ridgel had committed bigamy when he married Fannie Worthington earlier that year. Perhaps Ridgel's first wife, Frances, had read newspaper reports about the Liberian work of Ridgel and his new wife. Or possibly Dr. Derrick learned firsthand of the scandal when he attended the annual meeting of the Arkansas Conference, which met in November at St. Paul's Church in Brinkley, Ridgel's last parish. Derrick and the recording secretary for missions, John M. Henderson of Detroit, Michigan, began collecting evidence of Ridgel's crime.[24] In a meeting in New York of the missions board and several AME bishops, officials recalled Ridgel to America to answer the bigamy charge against him. Ridgel complained that while officials expected him to come back, they had paid him no salary in his ten months of work in Sierra Leone, nor did they send him any money to purchase transportation to America.[25]

While the missions board dropped Ridgel from the list of missionaries, Bishop Turner nonetheless directed him to go to Liberia to replace the Reverend Vreeland as presiding elder of the Liberia Conference. Malaria had seized Vreeland upon arrival in Liberia and never let go. He died without ever having a chance to do mission work. In March of 1894, Fannie Ridgel closed her school of 104 students and Alfred left his mission, which had claimed thirteen Africans for Christianity in his year of preaching.[26] After an eight-day voyage from Freetown and some time touring Liberia, the Ridgels settled in coastal Edina, in Bassa County, where Fannie opened another school for African children. Alfred spent much of his time traveling throughout the country supervising the sixteen existing AME congregations in the American settlements and establishing new missions.[27] The couple lived, rent free, in a three-story brick house in Edina owned by the president of the Republic of Liberia, Joseph J. Cheeseman. Within his first year in Liberia, Ridgel claimed to have organized three new mission congregations, received seventy-five persons into the church, baptized thirty children and adults, organized two district conferences, presided over forty-two quarterly district meetings, preached 225 sermons, and delivered forty lectures.[28]

Despite Ridgel's busy schedule, he found time to write numerous lengthy letters to black newspapers in the United States and continue the battle with his opponents within the AME Church hierarchy. AME Church officials evidently had tried to keep the bigamy charges from public knowledge to save embarrassment for the whole denomination. However, Ridgel's persistent attacks against Derrick and the mission department—for slighting African work, for allowing him and his wife "to starve 6000 miles away from home," and for misusing monies appropriated for missions—eventually drew blood.[29] By June 1894, Derrick and his assistant, Henderson, had made the bigamy charges public. Henderson even intimated that Ridgel had lost the money he had raised in his lecture tour before leaving for Africa "in the company of a Liverpool prostitute." In October, the supporting evidence—marriage licenses and affidavits by Ridgel's first wife and her supporters—were printed in the *Indianapolis Freeman*, which claimed to have more readers in Arkansas than any other nationally circulated black newspaper.[30] Ridgel insisted his detractors were not trying to fight him personally but attacking Africa missions in general.[31] A meeting of ninety-two members of the South Arkansas AME Conference, where Ridgel's ministry had begun and where his first wife still lived, voted to appoint a committee to investigate Ridgel's status, but other congregations and conferences in Arkansas continued to raise money for his work and seemed to ignore the controversy all together.[32]

Ridgel's struggle with the church came to a conclusion when Bishop Turner made his third visit to Liberia, in May 1895, and presided over a meeting of the Liberian Conference, which addressed the the bigamy charges against Ridgel.[33] Turner had consistently supported Ridgel, and Ridgel praised his mentor in all his communications to the United States, calling Turner the greatest living Negro. The Liberian Methodists also strongly supported their leader. In the summer of 1894, nine of the AME clergy serving under Ridgel had written to the bishops and missions board back in the United States expressing their distress over the church's efforts to recall their presiding elder. They called Ridgel a "noble, self-sacrificing young man . . . who has inspired new life all along the line," and his removal, they said, would be detrimental to missions in the country. J. R. Frederick, Ridgel's former coworker in Sierra Leone, also defended Ridgel against the "malicious falsehood" and slander by John Henderson.[34] It is no surprise then that under Turner's leadership, the Liberian Conference, by

REV. A. L. RIDGLEY,
Brinkley, Ark.

The Reverend Alfred L. Ridgel.
From the *Indianapolis Freeman*, 2
July 1892.

a unanimous vote, declared Ridgel not guilty of the charges against him, and
the matter was finally settled.[35]

Even after Ridgel's battle with the AME administration had ended, he found
new adversaries to engage. Charles Spencer Smith, the AME Sunday School
superintendent, whom Ridgel had met at the Arkansas annual meeting two
years before, made a well-publicized tour of the African continent in 1894. When
Smith returned to the United States and wrote forcefully against black American emigration to Africa, Ridgel blasted Smith for his stand. Ridgel said that
during his trip to Africa, Smith had never slept a night off of his steamship all
the way from Liverpool to the Congo, except for ten days when he was in Liberia, and for those ten days he never stepped outside the capital, Monrovia.
So what, Ridgel asked, did Smith really know about Africa?[36] The next year,
Ridgel wrote a blistering attack against Booker T. Washington just after the
noted leader gave his famous speech at the Atlanta Exposition in which he advocated that African Americans accommodate to white oppression by seeking
first economic prosperity rather than civil rights. In Ridgel's usual strong language, he denounced Washington as ignorant and poorly educated and his Atlanta speech as a "cringing, cowardly and niggardly declaration." Ridgel was so
harsh that even Bishop Turner, never one to mince words himself, printed the

letter in his monthly *Voice of Missions* with the disclaimer that it did not meet with his approval.[37] If that were not enough, Ridgel even went on to label Edward W. Blyden, the former Presbyterian minister and Liberia's most famous citizen, as a "strange man" because of his admiration of Islam. Ridgel said Blyden had "exchanged Christ for Mahomet. He laid down the Bible for the Koran."[38]

With his eloquent though biting prose, Ridgel perhaps made his mark more as a writer than a missionary. In his first year in Liberia, the missionary claimed he wrote 500 letters to individuals and articles for seven different American newspapers. Ridgel also wrote the booklet "A Pen Picture of the Republic of Liberia, West Africa," which was published by Bishop Turner in late 1895 and sold for fifteen cents. The next year he authored a longer book surveying Christian prospects in Africa, *Africa and African Methodism*.[39] In his voluminous writing, Ridgel echoed Bishop Turner's call for emigration as the solution to America's race problems. He believed black people had no future in America but misery and degradation. Separation from whites was the only answer.[40] Black people of the diaspora, Ridgel said, must come home to Africa so they could fully appreciate themselves and be "re-negroized." Africa did not need shiploads of helpless, ignorant Negroes but instead progressive, young, vigorous, self-reliant families. Most important, black Americans should take action to improve their lives. Ridgel especially encouraged those who lived in "mob-inflicted regions of the South to avail themselves of every opportunity to come to Africa, where they can have peace from the inhuman whitecaps and lynchers." He exhorted black southerners to "come out from among your enemies, and come among your friends. . . . Here you can have peace, prosperity, and fully enjoy the rights and privileges of citizens. Prejudice, caste, and race hate are unknown."[41] He concluded that "the Negro has no future in the United States of America. . . . Those of our people who elect to remain on American soil . . . deserve the punishment inflicted on them by the haughty white American."[42] Only in Liberia, Ridgel argued, could an African American "foster a great nationality, accumulate wealth, develop his moral, intellectual and social powers." In Africa, "He would be free to act as a man and not act as a slave."[43] Missionary Ridgel had clearly given up on America.

In Ridgel's last published letter to the United States, he noted his agreement with another black nationalist, Henry Highland Garnet, who had said, "I want to be buried in a soil that is congenial with my nature."[44] Garnet, who died shortly after he came to Liberia in 1881, got his wish. So would Alfred Ridgel. Ridgel's career as preacher, prolific writer, and missionary came to a sudden end in late September 1896. His wife Fannie had returned to Washington, D.C., to visit her mother in May, and Ridgel had been staying by himself in Monrovia. A. H. Watson, a Liberian pastor, said Ridgel had spoken from the pulpit about forebodings of imminent death and had suffered from fever through much of the month. On the evening of Saturday, 26 September, he jumped off the steamer *Sarah Ann* as he was traveling up the mighty St. Paul River near Monrovia. Watson intimated that the death was a suicide. However, another AME preacher, the Reverend Clement Irons, suggested that the engine of the steamer malfunctioned, the boat began racing away uncontrolled, and Ridgel jumped to save his life. The swift current carried Ridgel away, and his body was not found until a week later. Just as he had wished, missionary Ridgel arrived at his permanent rest in African soil outside the AME church in Millsburg, Liberia.[45]

The AME Church was not the only black denomination that supported African missions, nor was Ridgel the only missionary from Arkansas who served there. In 1893, the year Ridgel left for Liberia, a black Baptist minister in Hot Springs, the Reverend R. A. Jackson, planned for a career in African missions.[46] He received an appointment to become missionary to Africa from the Baptist Foreign Mission Convention in September 1893, but apparently that body failed to provide any financial support. By the end of the year, Jackson had saved $800 of his own money and had applied to the ACS in Washington for transportation from New York to Liberia for himself, his wife, Emma, and their two children. The ACS approved the passage of the Jackson family and another family from Georgia, the only people the society sent to Africa in 1894.[47] In the meantime, Bishop Turner had visited Hot Springs and announced that Jackson would be joining the AME Church's Liberian missions. In April, a week after this announcement, the Jackson family left for New York and sailed for Liberia on 17 April via Southampton, England.[48] But Jackson changed his mind about working for the AME Church, perhaps because of denominational loyalties, and his family traveled on down the West African coast to Capetown, where he established a Baptist church that spawned a number of daughter congregations.[49] At that time, Jackson was apparently the only American black Baptist missionary serving on the African continent.[50]

While Jackson's ministry was thriving in southern Africa in the late 1890s, a group of missionaries from Arkansas were preparing to go to Liberia for the black branch of the Methodist Episcopal Church. By 1892, the Reverend Joseph C. Sherrill, who had served several parishes in southern and central Arkansas, had finished studies at Philander Smith College, a black Methodist Episcopal school in Little Rock. A few years later, he decided to devote his career to African missions and received the Theodore Lewis Mason Scholarship

A steamship on the St. Paul River, Liberia. From Amanda Smith, *An Autobiography*, 1895.

to study at Gammon Theological Seminary in Atlanta, where he graduated in 1897 with a bachelor of divinity degree.[51] After his graduation, Sherrill and his wife returned to Little Rock, where he worked to recruit students at Philander Smith College to go with him to Liberia. Sherrill soon had more volunteers for Africa than the church body could accept. Eventually, Joseph Hartzell, the Methodist bishop for Africa, chose two Philander Smith graduates, Ferdinand Marcus Allen, a young man trained as a printer, and Joseph A. Davis, to accompany the Sherrill family to Liberia. Bishop Hartzell also appointed a graduate of the State Colored Normal School in Pine Bluff, Miss Amanda Davis, of no relation to Joseph, to teach in Liberia.[52]

On Sunday, 11 December 1898, Reverend Sherrill preached his last sermon in Little Rock, and his parishioners gave the new missionary and his wife a handsome new Bible as a parting gift. The missionary party left Little Rock for New York. Sherrill took with him a younger brother, as well as his wife and son. Ferdinand Allen brought his new bride, Ruby Estelle. The Sherrill and Davis families sailed for Africa on 17 December via Liverpool.[53] The trip to Africa, like Alfred Ridgel's before, was filled with one wondrous experience after another. Sailing on an English ship, *Roquelle*, from Liverpool to Liberia, Sherrill expressed amazement that English passengers treated him and his family "with the same courtesy and politeness they do the whites." He marveled at the mighty storms that blew through the Bay of Biscay. He noted that

Methodist missionaries from Arkansas pose in New York City en route to Liberia, 1898. Left to right, seated: Amanda Davis, Sherrill's son, Mrs. Sherrill, Ruby Allen; standing: Joseph A. Davis, Rev. Joseph C. Sherrill, brother of Rev. Sherrill, Ferdinand M. Allen. Courtesy Library of Congress.

his family dared not depart the ship when it landed in the Spanish Canary Islands, for the "Spaniards were still cursing the Americans" following their defeat in the recent war. At Gorée, Sherrill got his first glimpse of Africans in their flowing dress, who periodically fell to their knees to pray. Sherrill concluded after his studious observation of the Muslim Africans: "Though I must say that in the midst of the heathen darkness, there was a glimmer of moral intellectual and spiritual light."[54]

The Sherrills arrived in Liberia on 29 January 1899, and Reverend Sherrill took up his duties as pastor of the Methodist Episcopal Church in Monrovia, a large stone church with 300 members, the largest Christian congregation in the capital city. Sherrill also served as acting president of West Africa College, a Methodist day and boarding school in Monrovia. Sherrill reported back to Methodist Church officials in the United States that "the naked heathen are all about me, our own brothers and sisters," indicating his sense of both connection and distance to African people. He concluded, "I am happy in my work, I feel more and more each day that I am where God wants me."[55]

The Allens arrived soon after the Sherrill and Davis party. To inaugurate a church newspaper, Bishop Hartzell had purchased a cylindrical printing press, a paper cutter, and enough paper and ink to last two years. Allen had stayed in New York an extra month to collect the equipment and print a trial run on the press. The couple left New York with the precious equipment on 18 January. Once in Liberia, Allen set to work printing the *New Africa*, which soon published its first issue. Two years later, Allen reported that he had ten African boys in training to become printers and that the longer he stayed in Africa the better he liked his work. Joe Davis stayed in Liberia for five years working as a mathematics teacher at West Africa College. He married in 1900, when Cordelia Iris Durham, his fiancée from Little Rock, joined him in Monrovia. In 1902, the couple returned to Arkansas, but after a short stay they asked the ACS and the Methodist Church to send them back to Liberia as teachers. Ferdinand and Ruby Allen and the Reverend and Mrs. Sherrill remained in Liberia until 1909.

In the last years, the Sherrill family had moved some 350 miles down the Liberian coast to Cape Palmas, where Reverend Sherrill led a mission school he said was the largest in Liberia, with one hundred African students and even more American Liberians. Sherrill continued to preach and claimed that during a revival meeting in his last year in Liberia he won 170 conversions, most of them from the Grebo, Kru, and Bassa tribes. Although his last communications with the mission office back home echoed the familiar missionary complaints of insufficient funds and poor health, Sherrill continued to express his commitment to the evangelization of Africa.[56]

The year that the Sherrill, Davis, and Allen families arrived in Liberia, another Philander Smith College graduate, Eugene R. Gravelly, became the fourth man to win the Mason Scholarship at Gammon Seminary to prepare for the African mission field. In December 1900, the American Colonization Society sent Gravelly and his wife, who was a schoolteacher, to Liberia. The flow of black Methodist missionaries from Arkansas to Liberia continued as years passed. The Reverend John Hamilton Reed, pastor of Joseph Sherrill's former church, Wesley Chapel in Little Rock, received the appointment to the presidency at West Africa College in Monrovia in 1904. With several furloughs along the way, Reed, his wife, Marguerite, and their two children spent most of the next two decades in Liberia, returning to the United States in 1923.[57]

The missionary movement, from the societies, with their fund-raising, speech-giving, and conference-attending, to the departure for and work of these missionaries in Africa, demonstrates black Arkansans' fascination with Africa. The interest in missions especially grew in Arkansas after 1892, when the desire for Liberian emigration had swelled but the opportunity for actual settlement practically disappeared. Arkansas provided twelve of the fifty black adult missionaries who went to Africa from the United States between 1890 and 1900. For these missionaries and their families, and for the churches and clubs back home in Arkansas, the missionary movement allowed people, especially women, to express their race pride and sense of national identity. Just what Africa meant to the emigrants and these missionaries is the subject of the next chapter.

7

The Meaning of Africa

The preceding chapters demonstrate that blacks had compelling reasons to leave Arkansas, but they also possessed powerful motivations to come home to an ancestral continent. What did Africa, and Liberia in particular, mean to these black men and women who wished to move there either as permanent settlers or as missionaries? The very word "Africa" conjured up varied images of wonder in the minds of black Arkansans. And, in fact, part of the magnetic power of the image of Africa rested in its various and complex meanings. Africa functioned as a multireferential symbol, evoking different and sometimes paradoxical emotions. In the Christian religion, a cross represents suffering and redemption, death but also life, and the evocative power of the symbol comes partly from this complexity and texture of meanings. Similarly, for late-nineteenth-century black Arkansans, Africa connoted a bundle of dialectical oppositions: attraction and repulsion, hope and dread, an Eden but also a pagan savage place, a promised land but a dark continent.[1] Some black Americans promoted one set of these images over others, but, for many, all these meanings competed together to form a complex tapestry of the imagination. Many of these images bore little resemblance to the reality of late-nineteenth-century Africa, as those who actually emigrated would discover.

From the preceding discussion of the extreme racial oppression in Arkansas in the late 1800s comes one of the most obvious and important meanings of Africa: a refuge. In antebellum days, free blacks had seen Liberia as a symbol of banishment, and most of them clearly had opposed the American Colonization Society as the vehicle of their removal from North America. But in the late 1800s, thousands, perhaps millions, of black Americans began to see Liberia as a destination for escape from white oppression, and they became more than willing to work with that aging society, the ACS, to get away from America to Africa. Bishop Henry Turner, as always, made the point with force and eloquence: "Yes, I would make Africa the place of refuge because I see no other shelter from the stormy blast, from the red tide of persecution, from the horrors of American prejudice."[2]

Much of Arkansas's black population had come to the state from elsewhere in the South seeking political and economic opportunities. For example, the migrants to Arkansas from Edgefield and neighboring counties in South Carolina in the early 1880s had fled extreme conditions created by white rifle clubs organized there after the end of Reconstruction. Arkansas—"Rockansas"— was supposed to be the promised land for these black South Carolinians. But so many of these Edgefield black families settled in Conway County, where the black population percentage rose from 7 to nearly 40 percent, that a few years later they experienced in Arkansas a reprise of the same kind of terror they had fled in South Carolina. A migration to Liberia, instead of some American destination, offered an escape to an all-black world. Many of Arkansas's correspondents with the ACS spoke specifically of the desire to leave not just the state, or the South, but the entire country. As one black man from Menifee said, "We desire to Move out of these United States." A committee from Woodruff County similarly gave up hope on life in America: "Our country are getting in a deplorable condition and we are bound to do something and we want to leave the United States of America and our only hope to redeem our condition is to go to Africa."[3]

For those who wished to build a nation away from the control of white people, there seemed to be few alternatives to Liberia. Missionary Alfred Ridgel wrote back to the United States in 1896 lamenting that the "proud Caucasian holds sway" in so many parts of the earth that only Haiti, San Domingo, and Liberia stood as lands under black governments. Europeans, he said, had gobbled up nearly the entire African continent, leaving Liberia as the "only resort for civilized Negroes on all of the vast continent of Africa." If black Americans did not come to help build up the Liberian nation, Ridgel said, "soon the Negro will have no flag to which he can flee for protection and on which he can gaze with pride."[4] The Liberian Republic's particular attraction clearly stemmed from its offer of absolute escape from white oppression.

The "blackness" of Liberia attracted people who wished to get as far away as possible from white people, and letter writers wanted specific clarification that no whites lived there. One black man in Conway County wanted to know if "we wood be treaded as bad over in liBery as we ar in the U.S. Ar tha any White People over in liBery? If there is—none [of us] ar going there." Liberia's constitution forbade white citizenship or ownership of land anywhere in the country. This seemed too good to be true, and several Arkansans wrote the ACS to make sure the constitution was indeed followed. "Has any whites bought any [land] there?" asked a black man from Pine Bluff. From Cross County another asked, "Will a man be a free man in Liberia, and under a free Government, controlled by men of color?" ACS secretary William Coppinger repeatedly assured correspondents that whites could neither own land nor become citizens in Liberia, that slavery was forever prohibited by law, and that the government of Liberia rested in the hands of black people.[5]

The desire to escape whites to an all-black world also explains why Oklahoma appeared as such an attractive substitute for people who could not reach Africa. In retrospect, the talk of establishing Oklahoma as an all-black state was unrealistic, but it did not appear so in the early 1890s on the eve of mass settlement and with the development work of black leaders like William L. Eagleson and Edward P. McCabe. If Oklahoma failed to become an all-black state, several dozen new all-black towns offered African Americans the opportunity to live in relative isolation from whites under a local government of their own color. While only thirteen have survived to today, more than thirty all-black towns were established in Oklahoma between 1890 and 1907. By early 1892, Langston, the first and perhaps most successful, had seven grocery stores, two saloons, two blacksmiths, two barbershops, and a feed store. Within another year it added three restaurants, two meat markets, a bakery, two factories and a mill, a bank, two hotels, an opera house, and an ice cream parlor.[6] A resident of Langston could experience small-town American life just as it was anywhere else, with just one difference: one might never see a white person.

Some black developers also founded a few all-black towns in Arkansas. In southeastern Jackson County, in an area of intense interest in Liberia migration, Pickens W. Black, a prosperous black man, began acquiring land in the 1890s. He eventually founded Blackville, an all-black town of fifty-three families, with its own store, flour mill, gin, school, and blacksmith. When a black developer founded an all-black town in Desha County in 1904, he named it Liberia City in a conscious attempt to emulate black self-sufficiency symbolized by that black republic.[7] Long before Malcolm X and Louis Farrakhan talked about blacks' need to separate from white society, a separatist movement was alive and well among black farmers in Arkansas.

Africa represented the ultimate possibility to express black nationalism, the idea that African Americans were indeed a distinct and separate people. Liberia was a place where black Americans could come into their own, where they could control the government, economy, educational system, and cultural institutions of an entire country. They could demonstrate their ability to self-govern on a "civilized" Western basis. Numerous correspondents to the ACS yearned to go where blacks could govern themselves and be really free. One twenty-seven-year-old farmer, A. D. Allen of Damascus, explained his feelings to Coppinger: "Dear Sir, I hardly know how to address you I am so much hape up at the thoughts of such a glorious country for the colored man, as ruling and governing among themselves." After enduring white oppression, James Lattimer explained from western Arkansas that black people simply wanted "to get in a land and country of our own," or, as a black man from Woodruff County put it, to "become a nation among nations."[8]

In their rhetoric, the opportunity for nation-building in Liberia offered African Americans the chance to regain lost manhood. The late 1800s was a time of hypermasculinity in American culture, and manhood became a trope invoked continually to communicate a sense of personal and communal development.[9] Bishop Turner preached that slavery had stripped black Americans of their manhood, had convinced them of their own inferiority, and that emigration to Liberia offered blacks the chance to be men, to self-govern, to gain self-respect. Turner was convinced that black men could not truly be men in a country like the United States, where their manhood was neither recognized nor respected. Ridgel, Turner's hand-picked missionary from Arkansas to Liberia, agreed that racism had emasculated the black people of America. Only in Africa, Ridgel said, could "the Negro be a man. He can rise to eminence in common with other men." For Turner and Ridgel, black nation-building was a decidedly masculine affair.[10]

Whether people actually made it to Liberia or not, for black men and women Africa was linked to a emerging national identity. The correspondence to the ACS demonstrated a great deal of sentiment for Africa as an ancestral homeland, a sense of connection to Africa as a hearth of their culture and race. In countless letters, would-be emigrants referred to Africa as the "land of our forefathers," "motherland," "native land," or, simply, "home." An exodus club leader in Camden reported that one of his members who had recently died begged him on his death bed to "carry his children to Afrik."[11] Black Arkansans obviously felt connected to Africa in a way that could help them understand themselves.

The Africa of their imaginations was a mythical, romantic place more than a real location in time and space. Africa functioned as a totem, a symbol that helped black Americans identify themselves as a people, just as a sacred animal might symbolize the social unity of a Paleolithic community, a patron saint might crystallize the identity of a medieval European village, or a mascot today might unify sports fans behind a team. In the community that gathers around a totem pole and worships the owl, people know they are not owls, but owl people. Similarly, these black Arkansas farmers did not think of themselves as Africans but as people of Africa, people for whom Africa signified ancestry and cultural identity. However, they possessed a remarkable lack of curiosity about African peoples and cultures of the 1890s. Correspondents to the ACS asked every conceivable question about Africa, about climate, soil, crops, insects, snakes, diseases, money, railroads, and towns. They did not ask about the native people. These would-be emigrants saw Africa as a mythical place of the past, as a cultural legacy, somewhat as Zionist Jews might view Palestine before 1948. The Africa of the present or future appeared as an empty space ready to receive them.

The idea of Africa as a place, rather than people, formed an important part of the African American sense of national identity. In recent years, black nationalism has become conflated with Afrocentrism, or a celebration of traditional African culture. The civil rights and black power movements in the United States progressed in the 1960s as African colonies were becoming proud independent nation-states. The dashikis and Afros of the 1960s gave way to kente cloth and braids in the 1990s as the connection to, and celebration of, the culture of mother Africa remained. However, the black nationalism of the nineteenth century, and that displayed by Arkansas missionaries and aspiring emigrants, did not exalt Africa and despise Western culture. Instead, the emerging black nationalism of the late 1800s involved a sense of being black Americans. African ancestry formed part of that national identity. But so did the common heritage of slavery and then freedom that separated black Americans from black Africans.[12]

Black nationalist views incorporated a conflicted attitude toward America. Bishop Turner preached that the American government owed African Americans reparations for slavery, that blacks should spit on the Constitution of the United States, and that with incurable white racism, black people could never have rights or a real home in this country. Yet it was through American slavery, Turner believed, that a black nation was born. Slavery constituted part of a divine plan that had brought civilization and Christianity to the black race. America was the womb from which an African American nation came forth.

Slavery thus had been a curse but also a blessing. America was a place of misery but also a necessary preparation. The irony of these attitudes toward an American homeland had not originated with Henry Turner. He was indebted to Edward Blyden, Alexander Crummell, Martin Delany, and Henry Highland Garnet, who had all articulated these views in the mid-1800s. Turner, however, popularized these ideas through his mighty pen and countless sermons as bishop, especially in the Eighth District of the AME Church.[13]

Alfred Ridgel uncharacteristically disagreed with his mentor, insisting that the African American national identity was forged in freedom, not slavery. The problem was that America gave no place for free black men and women. Ridgel argued that God had nothing to do with an institution as vile as slavery. After the Civil War, the situation for black Americans had actually worsened, Ridgel said, for whites no longer valued blacks as property. A black man had become "a kind of unowned and unvalued chattel, at the disposal of any white rough who can shoot him down with impunity." For Ridgel, who left Arkansas for Liberia following the spectacle lynchings of 1892, "the spirit that instituted slavery has given birth to mob violence which has forever disgraced the American continent."[14]

Another black Arkansan agreed with Ridgel's assessment and suggested that black Americans would need to build their nation outside the United States. The Reverend A. H. Hill, an AME clergyman in Clarendon, argued in Bishop Turner's paper, *Voice of Missions*, that the black nation had been born from the trials that followed the Civil War and freedom. The Emancipation Proclamation prophesied and the Thirteenth Amendment brought about the birth of a nation of black Americans, Hill said. The Fourteenth and Fifteenth Amendments gave four million sons and daughters of the United States basic rights, which some states then denied through lynching, Jim Crow cars, and disfranchisement. But Hill believed in the moral authority of the Constitution and the legal tradition it represented. He just saw little hope for a black nation in America while the "prejudice of the Caucasian race is on the increase." In other words, white prejudice ruined a great system. In fact, the more black Americans educated and improved themselves, Hill said, the more intolerable whites seemed to find them. For Hill, "this new born nation, in order to gain recognition before the world, and to develop its national qualities, must build up a nation in some other land." This other land in Hill's view would be Africa.[15] Ridgel agreed, saying, "There is no such thing as two nations occupying the same territory on peaceful terms." The answer for the race problem was not accommodation and black servility in America, Ridgel said, but separation from white society through emigration to Liberia. Thus, black Arkansans dreamed of Africa as an opportunity to remake an American civilization without white people and racism. Liberia was an attempt to create a perfect America, with American institutions and culture, but with black people in control, demonstrating to the world their ability to self-govern. Only in Liberia, Ridgel asserted, could an African American "foster a great nationality, accumulate wealth, develop his moral, intellectual and social powers." In Africa, "he would be free to act as a man and not act as a slave."[16]

One of the most powerful ways black Arkansans internalized a meaning of Africa was through religious thinking, which meant infusing the back-to-Africa movement with the vocabulary and theology of Christianity. Historians now recognize that Christianity was an African religion long before it was a religion of white northern Europeans. But American slaves acquired the Christian faith west of the Atlantic Ocean, and by the late nineteenth century, Christianity had become an intrinsic part of black culture in the United States. As with their sense of national identity, black people preserved the framework of the Christian religion and merged it with surviving African and folk traditions, making "black" Christianity into something of their very own.[17] Christianity permeated almost every aspect of the back-to-Africa movement. The Liberia Exodus Arkansas Colony opened its convention in 1877 with singing and prayer, and the delegates held religious services, complete with preaching by the elected chaplain, the Reverend A. J. Smith.[18] Likewise, at the emigration club meetings in the 1890s, participants usually met in churches, sang hymns and spirituals, said prayers, and listened to rousing oration. Often clubs were organized around particular churches, with pastors writing to the ACS on behalf of members of their congregations. On several occasions when emigrants left their Arkansas homes, they said good-bye with a worship service to mark the event. They sang spirituals as their train traveled to the seaport. The McCrory emigrants, upon arriving in New York in 1892, held a prayer and singing ceremony before looking for a place to stay. When emigrants caught their first glimpse of Africa, the singing commenced again. It is not surprising, then, that black farmers in Arkansas thought about Liberia emigration in religious terms, especially invoking the biblical story of Exodus.

The Exodus story of the children of Israel enslaved in Egypt, led out of bondage to Canaan, an ancestral homeland, has figured prominently in black Christianity in America. Probably no other story so stirred the imagination of black men, women, and children in the nineteenth century, as is testified by the spirituals with Exodus themes, such as "Go Down, Moses" or "Joshua Fit De

Battle of Jericho." In one recent study, Eddie S. Glaude Jr., a scholar of black religion, argues that African Americans appropriated the Exodus story in the early 1800s because it allowed them to understand their identity as a people and to dream about a national destiny in the future. Glaude examined the free black conventions held in the late antebellum years to explain how black Americans thought of resistance to white oppression through the metaphor of Exodus. Glaude suggests that antebellum blacks imagined the promised land as a state of liberation, of freedom, more than a physical place. Whenever mass emigration movements were discussed, such as to Canada in the 1830s or to Kansas in the late 1870s, the Exodus language came forth. Eugene Genovese also explains how enslaved Christians fused their views of Moses and Jesus into one image. Jesus was a liberator, a deliverer, while Moses brought redemption from terrible suffering. The two figures collapsed into one powerful symbol.[19]

This well-worn Exodus metaphor became even more evocative when attached to a black mass movement for the return to the ancestral homeland, Africa. Black Arkansans spoke specifically of America as their Egypt, of emigration as the Exodus movement, and of Liberia as their promised land. James Matthews of Little Rock, for example, lapsed into this religious language as he begged Coppinger to accept his family as emigrants in 1891: "We ask you do you remember that god comand Moses to lead the children of isral out of bondage now declear before god that we is now in the same fixt the children of isral was in when god comanded Moses to lead them to the promiss land we prey in the name of god that you will . . . lead us and insist in geting to the land that is promiss to us."[20] Black Arkansans saw this migration to the promised land as a messianic culmination for themselves and for Africa. W. H. Holloway wrote to Coppinger from Cleveland County in 1891: "Dear Sir, as I am informed that you are one of the prominent men at the U.S. Capital that are assisting in the furtherance of the Exodus Movement to our Father's Home in the Eastern Continent of Africa, and as I appreciate the land of my Mother and Father, and [am] a Race lover of the deepest stain, and want to inhabit a free and independent Country, where Ethiopia can stretch forth her hands unto God and be a mighty nation unto God, I am prompted to write you for all the information touching the matter." He signed his letter, "a true and tried Afro-American, W. H. Holloway." In the same sentence, Holloway invoked the Exodus metaphor and the image of Ethiopia stretching forth her hand. This latter image comes from Psalms 68:31, a prophetic verse that points to a future time when Africa will come unto its own and when wrongs will be made right. A generation later, the Marcus Garvey movement would use this verse more than any other biblical allusion.[21] The cold, social-scientific language about a migration simply does not capture the awe and wonder conjured up when people whispered about Exodus, a promised land, and Ethiopia stretching forth her hand.

Christian beliefs encouraged African Americans to share the gospel of Jesus Christ with those who did not have it, particularly non-Christian Africans. Like white Euro-Americans of the late nineteenth century, black Arkansans believed that Christianity formed an essential element of civilization. Thus, blacks and whites together thought of Africa in the late 1800s as an environment awaiting civilization and conversion. Rather than a "white man's burden," as the English poet Rudyard Kipling put it, black Arkansans believed it was the civilized man's burden to convert, uplift, and educate the sons and daughters of Africa.[22]

Bishop Turner, again echoing views articulated earlier by Crummell, Garnet, and Delany, argued that it was specifically the black man's burden to bring civilization to Africa. God had chosen black Americans to carry out a master plan, a sort of black manifest destiny, for the salvation of Africa. Only such a divine plan could explain why God allowed whites to enslave Africans in the first place. As discussed above, Turner believed slavery brought Africans to America so that they could become Christian and enlightened, and only then could black Americans take back those gifts of Christian civilization to Africa. Anyone who opposed African emigration, Turner said, was "fighting the God of the universe, face to face."[23]

Turner strove to contradict those who denigrated Africa, who loved to hate the "dark continent." Especially after his four trips to Africa, in 1891, 1893, 1895, and 1898, Turner praised the continent as a virtual paradise of unlimited resources and her people as naturally intelligent and noble. In fact, Turner suggested in a letter he wrote during his first visit to Liberia in 1891 that "we poor American Negroes were the tail-end of the African races." Likewise, Alfred Ridgel said he opposed a wholesale emigration to Liberia, "not because the country is unfit for the people, but because millions of Afro-Americans are unfit for the country."[24] Ridgel even retooled the argument that civilization had emanated originally from Africa. Ancient Egypt, as the hearth of African culture, had given the gift of civilization to the world. Africa had thus been the mother of art, science, and civilization, Ridgel said, and black emigration from America should aim to build Africa back up, "to help restore the pristine glory of his ancestral home."[25]

Yet, despite their praise of Africa and Africans, Turner and Ridgel echoed the same sort of western chauvinism articulated by white American and European apologists for imperialism in the late 1800s. Turner emphasized the great "potential" of the native Africans, but he still viewed them as cultural inferiors who needed black Americans to instruct and uplift them, to bring them into membership of the civilized Christian black nation. In one of missionary Ridgel's first letters home after his arrival in Africa, he exclaimed that black Americans would be astonished to see "how degraded these poor heathens are. . . . You can see grown men naked, and women nearly the same way. Awful, awful, awful!"[26] With articulate leaders like Turner and Ridgel thus describing Africa, it is no wonder that images of "darkest" Africa abounded in the letters of prospective emigrants and in black church circles in Arkansas. In 1879, the constitution of the Liberia Exodus Arkansas Colony had dedicated the organization to uplift the African continent by bringing needed skilled human resources, "preachers, doctors and lawyers," as well as articles of material refinement, "sofas, lounges, pianos and organs." Sister Valinda Stewart, in a presentation to the Baptist Sunday School Convention in Dardanelle in July 1891, called for a new Africa, where "ignorance and savageness will have passed away." "In a word," she continued, "point us to the loveliest village that smiles upon a Scottish or New England landscape, compare it with the filthiness and brutality of the African coast, and we tell you our object is to render that African coast as happy and glad as that Scottish or New England village." Black Arkansans clearly wanted to "build up the Continent that has millions of people in gross darkness," as one Conway preacher put it. But as Sister Stewart and others imagined it, the new Africa would look a lot like Europe or America.[27]

Black American rhetoric about Africa in the late 1800s had a decidedly colonial ring to it. African Americans expressed ambivalent attitudes toward American imperialism with the acquisition of territories in the Pacific and Caribbean in the late 1890s. In fact, when the GOP staked out a pro-expansion policy in the 1900 election, some black Republicans shifted support to the Democratic Party, which took an anti-imperialist position under presidential candidate William Jennings Bryan. However, the African Americans who resisted imperialism did so because they did not want to see the expansion of white supremacy, particularly the possibility of Jim Crow–style racism over peoples of color in Cuba, the Philippines, and elsewhere.[28] While they might oppose white expansion abroad, Turner and Ridgel believed the development of Africa by black Americans benefited everyone. Here, again, they hearkened back to Martin Delany's earlier plan for black Americans to emigrate to Africa, develop its resources, and integrate the continent into the capitalist world economy.[29]

Ridgel called for African Americans to come "share in the glories of the rising Negro empire." African Americans, he said, could accomplish wonders in Liberia by developing railroads, steamships, and telegraphs and could bring Liberia into "the galaxy of nations what France, Germany, Portugal, Belgium and other nations are today." Ridgel even advocated sending teams of black explorers into central Africa to map and describe the continent to the world. Echoing Bishop Turner and foreshadowing the rhetoric of Marcus Garvey, Ridgel argued that black businessmen should develop the resources of Africa. As Europeans raced to stake out their African possessions, Bishop Turner said "the civilized negro should do the same and get a little foothold for their posterity." On the eve of the Berlin Congress, Turner had said black Americans should go now, not "wait till the whites go over and civilize Africa, and homestead all the land and take us along to black their boots and groom their horses."[30]

In the view of Bishop Turner, Ridgel, and the Arkansas missionaries, the goal of civilizing Africa was inseparable from the Christianization of the continent. The twin goals of civilizing and Christianizing Africa emerged self-consciously in the first Arkansas emigration movement in the late 1870s. The constitution of the Liberia Exodus Arkansas Colony began with this preamble:

> We feel it no less a duty than a pleasure to give the Gospel, christianity and civilization to our Fatherland. Africa must be redeemed and that by persons of African descent, and there are none so well prepared as are the American negroes. We have in this country been permitted to have the Gospel preached; we have been educated to believe in one Triune God, in the resurrection and ascension of our Lord Jesus Christ, and with all the other ennobling influences by which we have been surrounded, we, as a people, are better adapted to the work and for the work of redeeming Africa, than any other people on the earth; our identity, our interests are one and the same by ties strong and lasting; we are bound together in one interest.

The association's constitution required local chapters to begin each meeting with the singing of the popular mission hymn, the first verse of which went:

> From Greenland's icy mountains,
>   From India's coral strand,
> Where Africa's sunny fountains
>   Roll down their golden sand;
> From many an ancient river,

From many a palmy plain,
They call us to deliver
Their land from error's chain.[31]

The goal of winning the "dark continent" for Christianity figured large in the thinking of black Americans about Africa in the late 1800s. For African Americans, as for Euro-Americans in general in the late 1800s, Christian missions were just part of the package of Western civilization in its quest to control and uplift other parts of the globe.

In their letters to the ACS and discussions of missions, literate black Arkansans showed that they had embraced social Darwinian attitudes to a remarkable extent. Their views of themselves as superior and "civilized" in comparison to a "pagan" African other provided a sense of status they lacked in the American South.[32] The image of the Baptist preacher Judge Thornton emerging from his ship on the second leg of his journey to Africa carrying his battered lantern, which he thought he would need in the "dark continent," symbolizes the attitudes of Arkansas emigrants toward Africa. Thornton and the McCrory emigration club he led had pooled their money to buy the thick two-volume book by explorer Henry Morton Stanley, the cover of which showed a white man being rowed by natives down a river through a dense, dark green jungle. These black Arkansans clearly absorbed some of these prevailing late-Victorian images of Africa. In the Africa of their imaginations, they, not the white explorer, must have worn the pith helmets.

Africa meant many things to the black men and women of Arkansas. It served as a refuge, a foreign destination where they could separate themselves from the United States and the white race. But Africa was not entirely foreign, for African Americans thought of themselves as connected to the continent as an ancestral hearth, as a place that helped form their national identity. While the Africa of their imaginations was a mythical homeland of the past, the present-day Africa appeared as a canvas on which they would paint their portrait of the black nation. The people of Africa, conceived of only in the vaguest sense, were just part of the background scenery, a backdrop against which these black emigrants would fulfill their manifest destiny. While black Arkansans believed that building up Africa, developing it, civilizing it, and Christianizing it would all be good for the continent and its people, the real interest in Africa seemed to be as a promised land where they could come into their own.

8

The Last Voyages

While mission efforts absorbed some of the fascination with Africa in Arkansas after 1892, the dream of permanent emigration to Liberia refused to die among ordinary black farmers. After the American Colonization Society ended its support of emigration, black Arkansans found other ways to get to Africa in the mid-1890s. During the following three years, a few emigrants made their own way across the Atlantic the only way possible: by purchasing their passage aboard commercial sailing vessels. In 1894, several white businessmen formed the International Migration Society (IMS), a private company intended to profit from the desire of black southerners to emigrate to Liberia. Thousands of black people in Arkansas subscribed to the society in hopes that it would take them to Africa, and a number of them would indeed make it to African shores. More than half of all emigrants transported by the IMS hailed from Arkansas. And, in fact, about half of all the known emigrants to Liberia from Arkansas traveled on the two large IMS-sponsored expeditions aboard the ships *Horsa* and *Laurada* in 1895 and 1896. The *Laurada*'s voyage of March 1896 would transport the last boatload of American settlers to the Liberian Republic.

With the implementation of the disfranchisement laws and the rash of brutal lynchings, 1892 had been a debacle in Arkansas for people of color. Conditions hardly improved over the following few years, so black Arkansans still had powerful motivations to leave the state. In January 1893, just as Alfred Ridgel was leaving his church in Brinkley for the African missions, two black men accused of murder were brutally lynched there. A mob of 200 masked men took the accused African Americans from the city jail and hanged them from a shade tree in the jailhouse yard. In April, a crowd of leading citizens strung up a black man from a store sign in downtown Morrilton. And at the train depot in Bearden in Ouachita County the next month, a mob hanged from telegraph poles three black men accused of assaulting a young white business-man.[1] In St. Francis County, a group calling itself Gideon's Band rampaged through black precincts, burning houses, whipping black men, and demanding they move out of the area. White vigilantes similarly tried to oust black residents from their homes in Craighead County in April and Lawrence County in Jan-uary 1894.[2] Fire became a instrument of white terror. In March 1893, Wiley Jones's carhouse in Pine Bluff burned to the ground, destroying seventeen train coaches and doing $18,000 worth of damage. Local blacks boasted that Jones was the only black man in the world to own a railroad line, and they suggested the fire was deliberately set because of race prejudice. Also in March, the large, two-story building of the Arkansas Colored Female College burned to the ground, and it was believed to be arson. Twenty pupils were in the building, and six were injured when they jumped from second-story windows. A black Methodist church in Dexter (Jefferson County) burned in May at the hands of an unknown person.[3]

As the racial violence continued, Henry Turner, bishop of the Eighth Dis-trict of the AME Church, continued to preach the message of African migra-tion. Turner was probably at the peak level of his energy and influence in the mid-1890s. Still the sole black leader of national prominence who believed in the cause of African emigration, he tirelessly promoted it in his magazine, *Voice of Missions*, in letters to black newspapers nationwide, and from the speaker's rostrum. The two big meetings on Africa at Chicago and Cincinnati in 1893 gave this Moses a pulpit from which to preach his call for a mass exodus.

Turner had boasted at Cincinnati that two million black men and women were ready to leave for Africa at any moment and that he could fill 500 steam-ships within a month's time if he had the financial resources to do so.[4] While many delegates and speakers at the meeting disputed that claim, they did not make yearly rounds through rural Arkansas, as did Turner. Would-be emigrants in 1893 and 1894 continued to write to the American Colonization Society, claiming to speak for thousands of people ready to leave for Liberia. They sim-ply refused to believe the society had really ended its emigration work, even though the new secretary, J. Ormond Wilson, wrote back pointed form letters telling applicants to stop depending on "the pecuniary aid of others" in their am-bitions to emigrate. Bishop Turner claimed that he, too, received hundreds and hundreds of letters from black southerners who wished to leave for Liberia.[5]

Bishop Turner and the ACS referred potential emigrants to private shipping companies to arrange the Atlantic crossing. The trip was expensive and required changing ships in a European port, most likely Liverpool, but the ACS estimated that more than a hundred emigrants went at their own expense to Liberia in 1893 and 1894. One desperate Arkansas man, Ned Simure of Pine Bluff, even wrote the president of Liberia, Joseph Cheeseman, in care of the ACS, asking him to use Liberia's ships to come get American emigrants "to come home and build up our own country."[6] By 1893, Turner, like Marcus Garvey would a generation later, began to speak of organizing a new line of steamers, preferably black-owned, to ply the Atlantic directly between the southern United States and Africa for both passenger service and commercial purposes.[7]

Turner's dream came to fruition in January 1894 with the chartering of the International Migration Society, which was owned and led by four white businessmen of Birmingham, Alabama. Bishop Turner and several other black church leaders served on an advisory board for the corporation. The plan was deceptively simple. Applicants for emigration could join the IMS for a one-dollar membership fee and then make monthly payments of a dollar or more until they accumulated forty dollars. For that amount the IMS promised to transport the emigrant and provide three months of support in Liberia. Children would go at half that rate. When a sufficient number of subscribers had reached their full fare, then the society would charter a steamship to take the group to Liberia. A clause in the contract stated that members forfeited their contributions if they failed to keep paying. Evidently the company expected to make most of its money on forfeitures, for the rate of forty dollars for passage to Africa was slightly more than half that charged by other shipping lines that provided no support for emigrants after arrival. The Liberian government, eager for new immigrants, promised to support new settlers with land grants, just as it had done for settlers brought by the ACS. The IMS tried to establish relations with the American Colonization Society, but the ACS steadfastly refused to endorse its work.[8]

The IMS depended heavily on Bishop Turner to promote the new company and its monthly payment plan. He did so vigorously both in his *Voice of Missions* magazine and in his travels. The company eventually claimed to have secured the help of 138 local agents scattered in sixteen states who worked to recruit new members. But clearly Bishop Turner's preaching in Arkansas especially enthused black men and women for the new emigration scheme. In mid-August 1894, Turner went to Pine Bluff for an educational meeting with local AME Church leaders. Turner and the crowd that turned out to hear his speech processed in military fashion to Wiley Jones's grand racetrack on the outskirts of town. Dressed in African vestments, Turner regaled his audience with stories about his travels to Africa and stumped for emigration. Two months later, a correspondent from a rural precinct outside Pine Bluff reported to the *Indianapolis Freeman* that "since Bishop Turner's last lecture in Jefferson County, nearly everyone has taken the African fever. It seems to be somewhat contagious." And Willie Fletcher wrote the ACS from Pine Bluff that after Turner's visit, a crowd of 900 blacks were ready to go to Liberia. "We cant live hear," Fletcher concluded. "Every week som dam Negro kill so we haft to leave."[9]

By November 1894, the IMS arranged for its first party of emigrants to travel to Liberia, as a sort of advance guard that would prepare for the arrival of a larger group to follow. The group of thirteen traveled by commercial steamer to Liverpool and then on to Liberia. Eight of the thirteen settlers came from Arkansas, including the Donald Johnson family of six from Hot Springs and two men from Pine Bluff. The president of the IMS, Jeremiah McMullen, claimed that the Pine Bluff men traveled on behalf of Wiley Jones, one of the wealthiest black men in the South, who planned to sell his racetrack and stables, emigrate to Liberia, and invest his money there, provided his representatives sent back favorable reports about the country.[10] Wiley Jones never emigrated to Liberia, but several of his neighbors were anxious to go, for when the IMS organized its first major expedition a few months later, half of the 200 emigrants came from the Pine Bluff area of Arkansas.

By early 1895, the IMS claimed several thousand members and made plans to settle those who had paid their forty dollars. On Wednesday, 6 March, two train coaches filled with black families left Pine Bluff for Memphis, where they met T. D. Howard, a white officer of the IMS, and other emigrants from Mississippi and Tennessee. Unlike the Johnson family from Hot Springs, who reportedly took between $500 and $1,000 with them in November to Liberia, these emigrants lounging in the Memphis depot, sleeping on floors and benches, showed signs of obvious poverty. Most were ordinary farmers who had sold their possessions to get the seven dollars for train fare from Pine Bluff to Savannah and the forty dollars for the remaining passage to Liberia. A Memphis newspaper reported that when asked why they were leaving, the emigrants explained that "they were tired of a country where the white man is king and the negro the servant. . . . They argue that if the venture proves a failure that their condition could be but little worse."[11] Crowds of curious local black people in Memphis gathered at the depot to watch as the chartered train, draped with banners declaring the passengers were Liberia-bound, rolled out of the station.

The emigrants arrived in Savannah late on the following day only to find neither ship nor accommodations waiting for them. Agent Howard found a vacant warehouse for the passengers, and they settled down to wait for their ship to arrive. Meanwhile, Daniel J. Flummer, who had replaced McMullen as president of the IMS, was in Philadelphia busily searching for a ship to transport the emigrants. He secured a small Danish vessel, the *Horsa*, previously used to carry fruit from the Caribbean. Because the freighter had to be adapted to carry passengers, several more days passed before the ship sailed for Savannah. In the meantime, the IMS paid seventy-five dollars a day to house and feed the party of 200 travelers in Savannah.[12]

About the time the *Horsa* steamed out of Philadelphia, Charles Spencer Smith, the AME Church Sunday School leader, arrived in Savannah to make trouble for the movement. Smith had just returned from an African tour that had converted him into an outspoken opponent of emigration. In an article in the *Christian Recorder*, he had denounced the IMS as an organized swindle, denied that the government of Liberia wanted more settlers, and declared that nearly all of the emigrants who had traveled to Liberia the previous November were sick and suffering from lack of proper shelter. Missionary Ridgel responded from Liberia with stinging criticism of Smith and his "tour" of Africa. He declared that, contrary to Smith's charge, the Donald Johnson family, who alone formed half of the recent arrivals, was in good health, had just moved into a new house, and was placing fifty acres of land under cultivation.[13] While the emigrants waited in Savannah, Smith tried in vain to persuade them to abandon their plans. Ever hopeful, the emigrants refused to listen to him and boarded the *Horsa* when it arrived a few days later. Smith tried to keep the ship from sailing. He went to Savannah customs officials and charged that the *Horsa* was too small, old, and unsanitary to transport safely 200 passengers and 400 pieces of baggage. After a day of inspections, officials found the craft sufficiently seaworthy. They had refused Smith's request to board the ship and examine it for himself, so he hired a white lawyer to go aboard and write an evaluation he could use to counter the official report. When Smith failed on all counts to stop the voyage, he took his complaints to the press.[14]

Despite this reminder of the opposition to the back-to-Africa movement, a festive air pervaded the pier as a crowd of several thousand local people assembled to see off the ship on the afternoon of Tuesday, 19 March. Even white businessmen left their desks in Savannah to watch the ship's departure. Black clergy gave sermons to mark the occasion, a quartet of emigrants sang about their new land, and photographers snapped pictures. Men and women waved their handkerchiefs in the air. Three white officials of the IMS boarded the ship, announcing their intention to help settle the emigrants in Liberia and establish commercial ties there. As the gangplank was pulled up and the ship moved off, the emigrants began singing a song composed for the occasion, which began, "O let me go, I must obey. It is the Master called me; farewell my native land." Then they modulated into the old favorite hymn, "I'm Going Home to Africa's Shores," to which the crowd alongside the wharf joined in on the refrain. Not everyone enjoyed the festivities. Charles Spencer Smith lingered at the port long enough to note that two of the three white IMS officials who left aboard the *Horsa* returned to port with the tug that had pulled the ship out to sea. A Savannah newspaper said of the emigrants the day after: "By this time they are probably wishing themselves back in Arkansas."[15] On the contrary, several days later, passengers on a ship arriving in Savannah that had passed the *Horsa* at sea reported the emigrants up on deck singing "I'm Bound for the Happy Land."[16]

Upon arrival on the shores of Africa, the emigrants endured another round of confusion and disorganization on the part of the IMS. The telegraphed message that supposedly had been sent to announce their arrival had failed to reach its destination, and no one in Liberia was prepared to receive the new settlers. Moreover, the emigrants arrived without most of the three months worth of supplies the IMS had promised. The company had apparently purchased the goods and brought them to the dock in Savannah, but after the passengers and their baggage had been loaded, space remained for only a fraction of the food and supplies. Liberian government officials, working with Edwin Cottingham, the sole IMS officer who made the voyage, found the new settlers temporary accommodations in vacant buildings in the capital. Their baggage was stored, and some immigrants bunked in the American Colonization Society's decaying warehouse on Water Street. Good citizens of Monrovia fed the immigrants from their own tables. Within a month, the new arrivals were settled on their own land in communities outside Monrovia; Cottingham had long since returned to America on the *Horsa*. Bishop Turner arrived on his third visit to Liberia in May and, ever the optimist, declared the immigrants well pleased with their new surroundings.[17]

With all the publicity surrounding the sailing of the *Horsa*, emigration fever spread through Georgia, Alabama, and other southern states, as well as Arkansas. Some black Arkansans remained skeptical about the new company, however. The Reverend Thomas H. Jefferson wrote the ACS that "we can not trust that migration society. We have been humbuged so much." Even though he

Departure of the steamship *Horsa* from Savannah, 19 March 1895. From *Harper's Weekly*, 27 April 1895.

was a preacher himself, Jefferson thought there were too many "high toned colored preachers" in the movement for his liking. Some people wanted to hear the reports from the *Horsa* emigrants before they made up their minds. In Texarkana, a Mayday picnic ended with a public debate on the question, "Is it better for the Negro to go to Africa or to stay in America." After two men for each side spoke, the judges decided in favor of Africa.[18] By November 1895, Bishop Turner had returned to Arkansas to open the three annual AME conferences in the state, in Pine Bluff, Hot Springs, and Little Rock. He wrote the ACS in advance so he could bring information about Liberia to the meetings.[19]

By the end of the year, a sufficient number of subscribers in Arkansas and other states had paid their forty dollars for the IMS to plan another expedition. The company chartered a larger boat, a 1,200-ton steamer named the *Laurada*, and officials chartered a train again from Memphis to Savannah, making advance arrangements this time to accommodate the emigrants in the port city. The sailing of the *Laurada* on 1 March 1896 with 321 passengers marked the last, and one of the largest, mass migration voyage from the United States to Liberia.[20]

The *Laurada* passengers came from nearly every southern state, as well as from Oklahoma and Indian territories, Delaware, New York, and Illinois. Approximately half of the emigrants were from Arkansas. Members of the Arkansas group hailed from various parts of the state but particularly from the communities that had been most on fire for Liberia in past years, Woodruff, Jackson, Conway, Lonoke, Pulaski, St. Francis, Lee, and Ouachita Counties. The largest portion of emigrants came from the Forrest City and Madison communities of St. Francis County. In addition, two families from New York City were reported to have been part of the group of Arkansas emigrants stranded there in 1892.[21]

An even larger number of emigrants that left St. Francis County for Liberia never made it to Savannah. On the afternoon of 13 January 1896, the railroad depot in Forrest City looked like a camp meeting, as more than a hundred black men, women, and children arrived to buy tickets for Savannah. The emigrants brought with them a total of eighty-seven pieces of baggage, fourteen large boxes, five dogs, and a young hog. When a local white newspaper reporter asked them for information and their names, he "was silenced by a look."[22] The group got as far east as Birmingham, Alabama. Perhaps the group descended on the IMS headquarters to beg for transportation, as had the Arkansas refugees who went to New York in 1880 and 1892. Or possibly desperate black folks had been duped again. Reports suggested that scam artists once again had been working in the Forrest City area, promising that emigrants could get passage for a nine-dollar payment, with government money paying for the rest, or that emigrants could pay the $41 passage fee over ten years after they arrived in Liberia.[23] Whatever the reason, these St. Francis County emigrants became stranded in Birmingham. By March, a labor agent brought twenty of the Arkansas families back to work on the Tate brothers' plantation south of Memphis and the Hale plantation near Osceola, Arkansas.[24]

Despite the misfortune of these would-be African settlers, another group of IMS-approved and apparently paid-up emigrants set out from Forrest City on Sunday, 23 February. Before their departure, 450 people worshiped in a poignant good-bye service at the Colored First Baptist Church. The town's black newspaper reported: "During the whole service you could see tears flowing down the cheeks of someone. Now and then the people became so affected that they would scream and cry out so loud that the speakers would have to beg them to be quiet so that might be heard." So many clergymen wished to speak that each minister was limited to a six-minute oration. After the service, more than 600 black and many white people showed up at the train platform to see off the emigrants. The train took them to Memphis, where they held a prayer meeting in the station, slept overnight, and caught the chartered train the next morning for Savannah.[25]

On Sunday morning, a week after the Forrest City emigrants left home, a grand dockside send-off ceremony in Savannah took place. By seven in the morning, the emigrants and their baggage were aboard the *Laurada* and 5,000 people had arrived for singing, preaching, and farewells. Bishop Turner, who had come up from Atlanta for the occasion, enthused the crowd for more than an hour with the wonders of Liberia to frequent shouts of "Amen" and "Hallelujah." He repeated his views about the divine plan for African slaves to come to America so they could be Christianized and civilized and then enabled to take these gifts back to mother Africa. The bishop concluded by lifting eyes and hands heavenward and praying God's blessings on these pilgrims, "that they might be the pioneers and heroes of a nation—a nation where a dark skin would not be a stigma, but a recommendation." President Flummer and other white IMS officials also spoke, but surely they were a let down after the charismatic Turner. The crowd at the pier, by this time swelling to an estimated 10,000 to 15,000 people, and the emigrants on deck sang together "I Am Going Home to Part No More." Finally, at 1:25 P.M., as old men threw their hats into the air and hurrahed and old women tore off their aprons and waved them above their heads, the *Laurada* moved out to sea.[26]

The festive atmosphere lasted on the ship through most of the three-week journey. William K. Roberts, a white writer and photographer traveling with the emigrants, reported that older men and women passed their time singing, preaching, and praying. Younger ones courted, beat drums, played an accordion, laughed and joked, and marveled at the whales, porpoises, flying fish, and

Departure of the steamship *Laurada* from Savannah, 1 March 1896. From *Illustrated American Magazine*, 21 March 1896.

sea birds that they saw from deck. Evenings were spent singing spiritual songs; "Sunday Morning Band," "Job Says I Was Here," and "De Bells Done Rung and de Angels Done Sung" appeared to be the favorites. Three people died during the voyage, two infants and one elderly man. However, two babies were born in the crossing so that the ship arrived in Africa just one person short of the number that left the United States. When, on the afternoon of 23 March, the emigrants caught their first glimpse of Monrovia, many shouted and clapped with delight. African canoes swarmed around the big steamer as it lay anchor, and passengers threw coins from the deck, which Kru boys dived into the water to retrieve. Slowly and laboriously small surf boats brought passengers in groups to the shore, and most were housed temporarily in the old ACS warehouse. Missionary Alfred Ridgel, who had met the ship when it arrived, addressed the group at a meeting a few days later. He recognized several of the nearly one hundred St. Francis County emigrants from six years before, when he served as the AME preacher in Forrest City. Some of the Arkansas passengers were welcomed by family and friends who had emigrated earlier. The Coopers of Forrest City were kin to the Parkers, who had emigrated sixteen years before and were living in Brewerville. The *Laurada* passengers from Conway County—the Holman, Jenkins, and Shaver families—were all related to the Jenkins family, which had emigrated in 1891. During the following month, the settlers dispersed to various communities to receive their free land.[27]

Funeral for a passenger on the *Laurada*, 1896. Photo by William K. Roberts.

The departure of the *Laurada*, with all its fanfare, appeared to be a beginning when it was really an end. Although the IMS talked of further voyages, it never managed to organize any more. President Flummer had traveled on the *Laurada* and met with Liberian officials to discuss future expeditions and commerce between the United States and West Africa, and William Roberts toured and photographed the countryside. Upon their return to America, both men wrote pamphlets promoting Liberia, which the company distributed as recruiting material. On several occasions over the next few years, the IMS announced upcoming voyages, but the dates always came and went and no ship sailed. The company had little motive to charter ships, for the *Horsa* and *Laurada* ventures most certainly lost money, since the hope for profit lay in forfeited subscriptions. But with no ships sailing, people were reluctant to send in their monthly payments.[28]

In addition to a lack of ships, aspiring emigrants faced a scarcity of money. Even though the ACS had virtually ceased its emigration effort by the late 1890s, black farmers from Arkansas and elsewhere continued to write the society asking for assistance. They remembered the ACS sending emigrants for nothing or for whatever they could afford to contribute toward their passage. Unlike former ACS secretary William Coppinger, who had genuine sympathy for the difficult circumstances of the many black southerners who wished to emigrate, J. Ormond Wilson, the secretary in the ACS's last years, expressed an attitude

Laurada passengers step onto African soil, 1896. Photo by William K. Roberts.

of arrogant disdain. Wilson repeatedly responded to the many who still asked the ACS for assistance that they should stop begging and take responsibility for their own lives. With the ACS turning a cold shoulder, the IMS provided the only hope for would-be emigrants. And with the economic depression of the 1890s deepening in 1897 and cotton prices continuing to drop, few could pay in advance the $200 necessary to secure African passage for the average farm family of five. If emigrants were required to pay $41 per person to leave America, said A. B. Berry, a black farmer from Prairie County, "they will be here for ever and 2 or 3 days afterward." They could only afford to pay $20 for an entire family, Berry concluded. In late 1896, in an attempt to attract more subscribers, the IMS dropped its rate to $32 for adult passage with no promise of three-months' rations for new emigrants.[29]

A variety of other factors worked against the movement as well. Heightened political tension in American coastal waters, which soon culminated in the Spanish-American War in 1898, may have scared away some potential emigrants. In fact, when the *Laurada* sailed into Savannah to pick up the departing settlers in 1896, its previous captain sat in jail in Charleston under charges of smuggling guerrilla soldiers into Cuba. Shortly thereafter, the captain of the *Horsa* was charged with running guns to Cuba in the same holds that had transported emigrants the year before. This bad publicity for ships with names now associated with African emigration combined with the return of some unhappy emigrants from both the *Horsa* and *Laurada* expeditions to temper enthusiasm for emigration. White as well as black newspapers gave detailed coverage of the sickness and suffering of the emigrants in Liberia, giving the impression that the other settlers would return too if they had the chance. The IMS finally went under sometime in 1900.[30]

The New Orleans race riot of July of that year further damaged the emigration movement. When Robert Charles, a New Orleans agent of the IMS and salesman for Bishop Turner's *Voice of Missions*, pulled a gun and fired at a white policeman who harassed him for loitering in a residential neighborhood, the incident ignited a week of violence. An angry white mob marched through black neighborhoods searching for Charles and terrorized any black person they found on the way. At Charles's apartment, police and newspaper reporters found circulars of the IMS, pamphlets about Liberia, and copies of the *Voice of Missions*, which they declared to be evidence of his incendiary race hatred. Police finally shot and killed Charles, but not before he had killed a total of seven white people—four of them police officers—and wounded no fewer than twenty others. Before peace returned, the mob burned black homes and schools, and police arrested ten black men and women as accessories to Charles's crime. The episode made the Liberia emigration movement appear more threatening to white southerners and personally dangerous for blacks.[31]

By 1900, Booker T. Washington, a vocal opponent of emigration, had emerged as the indisputable leader of the black community. In a speech opening the new century, on 1 January 1900, Washington lambasted the Liberian emigration movement as a failure. Turner, whose influence was waning, nonetheless steadfastly preached the cause of African emigration until his death in 1915. Whom should we obey, asked an editor of a black Arkansas newspaper, the *Helena Reporter*? "'Stay here,' says Booker T. Washington, while Bishop Turner says, 'We must go to Africa.'" In the early 1900s, Bishop Turner, and even Daniel Flummer, tried to establish new emigration societies, steamship companies, conventions, and assorted schemes, but they all failed to send one emigrant to Africa.[32]

In Arkansas, interest in emigration declined after the *Laurada*'s 1896 voyage, but it refused to die. After 1896, Bishop Turner was transferred to the Georgia-Alabama district of the AME Church and he no longer made the yearly trips to Arkansas. The ACS continued to receive plaintive letters from black Arkansans wanting assistance with African emigration. Some writers expressed the desire to join their families who had emigrated earlier. In 1903, William Dickerson, a student at Philander Smith College, wanted the society to send him to Liberia as it had the Sherrill party of missionaries from the college in 1898; he, too, wanted to become "a missionary to the people of my fatherland." But most people dreamed the typical emigrant's dream, of a place offering freedom and prosperity lacking at home. When times were most difficult, Liberia remained a symbol of hope for a better life in this world rather than the next. As one black man in Beebe said in 1902, echoing letters from a decade before, "We are Suffering here and oppressed . . . and we are convinced that the best way to remedy our condition is to go to Liberia." Nearly all such requests to the ACS were in vain. But in January 1905, the Reverend John Hamilton Reed, his wife, Marguerite, and children, Florence and Walter, left Little Rock for mission work in Liberia. They were some of the last travelers ever assisted by the American Colonization Society.[33]

9

In Liberia

As immigrant ships arrived in Monrovia in the late 1800s, passengers invariably crowded on deck to glimpse the church steeples peeking through the palm trees and the gleaming zinc roofs of the impressive buildings that lined the main streets of the capital. At first glance, Liberia seemed everything immigrants' dreams were made of—civilization with a tropical backdrop. After they landed, however, a different Liberian reality set in. Upon closer inspection, the shining zinc roofs covered structures often crumbling with mold and decay. While the elevated Atlantic side of Monrovia commanded fine views and fresh sea breezes, the town sloped downward on its backside to a stagnant backwater, fetid with rot, mosquitoes, and fever. This swampy side of Monrovia was rimmed not with fine dwellings of brick or wood but with African huts of thatch and bamboo. Within a few weeks of their arrival, almost all immigrants came down with the chills and fever of malaria. Liberia's new settlers asked themselves the questions this chapter examines: was it worth it? Did they make the right choice?

The Arkansas settlers of the late 1800s arrived at a time when the continent of Africa and the Liberian Republic were experiencing great change. Western colonial powers were gobbling up great chunks of Africa in the 1880s and 1890s, and Europeans salivated from all directions over the territory claimed by this small republic with its historic ties to the United States. The settler elite who governed Liberia tried to shore up the country politically and economically into a more viable entity. Despite the enormous symbolic significance of the black Republic, Liberia in reality was a poor, undeveloped, and vulnerable land. The

British government pressured Liberia into signing a treaty in 1885 giving over territory west of the Mano River to augment the British colony of Sierra Leone. A few years later, the French encroached in the east from their colony in the Ivory Coast. By a treaty signed in 1892 in Paris, Liberia surrendered to France a fifty-mile strip of its coast between the San Pedro and Cavalla Rivers. Early in the next century, the French would annex even more of the Liberian hinterland neighboring their possessions in Ivory Coast and Guinea. Europeans demanded that Liberia observe the agreements made at the Berlin Congress of 1884 and 1885 that required countries colonizing Africa actually to control and administer their territories, not simply draw boundaries on a map. The Liberian government countered that it had neither participated in the Berlin meeting nor signed its agreements. But the areas claimed by Liberia that lacked American-Liberian settlement remained vulnerable nonetheless.[1]

The Liberian government only truly controlled the 200-mile coastal strip between Sierra Leone and the Ivory Coast. In this lowland ribbon of mangrove marshes, scrub forest, and cleared land, the scattered settler communities and African villages extended only about thirty miles into the interior before meeting a dense rainforest that was entirely the domain of indigenous people. The lush vegetation covered steep elevations that rose until joining the African plateau near the border with French Guinea, where the forest began to thin. By the 1890s, fewer than 20,000 settlers from America and recaptured returned slaves and descendants of both groups lived in the coastal communities with native Liberians who had acquired "civilization." But they were also in close proximity to a much larger group of indigenous people who lived in traditional ways. The total population in the area claimed by Liberia may have surpassed one million. The government of Liberia thus always wished for continued American emigration to replenish the coastal settlements and so it could maintain control of the country. In the latter part of the century, the government promoted settlement farther away from the coast, on higher ground believed to be healthier, and thus extending the administrative zone to a wider area. Several settlements up the St. Paul River from Monrovia took western-style civilization some thirty miles into the interior, at which point rapids made farther water travel upriver impossible.[2]

While the earlier settlement of black Americans in Liberia had concentrated in Monrovia and a few other market towns, new arrivals in the late 1800s generally dispersed onto the land to pursue farming. By the 1880s, it appeared that the struggling republic had finally found a cash crop, a tropical product in great demand around the world—coffee. New settlers were planting their immi-

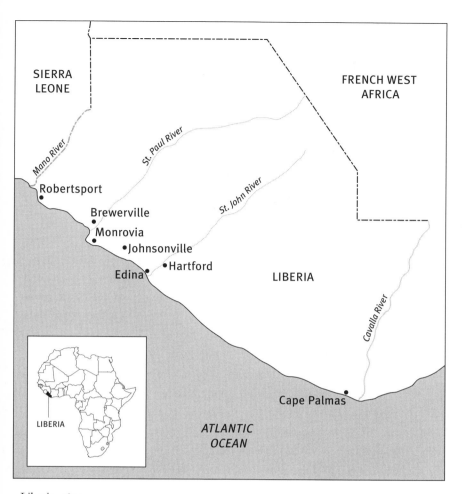

Liberia, 1895

grant land allotments with coffee trees, and some of the elite in Monrovia even began to acquire farms and go into large-scale production. Some contemporaries complained that American Liberians were still buying too much of their food from European traders instead of consuming the sustenance that grew naturally in West Africa. Even imported Indian rice largely had elbowed out African-grown rice in Monrovia's markets.[3] Small trading companies from England, Holland, and Germany had moved into Monrovia and other port cities and were trading directly with Kru, Vai, Dey, and other coastal peoples for coffee, palm oil and fiber, camwood, and other products. In return, native Africans began to order cloth and other manufactured goods directly from London, Liverpool, and Hamburg instead of buying it in Monrovia. American

Liberian businessmen began to lose their role as middlemen in the tropical trade. Lacking their own currency, Liberians used the British pound as a medium of exchange well into the twentieth century, when the American dollar replaced pound sterling.[4]

Despite the loss of their commercial monopoly, the American Liberian elite still ruled from Monrovia in the late 1800s. Most of the leading families had arrived before the American Civil War, and they formed an oligarchy closely linked by social and marriage ties. Almost every other man in Monrovia held some kind of political office, charged Charles H. J. Taylor, former American minister to Liberia. The president's cabinet included a secretary of the treasury and a secretary of the navy, even though the country had no currency or working ships. The postmaster general ruled over the nation's four post offices.[5] The capital, Monrovia, still made an impressive sight for visitors and new immigrants. During his visit to the city in 1894, Charles S. Smith counted 54 brick and 142 wooden houses, 35 shops, and a population of around 1,200. Broad thoroughfares separated the buildings, but, unlike in America, the streets grew with grass and weeds since there were no beasts of burden or wagons to traverse the city. Except for this feature and the tropical vegetation, downtown Monrovia looked much like any small southern American town.[6]

When the first group of Arkansas immigrants arrived in 1879, their leader, Dr. Anthony L. Stanford, settled in Monrovia and mingled with the Liberian elite. A physician with some experience in politics, Stanford quickly acquired the reputation as one of Monrovia's leading public figures. Although he, his wife, and son arrived without money in 1879, the ACS retained him to provide medical care to the Arkansas immigrants in 1879 and again for the other new arrivals of the early 1880s. He traveled out to rural settlements to tend to medical needs of immigrants while he maintained his own practice and drug shop in town. The Monrovia newspaper called Stanford the leading physician in the city, reporting as breaking news in 1881 that he removed a sixteen-foot tapeworm from a local woman. The ACS agent in Monrovia, C. T. O. King, however, thought Stanford was more gifted in oration than medicine and asked the society to send Liberia a "real physician."[7] In January 1880, less than a year after his arrival, Stanford addressed a joint session of the Liberian Senate and House of Representatives, and he later gave an entertaining public speech to a large audience on the power and influence of women in forming and shaping the character of men. In the fall of 1881, Stanford helped found a company in Monrovia, the Liberia Interior Association, to promote development of transportation and trade into the interior of the country. Stanford was elected pres-

Ashmun Street, Monrovia, Liberia, ca. 1892. Courtesy Library of Congress.

ident, and the company began selling ten thousand stock shares at five dollars each. No evidence suggests that the company ever accomplished anything, however. And the following year, the president of Liberia, Anthony W. Gardiner, appointed Stanford as a judge to the Court of Quarter Sessions, a position he held until his death in 1883.[8] After Stanford's death, the ACS continued to pay his wife, Susan, to treat immigrants using her husband's drugs and methods. Stanford's son, Willie Francis Stanford, was still living in Monrovia in 1891, and he visited Henry Turner when the bishop made his first African tour. Turner said the younger Stanford had grown to be "an industrious and bright young man."[9]

The town-dwelling Stanford family provided a contrast to the typical Arkansas immigrant. A class barrier separated the Liberian elite, who had arrived earlier in the century and were often of free black background, from the new arrivals of the late 1800s, who were mostly poor farmers from the rural American South. Amanda Smith, a black American missionary who spent most of the 1880s in Liberia, remarked that the newer immigrants did not mix with the established Liberian society any more than Italian, Irish, or Jewish immigrants in America found companionship with the native born.[10]

Daniel Warner, the ACS agent in Liberia at the time, and the Liberian government settled all but one of the first Arkansas immigrants on farmland in Brewerville, a new township being developed about ten miles up the St. Paul River from Monrovia. Moses L. Johnson of Poplar Grove, who insisted he had not signed on for any particular destination, against all advice decided to settle on the Poor River. Arriving there in a hired boat, he nearly killed himself and his whole family when he ordered the native Kru men to land the craft through a high surf despite their warnings of danger. The big waves swept over the small boat, washing Johnson and his whole family, including the baby born during the Atlantic crossing, into the river. Warner groused to Coppinger that stubborn Johnson "thinks he knows better to manage in Liberia than Liberians." After a few months there, the Johnsons were sick and destitute and begging for assistance from the ACS. The family eventually relocated to Brewerville, joining the rest of the farm families from Arkansas.[11]

The "Arkansas refugees," who had been stranded for weeks in New York City, also settled in Brewerville upon their arrival in Liberia in June 1880. In many ways, Brewerville was an ideal location for the new settlers. Founded in 1870 as an attempt to move settlers farther inland, Brewerville had become a thriving settlement by the end of the decade. Two miles back from the mangrove swamps surrounding the St. Paul River, Brewerville enjoyed slightly higher elevation and dryer productive land. By the time the Arkansas immigrants arrived, Brewerville already had a school, several churches, and three stores, which used coffee as currency.[12] The ACS had paid for the construction of several temporary cottages to accommodate new immigrants until they could build their own houses. Although crude and crowded, the shelters kept new settlers out of the incessant rain—both the 1879 and 1880 parties arrived in the rainy season—as they set about clearing their land and planting the first crops. The allotments for new settlers, however, lay on the edge of the settled area, far from the stores, churches, and school. Also, a shortage of timber in the area forced settlers to travel substantial distances to get wood for the construction of their homes.[13]

A few months after the Arkansas refugees had settled in Brewerville, Mrs. Mary Garnet Barboza, who had tended to their needs in New York, arrived in Liberia, with her husband and four children, to open a school for girls. The citizens of Monrovia tried to convince her to establish the school there, but instead she joined her Arkansas refugees in Brewerville. The daughter of elderly black leader Henry Highland Garnet, Barboza came to Liberia under an appointment of the Ladies Board of Missions of the Presbyterian Church. Her father followed her soon afterward, accepting the appointment as U.S. minister to Liberia. Garnet never recovered from his first bout of malarial fever, and he died and was buried in Palm Grove Cemetery in Monrovia. Barboza's school educated several daughters of the Arkansas immigrants. Other children attended the town school, whose teacher was paid by the ACS. The Arkansas refugees welcomed Barboza in January 1881 with a special worship service at Brewerville's Baptist Church, and the leader of their group, Richard Newton, declared the settlers' satisfaction with their new land, exclaiming he "would not go back to America to live for this house full of gold."[14] Professor Edward Blyden, who had lectured the Arkansas refugees about the attractions of Liberia when they were in New York, visited them in Brewerville less than a year after their arrival. He boasted about the success of the new immigrants and said some had pushed ahead of the old settlers there. The seven Arkansas immigrants who came in 1882 and 1883 joined the settlers in Brewerville.[15]

The other Arkansas arrivals, who came later in the 1880s, were settled much farther away from the capital. By 1887, the ACS had determined to strengthen the seacoast settlements north and south of Monrovia. The immigrant party of thirty-eight that arrived later that year, including Richard and Lucinda Bankhead and their six children from Helena, received land at Robertsport, in Cape Mount County, a remote location some fifty miles up the coast from Monrovia. A surveyor from the capital laid off their immigrant allotments on a high promontory overlooking the Atlantic Ocean. The settlement was adjacent to a village of recaptured slaves called Congo Town, and the ACS hired local men to help the surveyor cut the plot lines. The ACS even sent a teacher, Miss E. C. A. Payne, armed with a dozen spelling books, history texts, and second-through-fifth-grade readers, to open a one-room school for the settlers' children. Benjamin K. McKeever, who had come from Arkansas in 1879 and settled in Brewerville, joined the new party of immigrants in Robertsport. Perhaps he knew the Bankheads from years before in Phillips County.[16]

In May 1889, the next group of Arkansas immigrants arrived. John and Elissa Johnson and their six children from Conway were settled on the Liberian coast fifty miles south of Monrovia in Bassa County, where the mighty St. John River flows into the Atlantic. Two American Liberian settlements, Hartford and Fortsville, had been established a few miles inland about at the point where the falls set in. American Liberians in the area, glad to have new settlers, gave the new arrivals a cordial welcome. The new immigrants quickly set about collecting materials to build their homes and clearing land to plant coffee.[17]

The ACS decided to settle its last immigrants of the early 1890s in a new township known as Johnsonville, some twenty miles up the Mersurrado River from Monrovia. The Kru people lived in the area, with a few American Liberians nearby in the small community of Barnersville. The ACS hired a surveyor to lay out Johnsonville, named for Liberia's then-president Hilary Johnson, into the twenty-five-acre allotments for immigrant families, most of whom hailed from Arkansas's Conway and Pulaski Counties. The settlements commanded a beautiful landscape of rolling hills and fertile soil. Except for the mountain ridges and a few swampy areas, African inhabitants had years before cleared the high forest through shifting agricultural cultivation. A dense shrubbery of approximately five-years' growth covered the ground, broken by occasional clearings where Kru men and women had grown cassava and rice. The only access to Johnsonville was by canoe up the Mersurrado River.[18]

The new immigrants to the Johnsonville area in 1891 and 1892 immediately set about clearing their land, planting coffee and food crops, and building temporary shelters. Some educated their children at home; others attended the free school in neighboring Barnersville. Narcissie Moore, the single mother who brought her four children to Liberia in 1891, started a Baptist church in her home. She named it the Morning Star Baptist Church, after her home church back in Argenta (now North Little Rock), Arkansas. Another of the Argenta immigrants, Robert Lindsey, became the first pastor of the new church, which still meets today on the main street in Johnsonville. Within a few years, members had erected a small building with zinc siding and a plank floor. Johnsonville soon had two more churches and sturdy farmhouses, all surrounded by fields of coffee and rice. A mission school opened for the children of Johnsonville a few years later.[19] About a third of the *Horsa* passengers of 1895 settled in Johnsonville, with a third each going to Brewerville and neighboring Royesville. The *Laurada* passengers who came the next year dispersed throughout Liberia, but a few of them joined friends and family from Arkansas in Johnsonville.[20]

The experience of these immigrant farmers from Arkansas who arrived over a seventeen-year period followed similar patterns. The first year in their new country always proved the most difficult for the new settlers. The six months of assistance provided by the ACS or the International Migration Society proved invaluable for the new immigrants struggling though the most difficult phase. The ACS expeditions brought barrels of beef, pork, flour, cornmeal, and dried beans; cases of cheese, butter, and lard; and bags of Asian-grown rice. The Liberia-based ACS agent also doled out to settlers small amounts of sugar, salt, soda, tea, coffee, vinegar, and tobacco. The immigrants even received farm tools, such as shovels, axes, hatchets, hoes, and rakes, and cooking utensils, such as teapots, pans, and bowls.[21] The ACS agent kept supplies in the society's crumbling warehouse on Water Street in Monrovia and occasionally distributed additional rations in cases of dire need. One *Laurada* passenger bragged in a letter back home that his rations were so generous that some of his meal and

Road leading to the Morning Star Baptist Church, Johnsonville, Liberia, in 1998.
Photo by author.

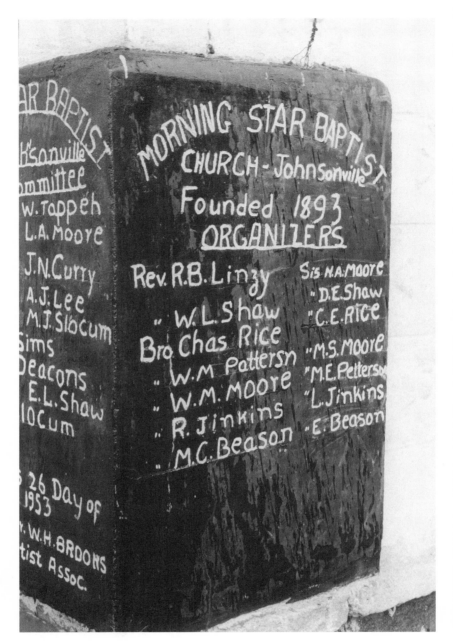

Cornerstone of the Morning Star Baptist Church, Johnsonville, Liberia. Photo by author.

The American Colonization Society's warehouse on Water Street, Monrovia, Liberia, ca. 1892. Courtesy Library of Congress.

flour had soured before he could use it and that he sold nearly ten dollars worth of the American food because his family soon had Liberian edibles in such abundance.[22]

While subsisting on this imported food, the settlers had to clear their land quickly and begin planting food crops that could bring a harvest by the time the rations ran out. If immigrants arrived during the rainy season, they had to slog through days of incessant rain in order to clear and plant. Settlers in Johnsonville helped each other in teams with the laborious task of cutting the tropical brush with hatchets and machetes.[23] They left the cut vegetation to dry and then burned the land to remove the dead brush and stumps. New settlers planted sweet potatoes, corn, melons, and other vegetables, often from seed they brought from America. But the ACS agent and established settlers encouraged the newcomers also to plant African crops of cassava, eddoes, rice, bananas, and plantains.[24] In Johnsonville, for example, Kru villagers living nearby taught the new settlers how to plant, harvest, and cook root vegetables such as the eddo and cassava, which has both an inner and outer peel.[25] Surely one of the major adjustments to life in Liberia must have been the shift from the American South's corn- and wheat-based diet (cornbread, hominy, grits, biscuits, and so forth) to meals centered around rice and starchy tropical tubers. Instead of turnip, mustard, and collard greens, the settlers began to eat the leaves of the cassava, sweet potato, and other plants. When Julius Stevens, the new ACS agent, arrived in Liberia in 1893, he found the Johnsonville settlers already eating much the same food as native Africans. In the home of Samuel David, formerly of Argenta, Stevens was served dumboy (a starchy paste of pounded cassava) with a chicken soup rich with palm oil. The meal also included chicken gravy, smothered chicken, rice, cassava, and sweet potatoes. Agent Stevens observed that banana trees grew in the yard and that water came from a clear running stream nearby.[26]

Settlers regularly supplemented their largely carbohydrate diet with animal protein. Besides chickens, they had ducks, turkeys, geese, pigs, and sheep. The settlers by the sea at Robertsport fished for mackerel in the bay and gathered oysters from nearby streams. In Johnsonville, on the edge of the high forest, settlers hunted wild game both for sport and for meat. Descendants of the Arkansas immigrants today explain that the original settlers were attracted to the area partly because of the opportunities for hunting. They brought their Winchester rifles and double-barrel shotguns with them and hunted for deer, bush goat, bush cow (a more aggressive animal than that American settlers were familiar with), monkeys, and leopards. Some immigrants even sold or traded meat to live.[27]

Immigrants also had to construct some form of shelter. The settlers at Brewerville in 1880 moved into crowded temporary cottages while they built their own homes. Several passengers from the *Horsa* and the *Laurada* moved into the homes of established settlers while they built their own dwellings. But many of the Arkansas settlers, such as the groups who settled in Johnsonville in 1891 and 1892, had to build their own temporary huts before they could contemplate more permanent structures. For their first homes they built small dwellings of palm thatch and sticks, much like those inhabited by African people and like many one can see in Liberia today. The settlers might paste the sticks together with a mortar of mud. Johnsonville settler Narcissie Moore hung blankets on the stick walls to keep out the drafts.[28] Within a year or two, the immigrants usually constructed a wood frame house with plank floors. In Brewerville, settlers cut black gum timber from the swamps, used pepperwood poles for rafters, and made bamboo mats for ceilings. The Arkansas immigrants in Johnsonville had brought with them a six-foot saw, so they felled larger trees to make chink-and-groove log homes. Others built substantial southern-style frame houses, sometimes two stories high with five and six rooms. Exterior walls and

A stick-and-thatch structure in Liberia, 1998. Photo by author.

ceilings were covered with shingles to keep out the rain; when settlers could afford it, they chose pieces of zinc siding instead. Immigrants usually built their houses on stone pillars about four feet off the ground, with stone steps leading up to the front door. They used the open crawl space underneath the floor for cooking and storing wood. After several years, the farmstead was complete: typically a large house with a yard filled with food trees—papaya, mango, guava, breadfruit, banana, avocado, and plantain. Soap trees, yielding a soaplike substance used for cleaning, were planted on the corners of property to mark boundaries. Tropical flowers such as bougainvillea and hibiscus and orange-red flame trees grew in the gardens year-round.[29]

Besides food and shelter, the greatest concern for new immigrants became their health. For any new arrivals in tropical West Africa from North America or Europe the most challenging disease clearly was malaria, or what westerners referred to as African fever. A parasitic disease, malaria in West Africa usually occurs in two forms, *Plasmodium malariae*, a chronic version of the disease, which brings fever, chills, and extreme weakness, and a more severe variety, *Plasmodium falciparum*, which produces the same symptoms but can quickly lead to death. Contrary to many perceptions, African Americans whose ancestors had left Africa centuries before had little more resistance to the malarial strains of West Africa than did white Americans or Europeans. The sickle cell trait, now known to provide some immunity to *falciparum*, occurs only in a small percent-

A settler house in Liberia, ca. 1892. Courtesy Library of Congress.

age of the African American population. *Falciparum*, as well as the less deadly form of malaria, existed in the southern United States well into the twentieth century. Coming from the lowland regions of the state, the Arkansas emigrants, like most adult southerners, would have had some resistance to the disease. While this resistance might provide some protection from the American strains of malaria, immigrants were relatively defenseless against the strains of *falciparum* or *malariae* they encountered in Liberia.[30]

Within a month of their arrival, immigrants usually came down with African fever, which might last for weeks and return periodically thereafter. In fact, everyone expected to undergo this "seasoning" or acclimating experience. Chances of a debilitating fever increased for immigrants who arrived right before or during the rainy season of May through November. After repeated infections with malaria, surviving immigrants gradually acquired some measure of resistance, but it was never a total immunity. Studies of mortality rates among the American immigrants to Liberia in the early nineteenth century suggest that the first year was devastating to health of the newcomers. One historian has estimated that 22 percent of American immigrants died within their first year in Liberia, while another suggests that 43 percent of immigrant deaths took place before the first anniversary of arrival. If settlers survived the first year, they had a much better chance for a normal life span thereafter.[31]

Mortality rates for immigrants in the 1880s and 1890s may have improved somewhat, although they were still alarmingly high. Although the anecdotal evidence varies considerably, clearly some newcomers in all the parties of Arkansas immigrants from 1879 to 1896 died of fever soon after arrival. In 1882, Dr. Anthony Stanford claimed that 195 of the immigrants at Brewerville under his care had survived acclimating fevers and thirteen had died. Stanford was able to give his patients quinine and other imported medications, and, of course, he had motivation to exaggerate his success to keep his employment. The immigrants in Johnsonville and elsewhere lacked such medical attention, although they learned from African neighbors how to make teas from local plants that provided some relief. Reliable reports in 1895 suggested that eighteen of the two hundred *Horsa* emigrants had died within their first seven months in Liberia.[32]

Settlers suffered with other diseases besides malaria, such as tuberculosis and whooping cough. They called one ailment that particularly plagued and puzzled them "eating ulcers," open sores, often on legs or feet, that grew to the size of silver dollars and refused to heal.[33] Probably caused by some type of burrowing parasite, the affliction provided just one more reminder of how different was the physical environment from their American homeland.

Beyond activities that insured basic physical survival, the new settlers' hope for a prosperous future lay in planting coffee, Liberia's cash crop in the late 1800s. The first American settlers in 1822 found coffee growing wild in the forests, and they planted it in their own gardens. In 1863, Edward S. Morris, a Philadelphia businessman and strong supporter of the ACS, came to Liberia to encourage the growth and export of coffee to Europe and America. He developed a machine to hull and clean the Liberian coffee bean and imported coffee from the republic himself for resale until his death in the late 1880s. The Liberian variety of coffee was a sturdy tree, with shiny green leaves that produced a robust berry that sold well on the world market. At the World's Columbian Exposition in Chicago in 1893, the Liberian bean beat out coffee from thirteen other countries in strength. With coffee prices rising rapidly in the 1880s and early 1890s, the new settlers in Liberia seemed to have a golden opportunity.[34]

As soon as they cleared their land and planted some food crops, the Arkansas immigrants purchased coffee scions (seedlings), priced at a dollar for a hundred, and planted their money crop. The scions were rooted, preferably in the rainy season, some ten feet apart in rows. David Rivers, one of the emigrants from Conway County to Johnsonville in 1892, had set out 5,000 coffee seedlings within four months of his arrival in Liberia. Farmers then needed simply to hoe the ground or chop grass with a machete once or twice a year to keep down the growth while the trees matured. Some growers fertilized the trees by distributing the soil from termite (Liberians called them bug-a-bug) hills, which could rise higher than a man's head. Unlike their old cash crop, cotton, coffee trees yielded no berries for at least three years and would not bring a full crop until seven years of maturity. Old trees brought the best-quality berries, and the life span of a coffee tree could easily exceed that of a human being. Growing coffee thus meant an investment for the future.[35]

Some of the first Arkansas immigrants to Brewerville in 1879 and 1880 became quite prosperous from coffee growing, for their trees matured just as coffee prices appreciated significantly in the late 1880s. Elijah Parker and Jack Allen, two of the 1880 immigrants from Phillips County, reported to William Coppinger a decade later that the Arkansas refugees were well satisfied with their land and had great prospects for the future with their coffee. He claimed they had 40,000 trees and expected to gather 25,000 pounds of coffee. William Lucas, an Arkansas emigrant of 1879, had become one of the wealthiest men in Brewerville.[36]

For the new settlers of the 1890s, coffee fortunes reversed dramatically. Just as the Arkansas immigrants were arriving in the greatest numbers in the early and mid-1890s, coffee prices on the Monrovia market peaked at eighteen cents per pound. By one estimate, Liberian farmers had planted fifteen million trees on some 50,000 acres by 1895, most of them not yet producing berries. By the time the trees came into full production in the late 1890s, the great fall in world coffee prices had begun. Producers in Brazil largely took control of the American coffee market, and enormous quantities of cheap Brazilian coffee traveled around the world. By the later 1890s, Brazil alone often sold four-fifths of the world's coffee. The price per pound of coffee in Liberia had fallen to six cents in 1898, and buyers in Liverpool and Hamburg were telling Liberian growers that it would not even pay to pick their berries.[37] Coffee prices remained low into the twentieth century. While some immigrants, such as John Dixon of Brewerville (formerly of Carlisle, Arkansas), grew ginger for export, it was not until the arrival of the Firestone Company in the 1920s that a new cash crop, rubber, took the place of coffee. At that time, farmers in the Johnsonville area, not far from the Firestone plantation, cut down their coffee trees and planted rubber saplings.[38]

Besides adjusting to tropical crops, foods, and diseases, the settlers from Arkansas learned to navigate their relationship with the African people. Upon arrival in Liberia, black immigrants from America made an immediate transition in status from an oppressed underclass to a local elite. With the gift of land, the new arrivals could become citizens, vote, and run for public office. On the other hand, indigenous people in Liberia, who lived traditional lifestyles and spoke African languages rather than English, possessed no voting or citizenship rights. The governing elite did not even use the term "Liberian" for Africans who lived a traditional lifestyle. They considered them aborigines who could become citizens only when they received some western education, became Christian, and lived like "civilized" westerners. The settlers from Arkansas were moving into an existing social hierarchy where they rose, if not to the top, immediately to a status above the large majority of the population.[39]

Indigenous people in Liberia belonged to sixteen ethnic groupings, or tribes, who spoke variations within three language families, Kwa, Mande, and Mel. The tribes' cultures varied considerably, and they differed in the degree to which they had assimilated aspects of western culture. The Kru, a seafaring and fishing people, lived along the coast in close contact with American Liberians. Kru towns clustered around most American settlements. Monrovia's Kru town, just across the swampy Mersurrado River, had a larger population than Monrovia proper, which was inhabited by American Liberians. People of the Dey, Vai, Bassa, and Gola tribes also lived near the coast in areas settled by Americans. On the frontiers, revolts were brewing in the 1890s among the Mende people, along the Sierra Leone border, and in 1892 the Grebo in the southeast waged a short war against the Liberian government. But the vast majority of Liberia's indigenous people lived in the interior of the country and had little or no contact with the government or American Liberians.

All English-speaking settlers, however, lived in close contact with some native Africans. When the Arkansas settlers came to Johnsonville in 1891 and 1892, for example, they found Africans in the area farming cassava and rice. New government surveys attempted to partition native and immigrant plots in a peaceful manner. But, according to Benjamin Anderson, the official surveyor, Africans resented the encroachment of American settlers and "being made to dwell cheek by jowl with their civilized brethren."[40] On the other hand, the Arkansas settlers were unhappy that their African neighbors failed to respect property boundaries and insisted on cultivating small plots that lay on immigrant allotments. In 1893, ACS agent Julius Stevens reported that one settler, Benjamin H. Miller, had sued Karna Bolla, a Kru leader who spoke no English, for criminal trespass. A magistrate eventually dismissed the case when both Miller and the chief presented deeds for the same land. The survey of 1892 had apparently ignored an earlier survey that had deeded part of the same land over to Karna Bolla. Lacking a resolution in court, Stevens feared it would be set-

An indigenous African village in Liberia, ca. 1892. Courtesy Library of Congress.

tled by force, for the Arkansas settlers, he said, had brought their Winchester rifles with them from America.[41]

Despite this rocky beginning in Johnsonville, descendants of these Arkansas settlers suggest that immigrants generally got along well with their indigenous neighbors. Tony Miller, the grandson of Benjamin Miller, explained that Africans showed settlers how to grow and cook traditional foods like cassava and eddoes. They also taught settlers how to use plants for medicinal purposes, to treat malaria, diarrhea, constipation, jaundice, and other complaints. Others said African neighbors helped settlers construct temporary shelters with available material such as palm thatch.[42] Settlers traded with African people, in some cases exchanging dried fish and tobacco for additional acres of land or other needed items, such as salt.[43]

The most intimate relationship between Arkansas settlers and native Africans came through the practice of apprenticeship, established by law in the early years of the republic. It was common for an American Liberian family to take an African boy or girl into the home and raise the child to adulthood, age eighteen for girls, twenty-one for boys. Settlers usually paid the child's parents a sum of money—fifteen dollars could buy a male apprentice for a term of several years—and provided food and clothing in exchange for the use of the child's labor. The apprentice would take a western name and learn English, might receive some education, very likely attend a Christian church, and otherwise become "civilized" through the experience. At adulthood, the apprentices became free either to return to their home villages or to become absorbed into the American Liberian population.[44] As the Arkansas immigrants became more settled and needed labor on their farms, they adapted to the apprentice system, and African children and settler children often lived under the same roof. Although regulated by law, the system bore resemblance to slavery and was clearly open to abuse. In 1930, the League of Nations formally investigated charges that the Liberian apprentice system constituted a form of slavery, and the Liberian president subsequently banned the practice. While clearly some settlers treated apprentices well—the term "godchildren" was frequently used to describe these laborers—others mistreated them and took advantage of their labor.[45]

Intimate contact between settlers and Africans took place through the apprentice system as well. Alexander Smart, whose mother came to Johnsonville from Conway County in 1896, recalls that one of the Arkansas settler children, Edward Slocum, married a Kpelle girl, Mary, who grew up as an apprentice in the neighboring Blassingam home. Isaac David, who emigrated with his family from Little Rock when he was five, passed over the two daughters of an American Liberian family to marry Rosalie, the family's godchild of Vai background. In some cases, female apprentices bore children of their male settler employers outside of marriage, a pattern reminiscent of plantation slavery.[46]

The Arkansas immigrants generally held the same sort of western chauvinistic ideas about African people they displayed before they emigrated, and their interaction with African neighbors in the late 1800s reflected these attitudes. The apprentice relationship allowed settlers to take advantage of African labor and offer in return the "benefits" of exposure to civilization. The settlers' churches and schools generally served their own population and the apprentices they brought into their homes, not Africans who maintained their traditional cultures and lived apart from settler society. A revival at the Methodist church in Brewerville in 1899 claimed to have converted a number of native Africans who could not speak a word of English.[47] But this attempt to reach out to Africans appears to be the exception to the rule. In addition, although marriages and sexual relations took place openly between male settlers and native women, settler culture forbade relationships the other way—between African men and settler women.[48]

Ironically, in general, Liberian society imitated the sort of Jim Crow segregation the emigrants had fled in the American South. Africans and American

Liberians occupied different compartments on the small steamers that ran on the St. Paul River. They sat in different pews in church, Africans always in the rear. Native apprentices and laborers were expected to enter by the back rather than front door of a settler home and might eat meals in the kitchen rather than at the table of the settler family.[49]

Although some Africans may have become assimilated into the American Liberian community by accepting western culture, language, and religion, movement in the other direction rarely took place. Descendants remember as exceptional the case of an Arkansas immigrant who voluntarily left settler society and "went native." Joe Parker of Brewerville, the son of one of the Phillips County emigrants of 1880, reportedly went into the bush and lived the rest of his life with Africans. Four children of an Arkansas settler family may have done so against their will. Donald and Flora Johnson and their four children of Hot Springs had emigrated to Liberia in 1894 on the first expedition of the International Migration Society. They were living in Sierra Leone when, in 1898, a group of Mende rebels killed Flora Johnson and took away the couple's four children. The ultimate fate of the children is unknown, but it is possible that they were assimilated into Mende society.[50]

The cultural views the Arkansas emigrants brought with them to Liberia prepared them to identify with only the American Liberian elite. The nation they proposed to build up on the fringe of the African continent would be only the faux America of the Liberian state, mimicking the institutions, values, and attributes of western civilization. The emigrants had scarcely any knowledge of Africa and its people before their departure other than a vague sense of connection to an ancestral land, and after they arrived in Liberia they appeared to have shown little desire to "become" African. Despite their struggle for sheer survival, the immigrants remained convinced that they were offering the gift of civilization to Africa. They and their descendants proudly wore these family names—Johnson, Taylor, Parker, Hays—as badges of American identity. But just how successful could this Liberian state ever be when built on a narrow base of 20,000 English speakers surrounded by a million indigenous Africans?

The Arkansas immigrants' new life in Liberia clearly brought both challenges and rewards. They asked themselves the question that still haunts this subject today: was the move worth it? Conclusive answers to this question remain elusive. Immigrants' views varied. Clearly, the settlers' first year in Liberia posed such significant challenges that many contemplated a return to the United States. During the first year, the immigrant family had to do the hardest physical work —clearing land, planting crops, building homes—at the time people felt the greatest mental stress of adjustment to new climate and disease environments. Many families lost at least one loved one to fever during the seasoning stage.

Some immigrants returned to the United States from nearly every expedition to Liberia in the 1880s and 1890s. Of the 118 Arkansas refugees who emigrated in 1880, 4 returned a year later dissatisfied with Liberia. Edward Talifero, the son-in-law of Richard Newton, the leader of this group, convinced his wife and mother-in-law of the disadvantages of Liberia, and they returned on the *Monrovia* in June 1881. They disembarked in the port of New York just as fifty-five emigrants, mostly from Charleston, South Carolina, prepared to board. Talifero spoke so strongly against Liberia that the majority of the Charleston emigrants changed their minds and returned to South Carolina.[51] Another family of Arkansas refugees, Moses and Melvina Crosston and their six children, returned to the United States two years later, claiming that they never could adjust to the Liberian diet of "roots and roots and roots and scarcely any fresh meat." Ironically, Mrs. Crosston came down with a cold when her family arrived in Philadelphia, and she died there of pneumonia.[52] Andrew and Maria Flowers and Maria's sister, Alice Johnson, who emigrated from Conway County in 1883, returned to the United States a year later after Mrs. Flowers had a debilitating attack of malaria.[53] After a year in Liberia, Richard Bankhead, whose family of ten had left Helena in 1888, begged Secretary Coppinger to send for his family, for he expected to die before Coppinger received the letter. Bankhead said his family had been sick since their arrival, and he believed they all would perish. He pleaded with Coppinger: "If taking us back will Cure us and save our lives, Do for god sake Help Us Back." The ACS did not assist emigrants in returning to the United States, and the fate of the Bankhead family is unknown.[54]

Those who returned to the United States generally possessed the greatest financial resources to do so. In fact, the ACS agent in Liberia in 1894 said the best settlers were the ones who came without money, for they had to pluck up their courage and endure the fevers and difficulties of settlement. The motto of the Republic of Liberia, "The love of liberty brought us here," had been expanded in popular discourse in the late 1800s to "The love of liberty brought us here and the want of money keeps us here."[55] Of the fifty emigrants from Morrilton who went to Liberia on the ACS's last expedition in March 1892, sixteen returned the next year. One of the returnees, David Rivers, had been one of the most successful settlers. He had planted 5,000 coffee trees and built his own frame house within a few months of arrival. Nonetheless, he and his teenaged son, Pagie, returned to the United States in the summer of 1893, leaving behind Mrs. Rivers and four daughters. Apparently Rivers and his son planned to work to raise the money to send for the rest of the family at a later time.[56]

Some evidence suggests that women were perhaps more dissatisfied with Liberian life than men. When the Arkansas refugees arrived in Brewerville in July 1880, Mrs. Henry Foster absolutely refused to stay in the temporary cottage provided by the ACS, deeming it too crowded and uncomfortable. Despite being in the late stages of pregnancy, she determined to return to America at the first chance. The ACS agent reported that Mrs. Foster was "set on it and he defers to her." Reports came back that the women among the 1889 emigrants to the Hartford/Fortsville area of Bassa County "longed for the flesh-pots of our American Egypt." When emigrants from Conway County arrived at their land in the summer of 1891, the women in the party cried and did not want to get off the boat. Within two months of his arrival, Walter Wade, who had come on his own in 1892 via Liverpool with his wife and five children, was in Monrovia planning to return because of his children's illness and his wife's constant appeals to leave.[57] With the nursing of sick family members and preparing new foods for the family to eat, surely women keenly felt the challenges of adjustment to a new life in Africa.

The most highly publicized returns were those of some of the passengers from the *Horsa* and the *Laurada*. Frank Shelton, J. R. Tucker, and Ebenezer Russell, three men from Jefferson County who had traveled to Liberia on the *Horsa* in 1895, stayed only two months before they obtained passage on a steamer bound for Liverpool. They worked their way back to the United States, arriving in Philadelphia in late July. From rented rooms at the Wayfarers Lodge on Lombard Street, they told newspaper reporters that the International Migration Society had failed to provide for the emigrants, that many had become sick and died, and that some pitiful settlers had resorted to eating the flesh of dead animals and snakes to survive. The men claimed they planned to work for enough money to get back home to Arkansas. The story of the "Disgusted Colonists" received wide coverage and appeared in the *Philadelphia Inquirer*, the *New York Times*, and the *Washington Post*.[58] Bishop Turner countered the bad press, arguing that 80 percent of the *Horsa* emigrants were still alive and that, with the abominable rate of racial violence in the United States, black people risked their lives in emigrating *or* staying home. As to emigrants eating dead animals and snakes, Turner asked, "Did they want live animals?"[59]

Similarly, a few of the *Laurada* immigrants returned a year later to widespread newspaper publicity. Within six months of the ship's arrival, J. N. and

Fannie Webb, formerly of Madison, Arkansas, had returned to the United States via Liverpool. They claimed that a third of the *Laurada*'s passengers had already died of fever and that the ones left behind were miserable with poverty.[60] Another former resident of Madison, Taylor Swift, even more vocally denounced Liberia when he returned in September 1896. Swift, who came back with his wife, Kate, and their three children, called Liberia unfit for civilization and said that most of the *Laurada* passengers were practically naked and crippled by disease due to the "miasma which spread over the land each night—the John Bull fever, as it is called." He also charged that England owned and controlled Liberia.[61] Swift traveled home to St. Francis County, where he rented fifteen acres of land from his former landlord, a wealthy black planter named Scott Bond.[62] While Swift resumed his former lifestyle as an Arkansas tenant farmer, the Reverend A. L. Brisbane, an AME preacher in Liberia, denounced Swift's stories, calling him a lazy scullion who had become homesick for the plantation.[63] Yet *Laurada* immigrants continued to trickle out of Liberia. Charlie Peterson arrived in New York in June 1897 with his family and began to look for work to get money to travel back to Arkansas. Others were stranded in England, trying to raise money to finish their trip home.[64] Some immigrants dissatisfied with Liberia moved to the British colonies of Sierra Leone and Gold Coast, today's Ghana.[65]

Were the returnees lazy scullions or jaded realists? ACS agents in Liberia suggested that dissatisfied settlers who chose to return to America had come to Liberia with false or unreasonably high expectations. None of the surviving printed material of the ACS and International Migration Society, nor any of the ACS correspondence, suggests that these societies oversold Liberia to prospective emigrants in a way that was less than truthful. However, we can never know what self-proclaimed emigration agents and charlatans actually said in the rural precincts of Arkansas. Agent Julius Stevens reported that some of the *Laurada* returnees had brought divining rods to locate gold and silver in Africa and, failing to find any precious metal, began to plan their return. According to Scott Bond, black people in St. Francis County had been told that gold and diamonds were present in such abundance in Liberia that one could gather them by the handful. Bond said people believed not only in instant wealth but that food lay on every hand, that "pancakes grew on trees, and that all one had to do was to shake the trees and feast."[66] Similarly, William Pickens, a field secretary for the NAACP, remembered from his childhood in Argenta, Arkansas, in the early 1890s that black neighbors were induced to emigrate to Africa "under the persuasion that bread trees grew there right on the brink of

Taylor Swift in St. Francis County, Arkansas, after his return from Liberia in 1896. From Rudd and Bond, *From Slavery to Wealth*.

molasses ponds, and wild hogs with knives and forks sticking in their backs trotted around ready baked." Although clearly this was a transparent fantasy, nearly all of the descendants of Arkansas emigrants whom I interviewed speak today of their settler ancestors coming with the belief that bread and butter grew on trees in Liberia. After arrival, they learned that the "bread" was actually breadfruit, a starchy staple that required considerable preparation before it could be put on the table, and "butter" was the butterpear, or what Americans know as avocado.[67] Johnsonville settlers of 1891 and 1892 told ACS agent Stevens that they expected to find jobs in factories, workshops, and railroads in Liberia but instead found no economic recourse but farming. When Taylor Swift arrived back in the United States, he complained that the St. Francis County emigrants had been "lied to, fooled, taken out there on contract between the emigration society and the Liberian government just as the slaves were taken from Africa a hundred years ago."[68] The collapse of the coffee prices in 1897 most likely intensified immigrants' sense of betrayal. The settlers clearly traded in their old set of trials—white oppression and falling cotton prices—for a new set—diseases, an unfamiliar climate, and new foods. But still they were hammered by world market forces which lay beyond their control.

While some settlers longed for their American homes, others appeared happy with their new life in Liberia. Elijah Parker and Jack Allen, two of the Arkansas refugees who settled in Brewerville in 1880, wrote to William Coppinger to report how they were doing after a decade in Liberia. The men reported that they were "better satisfied than they ever was" and "the prospect of the Arkansas Refugees, all of them which are living, is working very beautiful and we wish you would come and see how we getting along."[69] William Rogers, who left for Liberia with his wife, Sarah, in October 1891, admitted that he had earlier contemplated returning to the United States, but he grew out of those thoughts and aimed to stay in Africa forever. In 1895, he wrote a long letter to his family in Morrilton, Arkansas, describing his feelings toward his adopted homeland:

Dear Father—Yours of the past month came to hand, found all well, and hope when these few lines come to hand will find you all the same. I was glad to hear from you.

You was asking me about the times. The times are very hard with new people, but I would not exchange homes if some one would give me a place there and stock to work it. A man can live here when he has one or two years experience of the country and you won't have to work half as hard as you do over there.

We don't have everthing here as plentiful as there, but in a few years when we begin to raise our coffee we will have what we want. You may hear that you can't raise corn and hogs, but I raise my corn and hogs and have my own bread. There are some people who come out here and as soon as they get sick, or before they know anything about the country, they will go back and tell that they can't live here, but it is a mistake, any man can live here if he works. We have to work anywhere we go. One thing I like, there are no white men to give orders, and when you go in your house, there is no one to stand out, and call you to the door and shoot you when you come out. We have no foreman over us; we are our own boss. We work when we want to, and sit down when we choose, and eat when we get ready.

Pa, you had better make up your mind and come over here. You will not suffer, and if you will [come], let me know in your next letter. Write as soon as you get this.

A few words to Clara. Dearest Sister—I am glad to hear that you have professed a hope in Christ, but it is not anything to profess; but the thing is to live a Christian and to know that you are truly converted and born of

God, and live according. I trust we will meet again. Tell John Polk [brother-in-law] I want him to come out here before he gets too old, where your children will be free, and what you make will be yours.

A few words to Mary [illegible] to drop you a few words. Mary, I have not got those pictures, but I am going to try and get them. You and your husband must make up your mind to come out here. This is the colored man's home, the only place on earth where they have equal rights, and when you once get a start it will last you until death.

You can raise nearly everything here that you can there. We don't have the horse here, where we are, but they are here. We have the cow here, but they don't grow as large here as in the United States.

We raise chickens, geese, turkeys, guinea fowls and other fowls that you raise there; and you can live easier working three days in a week, than you can there working every day in the week and on Sunday too.

We have the same God here that you have there. Tell Aunt Mary howdy, tell her I want to hear from Thomas Strait, so I can write to him how times are.

Love to Bro. Toombs, tell him I am still in the faith, that I am an ordained deacon in the Morning Star Church.

Sarah says, write to her. Write soon and let us hear from you. Yours truly, N.[*sic*] M. Rogers[70]

Young Fannie Kettler emigrated from Marianna, deep in the Arkansas delta, aboard the *Laurada* with her parents and three brothers and sisters. On 2 October 1896, six months after her arrival in Liberia, Miss Kettler wrote glowingly to the readers of Bishop Turner's *Voice of Missions*:

Dear Editor—Please allow me space in your paper to advance a few thoughts to our American people in regards to Africa, our happy home. . . . Africa is the place for you. It's your home—a place of refuge and safety. Why not come? Oh, my dear friends, how happy I am, just to think that I am in a free country. In America you have Mr. White Man president, and here, my friend, we have Mr. Colored Man for president. That is grand. Oh, if you just knew how free you people could be if you would just only come to your home. Here you can be your own boss, hold your own office, and be a man of business. Makes no difference what is done to you all, you still say that you won't come. Now they have given you the jim-crow cars to ride on. What are you going to do [illegible] as a brute to the white people. They will shoot you as quick as they would a hog. Then to say that I will stay—no, never will I. Just think of this happy land being prepared for us—a lovely home waiting for you. I hope that God will enable me to see the day when all of you will reach this happy country. You can better your condition, and why not do so? Tell me, are you going to be a servant for the white people all your days, when you have got a chance to be as they are? . . . This is the place that you can come to—this lovely place our home. Oh, how free.[71]

For Fannie Kettler, Africa meant, in a word, home. Besides referring to Liberia as a "grand country," "free country," "happy country," "beautiful country," as well as a "place of refuge and safety," she used the specific word "home" no less than nine times as a euphemism for Africa.

Immigrants from Arkansas responded to the Liberian environment in a variety of ways—from the angry attacks of Taylor Swift to the sincere praise of William Rogers and Fannie Kettler. Although the evidence is fragmentary, it appears that for those immigrants motivated primarily by hopes for economic prosperity, such as Taylor Swift, who expected to pick gold and diamonds like berries from a tree, Africa was a bitter disappointment. But for those settlers, like William Rogers, who had dreamed of escape from white oppression, which denied them basic human rights and threatened physical violence, it appears that life in Liberia was a welcome change. The new settlers who stayed for more than a year, surviving the seasoning experience and weathering the disappointment upon learning that bread and butter did not really grow on trees, tended to stay in Liberia for a lifetime.

Conclusion

When William Rogers of the new settler community of Johnsonville wrote home to his family in Morrilton in 1895, he displayed a keen understanding of the meaning of Africa for black Arkansans. Wanting the rest of the family to join him and his wife, Sarah, in Liberia, he knew exactly what selling points to emphasize: "There are no white men to give orders; and when you go in your house, there is no one to stand out, and call you to the door and shoot you when you come out. We have no foreman over us; we are our own boss." The black republic represented the opposite of all the things Rogers's family would have hated about their home in Conway County, Arkansas. Liberia symbolized hope —hope for freedom, dignity, and a better life. "This is the colored man's home," Rogers said to sister Mary, "the only place on earth where they have equal rights, and when you once get a start it will last you until death."

This study demonstrates the profound motivations black people possessed to leave the United States. African emigration became a mass movement for black Arkansans precisely at those moments when political conditions worsened in the late 1870s and early 1890s. The federal government's and the Republican Party's retreat from Reconstruction after 1877 prompted a temporary crackdown on black political power in the east Arkansas delta region, as it did in the black-majority states of Mississippi, Louisiana, and South Carolina. Predictably, black migration movements arose in all of these areas, with Arkansas's Liberia Exodus Colony clearly imitating the exodus group organized earlier in South Carolina. A decade later, a coalition of white agrarian populists and black Republican voters in Arkansas threatened a revolt of the rural poor. By 1890, the white Democratic Party had responded with a campaign of fraud, terror, and then legal disfranchisement, which hammered the weakest link in the coalition, African Americans. Black people again looked to escape to a better place. As white authorities whittled away at black rights and racial violence intensified in the 1890s, the back-to-Africa movement became a contagious fever raging throughout black precincts in Arkansas.[1]

While these escape motives for black emigration in the late 1800s are obvious, it is more difficult to explain why black people in Arkansas in particular aspired to emigrate to Africa. Nearly half of all the known American emigrants to Liberia in the 1890s came from Arkansas, far more than from any other state, and the number of actual emigrants reflects the general interest level, as measured by letters and applications to the ACS. Although conditions in Arkansas clearly were horrible in the early 1890s, the situation was likely no better for black people in the Deep South states like Mississippi or the Carolinas.[2] In the 1880s, Arkansas had served as a leading destination for black migrants leaving the Deep South looking for economic and political opportunities west of the Mississippi River. But the fortunes for black Arkansans quickly reversed. The change in the perceived degree of oppression rather than the oppression's severity may explain the sudden and profound black interest in African emigration. The two moments of Liberia fever came when the high expectations of black Arkansans were crushed under the heel of white racism. In fact, Arkansas's emigration patterns reflect the concept of relative deprivation, of so-called revolutions of rising expectations articulated by political scientist James C. Davies in the 1960s and later expanded by Ted R. Gurr. This theory suggests that radical social action, such as revolution or, by extension, an emigration movement, will most likely take place after a period of rising expectations and well-being followed by a sudden reversal of fortune. People thus take action when the gap is greatest between their expectations and the reality of their existence.[3] The Liberia emigration movements in Arkansas came precisely at these junctures when improving conditions quickly reversed, when white Democrats thwarted real black power on the local level. Conditions for black families in the early 1890s may not have been worse in Arkansas than neighboring Mississippi, but Arkansas quickly moved from being a refuge for black people fleeing the Deep South to a place of Mississippi-style racial oppression.

When many black Arkansans could not leave for Africa, they moved to Oklahoma and Indian Territories in the 1890s, founding dozens of all-black towns in these federal territories lacking Jim Crow laws of the South. When the new Oklahoma legislature passed several disfranchisement laws between 1908 and

1911, a large number of black people left the state for Canada. Shortly thereafter, Alfred Charles Sam, a black man who spoke with an accent and claimed to be an African chief, began recruiting black families in eastern Oklahoma to move to Africa. He reportedly organized fifty emigration clubs and by late 1913 had hundreds of black people living in tents ready for an immediate departure for Africa. With the money he raised, Sam went to New York and bought a ship, renaming it the *Liberia*. The next year, the *Liberia* set sail from Galveston, Texas, for the British colony of Gold Coast. When British officials there levied a twenty-five-pound tax on each settler, however, Sam abandoned them, and the movement collapsed. Some emigrants returned to the United States, and a few found their way to Liberia. One man, Willie Taylor, settled with his family among the Arkansas emigrants in Johnsonville.[4] This last African exodus from Oklahoma—the last organized back-to-Africa expedition— thus echoed the hope-turned-to-despair that followed the crackdown on black freedom in Arkansas nearly two decades earlier.

Another explanation for the strength of the movement in Arkansas was the explosive potential of the black Republican and poor white agrarian populist alliance in the state and the heightened competition this alliance brought to local politics. Although letters and applications for emigration came to the ACS from most of Arkansas's counties in the late 1880s and 1890s, the areas of greatest interest were counties where black voters in coalition with white farmers controlled the balance of power. The political violence and fraud of the elections of 1888 and 1890 was most outrageous in the counties with black population percentages ranging from 40 percent, as in Conway, to 54 percent, as in Woodruff. Lynchings, whitecapping, and other racial violence in these counties attacked black power and spirits. Interest in emigration, as measured by letters and applications to the ACS and the actual number of emigrants, on the other hand, was less intense in those counties with the largest black percentage of the population. The three blackest counties, Chicot (88 percent), Crittenden (86 percent), and Desha (80 percent), which had small numbers of white residents, saw little interest in African migration. The one county that had both a sizable black majority and great interest in Liberian emigration, Jefferson (76 percent black), also possessed a large population of small white farmers (more than 10,000, nearly twice that of Chicot, Crittenden, and Desha Counties combined).[5] Thus, the counties with the most competitive political environments in the late 1880s and early 1890s were most likely to have strong back-to-Africa movements.[6]

A third explanation for Arkansas's intense interest in Liberia is Bishop Henry

McNeal Turner. Although Turner lived in Atlanta, he presided over the Eighth District of the AME Church, which included Arkansas, Mississippi, and Indian Territory. Thus, on a yearly basis, he visited Arkansas for church conferences. Several of the Arkansas towns that hosted these meetings, such as Morrilton, Augusta, Newport, Forrest City, Pine Bluff, and Little Rock, became centers of emigration activity. Clearly many black Arkansans embraced the bishop's exodus message and looked to Turner as their Moses. Turner's role, however, should not be overemphasized. Of those Arkansas emigrants who identified themselves to the ACS by religious denomination, Methodists were slightly less likely to emigrate to Liberia than Baptists. And while Liberia fever did sweep through parts of Indian Territory, the movement never caught on significantly in Mississippi, the easternmost part of Turner's Eighth District. Although the black population of Mississippi was four times that of Arkansas, five times as many Liberia-bound emigrants left Arkansas as departed from its near neighbor across the great river.[7]

The nine Arkansas counties that showed the greatest interest in African emigration, in descending order of interest, were Conway, Phillips, Pulaski, Lonoke, Jefferson, Woodruff, Faulkner, Lee, and St. Francis.[8] These counties defy easy categorization. Several were located in the delta, with flat, fertile land; the others were located in the Arkansas River valley in central Arkansas. They were neither Arkansas's blackest nor whitest counties. All had experienced rapid black population growth in the 1870s and 1880s, but no more so than most other Arkansas counties. When compared to the rest of Arkansas, these counties do not adhere to any particular pattern of black land ownership or tenancy, renting via sharecropping versus money payment, farm size, average indebtedness per farm acre, cotton dependency, or productivity in bales per acre. What each of these counties did experience was a high degree of political competition and/or racial violence. And at a time of great tension, Bishop Henry McNeal Turner came around the county seats of Morrilton, Helena, Little Rock, Pine Bluff, Augusta, and Forrest City, preaching about an African land of freedom, a black republic, where hardly a white man or woman was to be found.

Arkansas's Liberia exodus movement, with Turner as its Moses and the ACS as a vehicle, served a role for those who stayed home as well as for those who emigrated. For all, it meant a hope that black people could indeed self-govern, that somewhere justice existed, that the good life was still possible. When times became bad, there was always Liberia. Stories had circulated through black precincts in Arkansas that in Africa one could shake pancakes from the trees and that wild hogs trotted around ready baked, with knives and forks sticking from their backs. These same motifs appeared in eighteenth-century European peasant folktales, where they also underscored the reality of hunger and the allure of the open road.[9] Descendants of the Arkansas emigrants say today that their ancestors crossed over the Atlantic believing that bread and butter grew on trees in Liberia. That people could believe such claims speaks to black Arkansans's great need to believe in a land flowing with milk and honey. Such a need explains the ubiquity of scam artists like the Reverend Lightfoot, who with ease sold hope for quick money. It also explains how dangerous to aspiring emigrants were the returnees from Liberia, like James Dargan and Taylor Swift, who tried to destroy the dream, and how quickly they were discredited as "white agents" or "lazy scullions."

But the back-to-Africa movement was more than just a dream, a trope to think with, or an opiate for the black masses. Involvement in a migration movement constituted a form of resistance. To some degree, it was symbolic resistance, like a slave spitting in the master's soup. Black farmers wrote letters to the ACS as angry people write letters to the editor of newspapers today. Correspondents thought surely somebody in the ACS, with its Washington address and connection to the halls of government, would hear them when they described the appalling conditions of their lives in the South. Writing the ACS, organizing an exodus club, filling out the application forms, all of this meant action, *doing something*, to change the conditions of one's life. Getting involved in the back-to-Africa movement was an alternative to acquiescence. Writing the ACS or joining an exodus club was also a courageous act that involved taking a risk, the risk of retribution from white landowners who needed black labor. And blacks who left home for Africa, as opposed to another American destination like Oklahoma or a northern city, were taking an even greater risk of stepping into the truly unknown.

The idea of emigration was as likely to divide as to unite the black community. Like free black leaders in antebellum years, the most prominent black figures on the national stage in the late 1800s opposed African emigration. Both Frederick Douglass and Booker T. Washington consistently argued that emigration worked to avoid, rather than resolve, America's race problems. Other leaders, like black newspaper editors T. Thomas Fortune and Charles H. J. Taylor, were downright hostile to Bishop Turner and the emigration cause. Consequently, historians who have examined surviving printed records from the late 1800s, which most often reflect views of black elites, have underestimated the popular interest in African emigration among the ordinary black farmers of the South. As Bishop Turner argued, prosperous town-dwelling black people, "the Colored men of Charleston, Columbia, Cattanooga [*sic*], Mobile, Natchez, Vicksburg, and Montgomery[,] do not fully realize the condition of the southern negro . . . the southern negro is in the country, not in the cities." Those who said black people did not want to return to Africa, Turner argued, simply did not understand the thinking of rural black men and women.[10] While educated and middle-class blacks may have continued to aspire to get a seat at the American table, thousands of black farmers in Arkansas gave up on this American dream. They dreamed instead of a future in Africa, as far away from white people as possible.[11]

These would-be African emigrants showed a keen sense of black nationalism. As one black farmer said, "We wont to tread African soil for the sole purpose of helping to further the cause of Race nationality."[12] This national identity built upon a connection with Africa as an ancestral hearth, but it was forged in the American experience of slavery and thwarted freedom. Aspiring emigrants foresaw the culmination of this nationalism in leaving white America for an environment where black Americans could come into their own, where they could build a black society on western models and pass on the benefits of this civilization to the "dark continent."

In the 1920s, these sentiments surfaced again with Jamaican-born Marcus Garvey and his Universal Negro Improvement Association (UNIA). Garvey's black nationalist movement grew in response to the race riots and lynchings of the late 1910s and early 1920s, but it clearly built on foundations laid earlier by the back-to-Africa movement. Garveyites in the UNIA sang the same song, "From Greenland's Icy Mountains," quoted the same Bible verses, "Ethiopia stretched out her hand," and placed the theme of back-to-Africa and Liberia at the center of future plans for the black nation. Like the Liberia Exodus Arkansas Colony of 1878 and the emigration clubs of the 1890s, Garvey borrowed heavily from the trappings of Euro-American culture and secret-society symbolism, titles, and uniforms. And as did Bishop Henry Turner and Martin Delany before him, Garvey talked about black Americans commercially developing Africa and building a thriving trade between black people in the old and new worlds.

The literature about Garvey's UNIA, with its headquarters in New York City, has treated Garveyism primarily as a northern urban movement, leading some historians to forget how many black families in New York, Chicago, Detroit, and Philadelphia in the 1920s had recently arrived there from the rural South.[13] A recent study by Mary Rolinson has demonstrated that the UNIA flourished in the South, especially in the black-majority Cotton Belt. Moreover, the movement's ideology of African redemption, separatism, and resistance to white oppression, she argues, had evolved from the concerns of rural black southerners. Rolinson examined three areas of the South that were particularly rich fields for recruitment by Garvey's forces: southwestern Georgia, the Yazoo/Mississippi delta area of Mississippi, and the delta region of eastern Arkansas. At least forty-six UNIA divisions were organized in Arkansas, most of them in Phillips, Lee, Monroe, and St. Francis Counties, all areas enthused about African emigration a generation before.[14] Hundreds of Garvey supporters in several Arkansas locations sent donations to Garvey's legal defense fund when he faced federal prosecution on charges of mail fraud in 1923, and more than 28,000 Arkansans signed petitions or sent letters or telegrams to the Department of Justice requesting clemency for Garvey or that it review his case.[15] Garvey's movement apparently also rekindled dreams of Africa in eastern Arkansas. When the UNIA asked divisions to send contributions for its African colonization project in 1924, funds came in immediately from seven Arkansas divisions. The Blytheville division sent a representative to the UNIA convention that year specifically to gather information about the planned expedition that was to take 500 black emigrants to Liberia.[16] In the 1920s, the forty-six UNIA divisions in Arkansas were in contrast to the four chapters of the NAACP, an organization working for black rights through integration.[17] Clearly Garvey's black nationalism was a familiar tune that fell on receptive ears in Arkansas.

Garvey's second in command, William LeVan Sherrill, who became acting president of the UNIA when Garvey went to a federal prison, was born in Altheimer, Arkansas, in 1894, in rural Jefferson County, where more than a hundred black farmers were preparing to emigrate to Liberia aboard the *Horsa* the following year. Sherrill was probably related to Joseph Sherrill, who took his family to Liberia in 1898. William Sherrill attended Philander Smith College in Little Rock before going on to Northwestern University and then Baltimore, where he joined the UNIA in 1921.[18]

The back-to-Africa movement and black nationalism have been revived again and again since Garvey, usually appealing to America's most marginalized black citizens. In the late 1930s, a Louisiana-born black woman, Mittie Maud Lena Gordon, organized an effort in Chicago to get congressional funding for black repatriation to Africa, an idea Bishop Turner had promoted fifty years before. Theodore Bilbo, a racist white senator from Mississippi, took up Gordon's cause, just as white Alabama senator Matthew Butler had championed a similar plan years before. In 1938, Bilbo introduced the Greater Liberia bill, which called for a billion dollars in federal aid for black emigration and for negotiations with France and Britain to cede additional African lands near Liberia to accommodate a mass emigration from America. Surviving members of the UNIA threw their support to the bill, which died with the advent of World War II the next year. Even as late as 1969, a Pennsylvania congressman introduced a new back-to-Africa bill, actually crafted by a black Muslim constituent in Philadelphia, authorizing payments to black emigrants for transportation, property, a stipend, and, with a nod to cultural sensitivity this time, instruction in African languages and customs.[19] America's recent black nationalist movements, associated with Malcolm X and Louis Farrakhan, stand on foundations laid by Bishop Turner and his many followers in the rural South a hundred years earlier.

Although the pro-emigration forces defined a national identity, they could not foresee the future for the generations who would stay in America and those whose families crossed over the Atlantic. Few black Arkansans who stayed home would live long enough to witness significant changes in race relations in the state. When Jim Crow arrived in Arkansas in the early 1890s, it stayed for a very long time. By the 1910s and 1920s, thousands of black Arkansans were moving to new promised lands, not Liberia this time, but Kansas City, St. Louis, Chicago, and Detroit. At moments when the Great Migration north became particularly intense, it mimicked the rituals and symbolism of the earlier movement. Exodus language again abounded as trains traveled north from the delta with "Bound for the Promised Land" scrawled on the sides in chalk.[20]

World War I gave black Arkansans, especially returning soldiers, expectations for change that were bitterly dashed. In the summer of 1919, black farmers angry about conditions on the big farms in eastern Arkansas attempted to organize a union to protect their interests. When a white deputy sheriff and two other men showed up outside a union meeting in October at a black church near Elaine, in southern Phillips County, gunfire left a white man dead and another wounded. In the week that followed an orgy of violence broke out as a white vigilantes moved through the area, sending thousands of black people to hide in the swamps and canebrakes. Governor Charles Brough even arrived with hundreds of federal troops to assist the white posse in arresting suspected troublemakers. Before order returned, five whites and dozens of black men and women were dead. Estimates of blacks killed in the riot range from twenty-five to several hundred. More than 1,000 black men and women were arrested. Eventually, seventy-three black men were tried for murder and twelve were found guilty by all-white juries and sentenced to death in the electric chair. With legal support from the NAACP, appeals went all the way to the Supreme Court, which finally overturned the convictions of the condemned men. The Elaine race riot, like similar outbursts in Chicago, Knoxville, Omaha, Tulsa, and Longview, Texas, sent a resounding denial to black hopes for change. The rash of lynchings that followed in the 1920s equaled those of the 1890s in scale and brutality.[21]

A decade later, in the throes of the Great Depression, the organization of the Southern Tenant Farmers Union (STFU) in northeastern Arkansas provided one more failed opportunity for resistance and reform. Although most of its members were impoverished black sharecroppers, the STFU was a biracial co-alition of the rural poor, reminiscent of the Agricultural Wheel of the 1880s. One of the organizers of the Elaine union of 1919 was a founder of the STFU. Another black leader of the organization, preacher/farmer E. B. "Britt" McKin-ney, had been a devoted Garveyite in the 1920s. In organizing locals for the STFU, McKinney used the same rituals—preaching in black churches, singing hymns, using biblical references and prayers—that he employed to organize divisions of the UNIA a decade before and that clearly followed the traditions of back-to-Africa club meetings of the late 1800s. The STFU claimed to have 200,000 members within a few years. Local planters and lawmen harassed union leaders until they moved their headquarters to a safer location across the Mississippi River, in Memphis. The union achieved limited success by bringing attention of the national press and federal authorities to the conditions of Arkansas sharecroppers. But by 1937, charges of communist infiltration combined with a damaging flood in the area to bring the movement into decline.[22] Poor black farmers in eastern Arkansas demonstrated remarkable continuity of resistance from the late 1800s to the 1930s.[23]

Lasting change came only through the achievements of the civil rights movement two decades later. With the crisis at Little Rock's Central High School in 1957, Arkansas became the scene for some of the most dramatic moments in the dissolution of legal segregation. When Arkansas governor Orval Faubus called out the National Guard to prevent nine black children from attending the city's largest formerly all-white high school, President Dwight Eisenhower countered with force, deploying the 101st Airborne Division of the U.S. Army to escort these children to their classes and disperse the white mob that had gathered outside the school. People all over the United States and the world watched the affair on television. After the troops and television crews departed, Governor Faubus, using special authority given him by the state legislature, closed down all public high schools in Little Rock rather than allow integrated education. For the entire 1958–59 academic year, Arkansas's most populous city had no functioning public secondary school. Finally, in June 1959, the U.S. Supreme Court declared the school closing unconstitutional, and the schools opened again in the fall. In addition to taking a year of education away from both white and black high school students in Little Rock, the crisis had magnified racial animosity and probably delayed school integration in other areas of the state. The fight to integrate schools would continue through the 1960s, and even into the early 1970s in some areas. Meanwhile, the NAACP and Student Non-Violent Coordinating Committee (SNCC) organized sit-ins and boycotts to integrate public facilities and voter registration efforts, especially in the delta area. By the 1970s, the most visible forms of racism in Arkansas and the South had waned, if not disappeared. An African American man was elected to the state legislature in 1972, for the first time since the 1890s, and dozens of black officials served in elected posts throughout the state. Conditions for black Arkansans, especially in the struggling delta region, have followed the trends for the South as a whole, where political empowerment has far outpaced economic opportunities for most black citizens. By the 1990s, black Arkansans were still earning on average 40 percent less than their white neighbors.[24]

AS THE SITUATION FOR black Arkansans haltingly improved after many years, the Republic of Liberia has been moving toward a meltdown in recent times. Change came slowly after the organized migrations to Liberia ended in the 1890s. Most Arkansas settler families continued to engage in subsistence farming and coffee production, even though profits remained low after the great drop of world coffee prices in 1896. Not until the 1920s did these farm families find a cash crop to replace coffee. When the American rubber company Firestone moved into Liberia in the late 1920s, many of the Arkansas settlers and their children, especially in the Johnsonville area, cut down their coffee trees to plant rubber. By the 1930s, they had begun to tap the stately rubber trees and secure the milky-white latex fluid to sell to the huge American corporation.

In 1926, Harvey Firestone, the American rubber tycoon, negotiated a ninety-nine-year lease with the Liberian government for a million acres of land and an exemption from taxes in exchange for a two-million-dollar loan, most of which went to cover the republic's existing debt. The U.S. company agreed to pay six cents per acre for use of the land. Firestone workers cleared the dense vegetation and planted millions of neatly spaced Hevea rubber trees, native to the Amazon basin of South America. The company built its own schools, a hospital, roads, an electrical plant, and Liberia's first radio station. In 1930, Firestone was implicated in the League of Nation's investigation of slavery. In addition to examining the apprenticeship system, the league commission also investigated charges that Firestone benefited from a system whereby indigenous African leaders delivered forced laborers to the company with the approval of high officials in the Liberia government. Although the commission report did not find what it called outright slavery, its criticism of forced labor and the apprentice system prompted the president and vice president of Liberia to resign in December 1930. Liberians countered that powerful league members pushed the investigation in order to make the price of Liberian rubber more competitive with that of British and French rubber produced in Malaya and Indochina. Criticism notwithstanding, by the 1930s, the Firestone rubber plantation and processing facility, some forty miles southeast of Monrovia, had become the world's largest.[25]

Firestone was the first foreign corporation to arrive in Liberia, but others followed, all seeking favorable concessions like the ones Firestone received. The long presidency of William V. S. Tubman, from 1944 to 1971, promoted economic development by foreign companies. Other rubber companies, such as Goodrich and U.S. Rubber, established their own operations, and mining operations of rich iron deposits, as well as gold and diamonds, took foreign companies far into the interior. Tubman's development policies resulted in a greater integration of the backcountry into the life of Liberia. In fact, most of the country's road system and its only railroad were built by foreign companies to connect their resources in the interior with shipping facilities on the coast, mimicking colonial patterns of development elsewhere on the African continent.

American foreign policy interests in Liberia followed these economic investments. During World War II, the United States established an air base near the Firestone plantation at Robertsfield from which planes could bomb German operations in North Africa and the Mediterranean, and the U.S. Navy built a deep-water harbor and base at Monrovia. The American dollar replaced the British pound as Liberia's currency. During the Cold War, Liberia became the closest ally of the United States in the area, anchoring the CIA regional office for West Africa. From a transmitter outside Monrovia, the Voice of America beamed an American version of world news to the African continent. Tubman's close ties with the United States and his policy of economic development brought indigenous peoples of the hinterland into national life, and in the 1940s, they received legislative representation and voting rights that they had never before possessed. But this meant Africans accustomed to indirect rule through tribal leaders now came under the domination of American Liberians ruling from the coastal strip. Consequently, after World War II, indigenous people increasingly identified themselves as Liberians, but in so doing they became more aware that the wealth produced in their country remained largely in the hands of foreign corporations and their American Liberian partners in the government.[26]

Tensions between African people and American Liberians finally erupted in a violent coup in 1980, when Tubman's vice president and successor, President William Tolbert, was brutally assassinated. In the early morning hours of 12 April, six men wearing painted masks and loin cloths shot their way through the executive mansion in Monrovia and into the president's family quarters on the eighth floor; there they killed President Tolbert as his wife, Victoria, still dressed in her nightclothes, stood helplessly by. Mrs. Tolbert was the daughter of Isaac David, who, as a boy of five, emigrated with his family from Argenta (now North Little Rock), Arkansas. David had married a Vai girl who was apprenticed to a neighbor's family. The assassins spared Mrs. Tolbert's life, they said, because they considered her a Vai woman.[27]

A junta of military officers of indigenous background had planned the coup, and one of their leaders, a poorly educated but bright master sergeant named Samuel Doe, emerged as the leader. Under Chairman Doe's ten-year regime, the fortunes of the American Liberian oligarchy had reversed. It now was fashionable to have "country" origins. Some Liberians with names like Johnson, Smith, or Jones began to take on African family names and learn an African language in addition to English. However, as Liberia "Africanized," some common postcolonial patterns began to emerge. Doe filled high government and military positions with members of his own Krahn tribe and began to discriminate against others, notably the Gio and Mano ethnic groups. In 1985, Doe rigged the outcome of the presidential elections, which were held ostensibly to return Liberia to civilian rule, in his favor. During President Ronald Reagan's administration, the United States kept its close ties with Doe's administration and even recognized the elections of 1985 with the view that fraudulent elections were preferable to no elections.[28]

By the end of the 1980s, however, the corruption of Doe's regime, combined with ethnic tensions and opposition by American Liberians, led to Doe's free fall. An anti-Doe movement of Liberian exiles had grown outside the borders, supported by the neighboring African states of Côte d'Ivoire and Burkina Faso. One of their leaders was Charles Taylor, a former government paymaster accused of embezzling nearly a million dollars from the Doe regime. In

1983, Taylor fled to the United States, where he was arrested and placed in a county jail in Massachusetts. While awaiting extradition to Liberia, he escaped under mysterious circumstances and made his way back to Africa. Libya's Moammar Gadhafi, always on the lookout to support revolutionary movements against American client states, provided training and assistance to Taylor and other rebels. During the last week of December 1989, rebel fighters under Taylor's direction moved into the Liberian hinterland from Côte d'Ivoire, and the Liberian civil war began. By the summer of 1990, rebels were advancing toward Monrovia. Interethnic massacres abounded as the war degenerated into a conflict between pro-Doe Krahn and Mandingo fighters, sometimes in uniform of the Liberian army, against a largely Gio and Mano rebel force. Another group of poorly disciplined soldiers arrived from neighboring states, supposedly to help keep the peace under the banner of the Economic Community of West African States Cease-fire Monitoring Group (ECOMOG). The peacekeepers, mostly Nigerians, at times became combatants themselves in the civil war that followed. In September, President Doe was captured by a rebel force under Prince Johnson. With a video camera recording the scene, Johnson's men cut off the ears of the president, who was still alive and clad only in a camouflage shirt and his undershorts. A visibly drunk Johnson appeared on the video to chew on Doe's severed ear before he ordered the president's execution.[29]

Doe's death foreshadowed the savagery that would follow. Throughout most of the 1990s, Liberia remained a battleground. A rump government supported by the ECOMOG forces controlled downtown Monrovia but not all of the suburbs, where rebel fighters patrolled. The fighters had themselves fallen into warring factions. The atmosphere degenerated into one of surreal carnivalesque brutality. Soldiers fought while drunk, high on marijuana or amphetamines, and donning women's wigs, pantyhose, and Halloween masks, believing that such costumes protected them from enemy bullets. One fighter, Joshua Milton Blahyi, led his followers, known as the Butt Naked Brigade, into battle totally naked in the belief that their nudity garnered special magical powers. Preteenage children carried AK-47 assault rifles and grenades. Thousands of civilians were brutally murdered by all sides as political order dissolved. After the 1990 rebel offensive on Monrovia, twice again—in 1992 and 1996—rebel warlords tried to take the capital, each time with the ECOMOG fighting back, destroying much of the city and its environs in the process. It has been estimated that, before the war ended in 1997, as many as 80,000 people had been killed; some death estimates from the United Nations have ranged as high as

200,000, or nearly 10 percent of Liberia's population. The war at one time or another had displaced the majority of the surviving Liberians from their homes. Hundreds of thousands fled to Sierra Leone, Guinea, or Côte d'Ivoire; even more swelled Monrovia's population.[30]

A fragile peace came to Liberia after ECOMOG forces stopped the rebel offensive of 1996 and moved to secure large areas of the countryside. Under ECOMOG leadership and with international support, Liberia held elections on 19 July 1997 to choose a new government. Hailed as the most democratic and fairest elections in the republic's history, some 80 percent of eligible voters went to the polls. Charles Taylor, the strongest of the rebel warlords who had become rich in wartime by controlling the gold and diamond trade in the hinterlands and whose fighters had committed some of the most unspeakable atrocities, won a landslide victory. What Taylor failed to achieve through war, he gained through democracy. Some observers believe that Taylor, an educated man with some charisma, won because he had the appearance of a strong leader. Others think many Liberians voted for Taylor for fear that if he lost, the war would simply resume again.[31]

TO DO RESEARCH for this book, I arrived in Monrovia in July 1998, a year after the elections that brought Charles Taylor to the presidency. The rich records of the American Colonization Society had allowed me to learn much about the Arkansas emigrants before they left the United States, but once they set foot on their ships bound for Africa, they generally stopped writing letters. Thus, I knew very little about their experiences after they arrived in Africa. I traveled to Liberia in hopes that I would find descendants of the settlers from Arkansas and a surviving oral tradition about the settlers' experiences.

Liberia in the summer of 1998 still had the appearance of a war zone. Robertsfield, Liberia's international airport built thirty miles southeast of Monrovia for the convenience of Firestone, had just reopened, but the main terminal building lay empty, a burned-out shell. Refugees crowded the city, living alongside Monrovia's streets, afraid to go to their homes in rural areas, unsure that the war was really over. Government buildings and office complexes in downtown Monrovia sat gutted, burned, and pockmarked by shelling. I could imagine how the veneer of prosperity of the Tubman and Tolbert years must have looked in comparison to the reality after two decades of Doe and civil war. The hull of a modern metropolis grew dark after sundown because there was no electricity in the capital city. Government at all levels struggled to function again, lacking the ability even to pay employees a living wage. I had no budget item in my research grant for bribery, but I found it one of the most significant expenses of work in Liberia. I bribed to get my video camera past the customs official, to get my passport stamped, to pass through many of the military checkpoints on the highways manned by menacing-looking soldiers clad in camouflage and dark sunglasses, carrying AK-47s. These men had been Charles Taylor's fighters during the war, so I paid.

Many descendants of the Arkansas emigrants still lived in Brewerville and Johnsonville, and others had moved to Monrovia. In the presence of great suffering, my project seemed small and irrelevant, and I was embarrassed to ask people questions about events of a century ago when they had just lived through a historic traumatic upheaval. I knew little about the Liberia war, only what American newspapers had told me. Despite the brutal nature of this war, stories about Liberia throughout the 1990s were usually buried on inside pages of newspapers. The fall of Samuel Doe had taken place shortly after Iraq's invasion of Kuwait, and American reporters on the African beat had other stories to cover—American intervention in Somalia in 1992, the Rwandan genocide of 1994, and the gradual collapse of apartheid in South Africa. Thus, my interviewees taught me about the war, as well as about their family histories.

Most of the descendants of Arkansas settlers in Brewerville and Johnsonville lost their homes and material possessions during wartime. Johnsonville had been especially hard hit in the October 1992 rebel offensive. Rebel fighters, primarily of indigenous African backgrounds, looted and burned nearly all the homes owned by American Liberians. Then ECOMOG air strikes and artillery shelling attempted to push the rebels out of the area, destroying most of the remaining structures in the township. Residents fled into the bush and made their way to Monrovia. Nearly all the old settler houses built in the 1890s and early 1900s had burned to the ground.[32] When I asked descendants if they had any physical objects that the settlers brought from America, they remembered several—a silver spoon, a dish, an old swallowtail coat, some photographs— but they all had been lost in the war. The grandson of emigrant Benjamin Miller explained that the family had kept the old Winchester rifle, which Miller brought with him in 1891, but the owner, a cousin, had destroyed it during the war, fearing he would be killed if found with any type of arms.[33]

When I arrived for the first time in Johnsonville, on a Saturday morning, I came upon a group of men repairing the Morning Star Baptist Church, founded by Sister Narcissie Moore in 1893 and named after her home church back in Argenta, Arkansas. The roof had been badly damaged, and holes still remained from rocket blasts during the war. The men working were named Moore, Shaw, and Hart, all descendants of the original American settlers. Another crew was repainting the school building farther down the dirt road. Many of the residents had returned home to do subsistence farming. With the Firestone plantation out of operation during the war, the farmers had cut down most of the stately rubber trees to burn as charcoal for cooking fires.

Most descendants were more than willing to talk with me; several even sought me out to tell me their stories. Some had an ulterior motive for speaking with me: they wanted to emigrate to the United States. The word on the streets was that Liberians who could prove American ancestry, or who had family in the United States who "claimed" them, received preferential treatment in securing entry visas. Thus with my list of emigrants culled from ACS records, I could provide something these Liberians desperately wanted: documentary evidence. Many also asked me to locate their relatives in the United States and put families on both sides of the Atlantic in touch with one another, a difficult task given that Liberia still lacked a functioning mail system.

I had come to study an emigration movement, but I found myself personally involved in another one. Everyone had a story to tell of suffering, of atrocities witnessed firsthand. People spoke with the same tone of pleading I had heard before in countless letters by black Arkansas sharecroppers in the 1890s who wished to emigrate to Liberia. These letters had expressed the naive hope that if ACS officials and others in Washington simply knew what these correspondents had experienced, then they would surely help them get away. These grandchildren and great-grandchildren of Arkansas emigrants spoke to me with the same sort of earnest plea.

In the time since my visit to Liberia, conditions have only worsened. Rebel groups renewed the civil war in 1999, and the conflict has approached crisis proportions as this book goes to press in August 2003. Refugees by the hundreds of thousands crowded into the capital city, where Charles Taylor's government fighters made a last stand, stubbornly defending the bridges into central Monrovia against the rebel advance. Meanwhile, the people were dying daily from artillery shelling, as well as cholera and starvation. The Liberian people called out for American intervention, evoking the historic ties between the United States and the black republic.

The story of black migration to Africa reveals the ironic reality of American society in the late 1800s. It was a time of massive European influx to the United States but also a period in which thousands of black southerners became desperate to escape this country. The irony continues today, for many of the descendants of the Arkansas emigrants to Africa who have never seen the United States dream of America as a place of escape from the physical danger and economic privation of Liberia.

Notes

Introduction

1. *New York Times*, 11, 12 March 1892; *New York Evening Post*, 10 March 1892. A passenger list for the *Liberia* can be found in Journal of the Executive Committee of the American Colonization Society, 17 March 1892, reel 293, American Colonization Society Records, Library of Congress, Washington, D.C. (These manuscripts, hereafter cited as ACS, are filed chronologically within reels.) A passenger list for the *Werkendam* can be found through the Web site of the American Family Immigration History Center at Ellis Island: ‹http://www.ellisislandrecords.org›.

2. B. T. Willis to William Coppinger, 14 October 1890, ACS reel 135.

3. At the 1890 census, 4 percent of the country's black population lived in Arkansas (309,117 of 7,488,676). Yet 574 of the 1,665 known American emigrants to Liberia from 1879 to 1899, or nearly 35 percent, hailed from Arkansas. The figures include emigrants transported by the International Migration Society as well as the ACS. After 1892, some emigrants, including several black Arkansans, made their own way to Liberia; a definitive number of these emigrants is not known. These figures also do not reflect several dozen black American missionaries to Africa in the late 1800s, of which approximately a quarter hailed from Arkansas. North Carolina had the second largest number of Liberia emigrants from 1879 to 1899, with 273. These figures are compiled from emigrant lists that appeared in the *African Repository*, *Liberia Bulletin*, and *Voice of Missions*. The 1895 figure is an estimate of the 201 passengers on the *Horsa*, half of whom left from Jefferson County, Arkansas. The census numbers can be found in U.S. Bureau of the Census, *Negro Population, 1790–1915* (Washington, D.C.: Government Printing Office, 1918), 25, 777.

4. For an account of the founding of Sierra Leone, see John Peterson, *Province of Freedom: A History of Sierra Leone, 1787–1870* (Evanston: Northwestern University Press, 1969); and Christopher Fyfe, *A History of Sierra Leone* (Oxford: Oxford University Press, 1962).

5. For Cuffe's life and work and the early stirring of an African colonization movement in America, see Sheldon H. Harris, *Paul Cuffe: Black America and the African Return* (New York: Simon and Schuster, 1972); and Floyd J. Miller, *The Search for a Black Nationality: Black Emigration and Colonization, 1787–1863* (Urbana: University of Illinois Press, 1975), 3–53.

6. For the most thorough narrative of the founding of the American Colonization Society, see P. J. Staudenraus, *The African Colonization Movement, 1816–1865* (New York: Columbia University Press, 1961); for an early account that reproduces much of the speeches and proceedings, see Archibald Alexander, *A History of Colonization on the Western Coast of Africa* (1849; reprint, Freeport, N.Y.: Books for Libraries Press, 1971), 80–98. For the perspective of the free black community, see Philip S. Foner, *History of Black Americans: From Africa to the Emergence of the Cotton Kingdom* (Westport, Conn.: Greenwood Press, 1975), 579–94; and John Hope Franklin, *From Slavery to Freedom: A History of Negro Americans*, 4th ed. (New York: Alfred A. Knopf, 1974), 184–87.

7. Staudenraus, *African Colonization Movement*, 58–66; Miller, *Search for a Black Nationality*, 55–71; Tom W. Shick, *Behold the Promised Land: A History of Afro-American Settler Society in Nineteenth-Century Liberia* (Baltimore: Johns Hopkins University Press, 1977), 19–24.

8. Shick, *Behold the Promised Land*, 27–28; Staudenraus, *African Colonization Movement*, 50–55.

9. Penelope Campbell, *Maryland in Africa: The Maryland State Colonization Society, 1831–1857* (Urbana: University of Illinois Press, 1971), 30–44; Staudenraus, *African Colonization Movement*, 188–206; see also William Lloyd Garrison, *Thoughts on African Colonization, or an Impartial Exhibition of the Doctrines, Principles and Purposes of the American Colonization Society* (1832; reprint, New York: Arno Press and the *New York Times*, 1968); David Walker, *Walker's Appeal in Four Articles to the Colored Citizens of the World*, 2nd ed. (1830; reprint, New York: Arno Press and *New York Times*, 1969); and Howard Holman Bell, *A Survey of the Negro Convention Movement, 1830–1861* (New York: Arno Press and the *New York Times*, 1969), 15–34.

10. See the excellent discussion of these antebellum black-led emigration movements in Miller, *Search for a Black Nationality*, 170–249.

11. Staudenraus, *African Colonization Movement*, 246–48.

12. William Cohen, *At Freedom's Edge: Black Mobility and the Southern White Quest for Racial Control, 1861–1915* (Baton Rouge: Louisiana State University Press, 1991), 147; Edwin S. Redkey, *Black Exodus: Black Nationalist and Back-to-Africa Movements, 1890–1910* (New Haven: Yale University Press, 1969), 77–78; *Liberia Bulletin* 1 (November 1892): 1–3; Staudenraus, *African Colonization Movement*, 248–49. In the 1850s, yearly receipts of the ACS ranged between $50,000 and $160,000 while annual receipts by the 1880s slipped below $10,000. See a summary of annual income since 1817 in "Sixty-Ninth Annual Report of the American Colonization Society and Minutes of the Annual Meeting of the Board of Directors of January 17, 19, and 20, 1886," in *The Annual Reports of the American Colonization Society*, vol. 6: 1871–1910 (New York: Negro Universities Press, 1969), 25.

13. William Cohen, *At Freedom's Edge*, 142–48; a year-by-year listing of the number of emigrants settled in Liberia by the ACS, and the society's annual receipts, can be found in Staudenraus, *African Colonization Movement*, 251. After 1892, the society trans-

ported a small number of African Americans with specialized skills, mostly missionaries and teachers, but no more farmer-settlers.

14. For more information about the end of Reconstruction, see William Gillette, *Retreat from Reconstruction, 1869–1879* (Baton Rouge: Louisiana State University Press, 1979), 311–62; Stanley P. Hirshon, *Farewell to the Bloody Shirt: Northern Republicans and the Southern Negro, 1877–1893* (Bloomington: Indiana University Press, 1962), 21–44; James M. McPherson, *The Abolitionist Legacy: From Reconstruction to the NAACP* (Princeton, N.J.: Princeton University Press, 1975), 81–94; and Eric Foner, *Reconstruction: America's Unfinished Revolution, 1863–1877* (New York: Harper and Row, 1988), 564–601. While Hayes is said to have "withdrawn" the last federal troops from the South in April 1877, Foner (p. 582) clarifies that some troops physically remained in the South; they just ceased to operate in a political manner as an army of occupation.

15. Foner, *Reconstruction*, 559–60, 583–84; Gillette, *Retreat from Reconstruction*, 153–65.

16. Foner, *Reconstruction*, 575–79; Hirshon, *Farewell to the Bloody Shirt*, 48–56.

17. Foner, *Reconstruction*, 575; Vincent P. DeSantis, *Republicans Face the Southern Question: The New Departure Years, 1877–1897* (Baltimore: Johns Hopkins University Press, 1959), 102; U.S. Department of the Interior, Census Office, *Statistics of the Population of the United States at the Tenth Census, 1880* (Washington, D.C.: Government Printing Office, 1883), 398.

18. John Mardenborough to ACS, 11 April 1877, ACS reel 116A. For a discussion of violence in Edgefield County, see Orville Vernon Burton, "Race and Reconstruction: Edgefield County, South Carolina," *Journal of Social History* 12 (Fall 1978): 31–56.

19. For accounts of the *Azor* expedition, see George Brown Tindall, *South Carolina Negroes, 1877–1900* (Columbia: University of South Carolina Press, 1952), 153–68; William Cohen, *At Freedom's Edge*, 154–60; and A. B. Williams, "The Liberian Exodus: An Account of Voyage of the First Emigrants on the Bark 'Azor' and their Reception in Monrovia" (Charleston, S.C.: *Charleston News and Courier Press*, 1878), in vol. 5 of Colonization Pamphlets (a bound collection of miscellaneous printed materials drawn from the American Colonization Society Records, located in the Rare Book/Special Collections Division of the Library of Congress, Washington, D.C.; hereafter cited as Colonization Pamphlets).

20. William Cohen, *At Freedom's Edge*, 160–67; Nell Irvin Painter, *Exodusters: Black Migration to Kansas after Reconstruction* (New York: Knopf, 1977), 82–95; Henry Adams to John H. B. Latrobe, 31 August 1877, ACS reel 116A. For a list of all emigrants to Liberia transported by ACS after the Civil War, see Peter J. Murdza Jr., *Immigrants to Liberia, 1865 to 1904: An Alphabetical Listing* (Newark: University of Delaware and the Liberian Studies Association, 1975).

21. For excellent accounts of the Kansas migration, see Painter, *Exodusters*, 175–211; Hirshon, *Farewell to the Bloody Shirt*, 63–77; Robert G. Athearn, *In Search of Canaan: Black Migration to Kansas* (Lawrence: Regents Press of Kansas, 1978); and William Cohen, *At Freedom's Edge*, 168–83, 301–11. This rich historiography largely comes from the extensive testimony given to the Senate committee; see U.S. Congress, Senate, *Report and Testimony of the Select Committee of the United States Senate to Investigate the Causes of the Removal of the Negroes from the Southern States to the Northern States*, 3 parts, 46th Cong., 2nd sess., 1880, Senate Report 693 (Washington, D.C.: Government Printing Office, 1880).

Chapter One

1. "The First Convention of the Liberia Exodus Arkansas Colony," p. 2, vol. 6, Colonization Pamphlets. I am indebted to the earlier work of Adell Patton Jr., who located this report; see his "'Back-to-Africa' Movement in Arkansas," *Arkansas Historical Quarterly* 41 (Summer 1992): 164–77.

2. For the most detailed examination of Reconstruction in Arkansas, reflecting the Dunning school of interpretation, see Thomas S. Staples, *Reconstruction in Arkansas, 1862–1874* (New York: Columbia University Press, 1923); for an alternative interpretation by the Reconstruction governor, see Powell Clayton, *Aftermath of the Civil War in Arkansas* (New York: Neale Publishing, 1915). For more balanced assessments, see Carl H. Moneyhon, *The Impact of the Civil War and Reconstruction on Arkansas: Persistence in the Midst of Ruin* (Baton Rouge: Louisiana State University Press, 1994); and Thomas A. DeBlack, *With Fire and Sword: Arkansas, 1861–1874* (Fayetteville: University of Arkansas Press, 2003). For assessments of the efficacy of Clayton's policies, see Eric Foner, *Reconstruction: America's Unfinished Revolution, 1863–1877* (New York: Harper and Row, 1988), xxvi–xxvii, 292–307, 440; George C. Rable, *But There Was No Peace: The Role of Violence in the Politics of Reconstruction* (Athens: University of Georgia Press, 1984), 105; and Richard Current, *Those Terrible Carpetbaggers* (New York: Oxford University Press, 1988).

3. For more about the Brooks-Baxter War, see John Harrell, *The Brooks and Baxter War: A History of the Reconstruction Period in Arkansas* (St. Louis: Slawson, 1893); Earl F. Woodward, "The Brooks and Baxter War in Arkansas, 1872–1874," *Arkansas Historical Quarterly* 30 (Winter 1970): 315–36; and William Gillette, *Retreat from Reconstruction, 1869–1879* (Baton Rouge: Louisiana State University Press, 1979), 136–50.

4. See John William Graves, *Town and Country: Race Relations in an Urban-Rural Context, Arkansas, 1865–1905* (Fayetteville: University of Arkansas Press, 1990), 53–60; and Vincent P. DeSantis, *Republicans Face the Southern Question: The New Departure Years, 1877–1897* (Baltimore: Johns Hopkins University Press, 1959), 52. See also the testimony of V. Dell in U.S. Congress, Senate, *Report and Testimony of the Select Committee of the U.S. Senate to Investigate the Causes of the Removal of the Negroes from the Southern States to the Northern States*, 3 parts, 46th Cong., 2nd sess., 1880, Senate Report 693 (Washington, D.C.: Government Printing Office, 1880), pt. 3, 353–54. The anecdotes about Ned Hill and the attempted removal of Furbush come from Jerome R. Riley, *The Philosophy of Negro Suffrage* (Hartford, Conn.: American Publishing Company, 1895), 19–20, 58–59.

5. Graves, *Town and County*, 61–65. For an examination of how southern states took legislative action to control black labor, see Daniel A. Novak, *The Wheel of Servitude: Black Forced Labor after Slavery* (Lexington: University Press of Kentucky, 1978).

6. A. L. Stanford to William Coppinger, 15 August 1877, 8 October 1877, ACS reel 116A; Coppinger to Stanford, 1 September 1877, ACS reel 217.

7. This biographical information was culled from Stanford's obituary in the *Liberia Observer*, reprinted in Little Rock's black newspaper, *Arkansas Mansion*, 11 August 1883; M. M. Ponton, *Life and Times of Henry M. Turner* (New York: Negro Universities Press, 1970), 68; Stanford to Coppinger, 4 March 1879, ACS reel 118; and Harold J. Abrahams, *Extinct Medical Schools of Nineteenth-Century Philadelphia* (Philadelphia: University of Pennsylvania Press, 1966), 245. Although Stanford claimed to have matriculated in

1868 and 1869 and to have received his diploma in 1870, his name does not appear on Abrahams's list of students or graduates in those years (pp. 389–417, 426).

8. These charges were made in the AME Church's periodical, the *Christian Recorder*, 27 January 1872. The editor said Stanford had received money for the *Recorder* and other church publications but never delivered the goods or credited the account of the sender. By 9 March 1872, a new man had received the appointment in the publications office, and no more word appeared about Stanford. See the discussion about Stanford in William Seraile, *Fire in His Heart: Bishop Benjamin Tucker Tanner and the A.M.E. Church* (Knoxville: University of Tennessee Press, 1998), 29. On 10 March 1879, shortly before Stanford's departure for Liberia, he met with the AME district conference in Little Rock, where the presiding bishop, Thomas M. D. Ward, extolled Stanford's past service to the church, expressed regrets for the circumstances that led to his separation, and gave Stanford a hand of fellowship reinstating him into the AME Church (Minutes of 11th Annual Conference, 10 March 1879, Little Rock, in African Methodist Episcopal Church, Arkansas Annual Conference Minutes, original microfilms at Arkansas History Commission, Little Rock; hereafter cited as Arkansas AME Records).

9. Seraile, *Fire in His Heart*, 29; Stanford to Coppinger, 4 March 1877, ACS reel 118; *Historical Report of the Secretary of State of Arkansas* (Little Rock: Secretary of State, 1968), 339, 341. In his letters to the ACS in the late 1870s Stanford wrote in an elegant hand on stationary bearing the seal of the Arkansas Senate.

10. Dan A. Rudd and Theo Bond, *From Slavery to Wealth: The Life of Scott Bond* (Madison, Ark.: Journal Printing, 1917), 206.

11. Clubs were numbered consecutively in the order of their foundation. Delegates representing clubs numbering as high as twenty-eight attended the convention on 23–24 November (see "First Convention of the Liberia Exodus Arkansas Colony," 1).

12. Stanford to Coppinger, 4 November 1877, ACS reel 116B; "Constitution of the Liberia Exodus Arkansas Colony," vol. 6, Colonization Pamphlets. For a discussion of middle-class black views, see Kevin K. Gaines, *Uplifting the Race: Black Leadership, Politics, and Culture in the Twentieth Century* (Chapel Hill: University of North Carolina Press, 1996), 1–46.

13. "The First Convention of the Liberia Exodus Arkansas Colony." One member of the colony later complained that the money spent on the commissioners' trip could have sent a good number of permanent emigrants to Liberia. See Berry Colman to Coppinger, 4 April 1879, ACS reel 118. High-minded white neighbors were also skeptical of Stanford's mission. Alida Clark, an Indiana Quaker who had come with her husband to Phillips County during Reconstruction to open a school for black children, reported: "There has been great excitement on the Liberia question by unprincipled men, and money extorted from the people in the midst of their pinching poverty, to defray the expenses of sending two men to Liberia to 'spy out' the country" (letter of 10 January 1878, *Friends Review*, 26 January 1878).

14. Stanford to Coppinger, 4 November, 5 December 1877, ACS reel 116B; Coppinger to Stanford, 10 December 1877, ACS reel 217; Charles F. Hicks to Coppinger, 3 July 1879, ACS reel 119; Stanford to Coppinger, 9 June 1878, ACS reel 117.

15. S. M. Waters to Coppinger, 7 January 1878, ACS reel 117; *Arkansas Gazette*, 1 May 1878; Berry Colman to Coppinger, 12 August 1878, ACS reel 117.

16. A Phillips County planter recorded in his diary the Democratic company's campaign against potential black voters (13 August 1878, John Millinder Hanks Diaries, Special Collections, University of Arkansas, Fayetteville).

17. *New York Times*, 12, 14, 20 August 1878. The *Times* took its reports from accounts in the *St. Louis Globe Democrat*, the *Fort Smith New Era*, and the *Cincinnati Commercial*. The issue of 14 August contained a report sent directly from Phillips County. Helena planter John Hanks made his comment in his diary entry of 17 August 1878.

18. *New York Times*, 14, 20 August 1878.

19. *Arkansas Gazette*, 14, 23 August 1878.

20. *New York Times*, 20 August 1878; *Arkansas Gazette*, 23 August 1878.

21. *New York Times*, 14 August 1878.

22. Ibid., 14, 23 August 1878; *Arkansas Gazette*, 23 August 1878.

23. *Arkansas Gazette*, 4 September 1878; V. Dell testimony in U.S. Congress, Senate, *Report and Testimony*, pt. 3, p. 354; see also Powell Clayton's speech a decade later recounting the 1878 election, in *Arkansas Gazette*, 23 September 1888; and John Millinder Hanks Diaries, 2 September 1878.

24. In Crittenden, Lee, and Monroe Counties, Democrats had reportedly organized rifle clubs, and Democratic bulldozing was also alleged in Pulaski and Jefferson Counties (*Arkansas Gazette*, 14 August 1878; V. Dell testimony in U.S. Congress, Senate, *Report and Testimony*, pt. 3, p. 354); see also list of legislators in *Sharp County Record*, 17 October 1878. Statewide election returns from the September election did not get published in the newspapers as usual, and vote tallies are unavailable.

In the congressional elections of the following November, John Bradley, the Republican-Greenback candidate in southern Arkansas's Second District, complained that Democrats printed tickets for his opponent on election night after the polls had been closed. In Jefferson County, Bradley said Democratic authorities arrested the federal election supervisors and marshals on trumped-up charges, refused them bail, and released them only after the vote count was completed. Bradley charged that disguised men had burst into the home of a prominent black man, Castor McClelland, and brutally murdered him as he lay in bed with his wife and child. This kept many black voters home on federal election day. In Chicot County, Arkansas's blackest county at 85 percent, someone forged posters naming another man as the Republican candidate instead of Bradley, apparently to confuse black voters. The U.S. marshal for the Eastern District of Arkansas passed on Bradley's complaints to U.S. Attorney General Charles Devens, concluding, "we have a record of fraud that should cause honorable citizens regardless of party all over our land to hide their heads in shame that such things can be and the offenders go unpunished." See Bradley to James Torrans, 26 November, 20 December 1878; and James Torrans to Charles Devens, 5 January 1879; all in Letters Received from Arkansas, 1875–83, Eastern District, M1418, roll 2, U.S. Department of Justice, Record Group 60, National Archives, College Park, Md.

25. G. W. Hayden to Coppinger, 20 January 1879; H. H. Robinson to Coppinger, 29 October 1878; B. K. McKeever to Coppinger, 13 February 1879; all in ACS reel 118.

26. A. L. Stanford to Coppinger, 18 November 1878, ACS reel 118; Coppinger to Stanford, 25 November 1878, ACS reel 218. Coppinger told S. M. Waters of Galloway (28 March 1878, ACS reel 217) that it would require $20,000 paid in advance to char-

ter a ship from New Orleans for 200 passengers and six months of support after arrival. See also Coppinger to Shadrach Jenkins, 7 December 1878, ACS reel 218.

27. Coppinger to J. M. Waters, 12 January 1878, ACS reel 217; Coppinger to Shadrach Jenkins, 4, 27 March 1878, ACS reel 218; Coppinger to Berry Coleman, 4 September 1878, ACS reel 218; Coppinger to G. W. Hayden, 23 February 1879, ACS reel 218; A. L. Stanford to Coppinger, 29 March 1879, ACS reel 118.

28. Shadrach Jenkins to Coppinger, 23 December 1878, ACS reel 118; Coppinger to Jenkins, 6 April 1878, ACS reel 218.

29. G. W. Hayden to Coppinger, 2 February 1879; Berry Colman to Coppinger, 9 November 1878, 4 April 1879; all in ACS reel 118.

30. A. L. Stanford to Coppinger, 16 January 1879; B. K. McKeever to Coppinger, 18 January 1879; H. H. Robinson to Coppinger, 28 May 1879; all in ACS reel 118.

31. A. L. Stanford to Coppinger, 12 February 1879; G. W. Hayden to Coppinger, 17 March 1879; both in ACS reel 118.

32. William Lucas to Coppinger, 8 May 1879, ACS reel 118.

33. *Southern Standard*, 21 September 1878. Stanford's attendance in the state senate was poor both in the 1877 and 1879 sessions. He missed about a third of each session but was in attendance on the last day, 13 March 1879. See "Journal of the Senate of Arkansas, 21st Session, Little Rock, January 8, 1877," and "Journal of the Senate of Arkansas, 22nd Session, Little Rock, January 13, 1879," in A.1a, Arkansas, reel 7, Records of the States of the United States of America, a microfilm compilation prepared by the Library of Congress in association with the University of North Carolina.

34. A. L. Stanford to Coppinger, 24 February 1879; Stanford to Coppinger, 29 March 1879; both in ACS reel 118. Cabin passage for the three Stanfords cost $250. See Yates and Porterfield to Coppinger, 13 June 1879, ACS reel 118.

35. B. K. McKeever to Coppinger, 12 May 1879, ACS reel 118; Coppinger to McKeever, 17 May 1879, ACS reel 218.

36. Stanford had estimated $15 as the cheapest fare between Helena and New York, the water/train route via Cincinnati (Stanford to Coppinger, 4 March 1879, ACS reel 118). The Stanfords took a more leisurely trip through the South and up the East Coast with planned stops in Mississippi, Georgia, and North and South Carolina before heading to New York (Stanford to Coppinger, 29 March 1879, ACS reel 118). See also B. K. McKeever to Coppinger, 26 May 1879, ACS reel 118; and Yates and Porterfield to Coppinger, 9, 13 June, 1879, ACS reel 118; and Yates and Porterfield telegram to Coppinger, 1 August 1879, ACS reel 119. The birth of Aberdeen Johnson is recounted by his grandson, Johnny Johnson (interview with author, Brewerville, Liberia, 16 July 1998). Word about the births of the McKeever and Lucas children came from the ACS agent in Monrovia; see Daniel B. Warner to Coppinger, 5, 15 August 1879, ACS reel 164. A controversy resulted from the births, for Dr. Stanford charged each family $15 for assisting with the delivery, knowing surely that the families lacked the money to pay him. Ben McKeever and William Lucas complained that the ACS had hired Stanford to give medical care for the emigrants and thus they should not have to pay. See Warner to Coppinger, 15 October 1879; and McKeever and Lucas to Coppinger, 4 February 1880; both in reel ACS 164.

37. H. H. Robinson to Coppinger, 3 May 1879, ACS reel 118.

38. *New York Times*, 16 April, 20–21 May 1879.

39. William Cohen, *At Freedom's Edge: Black Mobility and the Southern White Quest for Racial Control, 1861–1915* (Baton Rouge: Louisiana State University Press, 1991), 306.

40. G. A. Walker to ACS, 12 July 1879, ACS reel 119.

41. Edward Larkin, a twenty-nine-year-old preacher at North Creek, wrote to Coppinger on 17 September 1879 concerning twenty to thirty families who wished to emigrate; Scipio Graves of Indian Bay, Monroe County, wrote to Coppinger on 5 September 1879 on behalf of four families; W. R. DeWitt of Ashley's Point in Lee County said in a letter of 20 September 1879 to Coppinger that twenty families there were ready to go; G. W. Hayden to Coppinger, 14 November 1879, all in ACS reel 119.

42. W. H. Green to Coppinger, 13 September 1879, ACS reel 119.

43. P. Clevoter to Coppinger, 7 December 1879, ACS reel 119. Clevoter was a white man who wrote on behalf of Elijah Parker and other black applicants from Poplar Grove in Phillips County (Annual Report of the American Colonization Society, January 18, 1881, pp. 12–13, ACS reel 287). See also Henry Foster to Coppinger, 4 February 1880, ACS reel 120. Foster, of DeView, Woodruff County, said he had sold everything and was just waiting to leave.

44. Yates and Porterfield to Coppinger, 16 February 1880, ACS reel 120.

45. Henry Phillips to Coppinger, 26 February 1880, ACS reel 120; Coppinger to [unknown], c. mid-February 1880, ACS reel 219; Yates and Porterfield to Coppinger, 26 February 1880, ACS reel 120.

46. Isaac Dickson to Coppinger, 1 March 1880; Yates and Porterfield to Coppinger, 20 March 1880; both in ACS reel 120.

47. *New York Times*, 27 March 1880.

48. Ibid., 27 March, 1, 20 April 1880; Yates and Porterfield to Coppinger, 31 March, 6 April 1880, ACS reel 120; clipping from the *New York Evening Telegram*, c. 15 April 1880, in ACS reel 120.

49. *New York Evening Telegram* clipping; Yates and Porterfield to Coppinger, 5 April 1880; Margaretta Scott to Coppinger, 6 April 1880; all in ACS reel 120. The Minute Book of St. Philip's Protestant Episcopal Church, a black congregation in New York, shows an entry of 13 April 1880 that included a resolution to take up a collection to assist the Arkansas refugees (Minute Book, St. Philip's Church Collection, Schomburg Center for Research in Black Culture, New York Public Library, New York). A list of those who gave to the Arkansas refugees included donors ranging from clergymen to anonymous women to the colored waiters at the Metropolitan Hotel. See *New York Times*, 25 April 1880.

50. [Unknown] to Coppinger, Philadelphia, 20 April 1880; Thomas S. Malcolm to Coppinger, 21 May 1880; both in ACS reel 120.

51. *New York Times*, 27 March, 5 April 1880.

52. *Arkansas Gazette*, 16 April 1880.

53. Yates and Porterfield to Coppinger, 16, 26 February 1880, ACS reel 120.

54. *New York Times*, 22, 25, 26 April 1880.

55. Printed flyer: "The Movement comes from our own Hearts; God put it there," 25 April 1880, ACS reel 120.

56. See receipts, May 1880; note from "Friend of the Oppressed," 14 May 1880;

Thomas Agan to Coppinger, 8 May 1880; and James McCormack to Edward Morris, 3 May 1880; all in ACS reel 120.

57. *African Repository* 56 (July 1880): 72; William V. Pettel to Coppinger, 11 May 1880, ACS reel 120; Journal of the Executive Committee of the ACS, 7 May 1880, pp. 283–84, ACS reel 293. Yates and Porterfield charged the ACS $5,114 for passage of the emigrants aboard the *Monrovia* and *Liberia*, and the society would pay even more for the provisions and supplies for each emigrant; see Yates and Porterfield to Coppinger, 14 June 1880, ACS reel 120. The relief committee in New York had disbursed $950.19 in expenses related to the care of the Arkansas refugees in that city; see *New York Times*, 27 June 1880.

58. Coppinger to Yates and Porterfield, 7 May 1880, ACS reel 219; Margaretta Scott to Coppinger, 6 April 1880; Berry Colman to Coppinger, 21 April 1880; [unknown] to Coppinger, 20 April 1880; all in ACS reel 120.

59. "Address to the Arkansas Refugees," *African Repository* 56 (July 1880): 70–72.

60. Thomas S. Malcolm to Coppinger, 19, 21 May 1880, ACS reel 120.

61. Coppinger to W. S. Phillips, 29 May 1880, ACS reel 219; Journal of the Executive Committee of the ACS, 5 June 1880, p. 286, ACS reel 293. The *Arkansas Gazette*, 1 June 1880, reported that some of the Arkansas refugees, after acquiring a taste for life in the big city, deserted the ship to stay in New York.

62. *African Repository* 56 (September 1880): 90; Yates and Porterfield to Coppinger, 16 July, 4 August 1880, ACS reel 120.

63. St. Francis County, which was 60 percent black, recorded five Republican votes in the gubernatorial election of 1880; Jefferson County, with a black population of more than 17,000, tallied only seven Republican votes. However, several black-majority counties, such as Ouachita, Monroe, Lafayette, Little River, and Woodruff, polled substantial numbers of Republican, presumably black, votes. See election returns by county in *Arkansas Gazette*, 19 September 1880.

Chapter Two

1. While the *Arkansas Gazette* failed to report about this meeting of black Republicans, accounts of the meeting appeared in the *New York Times*, 8 January 1882, and the *Edgefield Chronicle*, 11 January 1882. A similar meeting in August 1883 elected delegates to represent Arkansas in a national convention called by Frederick Douglass, to be held in Louisville, Kentucky; see *Arkansas Mansion*, 1, 8 September 1883.

2. See the chapter on Churchill by F. Clark Elkins in Timothy P. Donovan and Willard B. Gatewood Jr., eds., *The Governors of Arkansas: Essays in Political Biography* (Fayetteville: University of Arkansas Press, 1981), 68–72.

3. *Arkansas Gazette*, 16, 17 June 1881.

4. Ibid., 25 May, 22 June, 9 July, 22 August 1882.

5. See election returns for 1880 and 1882 in *Arkansas Gazette*, 19 September 1880; and *Biennial Report of the Secretary of State of the State of Arkansas, 1882* (Little Rock: Mitchell and Bates, 1882), 72–73.

6. Republicans accused Democrats of preventing several hundred black citizens

from voting at the courthouse in Helena. A ballot box was stolen in a black precinct in Monroe County, and a reporter sent by the *St. Louis Globe Democrat* to cover the Arkansas election claimed that people of color were afraid to leave their homes to vote in Little Rock. James T. White, a prominent black Republican and unsuccessful candidate for representative in Phillips County who had vowed to leave the country before he would allow high-handed outlaws to take away his rights, announced solemnly a few weeks after the election that his home in Helena was for sale at half its assessed value (*Arkansas Gazette*, 9, 12, 14 September 1882).

7. *Biennial Report of the Secretary of State of the State of Arkansas, 1884* (Little Rock: Mitchell and Bettis, 1884), 16–17; *Biennial Report of the Secretary of State of the State of Arkansas, 1886* (Little Rock: A. M. Woodruff, 1886), 37–39; *Biennial Report of the Secretary of State of the State of Arkansas, 1888* (Little Rock: Press, 1888), 39–41; *Arkansas Gazette*, 2 September 1884.

8. John William Graves, *Town and Country: Race Relations in an Urban-Rural Context, Arkansas, 1865–1905* (Fayetteville: University of Arkansas Press, 1990), 54; *Arkansas Gazette*, 6, 7, 8, 10, 12, 14 September 1882.

9. *Arkansas Gazette*, 6 September 1884, 9 September 1886.

10. U.S. Department of the Interior, Census Office, *Report on Population of the United States at the Eleventh Census, 1890* (Washington, D.C.: Government Printing Office, 1895), cvi.

11. Ibid.; U.S. Bureau of the Census, *Negro Population, 1790–1915* (Washington, D.C.: Government Printing Office, 1918), 777.

12. *Arkansas Mansion*, 1 September 1883; U.S. Department of the Interior, Census Office, *Report on the Productions of Agriculture as Returned at the Tenth Census, 1880* (Washington, D.C.: Government Printing Office, 1883), 3; U.S. Department of the Interior, Census Office, *Report on the Statistics of Agriculture in the United States of America at the Eleventh Census: 1890* (Washington, D.C.: Government Printing Office, 1895), 199. For more information about labor agents and the exploits of Peg Leg Williams, see William Cohen, *At Freedom's Edge: Black Mobility and the Southern White Quest for Racial Control, 1861–1915* (Baton Rouge: Louisiana State University Press, 1991), 257–73.

13. Colonel D. McD. Lindsey, *The Wrongs of the Negro: A Remedy*, 1888, reprinted in John David Smith, ed., *The American Colonization Society and Emigration: Solutions to the "Negro Problem"* (New York: Garland, 1993), 247 [9].

14. See George Brown Tindall, *South Carolina Negroes, 1877–1900* (Columbia: University of South Carolina Press, 1952), 174–80; and Frenise Avedis Logan, *The Negro in North Carolina, 1876–1894* (Chapel Hill: University of North Carolina Press, 1964), 127. See also the official newspaper of the Colored Methodist Episcopal Church, the Jackson, Tenn. *Christian Index*, June 1885.

15. William Pickens, *Bursting Bonds* (Boston: Jordon & More, 1923), 3–30.

16. Tindall, *South Carolina Negroes*, 164–65; George A. Devlin, *South Carolina and Black Migration, 1865–1940: In Search of a Promised Land* (New York: Garland, 1989), 127–33.

17. For information about the migration, see the *Charleston News and Courier*, 28, 30 December 1881, 2, 6, 24 January 1882; *New York Times*, 12 January 1882; Augusta, Ga., *Chronicle and Constitutionalist*, 7 January 1882; and *Edgefield Chronicle*, 28 December 1881, 4, 21 January 1882. See also Tindall, *South Carolina Negroes*, 170–77; and Devlin, *South Carolina and Black Migration*, 127–33.

18. *News and Courier*, 24 January 1882; *Edgefield Chronicle*, 4, 25 January 1882; U.S. Bureau of the Census, *Negro Population*, 777.

19. *Christian Index*, 23 June 1888. Turner wrote in the *Christian Recorder*, 13 December 1888; reprinted in *Indianapolis Freeman*, 5 January 1889.

20. Carl H. Moneyhon, *Arkansas and the New South, 1874–1929* (Fayetteville: University of Arkansas Press, 1997), 67.

21. U.S. Department of the Interior, Census Office, *Report on Cotton Production in the United States* (Washington, D.C.: Government Printing Office, 1884), pt. 1, p. 588; U.S. Department of the Interior, Census Office, *Report on the Statistics of Agriculture, 1890*, 393.

22. Moneyhon, *Arkansas and the New South*, 64, 68.

23. U.S. Department of the Interior, Census Office, *Report on Farms and Homes: Proprietorship and Indebtedness in the United States at the Eleventh Census, 1890* (Washington, D.C.: Government Printing Office, 1896), 288.

24. U.S. Bureau of the Census, *Negro Population*, 470; U.S. Department of the Interior, Census Office, *Report on the Statistics of Agriculture, 1890*, 123–24.

25. Moneyhon, *Arkansas and the New South*, 6. For more information about the postbellum cotton economy and conditions for black and white farmers, see Roger L. Ransom and Richard Sutch, *One Kind of Freedom: The Economic Consequences of Emancipation* (Cambridge: Cambridge University Press, 1977); Gavin Wright, *The Political Economy of the Cotton South: Households, Markets, and Wealth in the Nineteenth Century* (New York: W. W. Norton, 1978); Robert Higgs, *Competition and Coercion: Blacks in the American Economy, 1865–1914* (Cambridge: Cambridge University Press, 1977); Stephen J. Decanio, *Agriculture in the Postbellum South: The Economics of Production and Supply* (Cambridge: Harvard University Press, 1974); and Jay Mandle, *The Roots of Black Poverty: The Southern Plantation after the Civil War* (Durham: Duke University Press, 1978).

26. Pickens, *Bursting Bonds*, 24–30. See also the discussion of black family life in Stewart E. Tolnay, *The Bottom Rung: African American Family Life on Southern Farms* (Urbana: University of Illinois Press, 1999); and Jacqueline Jones, *Labor of Love, Labor of Sorrow: Black Women, Work, and the Family from Slavery to Present* (New York: Basic Books, 1985), 79–109. Also see Jerome C. Rose, ed., *Gone to a Better Land: A Biohistory of a Rural Black Cemetery in the Post-Reconstruction South* (Fayetteville: Arkansas Archeological Survey, 1985). Rose reports the findings of an archaeological team that excavated a turn-of-the-century black cemetery in Lafayette County, Arkansas. Skeletal remains showed a highly stressed population with nutritional deficiencies, degenerative joint disease indicating hard physical labor, and a high rate of infant mortality. For an informative look at daily life for rural Arkansans in the early 1890s, see the edited diary of a white woman in Desha County, Margaret Jones Bolsterli, ed., *Vinegar Pie and Chicken Bread: A Woman's Diary of Life in the Rural South, 1890–1891* (Fayetteville: University of Arkansas Press, 1982). For a description of the material conditions and daily routine of a rural black Arkansas family, see Ruth Polk Patterson, *The Seed of Sally Good'n: A Black Family of Arkansas, 1833–1953* (Lexington: University Press of Kentucky, 1985), 8–10.

27. See F. Clark Elkins, "Arkansas Farmers Organize for Action, 1882–1884," *Arkansas Historical Quarterly* 13 (Autumn 1954): 231–48; W. Scott Morgan, *History of the Wheel and Alliance and the Impending Revolution* (Fort Scott, Kan.: J. H. Rice, 1889); and Randy Hennsington, "Upland Farmers and Agrarian Protest: Northwest Arkansas and the Brothers of Freedom" (M.A. thesis, University of Arkansas, 1973). For an overview of

the movement, see Theodore Saloutos, *Farmer Movements in the South, 1865–1933* (Lincoln: University of Nebraska, 1964), 60–68.

28. Fon Louise Gordon, *Caste and Class: The Black Experience in Arkansas, 1880–1920* (Athens: University of Georgia Press, 1995), 15; Clifton Paisley, "The Political Wheelers and Arkansas' Election of 1888," *Arkansas Historical Quarterly* 25 (Spring 1966): 3; F. Clark Elkins, "The Agricultural Wheel in Arkansas, 1887," *Arkansas Historical Quarterly* 40 (Autumn 1981): 253–59. For a discussion of black populism, see Gerald Gaither, *Blacks and the Populist Revolt: Ballots and Bigotry in the "New South"* (Tuscaloosa: University of Alabama Press, 1977).

29. F. Clark Elkins, "The Agricultural Wheel: County Politics and Consolidation, 1884–1885," *Arkansas Historical Quarterly* 29 (Autumn 1970): 160, 165; F. Clark Elkins, "State Politics and the Agricultural Wheel," *Arkansas Historical Quarterly* 38 (Autumn 1979): 248–58; Moneyhon, *Arkansas and the New South*, 81–82. For more about the situation in Conway County, see Kenneth C. Barnes, *Who Killed John Clayton? Political Violence and the Emergence of the New South* (Durham: Duke University Press, 1998), 56–59.

30. For more about Turner, see Stephen Ward Angell, *Bishop Henry McNeal Turner and African-American Religion in the South* (Knoxville: University of Tennessee Press, 1992); Edwin S. Redkey, "The Flowering of Black Nationalism: Henry McNeal Turner and Marcus Garvey," in vol. 2 of *Key Issues in the Afro-American Experience*, ed. Nathan I. Huggins, Martin Kilson, and Daniel M. Fox (New York: Harcourt Brace Jovanovich, 1971), 107–15; Edwin S. Redkey, *Black Exodus: Black Nationalist and Back-to-Africa Movements, 1890–1910* (New Haven: Yale University Press, 1969), 24–46; Melbourne Stenson Cummings, "The Rhetoric of Bishop Henry McNeal Turner, Leading Advocate in the African Emigration Movement, 1866–1907" (Ph.D. diss., UCLA, 1972); and James T. Campbell, *Songs of Zion: The African Methodist Episcopal Church in the United States and South Africa* (New York: Oxford University Press, 1995), 79–99.

31. When Turner became bishop, most other AME bishops were living in the North and most rank-and-file members lived south of the Mason-Dixon Line. See Angell, *Bishop Henry McNeal Turner*, 142, 154–57.

32. Minutes of 14th Annual Conference, 23 February 1881, Batesville, p. 163; Minutes of 15th Annual Conference, 15–22 November 1882, Morrilton, p. 243; both in Arkansas AME Records.

33. See Redkey, *Black Exodus*, 41–42; and Minutes of 16th Annual Conference, November 21, 1883, p. 253, Arkansas AME Records. The *Arkansas Mansion*, 24 November, 1 December 1883, reported Turner's comments with its own editorials.

34. Berry Coleman to Coppinger, 30 April 1881, ACS reel 121.

35. E. S. Hughes to Coppinger, 24 April 1881, ACS reel 121. See also M. A. Guyton to Coppinger, 26 September 1881; T. J. Johnson to Coppinger, 17 October 1881; and T. S. Stewart to Coppinger, 2 November 1881; all in ACS reel 122. Letters arrived in the ACS office from St. Francis, Lee, and Woodruff Counties especially. Hughes was from Columbus in Cleveland County.

36. J. L. Judson to Coppinger, 12 January 1884, ACS reel 125. See also the letter of application of schoolteacher John Williams, who claimed to have attended Alcorn University and Shaw University in Mississippi before coming to Phillips County (John Williams to Coppinger, 2 February 1884, ACS reel 125). Green Williams explained that

twenty families in Lee County wished to emigrate after the fall harvest in 1883 (Green Williams to Coppinger, 5 July 1883, ACS reel 124).

37. *African Repository* 59 (January 1883): 28; 64 (January 1888): 39.

38. Barnes, *Who Killed John Clayton?* 46–47, 53–55.

39. Andrew Flowers to Edward S. Morris, 16 July 1881, ACS reel 122. The club also sent the ACS a copy of the preamble and resolution of the association. See Henderson Walker, president, and Jerry Jones, recording secretary, to Coppinger, 3 December 1882, ACS reel 122.

40. Andrew Flowers to Coppinger, 11 April 1882, ACS reel 122.

41. Ibid., 17 January 1883, ACS reel 124; Coppinger to Flowers, 20 January 1883, 27 August 1883, ACS reel 220; Coppinger's notes on applicants, series 6, volume 7, ACS reel 306; *African Repository* 60 (January 1884): 30–31.

42. M. E. Childress to Coppinger, 23 June 1884, ACS reel 125; Childress to Coppinger, 6 August 1884, ACS reel 126; Childress to Hon. Wayne McVeigh, Attorney General of the United States, 19 August 1881, U.S. Department of Justice, Letters Received from Arkansas, Eastern District, 1875–83, roll 2, U.S. Department of Justice, Record Group 60, National Archives, College Park, Md.

43. M. H. Keen to Coppinger, 28 January 1884, ACS reel 125; Keen to Coppinger, 4 July 1884, ACS reel 126.

44. R. R. Walting to Coppinger, 13 June 1883, ACS reel 124; *African Repository* 60 (January 1884): 32, 64.

45. R. R. Walting to Coppinger, 14 January, 26 March 1884, ACS reel 125; Coppinger to Walting, 26 February 1884, ACS reel 221; Coppinger to J. A. Allington, 13 March 1884, ACS reel 221; Henderson Walker to Coppinger, 24 August 1884, ACS reel 126.

46. R. R. Walting to Coppinger, 30 March 1884, ACS reel 125; C. T. O. King to Coppinger, 5 June 1884, ACS reel 166; Coppinger to King, 2 September 1884, ACS reel 221. King served as the ACS agent in Monrovia, Liberia.

47. R. A. Mitchell to Coppinger, 23 July, 27 September 1884; Henderson Walker to Coppinger, 21 September 1884; R. R. Walting to Coppinger, 28 October 1884; all in ACS reel 126.

48. Coppinger to A. A. Shelton, November 1886, ACS reel 222; J. C. Hazeley to Coppinger, 3, 24, 26 November 1885, ACS reel 127. Hazeley had visited Texarkana, Hot Springs, Prescott, Camden, Magnolia, Stephens, Lewisville, and other small communities. Black families in the area had reason to be interested in Hazeley's message. Just two years before, in the fall of 1883, a land dispute had evolved into a race riot in Howard and Hempstead Counties in southwestern Arkansas. After tensions flared over land, a black girl accused a white man of attempted rape. When white authorities refused to arrest the white man, black citizens organized a posse, hunted down the accused sex offender, and shot him dead. This attempt at extralegal justice unleashed a violent backlash as white gangs roamed the countryside near the Hempstead-Howard border. Black reports said whites went into houses, beat black women, and shot old men and boys "as they would shoot a squirrel." Finally the state militia was called in and order was restored. In the ensuing months, forty-three black men were taken to jail, and ten of them eventually received fifteen-year prison sentences. The alleged leader of the black posse was hanged the next year before an estimated crowd of 5,000 people. For a black

account of the race riot, see *Arkansas Mansion*, 11, 25 August; 1, 8 September; 10, 24 November; 8, 22 December 1883; 19 April 1884. For a white version, see *Arkansas Gazette*, 12, 14, 19 August 1883. See also Herbert G. Gutman's discussion of this incident in *The Black Family in Slavery and Freedom, 1750–1925* (New York: Pantheon Books, 1976), 439–41; and the most thorough study of the event, Peggy S. Lloyd, "The Howard County Race Riot of 1883," *Arkansas Historical Quarterly* 59 (Winter 2000): 353–87. Not surprisingly, when Hazeley came through the country two years after the riot, he found considerable interest in African emigration. In Saratoga, the center of the troubled area, George Byres led an emigration club that requested assistance from the ACS in 1886 to send delegates to Liberia to scout out the country. Byres said they were poor and badly treated and his group was mostly "waders [widows] that they husbands have been killed by the white man" (Byres to Coppinger, 24 May, 6 June 1886, ACS reel 128).

49. J. C. Hazeley to Coppinger, 3, 26 November, 7, 23 December 1885, ACS reel 127; Hazeley to Coppinger, 1 January, 19 February, 20 April 1886, ACS reel 128. Hazeley visited, for example, Pine Bluff, Augusta, Newport, Helena, and Fort Smith.

50. See the handbill from Hazeley's show in Parsons, Kansas, at 30 October 1886, ACS reel 129.

51. See the incoming correspondence of the ACS, December 1885–April 1886 in ACS reels 127 and 128.

52. J. C. Hazeley to Coppinger, 28 April 1886, ACS reel 128. Hazeley asked Coppinger to send copies of the *African Repository* to John Johnson and several other men in Faulkner County. Application lists were received on 10 February 1887, ACS reel 129, and 30 August 1887, ACS reel 130.

53. Faulkner County's black population in 1880 was 1,418, but by the 1890 census it had grown to 3,348 (U.S. Bureau of the Census, *Negro Population*, 777). In January 1883, near Pinnacle Springs, in the northern part of the county, night riders demanded that black homesteaders relocate south of the Cadron Creek. The family of Burrell Lindsey refused to go, prompting a firefight at the Lindsey cabin that left one white man dead and Lindsey in the state prison. In the following year, a band of masked men in Conway overpowered the local constable as he escorted a black man named Tom Wilson to jail. Wilson had reportedly attempted to sexually assault a married white woman. He was hanged by the men from an oak tree in Conway. For Lindsey's story, see Robert W. Meriwether, "'Bulldozing' on the Cadron (1883)," *Faulkner Facts and Fiddlings* 41 (Fall/Winter 1999): 67–70. For the Wilson lynching, see *Arkansas Gazette*, 21 February 1884.

54. John Johnson to ACS, 7 August 1888, ACS reel 131; Johnson to ACS, 22 January 1889, ACS reel 132; *African Repository* 65 (July 1889): 94.

Chapter Three

1. W. D. Leslie to Coppinger, 20 August 1890, ACS reel 134.

2. Carl H. Moneyhon, *Arkansas and the New South, 1874–1929* (Fayetteville: University of Arkansas Press, 1997), 85–87; Clifton Paisley, "The Political Wheelers and Arkansas' Election of 1888," *Arkansas Historical Quarterly* 25 (Spring 1966): 3–8; Conway, Ark., *Log Cabin Democrat*, 21 July 1888.

3. John William Graves, *Town and County: Race Relations in an Urban-Rural Context, Arkansas, 1865–1905* (Fayetteville: University of Arkansas Press, 1990), 68–69; *Arkansas Gazette*, 14, 16, 18 July 1888. As the black refugees scattered to points north, reports began to appear in northern newspapers. See Topeka, Kan., *American Citizen*, 17 August 1888; *St. Louis Globe Democrat*, 30 August 1888; and *Indianapolis Freeman*, 18 August 1888. See also the dramatic testimony about these events in U.S. Congress, House of Representatives, *Featherston vs. Cate*, 51st Cong., 1st sess., 1890, House Report 306 (Washington, D.C.: Government Printing Office, 1890), 2–12. Daniel Lewis, after fleeing to Memphis, moved a few years later to Oklahoma; see Daniel Webster Lewis Jr., "Judge Daniel Webster Lewis, Sr.: Early Arkansas Magistrate," clipping from *Boulé Journal*, file 1: Biographical Materials, Daniel W. Lewis Sr. Papers, Special Collections, University of Arkansas Library, Fayetteville.

4. Kenneth C. Barnes, *Who Killed John Clayton? Political Violence and the Emergence of the New South* (Durham: Duke University Press, 1998), 62; *St. Louis Globe Democrat*, 3 September 1888.

5. *Arkansas Gazette*, 4, 6, 7 September 1888; *New York Times*, 7 September 1890; Barnes, *Who Killed John Clayton?* 62–64; Paisley, "Political Wheelers and Arkansas' Election of 1888," 17–18.

6. Barnes, *Who Killed John Clayton?* 66–93.

7. Norwood won in black-majority Chicot, Drew, Desha, Jefferson, Lafayette, Lincoln, Monroe, Ouachita, and Phillips Counties. Democrats prevailed in the black-majority counties of Ashley, Crittenden, Lee, Mississippi, and Woodruff, suggesting some fraud occurred there. *Arkansas Gazette*, 8 September 1888, shows returns in the governor's race. See also the reports on county offices that appeared in the *Gazette* in the week following the election. The paper published a roster of House members on 14 September 1888.

8. William H. King to Coppinger, 28 September 1888, ACS reel 131; D. Williams Young to ACS, 2 October 1888, ACS reel 132; Ranson Perry to Coppinger, with application form, 22 October 1888, ACS reel 132. The election fraud in Conway and Crittenden Counties was so extreme in 1888 that a prominent leader of the Agricultural Wheel, W. Scott Morgan, later used real events as the basis of a novel, *The Red Light: A Story of Southern Politics and Election Methods* (Moravian Falls, N.C.: Yellow Jacket Press, 1904). In Morgan's version, Morrilton and Plumerville became Morriston and Hummersville while Crittenden County and its main town, Marion, became Critwell County and Maridon.

9. See, for example, letters to Coppinger from W. H. Tyler, 24 April 1889; Phillip James, 5 May 1889; Henry J. Jones, 7 June 1889; all in ACS reel 132. The request from Eureka Springs (23 May 1889, ACS reel 132) bore no name. At Eureka Spring's Fourth of July 1889 celebrations, a local white man, William Pitts, set up a sideshow whereby a black man's head appeared through a sheet as a target for people throwing eggs, at two shots for a nickel. The *Arkansas Gazette* (10 July 1889) reported, "The coon got considerable albumen in his wool during the day and Col. Pitts got a good many nickels out of the performance also." Pink Blair wrote first from Osceola, 30 September 1889; by the end of the year he had taken refuge in Memphis. See his pleading letters to Coppinger of 5 January and 9 February 1890, ACS reel 133.

10. Abner Downs to Coppinger, 6 April 1889, ACS reel 132; A. M. Lipscomb to

Coppinger, 20 August, 30 October 1889, and letter and application form, 23 November 1889; 7 January 1890, in ACS reel 133; and 21 April 1890, ACS reel 134; *African Repository* 66 (July 1890): 94–95.

11. See L. Wilson to Coppinger, 26 February 1890, ACS reel 133; W. K. Fortson to Coppinger, 22 April, 24 May 1890, ACS reel 134; and H. A. Anthony to Coppinger, 7 June 1890, ACS reel 134.

12. G. W. Pounds, president, and J. E. Walker, secretary, to Coppinger, 14 September 1889, ACS reel 133; Alex Samuel to Coppinger, 13 May 1890, ACS reel 134; J. P. Douglas to Coppinger, 9 May 1890, ACS reel 133.

13. See letters from Humphrey to Coppinger of S. W. Alexander, J. D. Thompson, S. S. Jacobs, 5 April 1890; J. B. Roberson to Coppinger, 12 May and 3 June 1890; and Tom Moss to Coppinger, 6 August 1890; all in ACS reel 134; William Moss to Coppinger, 23 September 1890; and J. B. Roberson to Coppinger, 28 October 1890, both in ACS reel 135; and Coppinger to William Moss, 26 September, 6 November 1890, ACS reel 224.

14. Graves, *Town and Country*, 142–43.

15. See discussion of the Lodge bill in C. Vann Woodward, *Origins of the New South* (Baton Rouge: Louisiana State University Press, 1951), 254–55; Edward L. Ayers, *The Promise of the New South: Life After Reconstruction* (New York: Oxford University Press, 1992), 50–51; and Richard E. Welch Jr., "The Federal Elections Bill of 1890: Postscripts and Prelude," *Journal of American History* 52 (December 1965): 511–26.

16. Barnes, *Who Killed John Clayton?* 97–100. See the vivid account in the *St. Louis Globe Democrat*, 31 August 1890; and *Arkansas Gazette*, 13 September 1890. See also the *Chicago Tribune* article quoted in *Arkansas Gazette*, 4 September 1890.

17. See election returns by county in *Arkansas Gazette*, 16 September 1890.

18. See Grave's discussion of the bill in *Town and County*, 150–63. Bell's and Lucas's speeches were printed verbatim in the *Arkansas Gazette*, 30 January and 21 February 1891, and in the *Indianapolis Freeman*, 21 February and 4 April 1891. Interestingly, George Bell was a native African. He was born in Ethiopia, and his family had been exiled during Bell's childhood to Malta because of his father's opposition to Ethiopian king Menelik I. Bell eventually joined the British Navy, emigrated to the United States, attended Lincoln University in Pennsylvania, and studied medicine in St. Louis before settling in Arkansas. See Walter L. Williams, *Black Americans and the Evangelization of Africa, 1877–1900* (Madison: University of Wisconsin Press, 1982), 158.

19. Graves, *Town and Country*, 164–73; J. Morgan Kousser, *The Shaping of Southern Politics: Suffrage Restrictions and the Establishment of the One-Party South* (New Haven: Yale University Press, 1974), 123–30; Michael Perman, *Struggle for Mastery: Disfranchisement in the South, 1888–1908* (Chapel Hill: University of North Carolina Press, 2001), 59–67. Of the southern states, Arkansas was one of the first to experience the challenge posed by the fusion of black Republicans and white agrarian radicals, and it became one of the first states to enact disfranchisement laws.

20. Richard E. Welch Jr., "Federal Elections Bill of 1890," 521–25.

21. Willard B. Gatewood Jr., "Arkansas Negroes in the 1890s: Documents," *Arkansas Historical Quarterly* 33 (Winter 1974): 297, 306–9. See also Joel Williamson, *The Crucible of Race: Black/White Relations in the American South since Emancipation* (New York: Oxford University Press, 1984).

22. See the speech by Professor Joseph A. Booker, president of Arkansas Baptist College of Little Rock, in *Arkansas Gazette*, 28 January 1891. For further discussion of this meeting and speech, see Graves, *Town and Country*, 154–55.

23. From the beginning of 1891 to 31 August, the last period for which Coppinger gave information to the executive board of the ACS, he reported that 468 of the 804 letters of application received at the Washington office, or 58.2 percent, were from Arkansas. The next largest group, 11.4 percent, came from Georgia (Coppinger's Report, 3 September 1891, Journal of the Executive Committee, ACS reel 293).

24. Using letters written to the ACS combined with the number of individuals who applied for emigration in 1888–93 as a measurement, the counties with the greatest interest in emigration were Conway (1,802 applications and letters), Lonoke (767), Pulaski (476), Woodruff (469), Faulkner (368), Ouachita (333), Jefferson (330), and Jackson (320).

25. H. C. Cade to Coppinger, 20 November 1890, ACS reel 135; B. H. Miller to Coppinger, 17 September 1890, ACS reel 135; William Jones to Coppinger, 23 January 1891, ACS reel 136; L. W. Wyatt to Coppinger, 10 October 1890, ACS reel 135.

26. G. W. Waters to Coppinger, 28 February 1891, ACS reel 136; G. W. Lowe to Coppinger, 19 September 1891, ACS reel 138.

27. J. S. Smith to Coppinger, 8 January 1890, ACS reel 135; I. W. Penn to Coppinger, 10 April 1891, ACS reel 137; Johnny Tewblie to Coppinger, 29 September 1991, ACS reel 138; John Jimison to Coppinger, 13 August 1891, ACS reel 138.

28. F. M. Gilmore to Coppinger, 15 April 1891, ACS reel 137.

29. R. W. Haffold to Coppinger, 1 August 1890, ACS reel 134; J. R. Jimison to Coppinger, 7 July 1892, ACS reel 141. A. W. Winfield of Germantown, Conway County, complained that crops had been short for the last two years; see Winfield to Coppinger, 17 April 1891, ACS reel 137.

30. W. P. Pennington to Coppinger, 12 May 1891, ACS reel 137; E. D. T. Davis to Coppinger, 13 February 1892, ACS reel 179; H. B. Blackwell to Coppinger, 19 October 1891, ACS reel 134.

31. James Yokeley to Coppinger, early February 1891, ACS reel 136; Sandy Lewis et al. to Coppinger, 22 December 1890, ACS reel 135; F. M. Gilmore to Coppinger, 15 April 1891, ACS reel 137.

32. James A. Miller to Coppinger, 12 August 1891, ACS reel 138; H. C. Cade to Coppinger, 20 November 1890, ACS reel 135.

33. W. P. Pennington to Coppinger, 3 April 1891, ACS reel 137.

34. J. H. Harris to Coppinger, 12 December 1890, ACS reel 135; H. C. Cade to Coppinger, 5 January 1891, ACS reel 136; J. M. Suggs to Coppinger, 24 December 1890, 3 February 1891, ACS reel 136.

35. Graves, *Town and Country*, 166.

36. E. H. Tate to Coppinger, 29 September 1890, ACS reel 135; W. P. Pennington to Coppinger, 12 May 1891, ACS reel 137; Eph Jones to Coppinger, 3 February 1891, ACS reel 136; Anderson Barnes to Coppinger, 10 March 1891, ACS reel 136.

37. H. S. Raney to Coppinger, 14 October 1891, ACS reel 138; Thomas Taylor to Coppinger, 8 November 1891, ACS reel 139.

38. The name Young Men's Association or Young Men's Working Association was

used in Menifee, Germantown, Pinnacle Springs, Pine Bluff, and Van Buren. See various correspondence in fall 1890 and 1891, ACS reels 134–39.

39. George Moore to Coppinger, 22 April 1890, ACS reel 134; Johnnie B. Hart to Coppinger, 23 October 1890, ACS reel 135.

40. Joseph H. Harris to Coppinger, 17 November 1890, ACS reel 135; E. W. Wofford to Coppinger, 8 December 1890, ACS reel 135. For Coppinger's frequent response to would-be agents in Arkansas, see his outgoing correspondence in December 1890, ACS reel 225.

41. W. H. Hafer to Coppinger, 20 April 1891, ACS reel 137; L. Vaughn to Coppinger, 21 April 1891, ACS reel 137; Daniel Simpson to Coppinger, 1 January 1891, ACS reel 136.

42. See, for example, Henry Jones to Coppinger, 7 June 1889, ACS reel 132; and L. T. Allington to Jeremiah Wilson, 2 June 1891, ACS reel 140.

43. Minutes of 22nd Annual Conference, 26 November–1 December 1889, Forrest City; Minutes of 23rd Annual Conference, 19 November 1890, Fort Smith; both in Arkansas AME Records.

44. Handbill located in mid-November 1890; H. C. Cade to Coppinger, 7 November 1890; both in ACS reel 135.

45. L. W. Wyatt to Coppinger, 9, 22 November 1890, ACS reel 135.

46. For an account of the U.S. and Congo Company, see Edwin S. Redkey, *Black Exodus: Black Nationalist and Back-to-Africa Movements, 1890–1910* (New Haven: Yale University Press, 1969), 150–69. A copy of the company's handbill can be found at 3 February 1891, ACS reel 136.

47. See Redkey's discussion of the House bill and the Butler bill in *Black Exodus*, 59–72, 151–53.

48. M. T. [illegible, writing from Humphrey] to Coppinger, 17 January 1891, ACS reel 136; J. Woodard to Coppinger, 27 August 1890, ACS reel 134; Woodard to Coppinger, 10 April 1891, ACS reel 137. C. W. Wofford of Malvern said he had read about the congressional emigration bill in the *St. Louis Globe Democrat;* see Wofford to Coppinger, 19 January 1891, ACS reel 179. See Coppinger's response to many correspondents in Arkansas in December 1890, in ACS reel 225.

49. J. M. Foster to Coppinger, 18 December 1890, ACS reel 132; S. W. Alexander et al. to Coppinger, 5 April 1890, ACS reel 134.

50. G. W. Pounds to Coppinger, 14 September 1889, ACS reel 133; Abner Downs to Coppinger, 4 May 1891, ACS reel 137; Harvey Hopson to Coppinger, 19 March 1891, ACS reel 136.

51. London Griggs to Coppinger, 21 September 1890, ACS reel 135; M. J. Miller to Coppinger, 24 October 1890, ACS reel 135.

52. G. W. Pounds to Coppinger, 14 September 1889, ACS reel 133; George Moore to Coppinger, 22 April 1890, ACS reel 134; H. M. Cook to Coppinger, 28 February 1891, ACS reel 136; John Abbot to Coppinger, 15 November 1891, ACS reel 139; Andrew Montgomery to Coppinger, 19 February 1890 (but located in February 1891 correspondence), ACS reel 136.

53. J. M. Foster to Coppinger, 18 November 1890, ACS reel 132; H. S. Raney to Coppinger, 14 October 1891, ACS reel 138; John Abbot to Coppinger, 15 November 1891, ACS reel 139.

54. M. J. Miller to Coppinger, 24 October 1890, ACS reel 135.

55. J. M. Foster to Coppinger, 18 November 1890, ACS reel 132; H. M. Cook to Coppinger, 28 February 1891, ACS reel 136; John Abbot to Coppinger, 15 November 1891, ACS reel 139.

56. Adaline Bailey to Coppinger, 29 February 1892, ACS reel 179; J. A. Miller to Coppinger, 6 March 1892, ACS reel 180; Thamy Smith to Coppinger, 11 September 1889, ACS reel 133. The black man from Conway who asked about European wars in Africa had read a treatise by Mr. Leighton Parks on the subject (unknown correspondent to Coppinger, 5 August 1891, ACS reel 138).

57. Solom Oliver to Coppinger, 6 January 1891, ACS reel 136; Miles West to Coppinger, 21 February 1891, ACS reel 136; James A. Willem to Coppinger, 21 September 1891, ACS reel 138; John Powers to Coppinger, 22 January 1892, ACS reel 179.

58. R. W. Haffold to Coppinger, 1 August 1890, ACS reel 134; Harvey Hopson to Coppinger, 29 March 1891, ACS reel 136; J. W. Waters to Coppinger, 16 October 1890, ACS reel 135. The absence of census information makes it difficult to establish the economic position of the Arkansas emigrants. The emigrants of 1879 and 1880 left the United States just before the census was taken in the summer of 1880. The manuscript returns of the 1890 census perished in a fire, and with them the detailed information for individuals, such as property values, state of birth, literacy, and other data.

59. Herbert G. Gutman, *The Black Family in Slavery and Freedom, 1750–1925* (New York: Pantheon Books, 1976), 443–45.

60. Coppinger to J. R. Riggins, 20 February 1891, ACS reel 225; Juda Parker to Coppinger, 15 April 1891, ACS reel 137; Coppinger to Juda Parker, 18 April 1891, ACS reel 225. Coppinger wrote W. K. Fortson of Menifee (15 April 1891, ACS reel 225) that the ACS did not send elderly people to Liberia. The emigration of Narcissus Moore and family is recorded in *African Repository* 67 (January 1892): 31. Few women wrote on their own initiative to go to Liberia. Mrs. Rosie Bowe, a widow in Conway, applied for herself and children and sent the ACS $15; she asked for her money back, however, when her teenaged child refused to go with her; see Rosie Bowe to Coppinger, 5 August 1891, ACS reel 138. The Bowe family was on the Conway application list of 12 December 1890, ACS reel 135. Sally Jenkins, a single woman in Menifee, applied to emigrate in 1892. Four years later, she had married Mack Shaver, and she and her husband paid their own way to Liberia aboard the *Laurada*. See Sallie Jenkins to Reginald Fendall, 6 July 1892, ACS reel 141; and *Voice of Missions*, May 1896. See also Alexander Smart (the grandson of Sallie Jenkins Shaver), telephone interview with author, Cambria Heights, N.Y., 18 February 1997.

61. Clifton Willis to Coppinger, 14 October 1890; James Dargan to Coppinger, 11 November 1890; W. D. Leslie to Coppinger, 20 August 1890; all in ACS reel 135.

62. W. K. Fortson to Coppinger, 14 October 1890; S. H. King to Coppinger, 3 October 1890; W. H. Westbrook to Coppinger, 19 October 1890; J. W. Polk to Coppinger, 24 November 1890; all in ACS reel 135.

63. W. H. King to Coppinger, 28 November 1890; James Dargan to Coppinger, 1 December 1890; both in ACS reel 135. Coppinger to James Dargan, 7 November 1890; Coppinger to John Polk, 14, 28 November 1890; and other outgoing correspondence in November–December acknowledging receipt of funds, all in ACS reel 225.

64. Coppinger to James Dargan, 22 November 1890; Coppinger to Andrew Ficklin, 24 November 1890; both in ACS reel 225.

65. Coppinger to Joseph Harris, 15, 20 December 1890, ACS reel 225; Joseph Harris to Coppinger, 27 December 1890, ACS reel 136.

66. James Dargan to Coppinger, 3, 9 January 1891, ACS reel 136; Coppinger to Dargan, 6, 13 January, 3 February 1891, ACS reel 225; Ines Dargan to Coppinger, 14 February 1891, ACS reel 136; Coppinger to Ines Dargan, 17 February 1891, ACS reel 225.

67. See Coppinger's outgoing correspondence of January–February 1891 in ACS reel 225. W. D. Leslie to Coppinger, 17 January 1891; John Rilhard to Coppinger, 18 February 1891; both in ACS reel 136.

68. W. K. Fortson to Coppinger, 30 March 1891, ACS reel 136; Coppinger to Fortson, 15 April 1891, ACS reel 225; *African Repository* 66 (July 1891): 95.

69. James Dargan to Coppinger, 9 January 1891, ACS reel 136.

70. Abner Downs to Coppinger, 13 May 1891; W. H. King to Coppinger, 8, 19 May 1891; D. H. Patterson to Coppinger, 26 May 1891; W. M. Jones to Coppinger, 6 July 1891; all in ACS reel 137.

71. Coppinger to John W. Polk, 13 May 1891; Coppinger to W. H. King, 12 May 1891; Coppinger to Abner Downs, 16 May 1891; Coppinger to D. H. Patterson, 30 May 1891; all in ACS reel 225.

72. W. H. King to Coppinger, 19 May 1891; Abner Downs to Coppinger, 17 June 1891; D. H. Patterson to Coppinger, 26 May 1891; all in ACS reel 137.

73. R. P. Davis and William Raggers [Rogers] to Coppinger, 13 July 1891, ACS reel 137; R. P. Davis to Coppinger, 10 August 1891, ACS reel 138; Coppinger to Andrew Ficklin, 10 July, 20 August 1891, ACS reel 225.

74. *Little Rock City Directory, 1890* (Little Rock: Arkansas Press, 1890), 515–39; Henry Moore, interview with author, Monrovia, Liberia, 16, 31 July 1998; J. Benedict Shaw I, interview with author, Johnsonville, Liberia, 18 July, 1998. The group that went ahead to New York included Andrew and Lizzie Ficklin and baby, William and Sarah Rogers, Narcissie Moore's family, Samuel and Maggie David and five children, and from Morrilton, Benjamin and Cora Miller and their two children and the Kelly and Bettie Whisenant family of four. See Coppinger to R. P. Davis, 1 October 1891; Coppinger to Andrew Ficklin, 3 October 1891; Coppinger to William Rogers, 21 October 1891; all in ACS reel 225; and Andrew Ficklin to Coppinger, 21 October 1891, ACS reel 138.

75. Yates and Porterfield to Coppinger, 31 October 1891, ACS reel 138; Coppinger to R. P. Davis, 10 November 1891, ACS reel 225; "List of emigrants left out of Bark 'Liberia' Oct., 31st., 1891," located in correspondence of 29 October 1891, ACS reel 179; Yates and Porterfield to Coppinger, 7 November 1891, ACS reel 139.

76. Handbill of Public Sale, 19 October 1891, ACS reel 138. The *African Repository* (67 [January 1892]): 32) listed these receipts by community. "Amounts paid by emigrants towards passage to Liberia," a single-page document in miscellaneous material at end of ACS reel 306, lists money the ACS received yearly from 1877 through 1891 from potential emigrants. These amounts ranged from a low of $65 in 1886, to $1,218.75 received in 1880, and $2,697.75 in 1891.

77. Coppinger to Abner Downs, 16 October 1891, ACS reel 225; W. A. Diggs to Coppinger, 9 November 1891; F. J. Jones to Coppinger, 30 December 1891; both in ACS reel 139.

78. W. H. Holloway to Coppinger, 11 November 1891, ACS reel 139.

Chapter Four

1. G. W. Angram to Coppinger, 8 November 1891; R. P. Pully to Coppinger, 16, 20 November 1891; all in ACS reel 139; A. C. Henry to Coppinger, 31 December 1891, ACS reel 139. Pully and his family had come to Little Rock from Atkins in Pope County.

2. Samuel Graham to Coppinger, 21 January 1892; Adaline Bailey to Coppinger, 29 February 1892; both in ACS reel 179. Coppinger's last letter was dated 19 January 1892 (ACS reel 225).

3. In the month he was in Liberia, Turner also visited with Willie Francis Stanford, the son of the Reverend Anthony Stanford, who had led the Helena party to Liberia in 1879 and who had died a few years before. See Stephen Ward Angell, *Bishop Henry McNeal Turner and African-American Religion in the South* (Knoxville: University of Tennessee Press, 1992), 218; and Edwin S. Redkey, *Black Exodus: Black Nationalist and Back-to-Africa Movements, 1890–1910* (New Haven: Yale University Press, 1969), 43–46. Edwin S. Redkey, ed., *Respect Black: The Writings and Speeches of Henry McNeal Turner* (New York: Arno Press and *New York Times*, 1971), 109, 117; this volume reprints all of Turner's letters written from Africa (pp. 85–134), which had been serialized in the *Christian Recorder*. See also R. Barr to Coppinger, 11 March 1892, ACS reel 180.

4. Yates and Porterfield to Reginald Fendall, 9, 12 February 1892, ACS reel 179; Fendall to Abner Downs, 13 February 1892, ACS reel 225.

5. Redkey, *Black Exodus*, 102–7; *New York Age*, 27 February 1892; *New York Times*, 22 February 1892; *New York Sun*, 24 February 1892; all in clippings file, ACS reel 322; *New York Tribune*, 22, 23 February 1892.

6. See applications from McCrory in correspondence of early December 1891, ACS reel 139; Coppinger to Peter Jones, 2 December 1891, ACS reel 225; *New York Times*, 23 February 1892; *New York Herald*, 23 February 1892; both in clippings file, ACS reel 322; *New York Sun*, 23, 26 February 1892.

7. *New York Herald*, 23 February 1892; *New York Sun*, 24 February 1892; both in clippings file, ACS reel 322.

8. Reginald Fendall to A. W. Russell, 29 February 1892, ACS reel 226; *New York Sun*, 24 February 1892; *New York Tribune*, 23 February 1892; *New York Evening Post*, 23 February 1892; all in clippings file, ACS reel 322. See also Redkey, *Black Exodus*, 120–21.

9. *New York Times*, 29 February 1892; an account of the second meeting with its formal resolution was printed in the *New York Age* and reprinted in the *Indianapolis Freeman*, 12 March 1892. See also Redkey, *Black Exodus*, 122–23. Turner's response to Fortune's attack appeared in the *Indianapolis Freeman*, 2 April 1892. For more information about Fortune, see his biography by Emma Lou Thornbrough, *T. Thomas Fortune: Militant Journalist* (Chicago: University of Chicago Press, 1972). Ironically, Fortune's last work as a journalist was for Marcus Garvey's paper, the *Negro World*. Fortune served as editor from 1923 until his death in 1928, although he never seemed to embrace Garvey's racial separatism and back-to-Africa posture.

10. Journal of the Executive Committee of the ACS, 4, 17 March 1892, ACS reel 293; editorial from the *New York Age*, reprinted in *The Statesman*, 24 February 1894, in clippings file, ACS reel 322. George Washington sailed for Liberia aboard the *Laurada* on 1 March 1896 (*Voice of Missions*, May 1896).

11. Journal of the Executive Committee of the ACS, 11 February, 4 March 1892, ACS reel 293; the new policies of the ACS were published in an article titled "Future Work of the American Colonization Society," in the *Liberia Bulletin* 1 (November 1892): 4–8. See Ida Coppinger's outgoing letters in March 1892 and J. Ormond Wilson's outgoing correspondence in April 1892, ACS reel 226. Letters continued to arrive from Arkansas addressed to William Coppinger for months following his death. Others wrote to Wilson, hoping vainly that he had not meant what he had said about the ACS's new policy regarding emigration. See incoming correspondence, March through June 1892. The meticulous recordkeeping of William Coppinger broke down after his death, and the ACS files after February 1892 are scattered and disorganized; some of this correspondence appears in ACS reel 139; other parts are located in ACS reel 180.

12. Stewart E. Tolnay and E. M. Beck, *A Festival of Violence: An Analysis of Southern Lynchings, 1882–1930* (Urbana: University of Illinois Press, 1995); Ida B. Wells, *A Red Record: Tabulated Statistics and Alleged Causes of Lynchings in the United States, 1892–1893–1894*, originally published in 1895, reprinted as Ida B. Wells-Barnett, *On Lynchings: Southern Horrors, A Red Record, Mob Rule in New Orleans* (New York: Arno Press, 1969), 20. In Wells's work, in which she records both white and black lynchings, Arkansas was exceeded by Louisiana, with 29 lynchings, and Tennessee, with 28 lynchings. NAACP, *Thirty Years of Lynching in the United States, 1889–1918* (1919; reprint, New York: Arno Press and *New York Times*, 1969). James Elbert Cutler, in *Lynch-Law: An Investigation into the History of Lynching in the United States* (1905; reprint, New York: Negro Universities Press, 1969), 160–61, 183, records 235 lynchings of whites and blacks, 20 of which took place in Arkansas. In his list, Arkansas tied with Tennessee for the greatest number. At the 1890 census, Arkansas's black population was 309,117, Tennessee's, 430,678, and Louisiana's, 559,193 (U.S. Census Bureau, *Negro Population, 1790–1915* [Washington, D.C.: Government Printing Office, 1918], 44).

13. For the Kelly lynching, see *American Citizen*, 19 February 1892. For more information about Jones and Havis, see Fon Louise Gordon, *Caste and Class: The Black Experience in Arkansas, 1880–1920* (Athens: University of Georgia Press, 1995), 78–79; and John William Graves, *Town and Country: Race Relations in an Urban-Rural Context, Arkansas, 1865–1905* (Fayetteville: University of Arkansas Press, 1990), 123–24. The *Echo* was just one of eight black newspapers known to be published in Arkansas the early 1890s. See Willard B. Gatewood Jr., "Arkansas Negroes in the 1890s: Documents," *Arkansas Historical Quarterly* 33 (Winter 1974): 293–94.

14. See the account in the *Arkansas Gazette*, 16, 21, 23 February, 22 March 1892; and Wells, *Red Record*, 61–62. The lynching was widely covered in the national and black press; see *American Citizen*, 19, 26 February 1892; *Richmond Planet*, 27 February 1892; and *Washington Post*, 21 February 1892. Another brutal lynching occurred on 9 February, the day of Coppinger's death. Hamp Biscoe, a black man in Lonoke County, after a dispute with a neighbor over a debt, engaged in a shooting match with the white constable who came to arrest him. Both Biscoe and the constable were wounded in the altercation, Biscoe so severely that he could not stand. The constable's deputies detained Biscoe, his pregnant wife, his thirteen-year-old son, and his infant, who was still nursing, and took them to a small frame building near the railroad depot in the town of England. Later that day, a party of white men burst into the building and shot Biscoe and his wife dead on the spot. The couple's teenaged son died later that evening of gunshot

wounds; the baby escaped with a slight injury on the upper lip. One man pulled off Mrs. Biscoe's stockings and took $220 of currency that she had hidden there. The men who killed the Biscoe family were never arrested for the crime (Wells, *Red Record*, 21–24; *Arkansas Democrat*, 11 February 1892).

15. *Arkansas Gazette*, 14, 15 May 1892.

16. For an examination of the correlation between cotton prices and lynching, see E. M. Beck and Stewart Tolnay, "The Killing Fields of the Deep South: The Market for Cotton and the Lynching of Blacks, 1882–1930," *American Sociological Review* 55 (August 1990): 526–99. See also Jacquelyn Dowd Hall, *Revolt against Chivalry: Jessie Daniel Ames and the Women's Campaign against Lynching* (New York: Columbia University Press, 1979); and Edward L. Ayers, *The Promise of the New South: Life after Reconstruction* (New York: Oxford University Press, 1992), 153–59. See also Fitzhugh Brundage's *Lynching in the New South: Georgia and Virginia, 1880–1930* (Urbana: University of Illinois, 1993), which reports that a large portion of lynching victims in Georgia and Virginia were described in newspapers as strangers or newcomers.

17. See Terrence Finnegan, "Lynching and Political Power in Mississippi and South Carolina," in *Under Sentence of Death: Lynching in the South*, ed. W. Fitzhugh Brundage (Chapel Hill: University of North Carolina, 1997), 189–218. Finnegan found that a spurt of lynchings followed disfranchisement in both Mississippi and South Carolina. Ida B. Wells is quoted in ibid., 214.

18. *Arkansas Gazette*, 6, 7 September 1892. The *Gazette* on 11 and 29 September reprinted accusations of fraud made by J. B. Settler, the populist leader and editor of the *Arkansas Political Farmer*, so that the newspaper could deny the charges. Settler also suggested that Democratic election judges in black precincts used their assistance to illiterate voters as a pretext to stall for time and ultimately disallow other voters from casting their ballots. The new law required all other voters to leave the room when a judge assisted an illiterate voter. Settler said judges would remove ten or fifteen voters and keep them waiting up to twenty minutes while the judges assisted one illiterate voter. Many black precincts had as many as 1,500 voters, and this tactic kept many literate blacks from casting their ballot.

19. See the analysis of the Arkansas vote in J. Morgan Kousser, *The Shaping of Southern Politics: Suffrage Restriction and the Establishment of the One-Party South* (New Haven: Yale University Press, 1974), 127–30; Graves, *Town and Country*, 173–74; Gordon, *Caste and Class*, 29–30; and Carl H. Moneyhon, "Black Politics in Arkansas during the Gilded Age, 1876–1900," *Arkansas Historical Quarterly* 44 (Autumn 1985): 244. Kousser estimates that the two laws reduced white voter turnout in Arkansas from 75 percent in 1890 to 56 percent in 1894 while black turnout dropped from 71 percent to 24 percent.

20. The 1892 election appears to have brought another bout of racial violence. Two weeks after the vote, a race war broke out in Calhoun County, and one report claimed black anger over the election law had caused the trouble. Problems had been brewing in the area for weeks. Before the election, Bob Jordan, a black man in the area, had been arrested for insulting a white woman. As the constable brought him to jail in Camden, a group of masked white men ordered the constable to surrender Jordan, and they shot him to his death. Whitecappers in the neighborhood then distributed circulars threatening that black laborers at Pott's Mill, a large sawmill eleven miles south of Camden, must leave the area or face death. Black men were arrested and brought to the county

jail for carrying weapons to defend themselves. A group of black men, reportedly angry over the whitecapping and the election, organized an armed band that roamed the country muttering threats against whites. On Saturday, 17 September, a posse of white men under the command of a deputy sheriff surrounded a house that the band of about thirty black men had fortified as their base. When the whites approached with warrants for the arrest of the leaders of the black gang, guards shot the deputy in the leg. Whites returned fire. Three black men were killed and as many as seven were wounded before the gang fled into the forest. Another black man was shot by whites a few days later while he gathered corn in a field. Deputies arrested a number of blacks thought to be associated with the uprising. One reportedly had in his possession a written oath by which the members of the black gang swore to kill every white man, woman, and child in the county. A general atmosphere of pandemonium prevailed for several weeks. Black citizens were reported to be leaving the area with all their possession tied in bundles. See *Arkansas Gazette*, 10, 28 August, 20, 21, 22, 24 September 1892; and *New York Times*, 21, 25 September 1892. Exactly what happened in Calhoun County remains unclear, for these newspaper accounts varied considerably in their information.

21. L. J. Allington and A. J. Johnson to kind sir, 2 May 1892, ACS reel 139; A. Jordan to Fendall, 2 March 1892, ACS reel 180; *Indianapolis Freeman*, 16 April 1892; C. M. Taylor to Coppinger, 16 October 1892, ACS reel 141; Robert Davis to Coppinger, 17 April 1892, ACS reel 139.

22. See Arthur L. Tolson, *The Black Oklahomans: A History, 1541–1972* (New Orleans: Edwards Printing, 1974), 51–55, 69–89; Jimmie Lewis Franklin, *Journey toward Hope: A History of Blacks in Oklahoma* (Norman: University of Oklahoma Press, 1982), 11–18; and Daniel F. Littlefield and Lonnie E. Underhill, "Black Dreams and 'Free' Homes: The Oklahoma Territory, 1891–1894," *Phylon* 34 (December 1973): 243–357. McCabe's boast appeared in the *Langston City Herald*, 17 November 1892, quoted in Littlefield and Underhill, "Black Dreams," 352.

23. Littlefield and Underhill, "Black Dreams," 343; *Arkansas Gazette*, 29 February, 11, 14 March 1891; R. Long to Coppinger, 25 August 1891, ACS reel 138.

24. *Arkansas Gazette*, 12, 13, 31 March 1892; *Indianapolis Freeman*, 16 April 1892. The *Gazette* reported the number of the travelers at Newport as 115, while the *Freeman* said there were 150.

25. *Indianapolis Freeman*, 30 April 1892; *Arkansas Gazette*, 31 May 1892, 25 January 1893. For an excellent overview of black emigration from Arkansas to Oklahoma, see Lori Bogle, "On Our Way to the Promised Land: Black Migration from Arkansas to Oklahoma, 1889–1893," *Chronicles of Oklahoma* 72 (Summer 1994): 160–77.

26. L. J. Allington and A. J. Johnson to ACS, 2 May 1892; W. D. Leslie to ACS, 1 April 1892; both in ACS reel 139. One desperate applicant for Liberian emigration, Pink Blair, who had fled Mississippi County in 1890 fearing for his life, was arrested in Phillips County in early 1892, according to his wife, for trying to organize families to emigrate to Oklahoma. Lou Vinnie Blair wrote President Benjamin Harrison, in care of the ACS, for assistance when her husband was not given a trial or allowed visitors at the county penal farm (Blair to Harrison, 23 April 1892, ACS reel 139); apparently the ACS did not forward Blair's letter to President Harrison but buried it in a file (W. H. King to Coppinger, 18 January 1892, ACS reel 179).

27. James Anderson to ACS, 9 November 1892, ACS reel 141; Yates and Porterfield to J. Ormond Wilson, 20 April 1892, ACS reel 140; Yates and Porterfield to Wilson, 5 December 1892, ACS reel 180.

28. A. G. Smith to ACS, 25 October 1892, ACS reel 141; Reginald Fendall to C. E. Dixon, 27 February 1892, ACS reel 226; C. E. Dixon to J. Ormond Wilson, 17 September, 21 November 1892, ACS reel 141; Wilson to Daniel Bacon, 31 October 1892, ACS reel 226; Wilson to A. J. Jackson, 28 January 1893, ACS reel 226. C. E. Dixon had been writing the ACS, asking to emigrate since 1876. See his frequent correspondence with Coppinger in fall 1876, ACS reel 217, and fall 1877, ACS reel 116B.

29. *Arkansas Gazette*, 18 November 1892; C. E. Dixon, from Brewerville, Liberia, 25 November 1893, 24 August 1894, ACS reel 143; "Seventy-Seventh Annual Report of the American Colonization Society, presented 16 January 1894," in *The Annual Reports of the American Colonization Society*, vol. 6: 1871–1910 (New York: Negro Universities Press, 1969). The *Gazette* printed the letter of Daniel Walker to his brother Joe Walker so that it could ridicule Walker and Liberia. The paper suggested that the letter was fiction; however, several details indicate that the author of the letter had actually been to Liberia. After receiving the letter, Joe Walker wrote to the ACS asking for information on how to send his brother a hundred-pound wooden box of clothing and other articles (J. J. Walker to J. Ormond Wilson, 17 September 1892, ACS reel 141).

30. *Richmond Planet*, 19 March 1892.

31. J. H. Harris to J. Ormond Wilson, 14 June 1892, ACS reel 141.

Chapter Five

1. P. Clevoter to Coppinger, 7 December 1879, ACS reel 119; see the testimonials written for the application of John Johnson and family of Conway, January 1889, ACS reel 132.

2. J. L. Cloninger to Albion Tourgée, 18 June 1892, reel 30, Albion W. Tourgée Papers, Chautauqua County Historical Society, Westfield, N.Y.

3. *Arkansas Gazette*, 18, 28 March 1880.

4. Ibid., 24 May, 28 August, 20 September, 23 October, 11, 24 December 1889, 15 January 1890.

5. Ibid., 15 January 1890; *New York Times*, 20 January 1890.

6. For example, when the first large party of emigrants left Morrilton for Liberia in February 1891, the local white newspaper reported the event with one line buried on page eleven: "About forty negroes left this place Monday for Africa" (*Morrilton Pilot*, 13 February 1891). The next year, the paper remained entirely silent about the departure of the second Morrilton party, while New York newspapers carried articles about the emigrants from Arkansas on their first pages.

7. Milton Keo to Coppinger, 21 April 1891, ACS reel 137; the Democratic paper to which Keo referred remains unclear.

8. B. K. McKeever to Coppinger, 10, 13 February 1879, ACS reel 118.

9. Joseph Harris to Coppinger, 4 December 1890, ACS reel 135; P. S. Buckingham to Coppinger, 28 February 1891, ACS reel 136; James Miller to ACS, 20 December 1892,

ACS reel 141; Clark Dothan to Coppinger, 15 February 1892, ACS reel 179; W. A. Diggs to Coppinger, 21 April 1891, and John R. Jimison to Coppinger, 22 April 1891, both wrote from Plumerville, ACS reel 137; Frank Little to ACS, 19 February 1895, ACS reel 147.

10. Theodore Steele to Coppinger, 1 October 1891, ACS reel 138; Andrew Thompson to Coppinger, 12 December 1891, ACS reel 139.

11. P. S. Buckingham to Coppinger, 28 February 1891, ACS reel 136; R. P. Pully to Coppinger, 24 November 1891, ACS reel 139; Shelton Leaphart to ACS, 15 June 1892, ACS reel 140; Marion Babb to ACS, 26 March 1893, ACS reel 141; Pully to Coppinger, 24 November 1891, ACS reel 139.

12. W. H. King to Coppinger, 26 January 1892, ACS reel 179; Pink Blair to Coppinger, 5 January 1890, ACS reel 133; Lou Vinnie Blair to President Benjamin Harrison, 23 April 1892, ACS reel 139; G. W. Angram to Coppinger, 8 November 1891, ACS reel 139; R. P. Davis to Coppinger, 20 November 1891, ACS reel 139.

13. W. M. Wilson to Coppinger, 6 November 1891, ACS reel 139; Adaline Bailey to Coppinger, 27 February 1892, ACS reel 179; Andrew Thompson to Coppinger, 12 December 1891, ACS reel 139.

14. R. T. Winters to ACS, 27 December 1892, ACS reel 141; unknown writer from Sans Souci to Coppinger, 15 September 1891, ACS reel 138.

15. For the story of the cotton pickers' revolt, see William F. Holmes, "The Arkansas Cotton Pickers' Strike of 1891 and the Demise of the Colored Farmers' Alliance," *Arkansas Historical Quarterly* 32 (Summer 1973): 107–19. See also accounts in the *Arkansas Gazette*, 2, 3 October 1891; *Richmond Planet*, 17 October 1891; and *Southwestern Christian Advocate*, 8 October 1891.

16. *Arkansas Gazette*, 11 October 1891.

17. Robert G. Weisbord, *Ebony Kinship: Africa, Africans, and the Afro-American* (Westport, Conn.: Greenwood Press, 1973), 17; Herbert Shapiro, *White Violence and Black Response: From Reconstruction to Montgomery* (Amherst: University of Massachusetts Press, 1988), 33–34. See also the discussion of Crummell, Douglass, and Turner in Leon Litwack and August Meier, eds., *Black Leaders of the Nineteenth Century* (Urbana: University of Illinois Press, 1988); Stephen Ward Angell, *Bishop Henry McNeal Turner and African-American Religion in the South* (Knoxville: University of Tennessee Press, 1992), 121; and Edwin S. Redkey, *Black Exodus: Black Nationalist and Back-to-Africa Movements, 1890–1910* (New Haven: Yale University Press, 1969), 185–86. The very old Frederick Douglass had softened by 1893, supporting emigration to Africa, just not a wholesale exodus.

18. For the debate on emigration in 1883, see the *Christian Recorder*, January–July 1883; William Seraile, *Fire in His Heart: Bishop Benjamin Tucker Tanner and the A.M.E. Church* (Knoxville: University of Tennessee Press, 1998), 87–90; and Redkey, *Black Exodus*, 32–41.

19. *Indianapolis Freeman*, 12 March 1892. The New Orleans *Southwestern Christian Advocate*, 31 March 1892, reprinted the resolution and a number of denunciations of Turner that appeared in black newspapers throughout the country. Turner's response to Fortune's attack appeared in the *Indianapolis Freeman*, 2 April 1892. See also Redkey, *Black Exodus*, 122–26.

20. For a discussion of the Chicago meeting, see Redkey, *Black Exodus*, 182–83; and Edwin S. Redkey, *The Meaning of Africa to Afro-Americans, 1890–1914* (Buffalo: Council on International Studies, State University of New York at Buffalo, 1971), 12–14.

21. A detailed description of the Liberian exhibit appeared in the *Liberia Bulletin* 3 (November 1893): 66–69; an itemized catalog of the Liberian exhibit can be found in "Liberian Commissioners to World's Columbian Exposition at Chicago, ILL., USA, 1893," in Lot 8555, Prints and Photographs Division, Library of Congress, Washington, D.C. Douglass's comment was quoted in Elliot M. Rudwick and August Meier, "Black Man in the 'White City': Negroes and the Columbian Exposition, 1893," *Phylon* 26 (Winter 1965): 359; Turner's quote appears in Redkey, *Meaning of Africa to Afro-Americans*, 12.

22. Redkey, *Black Exodus*, 183–93; Shapiro, *White Violence and Black Response*, 48–53. Excerpts from Turner's speeches at the conference appear in Edwin S. Redkey, ed., *Respect Black: The Writings and Speeches of Henry McNeal Turner* (New York: Arno Press and New York Times, 1971), 146–59. Reports of the Arkansas delegates elected to attend the Cincinnati meeting appeared in the *Indianapolis Freeman*, 18 November, 9 December 1893.

23. *Indianapolis Freeman*, November 25, 1893; Redkey, *Black Exodus*, 185–86.

24. *American Citizen*, 6 September 1889, 29 April 1892. See also Walter L. Williams, "Black American Attitudes toward Africa, 1877–1900," *Pan-African Journal* 8 (Spring 1971): 174–79; and Walter L. Williams, "Black Journalism's Opinions about Africa during the Late Nineteenth Century," *Phylon* 34 (September 1973): 224–35.

25. *American Citizen*, 6 September 1891, 15 January 1892; *Southwestern Christian Advocate*, 29 October 1891; *Richmond Planet*, 26 December 1891; *Indianapolis Freeman*, 4 April 1891. For more information about the black press on this issue, see Williams, "Black Journalism's Opinions," 224–35; Gilbert Anthony Williams, *The Christian Recorder, Newspaper of the African Methodist Episcopal Church: History of a Forum for Ideas, 1854–1902* (Jefferson, N.C.: McFarland Publishers, 1996), 91–102; and Shapiro, *White Violence and Black Response*, 39–53.

26. *Indianapolis Freeman*, 18, 25 November 1893. The *Freeman* on 8 August 1896 claimed that it had more readers in Arkansas than any other black newspaper. For more discussion about the opposition of black elites to African emigration, see William E. Montgomery, *Under Their Own Vine and Fig Tree: The African-American Church in the South, 1865–1900* (Baton Rouge: Louisiana State University Press, 1993), 199–210; and August Meier, *Negro Thought in America, 1880–1915: Racial Ideologies in the Age of Booker T. Washington* (Ann Arbor: University of Michigan Press, 1963), 66–68.

27. *American Citizen*, 30 May 1890, 7 July 1893; Redkey, *Black Exodus*, 54–55. Taylor's criticism of Liberia was so hostile it prompted a published response from the black republic: F. E. R. Johnson, *An Answer to the False and Slanderous Statements Made by C. H. J. Taylor, Late U.S. Minister and Consul General to Liberia; Concerning the Government and People of Liberia* (Monrovia: T. W. Howard, n.d.), folder 3, box 30, New York State Colonization Society Records, Schomburg Center for Research in Black Culture, New York Public Library, New York. For an examination of Taylor and other black American ministers to Liberia, see Elliot P. Skinner, *African Americans and U.S. Policy toward Africa, 1850–1924* (Washington, D.C.: Howard University Press, 1992).

28. "The First Convention of the Liberia Exodus Arkansas Colony," p. 2, vol. 6, Colonization Pamphlets.

29. Joseph Harris to Coppinger, n.d., but located in late December 1891, ACS reel 139; W. A. Diggs to Coppinger, 31 August 1891, ACS reel 138.

30. W. A. Diggs to Coppinger, 2, 9, 11 January 1892, 25 January 1892, ACS reel 179; Coppinger to Diggs, 11 January 1892, ACS reel 225; Reginald Fendall to Diggs, 26 February 1892, ACS reel 226; J. Ormond Wilson to C. J. Smith, 10 October 1892, ACS reel 226.

31. Milton McClain to Coppinger, 17 August 1891, ACS reel 138; James Miller to Ida Coppinger, 16 April 1892, ACS reel 139; for an example of an ACS response to such inquiries, see J. Ormond Wilson to Miller, 19 April 1892, ACS reel 226.

32. See Hollis R. Lynch, *Edward Wilmot Blyden: Pan-Negro Patriot, 1832–1912* (New York: Oxford University Press, 1967); and Redkey, *Black Exodus*, 47–58.

33. Andrew Ficklin to Coppinger, 7 July 1891, ACS reel 137; R. P. Davis to Coppinger, n.d. but located in mid-July 1891, ACS reel 137; J. T. Seak [unclear] to Coppinger, 20 August 1891, ACS reel 138; W. A. Diggs to Coppinger, 3 September 1891, ACS reel 138.

34. J. C. Carpenter to Coppinger, 25 July 1891, ACS reel 137; G. W. Lowe to Coppinger, 12 August 1891, ACS reel 138; C. J. Turner to Coppinger, 20 August 1891, ACS reel 138; Coppinger to Andrew Ficklin, 10 July 1891, ACS reel 225; and other outgoing mail of July and August explained that Blyden was an impostor; Edward Blyden [impostor] to Coppinger, 12, 13 July 1891, ACS reel 137, 13 August 1891, ACS reel 138; J. W. Turner to Coppinger, 24 August 1891, ACS reel 138; Moses King to Coppinger, 27 August 1891, ACS reel 138.

35. *New York Sun*, 10 December 1892, in clippings file, ACS reel 322; *Arkansas Gazette*, 10, 11, 14 December 1892; H. G. Love to ACS, 28 November 1892, ACS reel 141; C. M. Taylor to Coppinger, 4 December 1892, ACS reel 141.

36. *Arkansas Gazette*, 14 December 1892; *New York Times*, 12 December 1892; see also James Logan Morgan, "Dr. Lightfoot, 1892," *Streams of History* 16 (April 1978): 3–13; and R. T. Winters to ACS, 27 December 1892, ACS reel 141. For a discussion of black-on-black lynchings, see E. M. Beck and Stewart E. Tolnay, "When Race Didn't Matter: Black and White Mob Violence against Their Own Color," in W. Fitzhugh Brundage, ed., *Under Sentence of Death: Lynching in the South* (Chapel Hill: University of North Carolina Press, 1997), 137–44. Tolnay and Beck found that the number of black-on-black lynchings peaked in the early 1890s with most occurring in the three southern states of Mississippi, Louisiana, and Arkansas.

37. *Woodruff Vidette*, reprinted in *Arkansas Gazette*, 28 January 1893; *New York Times*, 18 February 1893.

38. *Woodruff Vidette*, reprinted in *Arkansas Gazette*, 28 January 1893; *Arkansas Gazette*, 10, 11 February, 9 March 1893; *New York Times*, 18 February 1893. A cluster of Arkansas-born black residents lived in Brunswick at the time of the 1900 census (manuscript census returns, Glynn County, Ga., 1900). In 1921, an Arkansas-born Baptist preacher in Brunswick, Georgia, invited an organizer for Marcus Garvey's United Negro Improvement Association (UNIA) into his church to speak on the topic "Freedom for Africa," and Brunswick's division of the UNIA was the first organized in Georgia; see Mary Gambrell Rolinson, "The Garvey Movement in the Rural South, 1920–1927" (Ph.D. diss., Georgia State University, 2002), 96, 99. Similar scams had occurred elsewhere in the South, wherever interest in emigration was particularly keen. For a description of a swindle of would-be emigrants in South Carolina in 1886, see George A.

Devlin, *South Carolina and Black Migration, 1865–1940: In Search of the Promised Land* (New York: Garland, 1989), 98–100.

39. Theodore Steele to ACS, 5 September 1893, ACS reel 145. See reports about the movement in the *Richmond Planet*, 27 January 1894; and *Arkansas Gazette*, 23 July 1893.

Chapter Six

1. For a listing of black American missionaries to Africa for the years 1877–1900, see Walter L. Williams, *Black Americans and the Evangelization of Africa, 1877–1900* (Madison: University of Wisconsin Press, 1982), 184–90.

2. Ibid., 4.

3. Ibid., 7–30. For a fascinating account of the career of William H. Sheppard, a black Presbyterian missionary to the Congo in the 1890s, see Pagan Kennedy, *Black Livingstone: A True Tale of Adventure in the Nineteenth-Century Congo* (New York: Penguin, 2002).

4. Sandy Dwayne Martin, *Black Baptists and African Missions: The Origins of a Movement, 1880–1915* (Macon, Ga.: Mercer University Press, 1989), 56–106; Sandy Dwayne Martin, "Black Baptists, Foreign Missions, and African Colonization, 1814–1882," in *Black Americans and the Missionary Movement in Africa*, ed. Sylvia M. Jacobs (Westport, Conn.: Greenwood Press, 1982), 63–76; L. G. Jordan, *Up the Ladder in Foreign Mission* (1901; reprint, New York: Arno Press, 1980), 88–90, 97–98; Walter L. Williams, *Black Americans and the Evangelization of Africa*, 39–40, 66–73. See also "Minutes of the 19th Annual Session of the Arkansas Baptist State Convention, Camden, August 23–28, 1887," p. 14, reel 14, African American Baptist Associations: Arkansas, 1867–1951, American Baptist–Samuel Colgate Historical Library, Colgate Rochester Divinity School, Rochester, New York (hereafter cited as AABA: Ark.); and E. C. Morris, *Sermons, Addresses and Reminiscences and Important Correspondence* (1901; reprint, New York: Arno Press, 1980), 68, 92.

5. James T. Campbell, *Songs of Zion: The African Methodist Episcopal Church in the United States and South Africa* (New York: Oxford University Press, 1995), 88–90; Carol A. Page, "Colonial Reaction to AME Missionaries in South Africa, 1898–1910," in Jacobs, ed., *Black Americans and the Missionary Movement in Africa*, 177–80; Stephen Ward Angell, *Bishop Henry McNeal Turner and African-American Religion in the South* (Knoxville: University of Tennessee Press, 1992), 218–30; and Walter L. Williams, *Black Americans and the Evangelization of Africa*, 50–54, 56. Bishop Turner often worked African missions into his sermons when he attended conferences in Arkansas. See his sermons at the annual conferences in 1882 in Morrilton and in 1890 in Fort Smith in Minutes of 15th Annual Conference, 15–22 November 1882, p. 243; Minutes of the 23rd Annual Conference, 19 November 1890, p. 311; both in Arkansas AME Records.

6. Fully 95.1 percent of reported black church members in Arkansas at the 1890 census were members of Methodist or Baptist churches. See U.S. Department of the Interior, Census Office, *Report on Statistics of Churches in the United States at the Eleventh Census: 1890* (Washington, D.C.: Government Printing Office, 1894), 38, 48–49. The black Baptist churches claimed 63,786 members in Arkansas, making this by far the largest denomination. The AME Church was the second largest church, with 27,956 members,

while the black branch of the Methodist Episcopal Church was a distant third, with 10,076 members. I am assuming that all or nearly all of the members of the Methodist Episcopal Church in Arkansas were black, for most white Methodists belonged to the Methodist Episcopal Church, South. See U.S. Department of the Interior, Census Office, *Report on Statistics of Churches*, 172, 505, 544.

7. "Minutes of the Arkansas Baptist State Sunday School Convention, Texarkana, June 23–24, 1892," reel 14, AABA: Ark.; Minutes of 25th Annual Conference, 16 November 1892, Newport, pp. 388–89, Arkansas AME Records.

8. "Minutes of the State Baptist Sunday School Convention, Newport, June 19–24, 1893," p. 23; and "Minutes of the Arkansas Sunday School Convention, Camden, June 19–21, 1895," pp. 7, 10; both in reel 14, AABA: Ark.

9. Minutes of 26th Annual Conference, 6 November 1895, Little Rock, Arkansas AME Records. Brown wrote a letter that appeared in *Voice of Missions*, May 1896.

10. Evelyn Brooks Higginbotham, *Righteous Discontent: The Women's Movement in the Black Baptist Church, 1880–1920* (Cambridge, Mass.: Harvard University Press, 1993), 68.

11. Campbell, *Songs of Zion*, 93–95; Angell, *Bishop Henry McNeal Turner*, 220.

12. *Voice of Missions*, September 1894, October 1895, August 1896. The 1884 General Conference of the AME Church in Baltimore had permitted women to serve as evangelists but barred them from serving as parish pastors. Bishop Turner favored the ordination of women and, in fact, ordained one in 1885. Another bishop subsequently removed her name from the clergy list, and the 1888 General Conference denied her appeal. See Angell, *Bishop Henry Turner*, 181–84.

13. *Voice of Missions*, December 1895, February 1896.

14. Ibid., July 1896. The three presenters were Mesdames M. E. Claybon, A. D. Read, and Mattie Adams.

15. See the discussion of black women's club work in Glenda Elizabeth Gilmore, *Gender and Jim Crow: Women and the Politics of White Supremacy in North Carolina, 1896–1920* (Chapel Hill: University of North Carolina Press, 1996), 45–48, 150–57; Cynthia Neverdon-Morton, *Afro-American Women of the South and the Advancement of the Race, 1895–1925* (Knoxville: University of Tennessee Press, 1989); Higginbotham, *Righteous Discontent*, 1–17; and Dorothy Salem, *To Better Our World: Black Women in Organized Reform, 1890–1920* (Brooklyn, N.Y.: Carlson, 1990), 7–100.

16. *Voice of Missions*, April 1895; Walter L. Williams, *Black Americans and the Evangelization of Africa*, 52–53.

17. Ridgel was born in Bradley County, Arkansas, in 1861, the son of Alfred Ridgel Sr., also a Methodist preacher, and his wife, Charlotte. As a young man, Alfred Ridgel Jr. lived in Monticello (Drew County), where he married Frances Graves, and the couple had two children, daughters Mattie and Lenora. Ridgel received his education in a country school. By the late 1880s, he was preaching at the AME congregation in Forrest City, where he also published a six-column weekly newspaper, the *Forrest City Enterprise*. He lived in the city in May 1889, when the Forrest City "riot" took place, the event that spelled the exclusion of blacks from political life of St. Francis County. Ridgel provided a biographical sketch in his *Africa and African Methodism* (Atlanta: Franklin Printing and Publishing Company, 1896), 13–20. Details of his marriage to Frances Graves appeared in the *Indianapolis Freeman*, 13 October 1894. For more information about the Forrest City race riot, see Melanie K. Welch, "Violence and the Decline of

Black Politics in St. Francis County," *Arkansas Historical Quarterly* 60 (Winter 2001): 360–93.

18. *Indianapolis Freeman*, 16 July, 6 August, 1892; J. Ormond Wilson to Rev. H. M. Turner, 28 October 1892, ACS reel 226.

19. Ridgel describes his American tour in *Africa and African Methodism*, 21–29; and *Indianapolis Freeman*, 29 September 1895. His flyer appears in late 1892 in ACS reel 141.

20. Worthington, who had his own family with wife, Louise, fathered a son and daughter with one of his slaves. He sent Fannie's father, James Mason, to Paris to be educated, and the daughter, Martha, attended Oberlin College in Ohio. James Mason returned to Arkansas and served two terms in the state senate during Reconstruction. Mason died when daughter Fannie was a child, and her mother remarried and moved to St. Louis and later Washington, D.C., where she worked as a clerk in the federal land office. Fannie had taken the name of her white grandfather Worthington and began teaching in the public schools of Maryland and New Jersey. Ridgel must have met Fannie when he was lecturing in Camden, Trenton, and Princeton, New Jersey. See Ridgel, *Africa and African Methodism*, 29, 113; and Mifflin Wistar Gibbs, *Shadow and Light: An Autobiography with Reminiscences of the Last and Present Century* (Washington, D.C.: n.p., 1902), 228–29. Mason's membership in the Arkansas Senate is noted in *Historical Report of the Secretary of State of the State of Arkansas* (Little Rock: Secretary of State, 1968), 330, 332. A copy of the couple's marriage license was printed in the *Indianapolis Freeman*, 13 October 1894.

21. Ridgel described his journey in *Africa and African Methodism*, 30–38; and *Indianapolis Freeman*, 28 July 1894. Oddly, Ridgel stayed in Liverpool for two weeks while his new bride and Bishop Turner toured London, before the entire party departed on a small ship for the west coast of Africa.

22. *Christian Recorder*, May 1893; letter of Ridgel to Rev. J. M. Conner, of Forrest City, 20 May 1893, published in the *Indianapolis Freeman*, 5 August 1893.

23. *Indianapolis Freeman*, 5 August 1893; letter from James A. F. Trice of Freetown, published in the *Richmond Planet*, 7 April 1894.

24. Derrick and Henderson retrieved copies of Ridgel's certificate of marriage to Frances Graves in Monticello, Arkansas, in 1881, and to Fannie Worthington in Camden, New Jersey, in 1893, with a signed and witnessed affidavit by Frances Ridgel, dated 23 November 1893, swearing that she was alive and well and still legally married to Alfred Ridgel. Frances Ridgel claimed that, during her husband's six months in Africa, she had received but one communication from him and that letter simply asked her to send a package of clothing he had left in her possession. See Minutes of Annual Conference, 7–12 November 1893, Brinkley, Arkansas AME Records; and *Indianapolis Freeman*, 13 October 1894.

25. *Indianapolis Freeman*, 10, 17 February 1894.

26. Ridgel reported the death of Vreeman in *Indianapolis Freeman*, 25 November 1893. Ridgel discussed his and his wife's work in Sierra Leone in *Voice of Missions*, September 1895; and *Indianapolis Freeman*, 10 March 1894.

27. *Voice of Missions*, August 1894; Minutes of Annual Conference, 31 October–5 November 1894, Fort Smith, Arkansas AME Records; an open letter from Ridgel of 12 September 1894 was read to the assembly.

28. *Indianapolis Freeman*, 1 September 1895; *Voice of Missions*, August 1895.

29. See Ridgel's stinging words in *Indianapolis Freeman*, 19 May, 2 June, 21 July 1894.

30. *Indianapolis Freeman*, 16 June, 4 August, 13 October 1894. The *Freeman* made the claim about its Arkansas readership in the 8 August 1896 issue.

31. *Voice of Missions*, August 1894.

32. Bishop Turner refused to publish in his magazine the resolution regarding Ridgel produced by the South Arkansas Conference of the AME Church, saying he would take it to Liberia for the conference there to consider (*Voice of Missions*, September 1894).

33. *Voice of Missions*, August 1895.

34. *Christian Recorder*, 20 September 1894; *Indianapolis Freeman*, 10 November 1895. Henderson went on to become the president of Morris Brown College, the AME college in Atlanta.

35. *Indianapolis Freeman*, 29 June, 24 August, 1895; *Voice of Missions*, October 1895. In 1896, H. B. Parks, a protégé of Bishop Turner, replaced Derrick as missions director, and Derrick, ironically, became bishop for Turner's Eighth District, which included Arkansas (*Voice of Missions*, October 1896).

36. *Voice of Missions*, June 1895.

37. Ibid., May 1896; see also Ridgel's criticism of Washington in *Indianapolis Freeman*, 14 March 1896.

38. *Voice of Missions*, February 1896. Ridgel must have become familiar with Blyden's book published in 1887, *Christianity, Islam and the Negro Race*, in which he argued that Islam had provided a more positive influence for the black race in Africa than, in many cases, Christianity. See Hollis R. Lynch, *Edward Wilmot Blyden: Pan-Negro Patriot, 1832–1912* (New York: Oxford University Press, 1967), 71–78. Ridgel had low regard for the faith of the Muslims. He believed that "Africa can never be civilized under the influence of Mohammedism" and that Islam was more dangerous than paganism. See his discussion of Islam in *Africa and African Methodism*, 65–72.

39. *Voice of Missions*, November 1895. I have been unable to locate a copy of "A Pen Picture of the Republic of Liberia."

40. See Ridgel's article, "Should Afro-Americans Return to Africa?" in *Voice of Missions*, February 1896, portions of which were reprinted in D. J. Flummer, *The Negro and Liberia* (Birmingham: International Migration Society, 1897), 9–12.

41. Ridgel, *Africa and African Methodism*, 50–51, 56, 88; *Indianapolis Freeman*, 10 March, 8 September 1894.

42. Ridgel, *Africa and African Methodism*, 86–88.

43. *Denver Statesman*, 1 September 1894, in clippings file, ACS reel 322.

44. Ridgel quoted Garnett in a letter to the *Voice of Missions*, October 1896.

45. *Voice of Missions*, May, December 1896. Edward Blyden, prejudiced against Ridgel because he was a mulatto, said the missionary, "after doing all the mischief he could in Liberia, committed suicide by jumping overboard in the St. Paul River" (Blyden to J. Ormond Wilson, 17 September 1897, in Hollis R. Lynch, ed., *Selected Letters of Edward Wilmot Blyden* [Millwood, N.Y.: KTO Press, 1978], 447). Ridgel's death was as enigmatic as his life. Had he committed suicide or was he fighting to save his life? Did he really commit bigamy? What had happened to his first wife? Had Fannie returned to America for a visit, or had she left Alfred for good? Fifteen months after Ridgel's death, in

January 1898, Mifflin W. Gibbs, a wealthy black businessman in Little Rock, received an appointment from President William McKinley to become the American consul to the French colony of Madagascar, off the coast of Africa. On his long journey there, he passed through Paris, where he visited an old friend from Arkansas, Mrs. James Mason, the mother of Fannie Worthington Ridgel. Mrs. Mason was living in well-appointed apartments in Paris, Gibbs said, with her daughter, "an artistic painter of some note, with studio adjoining, where I was shown many beautiful productions of her brush." What became of Fannie thereafter remains unknown. See Gibbs, *Shadow and Light*, 228–29; and *Voice of Missions*, December 1896.

46. Jackson was born in Holly Springs, Mississippi, in 1858, the son of a white man and a black slave. After graduating from the Mississippi State Normal School in 1883, he moved to Hot Springs, Arkansas. Jackson joined the Missionary Baptist Church in Gurdon (Clark County) in 1890 and became a preacher the next year. In 1893, he preached at the Roanoke Baptist Church in Hot Springs and worked as an upholsterer in a mattress factory. See R. A. Jackson to ACS, 22 February 1894, ACS reel 180; and "Arkansas Baptist Sunday Day School Convention, Camden, 1895," p. 22, reel 14, AABA: Ark.

47. R. A. Jackson to ACS, 8 December 1893, ACS reel 142; R. A. Jackson to ACS, 22 February 1894, ACS reel 180; Little Rock *Baptist Vanguard*, 20 October 1893; Journal of the Executive Committee of the ACS, 7 December 1893, ACS reel 293; *Liberia Bulletin* 6 (February 1895): 4.

48. The *Indianapolis Freeman*, 21 April 1894, reported that Turner preached at Visitor's Chapel and St. Paul's AME Church in Hot Springs. The Jacksons planned to arrive in New York on 16 April (R. A. Jackson to ACS, 20 March 1894, ACS reel 143). In the *Voice of Missions*, August 1894, Ridgel made a reference to Turner appointing R. A. Jackson to work in Liberia.

49. When their ship arrived in Liberia, the ACS agent there learned that the Jackson family had remained in the Canary Islands because Mrs. Jackson had become ill. The Jackson family apparently never set foot in Liberia. See J. C. Stevens to J. Ormond Wilson, 21 June 1894, 6 June 1895, ACS reel 170. See also Jordan, *Up the Ladder in Foreign Mission*, 101, 124–29; and Walter L. Williams, *Black Americans and the Evangelization of Africa*, 69–70. For more about Jackson's work in South Africa, see Kenneth C. Barnes, "'On the Shore Beyond the Sea': Black Missionaries from Arkansas in Africa during the 1890s," *Arkansas Historical Quarterly* 61 (Winter 2002): 346–50.

50. *Baptist Vanguard*, 27 April 1894; Martin, *Black Baptists and African Missions*, 93.

51. D. B. Gaines, *Racial Possibilities as Indicated by the Negroes of Arkansas* (Little Rock: Philander Smith College, 1898), 50–51. Gammon's president recommended Sherrill to the ACS as "one of our best-equipped men, of high character and large promise of usefulness, having expressed his abiding conviction of the call of God to missionary work in Africa," and he referred to Mrs. Sherrill as a cultured and devoted spouse who gave herself gladly to the African work. See "Annual Report of the American Colonization Society at the 81st annual meeting, January 18, 1898," *The Annual Reports of the American Colonization Society*, vol. 6: 1871–1910 (New York: Negro Universities Press, 1969), 7–8. The Methodist Episcopal Church, the northern branch of Methodism that emerged after the split over the slavery question, established the Gammon Theological

Seminary in Atlanta in 1883 to train black clergy. With 300,000 black members and 1,700 black clergy in 1890, this denomination had more black members than any other white-majority church. In 1894, a white Methodist preacher gave money to set up the Stewart Missionary Foundation at Gammon for the specific purpose of training black clergymen for African missions. The foundation made Gammon Seminary a repository of books, information, and expertise on Africa.

52. Walter L. Williams, *Black Americans and the Evangelization of Africa*, 15, 92, 184; Joseph C. Sherrill to Bishop Hartzell, 27 August, 28 October, 27 November, 3 December 1898, roll 5, Missionary Files, Missionary Correspondence, 1846–1912, United Methodist Church, General Commission on Archives and History, Madison, N.J. (hereafter cited as Missionary Correspondence).

53. *Southwestern Christian Advocate*, 29 December 1898.

54. Ibid., 30 March 1899.

55. Ibid., 25 May 1899; Sherrill to A. B. Leonard, 15 November 1901, roll 5, Missionary Correspondence.

56. The Sherrill and Allen families came to Liberia through a subsidy of the American Colonization Society (*Liberia Bulletin*, 14 [February 1899]: 2; 16 [February 1900]: 4). *Southwestern Christian Advocate*, 29 December 1898, 29 June 1899; Joe A. Davis to ACS, 18 October 1904, ACS reel 150; Davis to A. B. Leonard, 24 February 1900, 12 July 1902, 31 October 1904, roll 3, Missionary Correspondence; Walter L. Williams, *Black Americans and the Evangelization of Africa*, 15, 199 n. 55; F. M. Allen to Leonard, 29 May 1909, roll 2, Missionary Correspondence; Sherrill to Leonard, 6 October 1906, 28 July, 1 December 1908, 14 July 1909, roll 5, Missionary Correspondence.

57. *Liberia Bulletin* 16 (February 1900): 5; 18 (February 1901): 2, 4; John Hamilton Reed to Bishop J. C. Hartzell, 16 June 1904, roll 5, Missionary Correspondence. Mrs. Reed long outlived her husband. In 1952, she received an invitation from the Liberian government to attend the inauguration of President William V. S. Tubman. She made the long trip at the age of seventy-two with her daughter Florence, who grew up in Liberia, and they were greeted upon arrival by a host of Mrs. Reed's former students. See Doris Darnell, "Eighteen Years in Liberia," *World Outlook* (November 1956): 20–21, in John H. Reed, Mission Biographical Reference Files, 1880–1960, United Methodist Church General Commission on Archives and History, Madison, N.J.

Chapter Seven

1. This argument owes much to the work of Edwin S. Redkey; see his *Meaning of Africa to Afro-Americans, 1890–1914* (Buffalo: Council on International Studies, State University of New York at Buffalo, 1971).

2. Turner's comment appears in a letter of 22 February 1883 to the *Christian Recorder*, in Edwin S. Redkey, ed., *Respect Black: The Writings and Speeches of Henry McNeal Turner* (New York: Arno Press and *New York Times*, 1971), 54.

3. Unsigned letter from Menifee to Coppinger, 10 March 1890, ACS reel 133; Ben Lawrence, Andy Beezley, and Charly Eubanks to Coppinger, 21 February 1892, ACS reel 179.

4. *Voice of Missions*, August 1896.

5. B. T. Willis to Coppinger, 14 October 1890, ACS reel 135; unsigned letter from Pine Bluff to Coppinger, 13 February 1891, ACS reel 136; L. W. Wyatt to Coppinger, 10 October 1890, ACS reel 135; Coppinger to W. D. Leslie, 25 October 1890, ACS reel 225.

6. Kenneth Marvin Hamilton, *Black Towns and Profit: Promotion and Development in the Trans-Appalachian West, 1877–1915* (Urbana: University of Illinois Press, 1991), 99–110. The state legislature of Oklahoma in 1999 appropriated money for historical markers to commemorate the founding of Oklahoma's all-black towns, and in February 2000, the State Museum of History opened a new exhibit titled: "'Say, Have You Heard the Story': An Exhibition of the All-Black Towns of Oklahoma." The novel *Paradise*, by Nobel Prize–winning novelist Toni Morrison, tells the fictional story of blacks who fled oppression in Mississippi and founded an isolated all-black town in Oklahoma.

7. "Blackville: An All-Negro Community," *Stream of History* 9 (January 1971): 11–12; Alice Crawford Branch, "Desha County's Unique Town: Liberia City," *Desha County Historical Society 1983 Programs* 10 (Spring 1984): 62–70. Today Liberia City is called Masonville.

8. W. D. Leslie to Coppinger, 17 January 1891, ACS reel 136; A. D. Allen to Coppinger, 22 June 1891, ACS reel 137; James H. Lattimer to Coppinger, 7 April 1892, ACS reel 139; J. W. Penn to Coppinger, 1 July 1891, ACS reel 139.

9. See Gail Bederman, *Manliness and Civilization: A Cultural History of Gender and Race in the United States, 1880–1917* (Chicago: University of Chicago Press, 1995); and Michele Mitchell, "'The Black Man's Burden': African Americans, Imperialism, and Notions of Racial Manhood, 1890–1910," *International Review of Social History* 44 (1999, supplement): 77–99.

10. For an example of Turner's emphatic rhetoric about Africa and black manliness, see his speech given in Atlanta in 1895, "The American Negro and the Fatherland," in J. W. E. Bowen, ed., *Africa and the American Negro: Addresses and Proceedings of the Congress on Africa, December 13–15, 1895* (1896; reprint, Miami, Fla.: Mnemosyne Publishing, 1969), 195–98. See Ridgel, "Should Afro-Americans Return to Africa?" in *Voice of Missions*, February 1896, and Ridgel, *Africa and African Methodism* (Atlanta: Franklin Printing and Publishing Company, 1896), 56. See also the discussion of Turner in James T. Campbell, *Songs of Zion: The African Methodist Episcopal Church in the United States and South Africa* (New York: Oxford University Press, 1995), 82; and Mitchell, "'Black Man's Burden,'" 84.

11. H. C. Cade to Coppinger, 23 February 1891, ACS reel 136.

12. See Wilson Jeremiah Moses, *The Golden Age of Black Nationalism, 1850–1925* (Hamden, Conn.: Archon Books, 1978); and his introduction to *Classical Black Nationalism from the American Revolution to Marcus Garvey* (New York: New York University Press, 1996), 1–35. Moses argues that black nationalists in the late 1800s generally believed in the superiority of Western culture over African traditions and were concerned about spreading Anglo-American values into Africa.

13. See the discussion of Turner in Tunde Adeleke, *UnAfrican Americans: Nineteenth-Century Black Nationalists and the Civilizing Mission* (Lexington: University Press of Kentucky, 1998), 92–110; and Campbell, *Songs of Zion*, 74–89; or read Turner himself in Redkey, ed., *Respect Black*, 55, 74, 147.

14. *Voice of Missions*, February 1896. Ridgel was something of a sycophant in his relationship with Turner. In the article "Greatest Living Negro," Ridgel called Turner a scholar, writer, preacher, statesman, and "a great race lover and a truly patriotic man." By comparison, Ridgel said, "Mr Washington [Booker T.] can gather money and tell jokes" (*Indianapolis Freeman*, 14 March 1896).

15. *Voice of Missions*, September 1896.

16. *Denver Statesman*, 1 September 1894, in clippings file, ACS reel 322.

17. For an insightful discussion of the development of black Christianity in slavery days, see Eugene D. Genovese, *Roll, Jordan, Roll: The World the Slaves Made* (New York: Pantheon Books, 1974), 161–284; and Albert J. Raboteau, *Slave Religion: "The Invisible Institution" in the Antebellum South* (New York: Oxford University Press, 1978).

18. "The First Convention of the Liberia Exodus Arkansas Colony," pp. 1–3, vol. 6, Colonization Pamphlets.

19. Eddie S. Glaude Jr., *Exodus! Religion, Race, and Nation in Early Nineteenth-Century Black America* (Chicago: University of Chicago Press, 2000); Genovese, *Roll, Jordan, Roll*, 252–54.

20. James Matthews to Coppinger, 22 March 1891, ACS reel 136.

21. See Randall K. Burkett, *Garveyism as a Religious Movement: The Institutionalization of a Black Civil Religion* (Metuchen, N.J.: Scarecrow Press and the American Theological Library Association, 1978), 20, 34, 85–86.

22. See Walter L. Williams, "Black American Attitudes toward Africa, 1877–1900," *Pan-African Journal* 8 (Spring 1971): 179–85.

23. Turner letter to the *Christian Recorder*, 22 February 1883, in Redkey, ed., *Respect Black*, 55.

24. See Turner's letter in Redkey, ed., *Respect Black*, 124; Ridgel, *Africa and African Methodism*, 50–51, 88.

25. Ridgel, *Africa and African Methodism*, 42–44; *Voice of Missions*, February 1896. In these ideas Ridgel was probably influenced by the views of Edward Blyden or Martin Delany. See Hollis R. Lynch, *Edward Wilmot Blyden: Pan-Negro Patriot, 1832–1912* (New York: Oxford University Press, 1967), 55–57; and Adeleke, *UnAfrican Americans*, 53.

26. See the discussion of Turner's views of Africa in William E. Montgomery, *Under Their Own Vine and Fig Tree: The African-American Church in the South, 1865–1900* (Baton Rouge: Louisiana State University Press, 1993), 208–9; Gayraud S. Wilmore, *Black Religion and Black Radicalism* (New York: Doubleday, 1972), 168–75; and John Dittmer, "The Education of Henry McNeal Turner," in *Black Leaders of the Nineteenth Century*, ed. Leon Litwack and August Meier (Urbana: University of Illinois, 1988), 253–72. Ridgel was writing to the Reverend J. M. Conner; the letter was published in the *Indianapolis Freeman*, 5 August 1893. For a discussion, and visual examples, of late-nineteenth-century Western views of Africa, see Adeleke, *UnAfrican Americans*, 13–30; and Jan Nederveen Pieterse, *White on Black: Images of Africa and Blacks in Western Popular Culture* (New Haven: Yale University Press, 1992), 64–101.

27. "Constitution of the Liberia Exodus Arkansas Colony," vol. 6, Colonization Pamphlets; Valinda Smith's address, "The Object of Missions," can be found in Proceedings of the 18th Anniversary of the Antioch District Sunday School Convention, Dardanelle, July 20–22, 1891, p. 10, in reel 14, AABA: Ark.; Joseph M. Suggs to Coppinger, 9 January 1890, ACS reel 133.

28. See the excellent discussion of black attitudes toward American imperialism in Willard B. Gatewood Jr., *Black Americans and the White Man's Burden, 1898–1903* (Urbana: University of Illinois Press, 1975); and Mitchell, "'Black Man's Burden,'" 87–96.

29. Delany's plan called for African Americans to come to the Niger River area, then develop and oversee a cash crop economy based on cotton grown by native African labor. Before the Civil War interrupted Delany's plan, he had spent six months in Great Britain negotiating for partners to buy up African cotton. See the discussion in Adeleke, *UnAfrican Americans*, 62–64.

30. See Ridgel's letters in *Voice of Missions*, August 1894 and June 1895; and *Indianapolis Freeman*, 20 October 1894. Turner's letters of 1883 and 1895 can be found in Redkey, ed., *Respect Black*, 55, 162.

31. "Constitution of the Liberia Exodus Arkansas Colony," pp. 1, 4.

32. Kevin K. Gaines has examined the ethos of racial uplift among black elites in the late 1800s and 1900s in *Uplifting the Race: Black Leadership, Politics, and Culture in the Twentieth Century* (Chapel Hill: University of North Carolina Press, 1996). Gaines argues insightfully that black cultural elites adopted a paternalistic goal to uplift the race, itself a racist attitude that worked against any realistic effort in dismantling a racially oppressive system. While Gaines sees the attitude of racial uplift as an elite construct in the American context, the evidence within the back-to-Africa movement shows that both the educated and the ordinary shared common images of Africans in relation to self.

Chapter Eight

1. *Arkansas Gazette*, 11 January, 10 May, 9 December 1893; Morrilton *Pilot*, 21, 28 April 1893; *Southwestern Christian Advocate*, 18 May 1893; *Richmond Planet*, 22 July 1893. Other lynchings took place in Lincoln County in July and November, and in Cross and Greene Counties in December. See NAACP, *Thirty Years of Lynching in the United States, 1889–1918* (1919; reprint, New York: Arno Press and *New York Times*, 1969), 49.

2. *Arkansas Gazette*, 3, 6 February, 15 April, 24–30 October 1893; *Richmond Planet*, 29 April 1893; *Arkansas Gazette*, 17 January 1894.

3. *Richmond Planet*, 11 March 1893; *Indianapolis Freeman*, 25 March 1893; *Southwestern Christian Advocate*, 15 June 1893.

4. Herbert Shapiro, *White Violence and Black Response: From Reconstruction to Montgomery* (Amherst: University of Massachusetts Press, 1988), 53.

5. See, for example, the letter to the ACS of J. H. Barksdale from Pine Bluff (6 February 1893, ACS reel 141), who claimed to speak for 500 families wishing to go; or A. Buttes of Lollie, Faulkner County (1894 [date torn off], ACS reel 145), who said he had 500 people worked up to emigrate; or C. C. Dunham of Wheatley, St. Francis County (25 July 1893, ACS reel 145), who claimed he was part of a crowd of from 800 to 1,000 people who wished to leave. For an example of Wilson's form letters, see Wilson to S. C. Ruint of Cotton Plant, 28 February 1893, ACS reel 141. In *Voice of Missions*, March 1894, Turner claimed he had received hundreds of letters.

6. *Liberia Bulletin* 4 (February 1894): 3; 6 (February 1895): 4; Ned Simure to Joseph Cheeseman, 17 February 1894, ACS reel 145.

7. Turner to Byron Sunderland, 29 December 1892, ACS reel 140; *New York Times*, 12 February 1893.

8. See Edwin S. Redkey's excellent description of the founding of the company, in *Black Exodus: Black Nationalist and Back-to-Africa Movements, 1890–1910* (New Haven: Yale University Press, 1969), 195–201. A copy of the contract and application form can be found in ACS reel 319. According to the fine print of the contract, the IMS pledged to provide each emigrant upon arrival in Liberia with 1 barrel of flour, 2 barrels of meal, 35 lbs. of mess pork, 10 lbs. of lard, 25 lbs. of sugar, 15 lbs. of salt, 2 ounces of pepper, 8 bars of soap, and 1 lb. of yeast powder.

9. Redkey, *Black Exodus*, 197–201; *Indianapolis Freeman*, 18 August, 27 October 1894; Willie Fletcher to ACS, 9 September, 9 October 1894, ACS reel 145.

10. *Denver Statesman*, 17 November 1894; *Christian Recorder*, 15 November 1894; both in clippings file, ACS reel 322.

11. *Arkansas Gazette*, 8 March 1895; *Washington Post*, 8 March 1895; *Denver Statesman*, 17 November 1894; *Memphis Scimitar*, n.d., all in clippings file, ACS reel 322; *Christian Recorder*, 28 March 1895.

12. Redkey, *Black Exodus*, 210–14; *Memphis Commercial Appeal*, 7 March 1895.

13. *Christian Recorder*, 28 February 1895; *Voice of Missions*, June 1895.

14. Redkey, *Black Exodus*, 215–17. See Smith articles in *Christian Recorder*, 11 April 1895; and *New York Age*, 11 April 1895, both in clippings file, ACS reel 322; and his comments to the *Savannah Morning News*, 20 March 1895, printed in the *Indianapolis Freeman*, 30 March 1895. Smith republished his most scathing attacks against the IMS and its *Horsa* voyage in his book *Liberia in the Light of Living Testimony* (Nashville: A.M.E. Church Sunday School Union, 1895), 30–37.

15. Redkey, *Black Exodus*, 217–18; *Savannah Tribune*, 23 March 1895; *Indianapolis Freeman*, 30 March 1895; *New York Times*, 20 March 1895. Newspapers differed on the exact number in the emigrant party; some said 197 emigrants sailed, and others said 202.

16. Redkey, *Black Exodus*, 221.

17. "Annual Report of the American Colonization Society, Sixty-Ninth Session, 1896," in *The Annual Reports of the American Colonization Society*, vol. 6: 1871–1910 (New York: Negro Universities Press, 1969), 21–22; J. C. Stevens to J. Ormond Wilson, 10 May, 6 June, 10 November 1895, ACS reel 170; Redkey, *Black Exodus*, 221–23; *Voice of Missions*, July 1895; W. H. Heard to Wilson, 18 September 1895, ACS reel 170.

18. Thomas H. Jefferson to J. Ormond Wilson, 15 October 1894, ACS reel 143. A letter to the *Indianapolis Freeman*, 20 April 1895, from Lonoke said, "We have not got the Africa fever yet but are waiting to hear from those 202 that left on the ship *Horsa*." The Texarkana debate was reported in *Indianapolis Freeman*, 11 May 1895.

19. *Indianapolis Freeman*, 16, 30 November 1895; H. M. Turner to J. Ormond Wilson, 12 November 1895, ACS reel 145.

20. Redkey, *Black Exodus*, 225–27, 231–35.

21. A list of *Laurada* passengers over the age of five was printed in *Voice of Missions*, May 1896, showing passengers from Arkansas, Georgia, Mississippi, Texas, Tennessee, Florida, Alabama, South Carolina, Oklahoma, Indian Territories, Delaware, Illinois, and New York. Arkansas emigrants came from Forrest City, Madison, Little Rock, Galloway, England, Keo, Menifee, Marianna, Sweet Home, Gregory, and Bearden. Of the

277 passengers listed by name, 136 came from Arkansas and 141 from other states, including the former Arkansans in New York. The reference to the two New York families being stranded Arkansas emigrants from 1892 appears in D. J. Flummer, *The Negro and Liberia* (Birmingham: International Migration Society, 1897), 21.

22. *Forrest City Times*, 17 January 1896. The *Lonoke Weekly Democrat*, 23 January 1896, also reported the departure of the 102 blacks from Forrest City, concluding, "They will not be missed. Arkansas has plenty left—shoats, dogs, and darkeys."

23. Thomas H. Jefferson to Sir, 4 November 1895, ACS reel 145; *Forrest City Times*, 3 January 1896.

24. *Forrest City Times*, 27 March 1896.

25. *Forrest City Herald*, 14 March 1896; *Forrest City Times*, 28 February 1896; *Voice of Missions*, February 1896.

26. *Savannah Morning News*, 2 March 1896, reprinted in *Voice of Missions*, April 1896; Flummer, *Negro and Liberia*, 21–22; Redkey, *Black Exodus*, 236–37; *Illustrated American* 19 (21 March 1896): 371.

27. Flummer, *Negro and Liberia*, 21–23; William K. Roberts, *An African Canaan for the American Negro* (Birmingham: International Migration Society, 1896), 18–20. See also Ridgel's letter of 17 April 1896 to *Voice of Missions*, June 1896.

28. Redkey, *Black Exodus*, 242–48; see also Roberts, *African Canaan*, and Flummer, *Negro and Liberia*. Flummer cribbed large sections of his book from Roberts's earlier work.

29. A. B. Berry to ACS, 27 September 1895, ACS reel 145; Redkey, *Black Exodus*, 245–47.

30. Redkey, *Black Exodus*, 232, 239–41, 245–48. See the newspaper coverage of returning emigrants in the *New York Times*, 31 July 1895, 28 September 1896; *Southwestern Christian Advocate*, 15 October 1896; and clippings file, ACS reel 322. We know less about the decline of the back-to-Africa movement than its rise partly because few records of the IMS have survived.

31. See William Ivy Hair, *Carnival of Fury: Robert Charles and the New Orleans Race Riot of 1900* (Baton Rouge: Louisiana State University Press, 1976); Joel Williamson, *The Crucible of Race: Black/White Relations in the American South since Emancipation* (New York: Oxford University Press, 1984), 201–9; and Redkey, *Black Exodus*, 255–58. See also the discussion of the New Orleans riot and the waning of Bishop Turner's influence in Gayraud S. Wilmore, *Black Religion and Black Radicalism* (New York: Doubleday, 1972), 189–91.

32. See Redkey's description of the decline of the emigration movement, 1900–1910, in *Black Exodus*, 252–86; *Helena Reporter*, 1 February 1900, in clippings file, ACS reel 322.

33. See correspondence of 1897–1904 in ACS reels 147–50. A. J. Dixon to ACS, 16 March 1901, ACS reel 148; Rev. S. E. Jackson to ACS, 10 August 1902, ACS reel 149; both Dixon and Jackson wanted to join family already in Liberia. William Dickerson to ACS, 28 January 1903, ACS reel 149; "88th Annual Report of the American Colonization Society, presented January 17, 1905," in *Annual Reports of the American Colonization Society*, 5.

Chapter Nine

1. J. Gus Liebenow, *Liberia: The Evolution of Privilege* (Ithaca, N.Y.: Cornell University Press, 1969), 22–24; Yekutiel Gershoni, *Black Colonialism: The Americo-Liberian Scramble for the Hinterland* (Boulder, Colo.: Westview Press, 1985), 33–36.

2. Population estimates varied. The ACS claimed to have settled 16,202 people in Liberia by 1892 and to have assisted with the relocation of 5,722 recaptured slaves. See "75th Annual Report of the American Colonization Society, January 1892," in *The Annual Reports of the American Colonization Society*, vol. 6: 1871–1910 (New York: Negro Universities Press, 1969). Charles H. J. Taylor, the former American minister to Liberia, estimated that only 12,000 "civilized" people lived in the whole country. See his hostile descriptions in his Kansas City, Kansas, newspaper, the *American Citizen*, 29 April 1892. Joseph W. Yates, the Liberian consul to the United States and a senior partner of Yates and Porterfield, the shipping firm that engaged in trade with Liberia until 1892, estimated that there were 28,000 American settlers and their descendants in Liberia; see *Washington Star*, 16 February 1894, in clippings file, ACS reel 322. Other estimates ranged somewhere in between: for example, the *Liberia Bulletin* 3 (November 1893): 6, estimated 15,000–20,000 colonists and descendants and a total population of one to two million Africans.

3. *Monrovia Observer*, 25 February 1880.

4. See letter from Liberia by William K. Roberts in *Voice of Missions*, October 1896; and Alexander Smart, telephone interview with author, Cambria Heights, N.Y., 18 February 1997. Clement Irons, an AME Church pastor and emigrant on the *Azor* in 1878, reported that in 1895 five white businesses operated in Monrovia—three German, one Dutch, and one English, with three to four white businessmen working in each. European businesses also operated in Cape Palmas and Sinoe. See *Liberia Bulletin* 6 (February 1895): 44.

5. *American Citizen*, 29 April 1892.

6. See the descriptions of Monrovia in Charles Spencer Smith, *Glimpses of Africa* (Nashville: A.M.E. Sunday School Union, 1895), 269; Bishop Turner's letters from Liberia, in Edwin S. Redkey, ed., *Respect Black: The Writings and Speeches of Henry McNeal Turner* (New York: Arno Press and *New York Times*, 1971), 123–25; and G. G. Brownell, "The Lone Star Republic," *Harper's Weekly*, 27 April 1895.

7. *Monrovia Observer*, 20 July 1880, 27 January 1881, 8 September 1881; D. B. Warner to Coppinger, 25 August 1880, ACS reel 164; A. L. Stanford to C. T. O. King, 28 December 1882, ACS reel 165; King to Coppinger, July 1882, ACS reel 165.

8. D. B. Warner to Coppinger, 5 January 1880, ACS reel 164; *Monrovia Observer*, 22 July 1880, 22 September, 27 October 1881; obituary of Stanford in *Arkansas Mansion*, 11 August 1883, reprinted from the *Monrovia Observer*.

9. C. T. O. King to Coppinger, 10 March 1884, ACS reel 166; S. A. Stanford to Coppinger, 31 October 1884, ACS reel 166; Redkey, ed., *Respect Black*, 117.

10. Amanda Smith, *An Autobiography: The Story of the Lord's Dealings with Mrs. Amanda Smith, the Colored Evangelist* (1893; reprint, New York: Oxford University Press, 1988), 463.

11. D. B. Warner to Coppinger, 1 November 1879, ACS reel 164; Warner to Cop-

pinger, 16 April 1880, ACS reel 164; Warner to Coppinger, 2 August 1880, ACS reel 164. In July 1998, when I traveled to Liberia and reached Brewerville, I began shooting video, and an elderly resident walked over to see what I was doing. His name was Johnny Johnson, the grandson of Moses L. Johnson, who emigrated in 1879. Johnny Johnson became my first interview with a descendant of an Arkansas immigrant, and he went with me to locate and interview other descendants in the area.

12. Jesse Oliver Hayes, "A Brief History of the Founding of the Township of Brewerville," unpublished paper in the possession of Alexander M. Massey, New York, N.Y.; D. B. Warner to Coppinger, 11 June 1880, ACS reel 164.

13. D. B. Warner to Coppinger, 25 August 1880, ACS reel 164; C. T. O. King to Coppinger, 14 September 1883, ACS reel 165.

14. Edward Blyden to Coppinger, 18 January 1881, ACS reel 164; C. T. O. King to Coppinger, 17 February 1882, ACS reel 165; John Munden to Coppinger, 15 October 1881, ACS reel 165; Hayes, "Brief History of the Founding of the Township of Brewerville." The quarterly report of Sherwood Capps, the teacher at the ACS school in Brewerville, shows children of the Newton, Merritt, and Davis families from Arkansas attending the school in the fall of 1880; see correspondence of February 1881, ACS reel 164. The ACS quoted Newton's speech in the *African Repository* 58 (April 1882): 35.

15. Edward Blyden to Coppinger, n.d., located in correspondence of 20 March 1881, ACS reel 164; C. T. O. King to Coppinger, 18 December 1882, 28 August, 14 September 1883, ACS reel 165.

16. Coppinger to C. T. O. King, 12 February 1887, ACS reel 223; King to Coppinger, 17, 26 January 1888, ACS reel 167; Anderson (surveyor) to King, 17 February 1888, ACS reel 169. McKeever was there by March 1888, when Robertsport residents petitioned the ACS to send more immigrants to reinforce their settlement (Rev. B. K. McKeever et al. to Coppinger, 17 March 1888, ACS reel 169). The Robertsport residents received their mail in care of the post office in Manoh Salijah, Sierra Leone.

17. C. T. O. King to Coppinger, 28 May 1889, ACS reel 170; J. S. Smith to ACS, 18 September 1889, ACS reel 170; Coy Carver McLane Brown to Coppinger, 6 November 1889, ACS reel 170.

18. C. T. O. King to Coppinger, 23, 24 March 1891, ACS reel 179; Anderson to Ezekial Smith, 7 June 1892, in miscellaneous file, ACS reel 311; Ezekial Smith to Reginald Fendall, 19 April 1892, in late-June correspondence, ACS reel 140.

19. Tony Miller interview with author, Johnsonville, Liberia, 31 July 1998; Henry Moore interview with author, Monrovia, Liberia, 31 July 1998; J. Benedict Shaw interview with author, Johnsonville, Liberia, 18 July 1998. Charles Hays, an immigrant on the *Laurada* from Sweet Home, Arkansas, who settled in Johnsonville, declared that all his children went to school (Charles Hays to Green Battle, c/o ACS, 4 October 1897, ACS reel 170). See also the description of Johnsonville by H. W. White, the preacher of the local AME church, in *Voice of Missions*, December 1897; and the list of schools in Liberia in 1892 in *Liberia Bulletin* 1 (November 1892): 18–20.

20. J. C. Stevens to J. Ormond Wilson, 10 May 1895, 27 November 1896, ACS reel 170; Charles Hays to Green Battle, c/o ACS, 4 October 1897, ACS reel 170.

21. "Rations list for emigrants who came on the *Liberia*, December 6, 1891," 1 March 1892, ACS reel 179; "Invoice of Mdse. Shipped by American Colonization Society on

board Bark Liberia," 14 February 1891, ACS reel 225. "Bi-weekly ration list" shows rations drawn by the Bankhead family of Robertsport, 24 January 1888, ACS reel 169.

22. Charles Hays to Green Battle, c/o ACS, 4 October 1897, ACS reel 170.

23. Tony Miller interview. Liberians used the term "cutlass" for the small axlike devices. Many of my sources for this chapter are interviews I conducted with descendants of the Arkansas emigrants. Most of these descendants are grandchildren of the emigrants or, in a few cases, sons and daughters of emigrants who came themselves as children. The interviews were conducted in Liberia in the summer of 1998, in Monrovia, or in the Johnsonville and Brewerville communities. The political environment in 1998 was such that I could not travel safely throughout Liberia. Thus I used no sophisticated method of sampling in my choice of interviewees; I simply interviewed whomever I could find. One interview often led me to others in the community. Some interviewees became my guides who traveled with me to introduce me to other descendants. In the concluding chapter, I make some further remarks about the process and difficulties of doing fieldwork in war-torn Liberia. Little written documentary evidence regarding American immigrants exists in Liberia. I witnessed Liberians digging through the remains of the National Archives in Monrovia, which had burned to the ground, scavenging for materials of any value. It appears that civil war destroyed most of the paper records from the 1800s that had survived the tropical humidity.

24. *Liberia Bulletin* 6 (February 1895): 40. The cassava plant was native to Central America and brought to Africa by the Spanish in the 1500s.

25. Tony Miller interview.

26. J. C. Stevens to J. Ormond Wilson, 11 August 1893, ACS reel 170.

27. W. M. Rogers to Susan McCarroll, 28 July 1896, a letter from Johnsonville printed in *Voice of Missions*, October 1896; N.[*sic*] M. Rogers to Green Rogers, 26 September 1895, printed in *Voice of Missions*, February 1896; Anderson to C. T. O. King, 17 February 1888, ACS reel 169; Tony Miller interview; Henry Moore interview, 31 July 1998. For more about the transfer of American agricultural practices into Liberia and American settlers' adoption of African agriculture, see Santosh C. Saha, *A History of Agriculture in Liberia, 1822–1970* (Lewiston, N.Y.: Edwin Mellen Press, 1990).

28. Margo Cooper interview with author, Monrovia, Liberia, 15 July 1998; Tony Miller interview; Henry Moore interview, 31 July 1998.

29. Henry Jefferson Cooper described the settler homes in Brewerville (interview with author, Brewerville, Liberia, 16 July 1998). Cooper was born in 1916, twenty years after his father, Robert Lee Cooper, emigrated to Liberia aboard the *Laurada*. See also A. B. Smart Jr. interview with author, Monrovia, Liberia, 18 July 1998; Louise Blassingam Frank interview with author, Paynesville, Liberia, 16 July 1998; Tony Miller interview; and Henry Moore interview, 31 July 1998. My interviews are supported by descriptions of farmsteads in a few of the letters sent back to the ACS; see, for example, Charles Hays to Green Battle, c/o ACS, 4 October 1897, ACS reel 170.

30. For more about malaria, see John Duffy, "The Impact of Malaria on the South," in *Disease and Distinctiveness in the American South*, ed. Todd L. Savitt and James Harvey Young (Knoxville: University of Tennessee Press, 1988), 29–54; and Gordon Harrison, *Mosquitos, Malaria, and Man: A History of the Hostilities since 1880* (New York: E. P. Dutton, 1978).

31. Tom W. Shick, *Behold the Promised Land: A History of Afro-American Settler Society in Nineteenth-Century Liberia* (Baltimore: Johns Hopkins University Press, 1977), 27–28; Antonio McDaniel, *Swing Low, Sweet Chariot: The Mortality Cost of Colonizing Liberia in the Nineteenth Century* (Chicago: University of Chicago Press, 1995), 76–83. Both Shick and McDaniel make estimates for the early nineteenth century through analyses of passenger lists of the ACS voyages and returns of a census of Liberia in 1843. No similar census exists for the late nineteenth century.

32. "Sixty-Fifth Annual Report of the American Colonization Society, presented January 17, 1882," ACS reel 287; W. H. Heard to J. Ormond Wilson, 18 September 1895, ACS reel 170.

33. Medical report of F. J. Grant, 30 April 1888, ACS reel 169; "Sixty-Fifth Annual Report of the American Colonization Society." Reports of the eating ulcers appear in D. B. Warner to Coppinger, 11 June 1880, ACS reel 164; E. Skinner to Coppinger, 27 March 1888, ACS reel 169; and J. C. Stevens to J. Ormond Wilson, 11 August 1893, ACS reel 170.

34. See the article by coffee grower Alfred B. King, "Liberian Coffee," in *Liberia Bulletin* 6 (February 1895): 40–43; T. McCants Stewart, *Liberia: The Americo-African Republic* (New York: Edward O. Jenkins' Sons, 1886), 49; and Shick, *Behold the Promised Land*, 114–15.

35. *Liberia Bulletin* 1 (November 1892): 11; 6 (February 1895): 42; 7 (November 1895): 52–53; letter from W. K. Roberts, in *Voice of Missions*, October 1896.

36. Jack Allen and Elijah Parker to Coppinger, April 1890, ACS reel 178; Hayes, "Brief History of the Founding of the Township of Brewerville."

37. Alfred B. King, "Liberian Coffee," 43. See the descriptions of the plight of coffee farmers in J. C. Stevens to J. Ormond Wilson, 1 May, 25 June 1898, ACS reel 170; C. C. Brown to Wilson, May 1898, ACS reel 170; and W. M. Williams to Wilson, 8 March 1898, ACS reel 170. For a discussion of world market conditions for coffee in the 1880s and 1890s, see Steven C. Topik, "Coffee," in *The Second Conquest of Latin America; Coffee, Henequen, and Oil during the Export Boom, 1850–1930*, ed. Steven C. Topik and Allen Wells (Austin: University of Texas Press, 1998), 37–84; and Charles W. Berquist, *Coffee and Conflict in Columbia, 1886–1910* (Durham: Duke University Press, 1986), 21–23.

38. John Dixon to ACS, January 1895, ACS reel 144; Tony Miller interview; Henry Moore interview, 31 July 1998.

39. For a discussion of the evolution of privilege in the American Liberian community in the nineteenth century, see William Ndama, "Neither African nor American: An Analysis of Americo-Liberian Attitudes towards the Indigenous Africans in Liberia" (M.A. thesis, Indiana University, 1987).

40. There is some uncertainty as to the ethnicity of these Africans. While some descendants of settlers say the natives were Bassa, others and the ACS documents suggest that Kru (Kroo) people lived in the Johnsonville area when American settlers arrived. See Alexander Smart interview, 18 February 1997; Henry Moore interview, 31 July 1998; E. E. Smith's report in *Liberia Bulletin* 1 (November 1892): 9–10; and Benjamin Anderson (surveyor) to E. E. Smith, 17 June 1892, printed in the same issue, pp. 25–28.

41. J. C. Stevens to J. Ormond Wilson, 11 August 1893, ACS reel 170. Arthur Ficklin,

grandson of one of the Arkansas immigrants, said local Africans felt settlers were trying to take away their land (Arthur Ficklin interview with author, Paynesville, Liberia, 20 July 1998).

42. Tony Miller interview; Margo Cooper interview; Henry Jefferson Cooper interview; Henry Moore interview, 31 July 1998. The thousands of deaths in Liberia's 1980 coup and civil war of the 1990s can be attributed to African retribution for decades of oppression by American Liberians. When during interviews in 1998, a year after the end of civil war, I asked descendants about relations between settlers and Africans, I found it difficult to evaluate the answers I received because of the inherently political nature of the question.

43. Margo Cooper interview; John Baker Hart interview with author, Monrovia, Liberia, 18 July 1998.

44. See discussion of the legal framework for the apprentice system in Shick, *Behold the Promised Land*, 65–66; see also the description of the system by contemporaries: William K. Roberts, *An African Canaan for the American Negro* (Birmingham: International Migration Society, 1896),14; E. E. Smith's report in *Liberia Bulletin* 1 (November 1892): 21–23; and Stewart, *Liberia*, 71.

45. In 1892, the new ACS agent sent to Liberia, Ezekial E. Smith, defended the practice of apprenticeship (*Liberia Bulletin* 1 [November 1892]: 20–23). For more information about the League of Nations inquiry into the apprentice system, see Liebenow, *Liberia: Evolution of Privilege*, 65–69. The league commission that investigated the practice concluded that abuses with compulsory labor took place in Liberia, but it did not find outright slavery. The commission's report also acknowledged that similar practices were common in several European colonies in Africa.

46. Alexander Smart interview, 2 June 2000; Victoria Anna David Tolbert, *Lifted Up: The Victoria Tolbert Story* (Minneapolis: Macalester Park Publishing Company, 1996), 20–24; other descendants spoke of apprentices living with their families (Henry Jefferson Cooper interview; J. Nicholas Parker and Faraby M. Parker Gayedyu interview with author, Monrovia, Liberia, 17 July 1998; Johnny Johnson interview with author, Brewerville, Liberia, 14 July 1998; Helena McJunkins Saykiamien interview with author, Barnersville, Liberia, 26 July 1998; Tony Miller interview).

47. *Voice of Missions*, 1 January 1899.

48. Alexander Smart interview, 1 June 2000. Smart indicated that the Liberian system of "outside families," wherein settler men had African mistresses and children, was more common in some settler communities than others. He said it was less common, for example, in Johnsonville than in other settler towns, such as Careysburg and Arthington.

49. Although information is lacking on social intercourse between natives and Arkansas settlers specifically, these patterns generally prevailed among American Liberians in the period. See Roberts, *African Canaan*, 14; Charles H. J. Taylor's description of Liberian society in *American Citizen*, 29 April 1892, reprinted from 22 April 1888; Stewart, *Liberia*, 78; and Ndama, "Neither African nor American," 58–60.

50. J. Nicholas Parker III and Faraby M. Parker Gayedyu interviews; *Voice of Missions*, October 1898.

51. Edward Blyden to Coppinger, 18 January 1881, ACS reel 164; Coppinger to Blyden, 29 June 1881, ACS reel 220.

52. Ndama, "Neither African nor American," 54; "Sixty-Seventh Annual Report of the American Colonization Society presented January 15–16, 1884," ACS reel 287.

53. C. T. O. King to Coppinger, 5 June 1884, ACS reel 166; Mrs. S. A. Stanford to Coppinger, 31 October 1884, ACS reel 166; Coppinger to King, 2 September 1884, ACS reel 221.

54. Various immigrants at Cape Mount to Coppinger, 29 April 1889, ACS reel 170.

55. Julius Stevens to J. Ormond Wilson, 4 February 1894, ACS reel 170. Descendants disagreed on the question of immigrant satisfaction with Liberia. Tony Miller, son of child immigrant Roscoe Miller, believes that most emigrants would have returned to the United States if they had money to do so. Henry Moore, grandson of immigrant Narcissie Moore, argues that most immigrants were satisfied with Liberia. Miller and Moore engaged in a lively discussion on the issue when I interviewed them together on 31 July 1998. Charles H. J. Taylor noted the perversion of the Liberian motto as early as 1888 in his article about Liberia, reprinted in *American Citizen,* 29 April 1892. The slogan was still circulating when Walter Walker visited Liberia in 1908; see his article "Liberia and Emigration" in *Alexander's Magazine* 6 (15 August 1908): 162.

56. "Emigrants of Johnsonville Settlement," an undated list compiled by agent J. C. Stevens, filed in late August 1893, ACS reel 170; Stevens to J. Ormond Wilson, 4 February 1894, ACS reel 170.

57. D. B. Warner to Coppinger, 5 July 1880, ACS reel 164; J. E. Smith to ACS, 18 September 1889, ACS reel 170; Susan King to Coppinger, 16 July 1891, ACS reel 179; Ezekial Smith to J. Ormond Wilson, 17 May 1892.

58. Clippings file, July 1895, ACS reel 322.

59. *Voice of Missions,* September 1895; *Indianapolis Freeman,* 24 August 1895.

60. Unidentified clipping, located in late October 1896 clippings file, ACS reel 322.

61. *New York World* and *Boston Daily Globe,* in late December 1896 clippings file, ACS reel 322; *New York Times,* 28 September 1896. These newspapers mistakenly called him Taylor Smith. See also *Southwestern Christian Advocate,* 15 October 1896.

62. Daniel A. Rudd and Theo. Bond, *From Slavery to Wealth: The Life of Scott Bond* (Madison, Ark.: Journal Printing, 1917), 210–11.

63. See "Missionary Brisbane Takes the Skin off Taylor Swift," *Voice of Missions,* 1 April 1897.

64. *Boston Daily Globe,* 22 June 1897, in clippings file, ACS reel 322; *New York Times,* 22 June 1897; James Boyle, U.S. consul in Liverpool, to David J. Hill, assistant secretary of state, 26 June 1899, with attached clipping of *Liverpool Daily Post,* 26 June 1899, in ACS reel 149.

65. Some of the *Horsa* and *Laurada* passengers had made a secondary migration to Sierra Leone by the later 1890s (J. M. Woodson to the President of the United States, copy enclosed with memo from the Department of State to the ACS, 26 October 1897, ACS reel 144). One of the *Horsa* emigrants from Pine Bluff wrote a letter from Freetown, Sierra Leone, to the *Voice of Missions,* December 1897. Descendants of Arkansas settlers to Brewerville and Johnsonville recall that some families moved to Sierra Leone and Ghana (Margo Cooper interview; Henry Moore interview, 31 July 1998).

66. Stevens to J. Ormond Wilson, 25 June 1898, ACS reel 170; Rudd and Bond, *From Slavery to Wealth,* 206.

67. William Pickens, *Bursting the Bonds* (Boston: Jordan & More, 1923), 24. The "Bread and butter grow on trees" story obviously has become part of the national folklore of Liberia. Almost all the descendants in Brewerville and Johnsonville tell the same story. Henry Moore (interview of 31 July 1998) attributes the promise of bread and butter to Bishop Turner. Similarly, Helena McJunkins Saykiamien (interview of 26 July 1998) says a Methodist missionary came to her family's town in Arkansas and made this boast about bread and butter. Her grandfather, Charles McJunkins, lived in Morrilton, which hosted Bishop Turner and the Arkansas annual AME conference in 1882.

68. J. C. Stevens to J. Ormond Wilson, 11 August 1893, ACS reel 170; Swift's comments appeared in *Southwestern Christian Advocate*, 15 October 1896.

69. Jack Allen and Elijah Parker to Coppinger, April 1890, ACS reel 178.

70. Rogers discussed his contemplation of returning to America in a letter to Susan McCarroll, printed in *Voice of Missions*, October 1896. His letter to his family in Morrilton appeared in *Voice of Missions*, February 1896.

71. Fannie Kettler's letter of 2 October 1896 appeared in the *Voice of Missions*, December 1896.

Conclusion

1. Sociologists E. M. Beck and Stewart Tolnay have shown that black migration served as a form of resistance following outbreaks of mob violence. See Stewart E. Tolnay and E. M. Beck, "Rethinking the Role of Racial Violence in the Great Migration," in *Black Exodus: The Great Migration from the American South*, ed. Alferdteen Harrison (Jackson: University Press of Mississippi, 1991), 20–35.

2. For a comparative look at race relations in other southern states, see Neil R. McMillen, *Dark Journey: Black Mississippians in the Age of Jim Crow* (Urbana: University of Illinois Press, 1989); and Eric Anderson, *Race and Politics in North Carolina, 1872–1901: The Black Second* (Baton Rouge: Louisiana State University Press, 1981).

3. James C. Davies, "Toward a Theory of Revolution," *American Sociological Review* 27 (February 1962): 5–19; Ted Robert Gurr, *Why Men Rebel* (Princeton, N.J.: Princeton University Press, 1970).

4. Arthur L. Tolson, *The Black Oklahomans: A History, 1541–1972* (New Orleans: Edwards Printing, 1974), 88; for the story of the Oklahoma expedition to Africa, see William Bittle and Gilbert Geis, *The Longest Way Home: Chief Alfred C. Sam's Back-to-Africa Movement* (Detroit: Wayne State University Press, 1964); Fred Taylor telephone interview with author, Arlington, Tex., 13 April 1997.

5. These figures were computed from the U.S. Department of the Interior, Census Office, *Report on Population of the United States at the Eleventh Census: 1890* (Washington, D.C.: Government Printing Office, 1895), 490.

6. Joel Williamson, in his study of white racism around the turn of the century, suggests that racism was most extreme in areas of the South that were from one-third to two-thirds black. When the black percentage rose above two-thirds, he suggests, radical racism "seemed to be slightly less vociferous, less physical, and less overtly violent in its manifestations." See his *Crucible of Race: Black/White Relations in the American South since Emancipation* (New York: Oxford University Press, 1984), 181. The pattern of black

interest in Liberia migration corresponds to Williamson's generalization about radical white racism.

7. Information about emigrants was compiled from *African Repository, Liberia Bulletin,* and manuscript material. Of those Arkansas emigrants who identified a religious affiliation, eighty-five were Baptist and forty-one were Methodist, which presumably included several denominations besides the AME Church. Thus only 32 percent of these emigrants were Methodists, a slightly lower proportion than that relative to Baptists in the general black population of Arkansas, as reported in the 1890 census, which counted 37,445 Methodists and 63,786 Baptists. See U.S. Department of the Interior, Census Office, *Report on Statistics of Churches in the United States at the Eleventh Census: 1890* (Washington, D.C.: Government Printing Office, 1894), 38.

8. I make this determination by considering the number of applications, the letters written to the ACS, and the actual emigrants to Liberia.

9. The stories about Liberia were recounted by black Arkansans William Pickens in *Bursting Bonds* (Boston: Jordan & More, 1923), 24, and Scott Bond in Daniel A. Rudd and Theo. Bond, *From Slavery to Wealth: The Life of Scott Bond* (Madison, Ark.: Journal Printing, 1917), 206. For a discussion of these same food fantasies in European folktales, see Robert Darnton, "Peasants Tell Tales: The Meaning of Mother Goose," in *The Great Cat Massacre and Other Episodes in French Cultural History* (New York: Vintage, 1985), 43.

10. See, for example, Mary Frances Berry and John W. Blassingame, *Long Memory: The Black Experience in America* (New York: Oxford University Press, 1982), 39. Leon F. Litwack, in *Trouble in Mind: Black Southerners in the Age of Jim Crow* (New York: Knopf, 1998), 486, says that despite periodic revivals of interest in back-to-Africa solutions, "the vast majority of southern blacks expressed little interest or enthusiasm." Yet with Litwack's vast archival research for this magisterial work, he did not include in his bibliography the ACS records, with their numbing quantity of letters begging for emigration. Robert G. Weisbord views as extravagant Turner's boast that two million blacks would return to Africa if they had resources. See his *Ebony Kinship: Africa, Africans, and the Afro-American* (Westport, Conn.: Greenwood Press, 1973), 30. Turner made his claims in a letter to the *Washington Post* of 17 March 1890; see Edwin S. Redkey, ed., *Respect Black: The Writings and Speeches of Henry McNeal Turner* (New York: Arno Press and New York Times, 1971), 78.

11. V. P. Franklin discusses black migration movements of the late 1800s as an expression of the desire of African Americans to separate from whites and to free themselves from white domination; see *Black Self-Determination: A Cultural History of the Faith of the Fathers* (Westport, Conn.: Lawrence Hill, 1984), 194–95.

12. W. H. Holloway to Coppinger, 11 November 1891, ACS reel 139.

13. See, for example, Edwin S. Redkey, *Black Exodus: Black Nationalist and Back-to-Africa Movements, 1890–1910* (New Haven: Yale University Press, 1969), 1; Wilson Jeremiah Moses, *The Golden Age of Black Nationalism, 1850–1925* (Hamden, Conn.: Archon Books, 1978), 262–68; and E. David Cronon, *The Story of Marcus Garvey and the United Negro Improvement Association* (Madison: University of Wisconsin Press, 1972), 44. John H. Bracey Jr., August Meier, and Elliott Rudwick, eds., in *Black Nationalism in America* (Indianapolis: Bobbs-Merrill, 1970), 159, remind readers that Garvey's nationalist and separatist message was most attractive to "slum-shocked migrants who had been moving to the cities—especially to the cities of the North during and after the war." Mary

Rolinson, in her study, "The Garvey Movement in the Rural South" (Ph.D. diss., Georgia State University, 2002), 1–12, 113–14, points out that both rural southern membership and the culture of the rural South have been largely ignored in historical literature about Garvey and the UNIA.

14. Rolinson discusses the Arkansas divisions in "Garvey Movement in the Rural South," 104–11, 121. A UNIA division required at least seven dues-paying members. Rolinson compiled her list of UNIA divisions by culling references from the *Negro World*, the published Garvey papers, and a partial card file with UNIA materials housed at the Schomburg Center in New York.

15. Lists of donors to the Garvey legal defense fund appeared in various issues of *Negro World*, April through October 1923. In Rolinson's count of petitions for Garvey, Arkansas was surpassed in number only by Louisiana among southern states; see "Garvey Movement in the Rural South," 293.

16. Rolinson, "Garvey Movement in the Rural South," 176, 179.

17. Ibid., 246.

18. For biographical information on Sherrill, see *Negro World*, 15 September 1923, and Robert A. Hill, ed., *The Marcus Garvey and Universal Negro Improvement Association Papers* 4 (Berkeley and Los Angeles: University of California Press, 1985), 793–94 nn.

19. See Michael W. Fitzgerald, "'We Have Found a Moses': Theodore Bilbo, Black Nationalism, and the Greater Liberia Bill of 1939," *Journal of Southern History* 63 (May 1997): 293–320; and *Jet* 35 (3 April 1969): 8–9.

20. See Milton C. Sernett, *Bound for the Promised Land: African American Religion and the Great Migration* (Durham: Duke University Press, 1997), 59.

21. The facts about the Elaine riot still remain murky. For summaries, see Nan Elizabeth Woodruff, "African-American Struggles for Citizenship in the Arkansas and Mississippi Deltas in the Age of Jim Crow," *Radical History Review* 5 (Winter 1993): 41–43; Richard Cortner, *A Mob Intent on Death: The NAACP and the Arkansas Riot Cases* (Middleton, Conn.: Western University Press, 1988); and Grif Stockley, *Blood in Their Eyes: The Elaine Race Massacres of 1919* (Fayetteville: University of Arkansas Press, 2001). For a discussion of other race riots after World War I, see John Hope Franklin and Alfred A. Moss Jr., *From Slavery to Freedom: A History of Negro Americans*, 6th ed. (New York: McGraw-Hill, 1988), 313–16.

22. Donald H. Grubbs, *Cry from the Cotton: The Southern Tenant Farmers' Union and the New Deal* (Chapel Hill: University of North Carolina Press, 1971); for McKinney's role, see Rolinson, "Garvey Movement in the Rural South," 108–9.

23. M. Langley Biegert makes this argument in "Legacy of Resistance: Uncovering the History of Collective Action by Black Agricultural Workers in Central East Arkansas," *Journal of Social History* 32 (Fall 1998): 73–99.

24. For the best overview of the Central High Crisis and the civil rights movement in Arkansas, see John A. Kirk, *Redefining the Color Line: Black Activism in Little Rock, Arkansas, 1940–1970* (Gainesville: University of Florida Press, 2002); the information concerning percentage of black to white income in the 1990s appears on page xiii. For a discussion of the "lost year" of the Little Rock schools, see Sondra Gordy, "Empty Classrooms, Empty Hearts: Little Rock Secondary Teachers, 1958–1959," *Arkansas Historical Quarterly* 56 (Winter 1997): 427–42.

25. J. Gus Liebenow, *Liberia: The Evolution of Privilege* (Ithaca, N.Y.: Cornell University Press, 1969), 65–73; Stephen Ellis, *The Mask of Anarchy: The Destruction of Liberia and the Religious Dimension of an African Civil War* (New York: New York University Press, 1999), 44–45. For discussions of rubber in Liberia, see Charles Morrow Wilson, *Liberia* (New York: William Sloane, 1947), 80–158; and R. Earle Anderson, *Liberia: America's African Friend* (Chapel Hill: University of North Carolina Press, 1952), 129–37.

26. Liebenow, *Liberia: Evolution of Privilege*, 64–73, 77–80.

27. See Victoria Anna David Tolbert's account of the assassination in her memoirs, *Lifted Up: The Victoria Tolbert Story* (Minneapolis: Macalester Park Publishing, 1996), 128–41; for the background leading up to the 1980 coup, see J. Gus Liebenow, *Liberia: The Quest for Democracy* (Bloomington: Indiana University Press, 1987), 153–93.

28. For more on the Doe years, see Ellis, *Mask of Anarchy*, 54–72; and Liebenow, *Liberia: Quest for Democracy*, 197–296.

29. Ellis, *Mask of Anarchy*, 5–11, 65–74.

30. For the best detailed narrative of the war, see Ellis, *Mask of Anarchy*, 75–109, 267. Ellis discusses casualty figures in the appendix of his book, pp. 312–16. Also see *Washington Post* reporter Keith B. Richburg's evocative account of his trip to Liberia in war time, *Out of America: A Black Man Confronts Africa* (New York: Harcourt Brace, 1997), 133–36, and another American journalist's account of the war and the Doe years, Bill Berkeley, *The Graves Are Not Yet Full: Race, Tribe and Power in the Heart of Africa* (New York: Basic Books, 2001), 21–61.

31. Ellis, *Mask of Anarchy*, 109; Jon Lee Anderson, "The Devil They Know," *The New Yorker*, 27 July 1998, 34–43.

32. Arthur Ficklin interview with author, Paynesville, Liberia, 18 July 1998; Tony Miller interview with author, Johnsonville, Liberia, 31 July 1998; J. Benedict Shaw interview with author, Johnsonville, Liberia, 18 July 1998; Fred Taylor interview.

33. Helena McJunkins Saykiamien interview with author, Barnersville, Liberia, 26 July 1998; George Wesley Miller interview with author, Monrovia, Liberia, 16 July 1998; Henry Moore interview with author, Monrovia, Liberia, 18 July 1998.

Bibliography

Primary Sources

Manuscript Collections

College Park, Md.
    National Archives
        Letters Received from Arkansas, 1875–83, Eastern District, U.S. Department of
            Justice, Record Group 60 (microfilm)
Fayetteville, Ark.
    University of Arkansas Library, Special Collections
        James Millinder Hanks Diaries
        Daniel W. Lewis Sr. Papers
Little Rock, Ark.
    Arkansas History Commission
        African Methodist Episcopal Church, Arkansas Annual Conference Minutes,
            1868–95 (microfilm)
Madison, N.J.
    United Methodist Church, General Commission on Archives and History
        Mission Biographical Reference Files, 1880–1960
            F. M. Allen
            Joe Davis
            John H. Reed
            J. C. Sherrill
        Missionary Files, Missionary Correspondence, 1846–1912 (microfilm)
            Ferdinand Marcellus Allen
            Joe A. and Cordelia Iris Davis
            John Hamilton Reed
            Joseph Cephas Sherrill

New York, N.Y.
   Schomburg Center for Research in Black Culture, New York Public Library
      New York State Colonization Society Records
      St. Philip's Church Collection, Minute Book
Rochester, N.Y.
   American Baptist–Samuel Colgate Historical Library, Colgate Rochester Divinity
         School
      African American Baptist Associations: Arkansas, 1867–1951 (microfilm)
Washington, D.C.
   Library of Congress, Manuscripts Division
      American Colonization Society Records (microfilm)
      Records of the States of the United States of America, A.1a, Arkansas
         (microfilm)
   Library of Congress, Rare Book/Special Collections Division
      Colonization Pamphlets, 6 vols.
   National Archives
      Thomas Jefferson Cooper, Military Pension File, Records of Veterans Affairs,
         Record Group 15
Westfield, N.Y.
   Chautauqua County Historical Society
      Albion W. Tourgée Papers, 1890–92 (microfilm)

Government Documents

Biennial Reports of the Secretary of State of the State of Arkansas, 1882–1895. Little Rock,
   1882–95.
U.S. Bureau of the Census. *Negro Population, 1790–1915.* Washington, D.C.: Government Printing Office, 1918.
U.S. Congress. House of Representatives. *Featherston vs. Cate.* 51st Cong., 1st sess,
   1890, House Report 306. Washington, D.C.: Government Printing Office, 1890.
U.S. Congress. Senate. *Report and Testimony of the Select Committee of the United States Sen-
   ate to Investigate the Causes of the Removal of the Negroes from the Southern States to the
   Northern States,* 3 parts. 46th Cong., 2nd sess., 1880, Senate Report 693. Washing-
   ton, D.C: Government Printing Office, 1880.
U.S. Department of the Interior. Census Office. *Report on Cotton Production in the
   United States,* 2 parts. Washington, D.C.: Government Printing Office, 1884.
————. *Report on Farms and Homes: Proprietorship and Indebtedness in the United States at
   the Eleventh Census, 1890.* Washington, D.C.: Government Printing Office, 1896.
————. *Report on Population of the United States at the Eleventh Census, 1890.* Washington,
   D.C.: Government Printing Office, 1895.
————. *Report on Statistics of Churches in the United States at the Eleventh Census: 1890.*
   Washington, D.C.: Government Printing Office, 1894.
————. *Report on the Productions of Agriculture as Returned at the Tenth Census, 1880.* Wash-
   ington, D.C.: Government Printing Office, 1883.
————. *Report on the Statistics of Agriculture in the United States of America at the Eleventh
   Census, 1890.* Washington, D.C.: Government Printing Office, 1895.

———. *Statistics of the Population of the United States at the Tenth Census, 1880.* Washington, D.C.: Government Printing Office, 1883.

Newspapers

The American Citizen (Topeka and Kansas City, Kan.)
Arkansas City Journal
Arkansas Democrat (Little Rock)
Arkansas Gazette (Little Rock)
Arkansas Mansion (Little Rock)
Baptist Vanguard (Little Rock)
Charleston News and Courier
The Christian Index (Jackson, Tenn.)
Commercial Appeal (Memphis)
Edgefield Chronicle
Forrest City Herald
Forrest City Times
Fort Smith Times Record
Frank Leslie's Illustrated Newspaper (New York)
Helena Reporter
Indianapolis Freeman
Log Cabin Democrat (Conway, Ark.)
Lonoke Weekly Democrat
The Observer (Monrovia, Liberia)
Negro World (New York)
New York Age
New York Sun
New York Times
New York Tribune
Osceola Times
Richmond Planet
St. Louis Globe Democrat
Savannah Tribune
Sharp County Record (Evening Shade, Ark.)
Southern Standard (Arkadelphia, Ark.)
Southwestern Christian Advocate (New Orleans)
Washington Post

Magazines and Periodicals

The African Repository
Christian Recorder
Harper's Weekly
Liberia Bulletin
Southern Recorder
Voice of Missions

Interviews by Author

Louise Avery. Monrovia, Liberia. 21 July 1998.

Zebulon Avery. Monrovia, Liberia. 21 July 1998.

Altrine Brisbane. Brewerville, Liberia. 24 July 1998.

Rachel Chesson Brown. Telephone. Hackettstown, N.J. 22 June 1999.

Henry Jefferson Cooper. Brewerville, Liberia. 16 July 1998.

Margo Cooper. Monrovia, Liberia. 15 July 1998.

Titus Lee Cooper. Gbarnga, Liberia. 1 August 1998.

Jerome Curry. Johnsonville, Liberia. 15 July 1998.

Arthur Ficklin. Paynesville, Liberia. 18 July 1998.

James Stephen Ficklin. Monrovia, Liberia. 18, 20 July 1998.

Louise Blassingam Frank. Paynesville, Liberia. 16 July 1998.

Eddie Garnett. Monrovia, Liberia. 17, 28 July 1998.

Faraby M. Parker Gayedyu. Monrovia, Liberia. 17 July 1998.

Arthur Hart. Johnsonville, Liberia. 18 July 1998.

John Baker Hart. Monrovia, Liberia. 18 July 1998.

Doris Cooper Hays. Monrovia, Liberia. 29 July 1998.

Patricia Hill. Telephone. Arlington, Tex. 13 April 1997.

Eugene Holman. Johnsonville, Liberia. 18 July 1998.

Sophie Chesson Itoka. Telephone. Baltimore, Md., 18 June 1999.

Johnny Johnson. Brewerville, Liberia. 14 July 1998.

James Maximo. Monrovia, Liberia. 20 July 1998.

Edwin Nathaniel Miller. Monrovia, Liberia. 16 July 1998.

George Wesley Miller. Monrovia, Liberia. 16 July 1998.

Tony Miller. Johnsonville, Liberia. 31 July 1998.

Henry Moore. Monrovia, Liberia. 16, 31 July, 1 August 1998.

Verlene Brisbane Olson. Monrovia, Liberia. 24 July 1998.

Gabriel Parker. Brewerville, Liberia. 16 July 1998.

J. Nicholas Parker III. Monrovia, Liberia. 17 July 1998.

Isaac Roland. Monrovia, Liberia. 15 July 1998.

Mary Shaw Roberts. Brewerville, Liberia. 16 July 1998.

Helena McJunkins Saykiamien. Barnersville, Liberia. 26 July 1998.

J. Benedict Shaw. Johnsonville, Liberia. 16 July 1998.

McKinley Slocum. Monrovia, Liberia. 17 July 1998.

Alexander Smart. Telephone. Cambria Heights, N.Y. 18 February 1997; 1, 2 June 2000.

A. B. (Oscar) Smart Jr. Monrovia, Liberia. 18 July 1998.

Eddie Taylor. Telephone. Arlington, Tex. 13 June 1997.

Fred Taylor. Telephone. Irving, Tex. 13 April 1997.

Alexander Tubman. Johnsonville, Liberia. 17 July 1998.

Published Primary Sources

The Annual Reports of the American Colonization Society. Vol. 6: 1871–1910. New York: Negro Universities Press, 1969.

Arkansas State Gazetteer and Business Directory, 1888–1889. Atlanta: R. L. Polk, 1888.

Arkansas State Gazetteer and Business Directory, 1892–1893. Detroit: R. L. Polk, 1892.

Bolsterli, Margaret Jones, ed. *Vinegar Pie and Chicken Bread: A Woman's Diary of Life in the Rural South, 1890–1891.* Fayetteville: University of Arkansas Press, 1982.

Bowen, J. W. E., ed. *Africa and the American Negro: Addresses and Proceedings of the Congress on Africa, December 13–15, 1895.* 1896. Reprint, Miami, Fla.: Mnemosyne Publishing, 1969.

Camphor, Alexander Priestley. *Missionary Story Sketches: Folklore from Africa.* 1909. Reprint, Freeport, N.Y.: Books for Libraries Press, 1971.

The City of Little Rock: Guide to the "City of Roses". Little Rock: Guide Publishing, 1890.

Flummer, D. J. *The Negro and Liberia.* Birmingham: International Migration Society, 1897.

Gaines, D. B. *Racial Possibilities as Indicated by the Negroes of Arkansas.* Little Rock: Philander Smith College, 1898.

Garrison, William Lloyd. *Thoughts on African Colonization, or an Impartial Exhibition of the Doctrines, Principles and Purposes of the American Colonization Society.* 1832. Reprint, New York: Arno Press and the *New York Times,* 1968.

Gibbs, Mifflin Wistar. *Shadow and Light: An Autobiography with Reminiscences of the Last and Present Century.* Washington, D.C.: n.p., 1902.

Heard, William H. *From Slavery to the Bishopric in the A.M.E. Church.* 1924. Reprint, New York: Arno Press and the *New York Times,* 1969.

Hewett, Janet B., ed. *Roster of Union Soldiers, 1861–1865: United States Colored Troops.* Wilmington, N.C.: Broadfoot Publishing, 1997.

Hill, Robert A., ed. *The Marcus Garvey and United Negro Improvement Association Papers.* Vols. 4–7. Berkeley and Los Angeles: University of California Press, 1985–90.

Jordan, L. G. *Up the Ladder in Foreign Mission.* 1901. Reprint, New York: Arno Press, 1980.

Lindsey, D. McD. *The Wrongs of the Negro: A Remedy.* 1888. Reprinted in John David Smith, ed. *The American Colonization Society and Emigration: Solutions to the "Negro Problem."* New York: Garland, 1993.

Lynch, Hollis R., ed. *Selected Letters of Edward Wilmot Blyden.* Millwood, N.Y.: KTO Press, 1978.

Morgan, W. Scott. *History of the Wheel and Alliance and the Impending Revolution.* Fort Scott, Kan.: J. H. Rice, 1889.

Morris, E. C. *Sermons, Addresses and Reminiscences and Important Correspondence.* 1901. Reprint, New York: Arno Press, 1980.

Moses, Wilson Jeremiah, ed. *Liberian Dreams: Back-to-Africa Narratives from the 1850s.* University Park: Pennsylvania State University Press, 1998.

Murzda, Peter J., Jr. *Immigrants to Liberia, 1865–1904: An Alphabetical Listing.* Newark, Del.: Liberian Studies Association, 1975.

Parks, H. B. *Africa, the Problem of the New Century.* New York: A.M.E. Missions Board, 1899.

Pickens, William. *Bursting Bonds.* Boston: Jordan & More, 1923.

Rawick, George P., ed. *The American Slave: A Composite Autobiography.* Vol. 11: Arkansas Narratives. 1941. Reprint, Westport, Conn.: Greenwood Press, 1977.

Redkey, Edwin S., ed. *Respect Black: The Writings and Speeches of Henry McNeal Turner.* New York: Arno Press and *New York Times,* 1971.

Ridgel, Alfred Lee. *Africa and African Methodism*. Atlanta: Franklin Printing and Publishing Company, 1896.

Riley, Jerome R. *The Philosophy of Negro Suffrage*. Hartford, Conn.: American Publishing Company, 1895.

Roberts, William K. *An African Canaan for the American Negro*. Birmingham: International Migration Society, 1896.

Robinson, David. "To the Land of Their Fathers." *Illustrated American*, 21 March 1896, 371.

Smith, Amanda. *An Autobiography: The Story of the Lord's Dealings with Mrs. Amanda Smith, the Colored Evangelist*. 1893. Reprint, New York: Oxford University Press, 1988.

Smith, Charles Spencer. *Glimpses of Africa*. Nashville: A.M.E. Church Sunday School Union, 1895.

————. *Liberia in the Light of Living Testimony*. Nashville: A.M.E. Church Sunday School Union, 1895.

Smith, John David, ed. *The American Colonization Society and Emigration: Solutions to "The Negro Problem."* New York: Garland, 1993.

Stewart, T. McCants. *Liberia: The Americo-African Republic*. New York: Edward O. Jenkins' Sons, 1886.

Thanet, Octave. "Town Life in Arkansas." *Atlantic Monthly*, September 1891, 332–40.

Tolbert, Victoria Anna David. *Lifted Up: The Victoria Tolbert Story*. Minneapolis: Macalester Park Publishing, 1996.

Walker, Walter F. "Liberia and Emigration," *Alexander's Magazine* 6 (15 August 1908): 162–65.

Wells-Barnett, Ida B. *On Lynchings: Southern Horrors, A Red Record, Mob Rule in New Orleans*. 1892, 1895, 1900. Reprint, New York: Arno Press, 1969.

Wiley, Bell I., ed. *Slaves No More: Letters from Liberia, 1833–1869*. Lexington: University Press of Kentucky, 1980.

Secondary Sources

Adeleke, Tunde. *UnAfrican Americans: Nineteenth-Century Black Nationalists and the Civilizing Mission*. Lexington: University Press of Kentucky, 1998.

Alexander, Archibald. *A History of Colonization on the Western Coast of Africa*. 1849. Reprint, Freeport, N.Y.: Books for Libraries Press, 1971.

Anderson, Eric. *Race and Politics in North Carolina, 1872–1901: The Black Second*. Baton Rouge: Louisiana State University Press, 1981.

Anderson, James D. *The Education of Blacks in the South, 1860–1935*. Chapel Hill: University of North Carolina Press, 1988.

Anderson, Jon Lee. "The Devil They Know." *The New Yorker*, 27 July 1998, 34–43.

Angell, Stephen Ward. *Bishop Henry McNeal Turner and African-American Religion in the South*. Knoxville: University of Tennessee Press, 1992.

Athearn, Robert G. *In Search of Canaan: Black Migration to Kansas 1879–1880*. Lawrence: Regents Press of Kansas, 1978.

Ayers, Edward L. *The Promise of the New South: Life after Reconstruction*. New York: Oxford University Press, 1992.

Barnes, Kenneth C. *Who Killed John Clayton? Political Violence and the Emergence of the New South, 1861–1893.* Durham: Duke University Press, 1998.

Bay, Mia. *The White Image in the Black Mind: African-American Ideas about White People, 1830–1925.* New York: Oxford University Press, 2000.

Bederman, Gail. *Manliness and Civilization: A Cultural History of Gender and Race in the United States, 1880–1917.* Chicago: University of Chicago Press, 1995.

Berkeley, Bill. *The Graves Are Not Yet Full: Race, Tribe, and Power in the Heart of Africa.* New York: Basic Books, 2001.

Berry, Mary Frances, and John W. Blassingame. *Long Memory: The Black Experience in America.* New York: Oxford University Press, 1982.

Beyan, Amos J. *The American Colonization Society and the Creation of the Liberian State: A Historical Perspective, 1822–1900.* Lanham, Md.: University Press of America, 1991.

Biegert, M. Langley. "Legacy of Resistance: Uncovering the History of Collective Action by Black Agricultural Workers in Central East Arkansas." *Journal of Social History* 32 (Fall 1998): 73–99.

Bittle, William, and Gilbert Geis. *The Longest Way Home: Chief Alfred C. Sam's Back-to-Africa Movement.* Detroit: Wayne State University Press, 1964.

"Blackville: An All-Negro Community." *The Stream of History* 9 (January 1971): 11–12.

Bogle, Lori. "On Our Way to the Promised Land: Black Migration from Arkansas to Oklahoma, 1889–1893." *The Chronicles of Oklahoma* 72 (Summer 1994): 160–77.

Bracey, John H., Jr., August Meier, and Elliott Rudwick, eds. *Black Nationalism in America.* Indianapolis: Bobbs-Merrill, 1970.

Branch, Alice Crawford. "Desha County's Unique Town, Liberia City." *Desha County Historical Society 1983 Programs* 10 (Spring 1984): 62–70.

Brundage, W. Fitzhugh, ed. *Under Sentence of Death: Lynching in the South.* Chapel Hill: University of North Carolina Press, 1997.

Burkett, Randall K. *Garveyism as a Religious Movement: The Institutionalization of a Black Civil Religion.* Metuchen, N.J.: Scarecrow Press and the American Theological Library Association, 1978.

Campbell, James T. *Songs of Zion: The African Methodist Episcopal Church in the United States and South Africa.* New York: Oxford University Press, 1995.

Campbell, Penelope. *Maryland in Africa: The Maryland State Colonization Society, 1831–1857.* Urbana: University of Illinois Press, 1971.

Cartwright, Joseph H. *The Triumph of Jim Crow: Tennessee Race Relations in the 1880s.* Knoxville: University of Tennessee Press, 1976.

Cecelski, David S., and Timothy B. Tyson. *Democracy Betrayed: The Wilmington Race Riot of 1898 and Its Legacy.* Chapel Hill: University of North Carolina Press, 1998.

Cohen, Robin, ed. *Theories of Migration.* Cheltenham, U.K.: Edward Elgar, 1996.

Cohen, William. *At Freedom's Edge: Black Mobility and the Southern White Quest for Racial Control, 1861–1915.* Baton Rouge: Louisiana State University Press, 1991.

Cortner, Richard. *A Mob Intent on Death: The NAACP and the Arkansas Riot Cases.* Middleton, Conn.: Wesleyan University Press, 1988.

Cronon, E. David. *The Story of Marcus Garvey and the Universal Negro Improvement Association.* Madison: University of Wisconsin Press, 1972.

Crowder, Michael. *West Africa under Colonial Rule.* Evanston: Northwestern University Press, 1968.

Cummings, Melbourne Stenson. "The Rhetoric of Bishop Henry McNeal Turner, Leading Advocate in the African Emigration Movement, 1866–1907." Ph.D. diss., UCLA, 1972.

Dailey, Jane. *Before Jim Crow: The Politics of Race in Postemancipation Virginia.* Chapel Hill: University of North Carolina Press, 2000.

Davies, James C. "The J-Curve of Rising and Declining Satisfactions as a Cause of Some Great Revolutions and a Contained Rebellion." In *Violence in America: Historical and Comparative Perspectives,* edited by Hugh Davis Graham and Ted Robert Gurr, 2:547–76. Washington, D.C.: Government Printing Office, 1969.

——. "Toward a Theory of Revolution." *American Sociological Review* 27 (February 1962): 5–19.

Davis, Lenwood G. "Black American Images of Liberia, 1877–1914." *Liberian Studies Journal* 6 (1975): 53–72.

Decanio, Stephen J. *Agriculture in the Postbellum South: The Economics of Production and Supply.* Cambridge: Harvard University Press, 1974.

DeSantis, Vincent P. *Republicans Face the Southern Question: The New Departure Years, 1877–1897.* Baltimore: Johns Hopkins University Press, 1959.

Devlin, George A. *South Carolina and Black Migration, 1865–1940: In Search of the Promised Land.* New York: Garland, 1989.

Donovan, Timothy P., and Willard P. Gatewood Jr., eds. *The Governors of Arkansas: Essays in Political Biography.* Fayetteville: University of Arkansas Press, 1981.

Duffy, John. "The Impact of Malaria on the South." In *Disease and Distinctiveness in the American South,* edited by Todd L. Savitt and James Harvey Young, 29–54. Knoxville: University of Tennessee Press.

Du Bois, W. E. B. *Dusk of Dawn: An Essay Toward an Autobiography of a Race Concept.* New York: Harcourt, Brace, and Co., 1940.

Dunn, D. Elwood, and S. Byron Tarr. *Liberia: A National Polity in Transition.* Metuchen, N.J.: Scarecrow Press, 1988.

Elkins, F. Clark. "The Agricultural Wheel: County Politics and Consolidation, 1884–1885." *Arkansas Historical Quarterly* 29 (Autumn 1970): 152–75.

——. "The Agricultural Wheel in Arkansas, 1887." *Arkansas Historical Quarterly* 40 (Autumn 1981): 249–58.

——. "Arkansas Farmers Organize for Action, 1882–1884." *Arkansas Historical Quarterly* 13 (Autumn 1954): 231–48.

——. "State Politics and the Agricultural Wheel." *Arkansas Historical Quarterly* 38 (Autumn 1979): 248–58.

Elliott, Mark. "Race, Color Blindness, and the Democratic Public: Albion W. Tourgée's Radical Principles in *Plessy v. Ferguson.*" *Journal of Southern History* 67 (May 2001): 287–330.

Ellis, Stephen. *The Mask of Anarchy: The Destruction of Liberia and the Religious Dimension of an African Civil War.* New York: New York University Press, 1999.

Fitzgerald, Michael W. "'We Have Found a Moses': Theodore Bilbo, Black Nationalism, and the Greater Liberia Bill of 1939." *Journal of Southern History* 63 (May 1997): 293–320.

Fligstein, Neil. *Going North: Migration of Blacks and Whites from the South, 1900–1950.* New York: Academic Press, 1981.

Franklin, Jimmie Lewis. *Journey toward Hope: A History of Blacks in Oklahoma*. Norman: University of Oklahoma Press, 1982.

Franklin, John Hope, and Alfred A. Moss Jr. *From Slavery to Freedom: A History of Negro Americans*. 6th ed. New York: McGraw-Hill, 1988.

Franklin, V. P. *Black Self-Determination: A Cultural History of the Faith of the Fathers*. Westport, Conn.: Lawrence Hill, 1984.

Gaither, Gerald H. *Blacks and the Populist Revolt: Ballots and Bigotry in the "New South."* Tuscaloosa: University of Alabama Press, 1977.

Gates, Henry Louis, Jr. *Loose Canons: Notes on the Culture Wars*. New York: Oxford University Press, 1992.

———. *The Signifying Monkey: A Theory of Afro-American Literary Criticism*. New York: Oxford University Press, 1988.

Gatewood, Willard B., Jr. "Arkansas Negroes in the 1890s: Documents." *Arkansas Historical Quarterly* 33 (Winter 1974): 293–325.

———. *Black Americans and the White Man's Burden, 1898–1903*. Urbana: University of Illinois Press, 1975.

———. "Negro Legislators in Arkansas, 1891: A Document." *Arkansas Historical Quarterly* 31 (Autumn 1972): 220–33.

Genovese, Eugene D. *Roll, Jordan, Roll: The World the Slaves Made*. New York: Pantheon Books, 1974.

Gershoni, Yekutiel. *Black Colonialism: The Americo-Liberian Scramble for the Hinterland*. Boulder, Colo.: Westview Press, 1985.

Gilmore, Glenda Elizabeth. *Gender and Jim Crow: Women and the Politics of White Supremacy in North Carolina, 1896–1920*. Chapel Hill: University of North Carolina Press, 1996.

Ginger, Ray. *Age of Excess: The United States from 1877 to 1914*. 2nd ed. New York: Macmillan, 1975.

Glaude, Eddie S., Jr. *Exodus! Religion, Race, and Nation in Early Nineteenth-Century Black America*. Chicago: University of Chicago Press, 2000.

Gordon, Fon Louise. *Caste and Class: The Black Experience in Arkansas, 1880–1920*. Athens: University of Georgia Press, 1995.

Gordy, Sondra. "Empty Classrooms, Empty Hearts: Little Rock Secondary Teachers, 1958–1959." *Arkansas Historical Quarterly* 56 (Winter 1997): 427–42.

Graves, John William. *Town and Country: Race Relations in an Urban-Rural Context, Arkansas, 1865–1905*. Fayetteville: University of Arkansas Press, 1990.

Grossman, James R. *Land of Hope: Chicago, Black Southerners, and the Great Migration*. Chicago: University of Chicago Press, 1989.

Grubbs, Donald H. *Cry from the Cotton: The Southern Tenant Farmers' Union and the New Deal*. Chapel Hill: University of North Carolina Press, 1971.

Gurr, Ted Robert. *Why Men Rebel*. Princeton, N.J.: Princeton University Press.

Gutman, Herbert G. *The Black Family in Slavery and Freedom, 1750–1925*. New York: Pantheon Books, 1976.

Hair, William Ivy. *Carnival of Fury: Robert Charles and the New Orleans Race Riot of 1900*. Baton Rouge: Louisiana State University Press, 1976.

Hall, Raymond L. *Black Separatism in the United States*. Hanover, N.H.: University Press of New England, 1978.

Hamilton, G. P. *Beacon Lights of the Race*. Memphis: P. H. Clarke, 1911.

Hamilton, Kenneth Marvin. *Black Towns and Profit: Promotion and Development in the Trans-Appalachian West, 1877–1915*. Urbana: University of Illinois Press, 1991.

Harris, Sheldon H. *Paul Cuffe: Black America, and the African Return*. New York: Simon and Schuster, 1982.

Harrison, Alferdteen, ed. *Black Exodus: The Great Migration from the American South*. Jackson: University Press of Mississippi, 1991.

Harrison, Gordon. *Mosquitos, Malaria, and Man: A History of the Hostilities since 1880*. New York: E. P. Dutton, 1978.

Hendrix, Thomas Christian. "'The Love of Liberty': A Study of the Religious Factor in the Nineteenth-Century Settlement of Afro-Americans in Liberia." Ph.D. diss., University of Illinois, Chicago, 1985.

Hennsington, Randy. "Upland Farmers and Agrarian Protest: Northwest Arkansas and the Brothers of Freedom." M.A. thesis, University of Arkansas, 1973.

Higginbotham, Evelyn Brooks. *Righteous Discontent: The Women's Movement in the Black Baptist Church, 1880–1920*. Cambridge, Mass.: Harvard University Press, 1993.

Higgs, Robert. *Competition and Coercion: Blacks in the American Economy, 1865–1914*. Cambridge: Cambridge University Press, 1977.

Hirshon, Stanley P. *Farewell to the Bloody Shirt: Northern Republicans and the Southern Negro, 1877–1893*. Bloomington: Indiana University Press, 1962.

Hodes, Martha. *White Women, Black Men: Illicit Sex in the Nineteenth-Century South*. New Haven: Yale University Press, 1997.

Hunter, Tera. *To 'Joy My Freedom: Southern Black Women's Lives and Labors after the Civil War*. Cambridge, Mass.: Harvard University Press, 1997.

Jacobs, Sylvia M., ed. *Black Americans and the Missionary Movement in Africa*. Westport, Conn: Greenwood Press, 1982.

Jenkins, David. *Black Zion: Africa, Imagined and Real as Seen by Today's Blacks*. New York: Harcourt Brace Jovanovich, 1975.

Johnson, Charles S. *Bitter Canaan: The Story of the Negro Republic*. New Brunswick: Transaction Books, 1987.

Johnson, Daniel M., and Rex R. Campbell. *Black Migration in America: A Social Demographic History*. Durham: Duke University Press, 1981.

Johnston, Harry. *Liberia*. 2 vols. 1906. Reprint, New York: Negro Universities Press, 1969.

Jones, Jacqueline. *Labor of Love, Labor of Sorrow: Black Women, Work, and the Family from Slavery to the Present*. New York: Basic Books, 1985.

Kennedy, Thomas C. "Southland College: The Society of Friends and Black Education in Arkansas." *Arkansas Historical Quarterly* 42 (Autumn 1983): 207–38.

Kenzer, Robert C. *Enterprising Southerners: Black Economic Success in North Carolina, 1865–1915*. Charlottesville: University of Virginia Press, 1997.

Kirk, John A. *Redefining the Color Line: Black Activism in Little Rock, Arkansas, 1940–1970*. Gainesville: University of Florida Press, 2002.

Kousser, J. Morgan. *The Shaping of Southern Politics: Suffrage Restriction and the Establishment of the One-Party South*. New Haven: Yale University Press, 1974.

Lewis, Todd Everett. "Race Relations in Arkansas, 1910–1929." Ph.D. diss., University of Arkansas, 1995.

Liebenow, J. Gus. *Liberia: The Evolution of Privilege*. Ithaca, N.Y.: Cornell University Press, 1969.

————. *Liberia: The Quest for Democracy*. Bloomington: University of Indiana Press, 1987.

Litwack, Leon F. *Trouble in Mind: Black Southerners in the Age of Jim Crow*. New York: Knopf, 1998.

Litwack, Leon, and August Meier, eds. *Black Leaders of the Nineteenth Century*. Urbana: University of Illinois Press, 1988.

Lloyd, Peggy S. "The Howard County Race Riot of 1883." *Arkansas Historical Quarterly* 59 (Winter 2000): 353–87.

Logan, Frenise Avedis. *The Negro in North Carolina, 1876–1894*. Chapel Hill: University of North Carolina Press, 1964.

Lynch, Hollis R. *Edward Wilmot Blyden: Pan-Negro Patriot, 1832–1912*. New York: Oxford University Press, 1967.

Mandle, Jay. *The Roots of Black Poverty: The Southern Plantation after the Civil War*. Durham: Duke University Press, 1978.

Martin, Sandy Dwayne. *Black Baptists and African Missions: The Origins of a Movement, 1880–1915*. Macon, Ga.: Mercer University Press, 1989.

McDaniel, Antonio. *Swing Low, Sweet Chariot: The Mortality Cost of Colonizing Liberia in the Nineteenth Century*. Chicago: University of Chicago Press, 1995.

McPherson, James M. *The Abolitionist Legacy: From Reconstruction to the NAACP*. Princeton, N.J.: Princeton University Press, 1975.

McMillen, Neil R. *Dark Journey: Black Mississippians in the Age of Jim Crow*. Urbana: University of Illinois Press, 1989.

Meier, August. *Negro Thought in America, 1880–1915: Racial Ideologies in the Age of Booker T. Washington*. Ann Arbor: University of Michigan Press, 1963.

Meriwether, Robert W. "A Lynching Thwarted, 1891." *Faulkner Facts and Fiddlings* 33 (Fall/Winter 1991): 9–11.

Miller, Floyd J. *The Search for a Black Nationality: Black Emigration and Colonization, 1787–1863*. Urbana: University of Illinois Press, 1975.

Mitchell, Michele. "'The Black Man's Burden': African Americans, Imperialism, and Notions of Racial Manhood, 1890–1910." *International Review of Social History* 44 (1999, supplement): 77–99.

Moneyhon, Carl H. *Arkansas and the New South, 1874–1929*. Fayetteville: University of Arkansas Press, 1997.

————. "Black Politics in Arkansas during the Gilded Age, 1876–1900." *Arkansas Historical Quarterly* 44 (Autumn 1985): 222–45.

Montgomery, William E. *Under Their Own Vine and Fig Tree: The African-American Church in the South, 1865–1900*. Baton Rouge: Louisiana State University Press, 1993.

Morgan, James Logan. "Dr. Lightfoot, 1892." *Stream of History* 16 (April 1978): 3–13.

Morris, Milton D. *The Politics of Black Nationalism*. New York: Harper and Row, 1975.

Moses, Wilson Jeremiah. *The Golden Age of Black Nationalism, 1850–1925*. Hamden, Conn.: Archon Books, 1978.

Mudimbe, V. Y. *The Invention of Africa: Gnosis, Philosophy, and the Order of Knowledge*. Bloomington: Indiana University Press, 1988.

Nederveen Pieterse, Jan. *White on Black: Images of Africa and Blacks in Western Popular Culture*. New Haven: Yale University Press, 1992.

Neverdon-Morton, Cynthia. *Afro-American Women of the South and the Advancement of the Race, 1895–1925*. Knoxville: University of Tennessee Press, 1989.

Novak, Daniel A. *The Wheel of Servitude: Black Forced Labor after Slavery*. Lexington: University Press of Kentucky, 1978.

Ofari, Earl. *"Let Your Motto Be Resistance": The Life and Thought of Henry Highland Garnet*. Boston: Beacon Press, 1972.

Okonkwo, Rina L. "Orishatukeh Faduma: A Man of Two Worlds." *Journal of Negro History* 68 (Winter 1983): 24–36.

Olsen, Otto H. *Carpetbagger's Crusade: The Life of Albion Winegar Tourgée*. Baltimore: Johns Hopkins University Press, 1965.

Painter, Nell Irvin. *Exodusters: Black Migration to Kansas after Reconstruction*. New York: Knopf, 1977.

———. *Standing at Armageddon: The United States, 1877–1919*. New York: W. W. Norton, 1987.

Paisley, Clifton. "The Political Wheelers and Arkansas' Election of 1888." *Arkansas Historical Quarterly* 25 (Spring 1966): 3–21.

Patterson, Ruth Polk. *The Seed of Sally Good'n: A Black Family of Arkansas, 1833–1953*. Lexington: University Press of Kentucky, 1985.

Patton, Adell, Jr. "The Back-to-Africa Movement in Arkansas." *Arkansas Historical Quarterly* 51 (Summer 1992): 164–77.

Perman, Michael. *Struggle for Mastery: Disfranchisement in the South, 1888–1908*. Chapel Hill: University of North Carolina Press, 2001.

Peterson, John. *Province of Freedom: A History of Sierra Leone, 1787–1870*. Evanston: Northwestern University Press, 1969.

Pinkney, Alphonso. *Red, Black, and Green: Black Nationalism in the United States*. Cambridge: Cambridge University Press, 1976.

Ponton, M. M. *Life and Times of Henry M. Turner*. New York: Negro Universities Press, 1970.

Raboteau, Albert J. *Canaan Land: A Religious History of African Americans*. New York: Oxford University Press, 1999.

———. *Slave Religion: "The Invisible Institution" in the Antebellum South*. New York: Oxford University Press, 1978.

Ransom, Roger L., and Richard Sutch. *One Kind of Freedom: The Economic Consequence of Emancipation*. Cambridge: Cambridge University Press, 1977.

Redkey, Edwin S. *Black Exodus: Black Nationalist and Back-to-Africa Movements, 1890–1910*. New Haven: Yale University Press, 1969.

———. "The Flowering of Black Nationalism: Henry McNeal Turner and Marcus Garvey." In vol. 2 of *Key Issues in the Afro-American Experience*, edited by Nathan I. Huggins, Martin Kilson, and Daniel M. Fox, 107–24. New York: Harcourt Brace Jovanovich, 1971.

———. *The Meaning of Africa to Afro-Americans, 1890–1914*. Buffalo: Council on International Studies, State University of New York at Buffalo, 1971.

Rose, Jerome C., ed. *Gone to a Better Land: A Biohistory of a Rural Black Cemetery in the Post-Reconstruction South*. Fayetteville: Arkansas Archeological Survey, 1985.

Roth, Donald Franklin. "'Grace Not Race': Southern Negro Church Leaders, Black

Identity, and Missions to West Africa, 1865–1919." Ph.D. diss., University of Texas, Austin, 1975.

Rudd, Dan A., and Theo Bond. *From Slavery to Wealth: The Life of Scott Bond*. Madison, Ark.: Journal Printing, 1917.

Rudwick, Elliot M., and August Meier. "Black Man in the 'White City': Negroes and the Columbian Exposition, 1893." *Phylon* 26 (Winter 1965): 354–61.

Saha, Santosh C. *Culture in Liberia: An Afrocentric View of the Cultural Interaction between the Indigenous Liberians and the Americo-Liberians*. Lewiston, N.Y.: Edwin Mellen Press, 1998.

———. *A History of Agriculture in Liberia, 1822–1970: Transference of American Values*. Lewiston, N.Y.: Edwin Mellen Press, 1990.

Salem, Dorothy. *To Better Our World: Black Women in Organized Reform, 1890–1920*. Brooklyn, N.Y.: Carlson, 1990.

Saloutos, Theodore. *Farmer Movements in the South, 1865–1933*. Lincoln: University of Nebraska Press, 1964.

Scott, James C. *Domination and the Arts of Resistance: Hidden Transcripts*. New Haven: Yale University Press, 1990.

Scott, William R. "Rabbi Arnold Rod's Back-to-Ethiopia Movement: A Study of Black Emigration, 1930–1935." *Pan-African Journal* 8 (Summer 1975): 191–202.

Seraile, William. "Black American Missionaries in Africa, 1821–1925." *Social Studies* 63 (October 1972): 192–202.

———. *Fire in His Heart: Bishop Benjamin Tucker Tanner and the A.M.E. Church*. Knoxville: University of Tennessee Press, 1998.

Sernett, Milton C. *Bound for the Promised Land: African American Religion and the Great Migration*. Durham: Duke University Press, 1997.

Shapiro, Herbert. *White Violence and Black Response: From Reconstruction to Montgomery*. Amherst: University of Massachusetts Press, 1988.

Shaw, Stephanie J. *What a Woman Ought to Be and to Do: Black Professional Women Workers during the Jim Crow Era*. Chicago: University of Chicago Press, 1996.

Shick, Tom W. *Behold the Promised Land: A History of Afro-American Settler Society in Nineteenth-Century Liberia*. Baltimore: Johns Hopkins University Press, 1977.

Singler, John Victor. "Plural Markings in Liberian Settler English, 1820–1980." *American Speech* 64 (Spring 1989): 40–64.

Skinner, Elliot P. *African Americans and U.S. Policy toward Africa, 1850–1924*. Washington, D.C.: Howard University Press, 1992.

Stein, Judith. *The World of Marcus Garvey: Race and Class in Modern Society*. Baton Rouge: Louisiana State University Press, 1986.

Stuckey, Sterling. *Slave Culture: Nationalist Theory and the Foundations of Black America*. New York: Oxford University Press, 1987.

Thornbrough, Emma Lou. *T. Thomas Fortune: Militant Journalist*. Chicago: University of Chicago Press, 1972.

Tindall, George Brown. *South Carolina Negroes, 1877–1900*. Columbia: University of South Carolina Press, 1952.

Tolnay, Stewart E. *The Bottom Rung: African American Family Life on Southern Farms*. Urbana: University of Illinois Press, 1999.

Tolnay, Stewart E., and E. M. Beck. *A Festival of Violence: An Analysis of Southern Lynch-ings, 1882–1930*. Urbana: University of Illinois Press, 1995.

Tolson, Arthur L. *The Black Oklahomans: A History, 1541–1972*. New Orleans: Edwards Printing, 1974.

Trimiew, Darryl M. *Voices of the Silenced: The Responsible Self in a Marginalized Community*. Cleveland: Pilgrim Press, 1993.

Vogler, Myrtle Clarine. "Negroes of Area Joined Back to Africa Movement of 1892." *Independence County Chronicle* 16 (January 1975): 46–57.

Walker, Clarence E. *Deromanticizing Black History: Critical Essays and Reappraisals*. Knox-ville: University of Tennessee Press, 1991.

Weisbord, Robert G. *Ebony Kinship: Africa, Africans, and the Afro-American*. Westport, Conn: Greenwood Press, 1973.

Welch, Melanie K. "Violence and the Decline of Black Politics in St. Francis County." *Arkansas Historical Quarterly* 60 (Winter 2001): 360–93.

Welch, Richard E., Jr. "The Federal Elections Bill of 1890: Postscripts and Prelude." *Journal of American History* 52 (December 1965): 511–26.

West, Richard. *Back to Africa: A History of Sierra Leone and Liberia*. New York: Holt, Rinehart and Winston, 1970.

White, Deborah Gray. *Too Heavy a Load: Black Women in Defense of Themselves, 1894–1994*. New York: W. W. Norton, 1999.

Williams, Gilbert Anthony. "The A.M.E. *Christian Recorder*: A Forum for the Social Ideas of Black Americans." Ph.D. diss., University of Illinois, 1979.

Williams, Walter L. "Black American Attitudes toward Africa, 1877–1900." *Pan-African Journal* 8 (Spring 1971): 173–94.

———. *Black Americans and the Evangelization of Africa, 1877–1900*. Madison: University of Wisconsin Press, 1982.

———. "Black Journalism's Opinions about Africa during the Late Nineteenth Cen-tury." *Phylon* 34 (September 1973): 224–35.

Williamson, Joel. *The Crucible of Race: Black/White Relations in the American South since Emancipation*. New York: Oxford University Press, 1984.

Wilmore, Gayraud S. *Black Religion and Black Radicalism*. New York: Doubleday, 1972.

Woodruff, Nan Elizabeth. "African-American Struggles for Citizenship in the Arkan-sas and Mississippi Deltas in the Age of Jim Crow." *Radical History Review* 55 (Win-ter 1993): 33–51.

Wright, Gavin. *The Political Economy of the Cotton South: Households, Markets, and Wealth in the Nineteenth Century*. New York: W. W. Norton, 1978.

Zald, Mayer N., and John D. McCarthy, eds. *The Dynamics of Social Movement: Resource Mobilization, Social Control, and Tactics*. Cambridge, Mass.: Winthrop Publishers, 1979.

Index

Hartford, Liberia, 155, 170
Hartzell, Joseph, 119
Havis, Ferd, 81
Hayden, George, 22
Hayes, Rutherford B., 9
Hazeley, J. C., 10, 46–47
Helena, Ark., 101, 108, 180; emigration activity in, 13, 17–19, 25; and 1878 election, 20–21; emigration to Liberia from, 44; efforts to promote white immigration to, 92; missionary work in, 111
Hempstead County, Ark., 207 (n. 48)
Henderson, John M., 114–15
Hicks, Charles F., 19
Hill, A. H., 128
Hill, Cicely, 111
Hill, Ned, 15–16
Hilzheim, Sam, 34
Holloway, W. H., 73, 130
Holman family, 144
Holmes, Ephraim, 28, 30
Hopson, Harvey, 68
Horsa (ship), 139–41, 156, 170
Hot Springs, Ark., 118, 138, 142
Howard, T. D., 138–39
Howard County, Ark., 207 (n. 48)
Hughes, E. S., 44
Hughes, Simon P., 50
Humphrey, Ark., 53

Illinois, 142
Immigration: efforts to attract white immigrants, 92–93
In Darkest Africa, 63, 77
Indian Territory, 77, 79, 85–87, 142
International Migration Society, 135, 137–47
Irons, Clement, 118
Ivory Coast, 150, 188–90

Jackson, R. A., 118
Jackson County, Ark., 125; white opposition to emigration in, 95; frauds against would-be emigrants in, 104; emigration from, 142

James, Henry, 81–83
Jefferson, Thomas H., 140–41
Jefferson County, Ark., 34, 55, 60, 69; politics in, 15, 21–22, 34, 84, 200 (n. 24), 203 (n. 63); emigration activity in, 53, 85, 180; and migration to Oklahoma, 86; arson against black property in, 136. *See also* Pine Bluff
Jenkins, Sally, 213 (n. 60)
Jenkins, Shadrach, 22
Jenkins family, 144
Jennifer, J. T., 101
Jewel, Mrs. Henry, 81
Jimison, John, 59–60
Johnson, Alice, 45–46, 169
Johnson, Donald, 138, 139, 168
Johnson, Flora, 168
Johnson, George, 95
Johnson, H. T., 113
Johnson, Hilary, 155
Johnson, John, 47, 155
Johnson, Lewis R., 109
Johnson, Moses L., 153–54
Johnson, Prince, 189
Johnson, R. H. 34
Johnson, Sarah, 23–24
Johnson County, Ark., 68
Johnsonville, Liberia, 155–60, 163–67, 172, 177, 179, 186, 191
Jones, Eph, 62
Jones, F. J., 73
Jones, Wiley, 81, 136, 138
Jones, William, 58
Jonesboro, Ark., 111
Jordan, Benjamin, 28
Jordan, Bob, 217 (n. 20)

Kansas, migration to, 12, 130
Keen, M. H., 45–46
Kelly, John, 81
Keo, Ark., 72
Kettler, Fannie, 174–75
King, C. T. O, 79, 152
King, William H., 52, 70, 87, 96
Knights of Labor, 49–50
Kpelle people, 167

Meingault, 103

Memphis, Tenn., 138, 142, 143, 185

Mende people, 165, 168

Menifee, Ark., 67, 93, 96; Liberia exodus clubs in, 53, 62–63, 73; emigration activity in, 70, 213 (n. 60); black opposition to emigration in, 101

Mersurrado River (Liberia), 155–56

Methodist Episcopal Church, 118–21

Methodists: and emigration, 180. *See also* African Methodist Episcopal Church; African Methodist Episcopal Church Zion; Methodist Episcopal Church

Migration: into Arkansas, 35–39; to Oklahoma, 57, 85–87, 125, 177; to northern cities, 184

Miller, Benjamin H., 57, 165–66, 191, 214 (n. 74)

Miller, James, 93

Miller, M. J., 68

Miller, William, 21

Missionary work, 107–22; children's organizations for, 110–11; women's organizations for, 110–12, 154

Mississippi, 9, 183

Mississippi County, Ark., 68; white opposition to emigration in, 96; frauds against would-be emigrants in, 106

Mitchell, John, 88

Monroe County, Ark., 22, 50, 103; emigration activity in, 25, 58–59; white opposition to emigration in, 95; Garvey movement in, 183; politics in, 200 (n. 24), 204 (n. 6)

Monrovia, 140, 150–51, 153, 187; early settlement, 4; missionaries in, 120–21; ships arrival in, 144; description of, 149, 152; and civil war, 190–92

Monrovia (ship), 31, 45, 87, 169

Moore, Dora, 72

Moore, George, 67

Moore, Narcissie (Narcissus), 69, 71–72, 156, 160, 192, 214 (n. 74)

Morning Star Baptist Church, 156–58, 191–92

Morrilton, Ark., 38, 43, 51, 61, 169, 173,

177, 180; emigration from, 1, 53, 70–72, 76–77, 219 (n. 6); emigration activity in, 45, 52–53, 58, 73; Liberia exodus clubs in, 53, 63, 70, 73; political violence in, 54; white opposition to emigration in, 95; lynching in, 136

Morris, Edward S., 28, 163

Moss, William, 53

Nat Turner rebellion, 5

National Association for the Advancement of Colored People (NAACP), 183, 184, 185

Neel Guards, 34

New Africa (newspaper), 121

Newberry County, S.C., 38

New Orleans, 11, 147

Newport, Ark., 86, 109, 112, 180

Newton, R. L., 34

Newton, Richard, 26, 27, 30, 155, 169

New York, N.Y., 142; Arkansas emigrants in, 25–31, 46, 72, 77–79, 98, 129

Nigeria, 6

Noble Lake, Ark., 62

North Carolina, 92

North Creek, Ark., 22, 25

North Little Rock, Ark. *See* Argenta

Norwood, C. M., 50–51

Nubia, Ark., 62

Oklahoma, 142; black migration to, 57, 85–87, 125, 177; emigration from, 178

Osceola, Ark., 52, 95, 111, 143

Ouachita County, Ark., 136, 142

Parker, Caroline, 25, 144

Parker, Elijah, 25, 144, 164, 173

Parker, Joe, 168

Parker, Juda, 69

Patterson, William, 76

Payne, E. C. A., 155

Penn, I. W., 59

Pennington, W. P., 62

People's Party, 84

Perry County, Ark., 34